The Gospel of Matthew Through New Eyes

Volume Two:
Jesus as Israel

Peter J. Leithart

WEST MONROE, LOUISIANA

The Gospel of Matthew Through New Eyes
VOLUME TWO: *Jesus as Israel*
Copyright © 2018 by Peter Leithart
Athanasius Press
715 Cypress Street
West Monroe, Louisiana 71291
www.athanasiuspress.org

ISBN: 978-1-7335356-0-1 (softcover)

All rights reserved. No part of this publication may be reproduced, stored in a retrieval system, or transmitted in any form or by any means— electronic, mechanical, photocopy, recording, or any other—except for brief quotations in printed reviews, without the prior permission of the publisher.

This publication contains The Holy Bible, English Standard Version®, copyright © 2001 by Crossway Bibles, a publishing ministry of Good News Publishers. The ESV® text appearing in this publication is reproduced and published by cooperation between Good News Publishers and Athanasius Press and by permission of Good News Publishers. Unauthorized reproduction of this publication is prohibited.

The Holy Bible, English Standard Version (ESV) is adapted from the Revised Standard Version of the Bible, copyright Division of Christian Education of the National Council of the Churches of Christ in the U.S.A. All rights reserved.

English Standard Version®, ESV®, and the ESV® logo are trademarks of Good News Publishers located in Wheaton, Illinois. Used by permission.

Contents

4   **KINGDOM OF HEAVEN | MATTHEW 13-17**   **1**
    Many Things in Parables - 13:1-23   3
    Seeds and Leaven - 13:24-43   12
    Seek the Kingdom - 13:44-58   22
    Two Feasts, Two Kingdoms - 14:1-36   30
    Defilement - 15:1-20   41
    Crumbs - 15:21-39   50
    Food Test - 16:1-12   57
    On this Rock - 16:13-28   66
    Death and Glory - 17:1-13   75
    Down from the Mountain - 17:9-27   83

5   **TOWARD THE TEMPLE | MATTHEW 17-22**   **91**
    Greatest in the Kingdom - 17:24 - 18:14   91
    Brothers - 18:15-20   99
    Seventy Times Seven - 18:21-35   105
    Marriage from the Beginning - 19:1-15   114
    Last and First - 19:16 - 20:16   121
    Servant of All - 20:17-34   131
    The King and His House - 21:1-17   138
    The Fig Tree and the Vineyard - 21:18-46   147
    Caesar's Coin - 22:1-22   156
    Battle for the Temple - 22:23-46   164

6   **NOT ONE STONE | MATTHEW 22-25**   **175**
    Woe to You - 22:41 - 23:12   175
    Weighty Things of the Law - 23:13-28   184
    Jerusalem, Jerusalem - 23:29 - 24:2   193
    Not One Stone - 23:37 - 24:14   200
    Abomination of Desolation - 24:15-28   208
    Cosmic Collapse - 24:29-35   216
    Be on the Alert - 24:36-51   223
    Parables of the Kingdom - 25:1-30   231
    The Least of These - 25:31-46   238

Contents

7	**THE CHRIST CRUCIFIED	MATTHEW 26-27**	**249**
	The Christ Crucified - 26:1-16	*249*
	Body and Blood - 26:17-30	*259*
	In Gethsemane - 26:31-56	*267*
	God on Trial - 26:57 - 27:2	*274*
	Innocent Blood - 27:1-10	*281*
	King of the Jews - 27:11-26	*289*
	God is Mocked - 27:27-44	*298*
	The Death of God - 27:45-54	*308*
	Dead and Buried - 27:55-66	*316*
8	**HE IS RISEN!	MATTHEW 28**	**327**
	He is Risen - 28:1-10	*327*
	Go! - 28:11-20	*333*

4

Kingdom of Heaven

Matthew presents Jesus as Israel, as the "son" who is called from Egypt (Matt. 2:15). His life recapitulates the life of Israel, from two angles. On the one hand, He lives through the entire history of Israel. Matthew begins his Gospel with the phrase *biblos geneseos*, "the book of genesis," and immediately follows with a genealogy that reminds us of the *toledoth* (generations) statements of Genesis. Jesus' human father is named Joseph, and he has dreams that enable his family to escape from a murderous Pharaoh-like king, Herod. Jesus goes to Egypt and returns, is tempted in the wilderness, ascends a mountain to teach about the law, carries out a merciful conquest of the land by healing and driving out demons, forms a new Israel within Israel, is sent outside the gate to suffer exile from His Father on a Roman cross, but then returns in glory from the exile of the grave and, with authority greater than the authority of Cyrus, sends His disciples out to build the house of God in all nations.

The five large discourses of Matthew fit into this scheme. In the Sermon on the Mount, Jesus is Moses delivering the law from a new Sinai. When Jesus sends out the Twelve to the tribes of Israel (Matthew 10), He is a new Joshua heading up a new conquest of the land. Telling parables of the kingdom (Matthew 13), Jesus is the philosopher-king Solomon, and when He gives instructions to His disciples about forgiveness and community life (Matthew 18), He is like Elisha leading a company of prophets. He denounces the temple like Jeremiah and Ezekiel, warning of its imminent destruction because of the hypocrisy of the scribes and Pharisees (Matthew 23-25).

Jesus assumes the role of every major leader in Israel's history, but at the same time He is also taking Yahweh's role in Israel's history. Moses receives the law from Yahweh and delivers it to the people, but Jesus speaks in His own authority. Joshua, Solomon and the kings who followed him, Elisha, Jeremiah, Ezekiel and all the prophets were messengers of the Lord, but Jesus is the Lord Himself. The Word becomes flesh — the flesh of Moses, Solomon, Elijah, Jeremiah, and all the rest. In Jesus, the Lord who created Israel *becomes* Israel to live Israel's history again, and to redeem the times.

Jesus' interactions with the leaders of Israel thus recapitulate Yahweh's tortured interactions in the Old Testament. Yahweh sent Moses and the people refused to hear. But Yahweh kept coming, He continued to speak; He sent Joshua and David and the prophets, and at each stage Israel rejected Him and His spokesmen. Yet Yahweh never gave up on His beloved; He remained faithful to His covenant people. And now, at the end of the ages, He comes in person to meet His people face-to-face, to woo them back from the wilderness. And they reject Him again. Yahweh comes in person, and the Jews turn Him over to the Romans to be crucified. But death does not stop Yahweh, whose love is stronger than death. He comes back again, comes back as the world-emperor to send His new Israel to disciple the nations.

This second volume begins in the middle of the story. Jesus-as-Moses called Israel to keep a renewed Torah, a way of peace and justice, a righteousness that surpassed that of the scribes and Pharisees. He gave authority to His disciples to carry on His mission to the twelve tribes, by healing, casting out demons, proclaiming the good news, raising the dead. Multitudes follow Jesus, but He also faces opposition, especially from the official and unofficial leaders of Israel, the scribes, Pharisees, and priests. They do not want to follow this Teacher; they stop their ears to His words. And so Jesus begins to speak in riddles and parables, confirming them in their deafness. That is where we start in this chapter.

By the time we get to Matthew 18, Jesus has withdrawn from the mainstream of Judaism to focus attention on His disciples. After the great Solomonic discourse on the kingdom (Matthew 13) comes a "divided kingdom," Jesus as the true son of David forming a counter-kingdom within the kingdom of the Herods and the Jewish elites. In Matthew 18, He teaches His disciples what kind of kingdom they are called to be — a kingdom of humility, compassion and forgiveness, a community of mutual, loving correction. And eventually the Jews will seal their fate further by trying to trap Jesus and plotting to kill Him. In a final discourse (Matthew 23-25), Jesus will predict the catastrophe that will engulf Jerusalem and Judea, the fall of Jerusalem in AD 70.

Many Things in Parables
Matthew 13:1-23

That day Jesus went out of the house and was sitting by the sea. ² And large crowds gathered to Him, so He got into a boat and sat down, and the whole crowd was standing on the beach. ³ And He spoke many things to them in parables, saying, "Behold, the sower went out to sow; ⁴ and as he sowed, some seeds fell beside the road, and the birds came and ate them up. ⁵ Others fell on the rocky places, where they did not have much soil; and immediately they sprang up, because they had no depth of soil. ⁶ But when the sun had risen, they were scorched; and because they had no root, they withered away. ⁷ Others fell among the thorns, and the thorns came up and choked them out. ⁸ And others fell on the good soil and yielded a crop, some a hundredfold, some sixty, and some thirty. ⁹ He who has ears, let him hear." ¹⁰ And the disciples came and said to Him, "Why do You speak to them in parables?" ¹¹ Jesus answered them, "To you it has been granted to know the mysteries of the kingdom of heaven, but to them it has not been granted. ¹² For whoever has, to him more shall be given, and he will have an abundance; but whoever does not have, even what he has shall be taken away from him. ¹³ Therefore I speak to them in parables; because while seeing they do not see, and while hearing they do not hear, nor do they understand. ¹⁴ In their case the prophecy of Isaiah is being fulfilled, which says, 'You will keep on hearing, but will not understand; you will keep on seeing, but will not perceive; ¹⁵ for the heart of this people has become dull, with their ears they scarcely hear, and they have closed their eyes, otherwise they would see with their eyes, hear with their ears, and understand with their heart and return, and I would heal them.' ¹⁶ But blessed are your eyes, because they see; and your ears, because they hear. ¹⁷ For truly I say to you that many prophets and righteous men desired to see what you see, and did not see it, and to hear what you hear, and did not hear it. ¹⁸ Hear then the parable of the sower. ¹⁹ When anyone hears the word of the kingdom and does not understand it, the evil one comes and snatches away what has been sown in his heart. This is the one on whom seed was sown beside the road. ²⁰ The one on whom seed was sown on the rocky places, this is the man who hears the word and immediately receives it with joy; ²¹ yet he has no firm root in himself, but is only temporary, and when affliction or persecution arises because of the word, immediately he falls away. ²² And the one on whom seed was sown among the thorns, this is the man who hears the word, and the worry of the world and the deceitfulness of wealth choke the word, and it becomes unfruitful. ²³ And the one on whom seed was sown on the good soil, this is the man who hears the word and understands it; who indeed bears fruit and brings forth, some a hundredfold, some sixty, and some thirty."

> Brother will deliver up brother to death, and a father his child; and children will rise against parents, and cause them to be put to death.[1]

> Do not think that I came to bring peace on earth; I did not come to bring peace, but a sword. For I came to set a man against his father, and a daughter against her mother, and a daughter-in-law against her mother-in-law; and a man's enemies will be the members of his household.[2]

According to Jesus, these are the effects of His coming, and even in some sense the *purpose* of His ministry. God brings salvation to the world by dividing between the Jews and Gentiles, by cutting into the human race and circumcising it, cutting it up for sacrificial slaughter, before reuniting it through the resurrection of Jesus. And Jesus' ministry follows this deep structure of human history. He comes to Israel and does to Israel what Yahweh has already done to the human race. He comes to Israel with a sword, in order to divide it, but He divides it in order to one day reunite it as a new Israel, a living Israel, in His resurrection.

We have seen that happening up to this point in Matthew. Jesus sends out the Twelve, but the cities of Chorazin, Capernaum, and Bethsaida do not receive Him or His disciples. Jesus heals and gives relief. He practices true Sabbath. But the Pharisees criticize Him for not keeping Sabbath, and then go out to plot Jesus' death. The Pharisees accuse Jesus of being in league with Satan, casting out devils by the power of the prince of the devils. The scribes and Pharisees come looking for a sign, but Jesus discerns that they are really looking for another savior, another husband. The gap continues to widen between Jesus and the "wicked and adulterous generation" among whom He ministers; the gap widens between Jesus' disciples and the leaders of Israel.

This is evident in the frame verses that surround Matthew 13. Matthew 12 ended, with Jesus teaching about His re-constituted family (Matt. 12:46-50). The ones who welcome Him and do His

---

1 Matt. 10:21
2 Matt. 10:34-36

will are His family — His brother and sister and mother. Jesus returns to this point at the end of Matthew 13, where He reiterates that a prophet is without honor in His home town (vv. 53-58). In fact, at the end of Matthew 13, Jesus appears in "their synagogue" for the last time (vv. 53-58).

Jesus' placement and posture here reinforce this separation. Jesus leaves the house, and a crowd "gathers" to Him. Matthew uses the verb form of "synagogue"; the gathering is a synagogue for Jesus, and Jesus adopts the typical posture of a synagogue teacher, sitting to teach a crowd that is standing on the beach. This is the first time Jesus has sat down, and it is a posture not only of an authoritative teacher but also of a king. Jesus sits down as a new Solomon, with a new people, a new gathering, a new synagogue. But Jesus is not with the gathering; He has separated from them. They are all standing on the beach, and He is sitting in a boat a little off shore. He has not yet crossed the sea. He has not left the "synagogue" that gathers to Him, but He is shoving off. He is not in the middle of the sea, but He is not on land either. He is moving out from the synagogue, as He does literally at the end of the chapter.

This scene has been the subject of countless paintings, and it is a charming scene. It seems *so* Jesus, talking about birds and lilies. It is usually interpreted as a logistical necessity: The crowds are so huge that the only way that Jesus can be seen and heard by everybody is by shoving out from the land a bit in a boat. It is possible there was a pragmatic reason for Jesus to go into the boat. But the text does not say that, and it may point in a different direction. In the Bible, the sea is the symbol of the Gentiles, the land of the Jews, and the beach is the margin between them. A boat is a little piece of land floating on the sea, a perfect picture of Jesus' little flock of disciples who are tossed here and there among the Gentiles, a little bit of Israel, with Jesus inside, looking threatened and small in the heart of the sea. Jesus' position in the little boat is an enacted parable, a picture of the kingdom of heaven that is small like a mustard seed, like a little leaven shoved into a lump of dough. Eventually, though, the seed grows into a tree, the leaven leavens the whole lump. Jesus stands in a boat alone on the sea, but He is gathering fishers of men. Later, Paul travels across the sea, like Jonah, with a large shipload of Gentiles, and Paul hosts a meal aboard the ship. At the last, Revelation tells us, there shall be no more sea. Gentiles will be transformed into Jews, the sea into the land, and we will all walk across the sea, like Peter, and not sink; the church will become a boat that is as big as the sea. And it all starts with Jesus alone in the boat.

This story of separation and division is the context for Jesus' teaching in Matthew 13. With Israel growing dull of hearing, Jesus begins teaching in parables (v. 15). Matthew 13 is a chapter of parables. "Parable" is used twelve times in the passage, and there are seven parables: 1) the sower, 2) the wheat and tares, 3) the mustard seed, 4) leaven, 5) the treasure in the field, 6) the merchant seeking pearls, 7) the dragnet.[3] Jesus says the parables express the nature of the kingdom: "The kingdom of heaven may be compared to a man who sowed good seed (v. 24). . . . the kingdom of heaven is like a mustard seed (v. 31) . . . the kingdom of heaven is like leaven (v. 33) . . . the kingdom of heaven is like a treasure hidden in the field (v. 44) . . . the kingdom of heaven is like a merchant seeking fine pearls (v. 45) . . . the kingdom of heaven is like a dragnet (v. 47)." The parables reveal to the disciples the "mysteries of the kingdom," mysteries being things that have been hidden, perhaps since the foundation of the world, but now unveiled. Jesus the new Solomon is untying knots and solving riddles of history.

Matthew 13 divides into three sections, each of which begins with a parable and ends with an interpretation of that parable.

---

[3] There is an eighth saying that resembles a parable in Matt. 13:52: the disciple of the kingdom is like a head of household who brings good things out of his treasure. The seven parables may match the seven days of creation: The separation of wheat and tares resemble the firmament (Day Two), the mustard plant is a creation of Day Three, the merchant is an Adam (Day Six), and the dragnet is an image of Sabbatical final judgment. Fill in the remainder at your leisure.

1. The first section includes the parable of the sower (vv. 1-9), an explanation of Jesus' use of parables with a quotation from Isaiah (vv. 10-17), and an interpretation of the parable (vv. 18-23).
2. Part two begins with the parable of the tares (vv. 24-30), adds two complementary parables (vv. 31-33), and ends with Jesus' interpretation of that parable (vv. 36-43).
3. The third section begins with the parable of the treasure (v. 44), adds two more parables (vv. 45-48), and ends with a reference to the treasure (vv. 51-52).

Each section includes a question that Jesus answers (vv. 10, 36, 51).

Jesus teaches us three things about parables, and a few other things are implied. First, He teaches in parables in order to hide His message from those who refuse to receive Him (vv. 13-17). Jesus does not *begin* his ministry with parables. At the outset, He openly proclaims the kingdom of heaven. Only after Israel resists His call to repentance does He begin talking in riddles. Teaching in parables is an act of judgment (vv. 14-15), and furthers the division within Israel (vv. 11-12). Parables veil the truth of the kingdom from those who have refused to come into the kingdom. Jesus justifies His case for parables by quoting from Isaiah's commission (Isa 6). When Isaiah sees the Lord exalted on His throne, the Lord commissions Him to go to Israel to prophesy. Isaiah is told to proclaim to deaf people, and this proclamation is a prelude to destruction. The Lord commissions him to prophesy until "cities are devastated and without inhabitant, houses are without people, and the land is utterly desolate." The Lord will save a tithe of the people, a stump that is saved from the burning. Otherwise, the nation will be destroyed. Jesus' ministry follows the pattern of Isaiah's. He veils His teaching to those who have become blind and deaf, in the expectation that Israel will soon face a day of judgment, when the nation will be desolated.

There is a pattern for the church here as well. We do not start out speaking obscurely. We do not start out telling riddles. We openly proclaim the gospel. But when people's ears are dull, when they refuse to hear, we start speaking in parables. We rarely follow Jesus' example. When people do not understand our message, we explain again, and again, and again. We assume our lack of clarity keeps them from understanding us. Jesus knows better. It is not His lack of clarity; the Jews know perfectly well what Jesus demands of them. The problem is hardness of heart. So He begins teaching in a way that reinforces that lack of understanding.

Second, Jesus' parables bring about the very division that He is talking about. Parables are not merely informative; they are effective. To teach in parables is to teach with a sword. Parables are acts of judgment, reinforcing the divisions that He has already caused within Israel. For instance: Jesus tells the parable of the sower to a large crowd, but not all are given the privilege of knowing the mysteries of the kingdom. Jesus explains the parable only to His disciples (vv. 10ff), and the rest hear only the parable, which is a riddle and a veil. To some it is given — by God — to understand the mysteries of the kingdom that are being revealed. To some it is *not* given, and even what they have is taken away from them. The parables not only talk *about* an "inside" and "outside" group but *form* those groups. Those who come to Jesus seeking explanations are the ones who receive the mysteries; those who listen but do not ask are the ones who fail to receive the kingdom. Parables are effective in another way as well. Jesus is not giving instruction about what to do so much as re-imagining how the world is. Jesus is giving a picture of reality and inviting us to inhabit that reality. Those who hear and cling to Jesus live in a different communal and imaginative world than those outside.

Third, this chapter helps us to see the meaning and proper interpretation of parables. The word "parable" has come to mean "story," but the Hebrew word behind the New Testament usage, and the New Testament word itself, has a broader meaning. A parable might be a similitude, a simple simile or metaphor, as some of Jesus' parables are in this chapter – the comparison of the kingdom to leaven does not tell a story, but only draws a comparison between the kingdom of heaven and a woman putting leaven into a lump of dough. Sometimes parables are simply proverbs – the Hebrew word translated as parable can mean either a parable or a proverb. In verse 35, Jesus quotes from Psalm 78, which is a Psalm that summarizes the history of Israel, drawing instruction from history, and Jesus, following the Psalmist, calls this a "parable."

We have heard many of Jesus' parables so often that we do not consider them to be mysterious. But Jesus says that His parables are mysterious, veiling their meaning. They are riddles, and we need the key to understand them. Jesus makes it plain that parables should be interpreted as allegories. In His interpretation of the parable of the sower, every detail has a symbolic meaning – the sower, the seed, the different sorts of ground, the thorns. He does the same when he explains the parable of the tares and wheat – the sower, the seed, the tares, the enemy, even the reapers represent specific realities. It is entirely legitimate to ask, when Jesus does not explicitly explain it, what the details signify. What is the mustard seed? What are the birds of the air in that parable? Who is the woman who puts the leaven in the lump of dough? What is the leaven? Though Jesus does not say it explicitly, He implies that His parables are explanations of His own work and ministry. They are about the "mysteries of the kingdom," the kingdom that He has been proclaiming. And most of the parables become much clearer when we recognize the parables are not moral stories in general, but are commentaries on the situation of Jesus, His disciples, and the Jews of His time. They tell us about Jesus' ministry and its effects.

At one level, the sower parable is fairly easy to understand, especially after Jesus explains it. The sower is a preacher of the Word, and the seed is the Word of the kingdom, the proclamation of the kingdom. That word is broadcast, spread out indiscriminately, but there are different responses to it, represented by different kinds of soil. Adam was made from dust, and so it is fitting that dirt should represent people receiving the word. Some dirt is hard and packed down; that is, some people hear the word but do little more than hear it. It does not mean anything to them (v. 19). That seed lies on the ground, until Satan snatches it away. On rocky places, the seed springs up. There is real life, and real growth and real joy in receiving the word of the kingdom, but the seed does not go deep and has no root. When this hearer faces difficulties, he fades. The third receives the word, and it begins to grow, but it is too entangled in worries and the deceitful pursuit of riches, and it is choked out. The good soil is distinguished primarily by its fruitfulness: Hearers receive the seed of the word, and the word multiplies. Is that you?

So far, so simple. But there are signs that something else is going on. In Daniel 2, Daniel recalls and interprets the dream of Nebuchadnezzar, who sees a statue of four materials. A stone cut without hands breaks down the statue and grinds it to powder. The stone then begins to grow into a mountain that fills the whole earth. There are multiple connections with Matthew 13. In the Greek Old Testament, the word "mystery" appears only in Daniel 2, and Daniel 2 also talks about the "kingdom" that will be set up by the "God of heaven." Both Daniel 2 and Matthew 13 have a four-fold structure: Nebuchadnezzar sees a statue of four materials, which Daniel interprets as four kingdoms, beginning with Babylon and ending with Rome. Jesus says that He reveals the mystery of the kingdom of heaven in talking about a sower whose seed goes on four different types of soil. The connections suggest that, like Daniel, Jesus is explaining the history of Israel over a lengthy period of time.

Why would Jesus use the notion of "sowing" to explain the mystery of the kingdom? Why not a statue and a stone, like Daniel? Or a series of four beasts that come out of the sea, as in Daniel 7? In the prophets, "sowing" is a common image of the return from exile (Isa. 61:11; Jer. 31:27; Ezek. 36:9; Hos. 2:23). When Babylon invaded Judah, they emptied the land of people and animals. At the return, Yahweh will sow the land again with man and beast.[4] Alongside the promise of physical return, Yahweh promises to sow the land with the word, so that it produces righteousness and

---

4   There is a literal dimension to this: During the exile, the land remained fallow, uncultivated. The return of the people of Israel was also the return of sowing.

peace (Isa. 55:10-11; 61:11). Jesus is talking about the Lord's sowing, and the effects of that sowing, and He is talking about His *own* sowing as the climax to the Lord's re-sowing of the land with the word. Over centuries, the Lord spread out seed indiscriminately. Satan snatches away the seed, some fall away during persecution because they are shallowly rooted, and some are choked by love of the world. Previous sowings have not had much effect. A few seeds spring up here and there, briefly, but there has been no fruit and no harvest. Even now, in Jesus' own ministry, it does not look very promising. Capernaum and Bethsaida will not listen, and when He goes to His home synagogue at the end of the chapter, everyone is offended because of Him.

But the Lord has not given up. He comes back for one last sowing, the sowing of Jesus. And Jesus' parable assures us that, this time, there *will* be a harvest, the word will not return void, the seed will go into the ground, die, and rise to bear much fruit. Though Jesus' disciples are only a small boat tossed on the sea, someday there will be no more sea, and the earth will be filled with the knowledge of the Lord as the waters now cover the sea. Though Jesus' ministry looks like a failure, it is the small stone aimed at the feet of the imperial statue, which will grind the statue to powder and then grow into a mountain that fills the whole earth. It looks small as a seed, but it will spring up thirty-, sixty-, and hundred-fold.

If you know this, you have been given to know the mysteries of the kingdom of heaven.

Seeds and Leaven
Matthew 13:24-43

[24]Jesus presented another parable to them, saying, "The kingdom of heaven may be compared to a man who sowed good seed in his field. [25] But while his men were sleeping, his enemy came and sowed tares among the wheat, and went away. [26] But when the wheat sprouted and bore grain, then

the tares became evident also. ²⁷ The slaves of the landowner came and said to him, 'Sir, did you not sow good seed in your field? How then does it have tares?' ²⁸ And he said to them, 'An enemy has done this!' The slaves said to him, 'Do you want us, then, to go and gather them up?' ²⁹ But he said, 'No; for while you are gathering up the tares, you may uproot the wheat with them. ³⁰ Allow both to grow together until the harvest; and in the time of the harvest I will say to the reapers, "First gather up the tares and bind them in bundles to burn them up; but gather the wheat into my barn."'" ³¹ He presented another parable to them, saying, "The kingdom of heaven is like a mustard seed, which a man took and sowed in his field; ³² and this is smaller than all other seeds, but when it is full grown, it is larger than the garden plants and becomes a tree, so that the birds of the air come and nest in its branches." ³³ He spoke another parable to them, "The kingdom of heaven is like leaven, which a woman took and hid in three pecks of flour until it was all leavened." ³⁴ All these things Jesus spoke to the crowds in parables, and He did not speak to them without a parable. ³⁵ This was to fulfill what was spoken through the prophet: "I will open my mouth in parables; I will utter things hidden since the foundation of the world." ³⁶ Then He left the crowds and went into the house. And His disciples came to Him and said, "Explain to us the parable of the tares of the field." ³⁷ And He said, "The one who sows the good seed is the Son of Man, ³⁸ and the field is the world; and as for the good seed, these are the sons of the kingdom; and the tares are the sons of the evil one; ³⁹ and the enemy who sowed them is the devil, and the harvest is the end of the age; and the reapers are angels. ⁴⁰ So just as the tares are gathered up and burned with fire, so shall it be at the end of the age. ⁴¹ The Son of Man will send forth His angels, and they will gather out of His kingdom all stumbling blocks, and those who commit lawlessness, ⁴² and will throw them into the furnace of fire; in that place there will be weeping and gnashing of teeth. ⁴³ Then the righteous will shine forth as the sun in the kingdom of their Father. He who has ears, let him hear."

One of the keys to the parable of the wheat and tares is to understand the time frame. Jesus is speaking in pictures and symbols about some period of history, but *which*? What is the beginning, and what is the end of the parable? Is Jesus talking about what happens *after* Him, what happened *before* Him, or something else?

Typically, the parable of the tares and wheat has been understood as a description of church history (cf. Augustine). Jesus is the owner sowing the field, the devil sows tares into the church (like Judas), and for that reason the church remains a "mixed multitude" until the end. We have to be patient with evil members of the church until the world ends and the Lord clears the tares from His people. The parable of the mustard seed is read as a parable about the history of the church as well: Jesus has only a handful of close disciples during His lifetime, but over the centuries the mustard seed becomes a tree in which the birds find shelter. During Jesus' ministry, the leaven is put in the loaf, and through the history of the church the loaf is permeated until it is entirely leavened.

Those readings are not entirely wrong. The history of the church *does* follow these patterns. The church is a mixed multitude, and, while we are responsible to exercise church discipline, we cannot read hearts. There are hypocrites in the church who will not be revealed as such until the last judgment. The church did start small, and become great. The church is like a packet of leaven permeating the lump of the universe. We can even say that these stories reveal a movement that recurs over and over in the history of the church. Luther was a mustard seed, but from him came a great tree. Missionaries sent to nineteenth-century Africa pressed leaven in the lump of Africa, and which has been leavening the lump ever since. These parables teach us about God's ways and help us to anticipate what happens next. Whenever a field is planted with wheat, whenever we see the word spreading out through the world, we can expect the devil to spread his own seed, and the two grow up until a harvest. Whenever the gospel enters a new field, we expect it to operate secretly, like leaven in dough. These are mysteries of God's dealings throughout the ages. By learning to interpret parables, God forms us into prophets who know the times and can anticipate trajectories.

For several reasons, though, I think Jesus is talking primarily about the history of Israel that climaxes in His own ministry. We tend to read the parables as if Jesus' ministry is at the *beginning* of the parables. He is the Son of Man sowing seed; He is the one planting the mustard seed; He is the one who puts the leaven in the lump. He is the beginning of the story, and the rest of the story is what happens after Jesus. I am suggesting that we consider the possibility that Jesus comes at the *end* of the story. For example: The parable of wheat and tares ends with a harvest when the wheat and tares are separated from one another. Jesus has already observed that Israel is ready for harvest: "The harvest is plentiful, but the workers are few. Therefore beseech the Lord of the harvest to send out workers into His harvest" (Matt. 9:37-38). In the next breath, Jesus gives authority to the Twelve to harvest Israel – both gathering in the wheat and dividing between wheat and tares. For Jesus, harvest time is not in the distant future, but now. And that means He comes at the end of the story of the wheat and tares, rather than at the beginning.

In some parables, this time frame is obvious, and everyone recognizes that Jesus comes at the end of the story rather than the beginning. The most obvious of these is the parable of the vineyard and the tenants (Matthew 21). An owner leases his vineyard to tenants and then sends His servants to collect rent. The tenants abuse the servants and chase them away. Finally, at the *end* of the story, the owner sends his son, whom the tenants kill in hopes of seizing the vineyard for themselves. Obviously, this is about Israel rejecting the prophets who were sent to her; the Son's coming is the coming of Jesus, and He comes at the *end* of the story and is followed by a judgment that crushes the rebellious tenants to dust. I am suggesting that we think about reading the parables of Matthew 13 in the same framework.

Matt. 13:34-35 shows that Jesus is retelling the story of Israel, not foretelling the story of the church. Matthew pauses to explain, again, why Jesus teaches in parables, saying that Jesus' teaching fulfills what he calls the "prophecy" of Psalm 78. The quotation in Matt. 13:35 is from the opening of Psalm 78. The "parable" or "dark sayings" of Psalm 78 are not prophecies but histories: "which we have heard and known, and our fathers have told us" (Psalm 78:3). Psalm 78 describes the exodus; Israel's rebellion in the wilderness; the Lord's provision of water, manna, and meat in the desert; and the incident at Shiloh when the Philistines captured the ark. It is about Yahweh's wonders for Israel, Israel's forgetfulness of Yahweh, and Yahweh's work in Egypt and the wilderness. Psalm 78 ends with Yahweh awakening from sleep, driving His enemies away, building His sanctuary, and choosing David to shepherd Israel. The Psalm is about Yahweh's intervention in the history of rebellious Israel and His goodness in giving them a faithful shepherd. Matthew's quotation of Psalm 78 indicates that the "parables" Jesus is telling are the hidden things of Israel's history, the secret that Yahweh will justify and deliver Israel not for their own obedience but for the sake of His own name. The secret that Yahweh will not leave Israel bereft but will justify the ungodly, the secret that David the good shepherd comes at the *end* of a history of rebellion, not at the beginning

With this in mind, let us look back at the parable of the wheat and tares. If Jesus is talking about the history of Israel, which comes to the *climax* in Jesus, what is He saying? As we have seen, the Lord "sows" Israel back into the land after exile, but Matt. 13:38 says that the field is not the land but the "world." So, the sowing is the scattering of the seed of Israel at the time of the exile. Israel is scattered to the four corners of the earth and begins to grow. From the Babylonian exile until the time of Jesus, wheat is growing throughout the Mediterranean world, and Israel is the bread of God to the nations, manna scattered to the Gentiles. But there are rotten figs among the ripe figs, tares among the wheat. At the same time that Israel is scattered to the corners of the earth, the devil scatters weeds among them. This is why Israel is such a mixed people, and why there is so much opposition to Jesus during His lifetime. This is why some Jews in the intertestamental period remain faithful to Yahweh and His Torah, while many

Jews compromise, adopting Greek customs and culture and ways of thinking. Israel is the wheat of the world, but there are tares among the wheat.

To the wheat-plant among the Jews of the first century, it might look as if the Lord is doing nothing, as if He is tolerating the weeds that make the nations blaspheme (Romans 2). The tares seem to be growing and prospering, threatening to take over the wheat field, and the owner of the field has not removed them – no herbicides, no weeding, no effort to deal with the wicked in Israel. Jesus' good news is: *Now* is the judgment of this world; *now* is the prince of this world cast out – along with the weeds that he sowed. The Lord left the wheat and weeds to grow up side-by-side until the harvest, that is, *until Jesus comes*. Now Jesus and His apostles will separate the wheat from the tares, gathering the wheat and leaving the weeds to be burned in fire. Now, at the *end* of the age, the Son of Man will send His angels into the world to gather the wheat and burn the chaff. There is a judgment coming on the wheat field, Israel scattered throughout the world, and this judgment is going to separate wheat and tares.

It is starting already, as Jesus and His disciples go into a field white with harvest. Jesus' quotation from Dan. 12:3 (in Matt 13:43) supports this. Daniel predicts a "time of distress," which is followed by a "resurrection" and glorification of "those who have insight" and "those who lead the many to righteousness" (Dan. 12:1-3).[5] This is usually taken as a prediction of the end of the world, but the "time of distress" refers to the same "time of tribulation" that Jesus speaks of in Matthew 24, which Jesus says will happen before the end of this generation (Matt. 24:34). Daniel predicts the same sequence as Jesus' prophecy in Matthew 24, which is about the destruction of Jerusalem (cf. 24:9, 21, 31, 34-35). Daniel and Jesus are both talking about the end of the seventy weeks of years. Of course, the church *is* a mixed community, including both faithful sons and traitors. But Jesus' parable focuses on the events surrounding the end of the Old Covenant

---

[5] James Jordan, *Handwriting on the Wall* (Atlanta, Ga.: American Vision, 2007).

order. That is the "end of the age." The separating of tares and wheat will take place within the generation of His disciples, when the righteous will shine like the sun.

Can we say the same about the other two parables in this section of Matthew 13? Is the mustard seed planted at the time of the exile or the return from exile? Is the leaven placed within the lump at the time of Jesus, or Pentecost, or earlier? Again, patterns in these parables apply to the history of the church and to many specific episodes in the history of the church. But the question is what Jesus' words mean in the first century. The planting of the mustard seed might refer to the return from exile, but it might also refer to the diaspora, Israel's "sowing" and "scattering" among the Gentiles. The reference to birds in the "tree" might refer to the nations that find refuge in Yahweh's kingdom. The fact that the man sows the mustard seed in his "field" points in the same direction. In the parable of the wheat and tares, the field is the "world," and this is plausibly the same field. Israel is the tiny mustard seed planted among the nations, in the Lord's garden. Yahweh planted the tiny mustard seed of Israel, but as it comes to fruition, it becomes a "tree."

Now, that is not scientifically accurate. The mustard seed produces a bush, a shrub – a large shrub to be sure (8-10 feet high), but a shrub, not a tree. What is Jesus up to then? Is He ignorant of botany? Had He never seen a tree larger than a mustard shrub? That is unlikely, since there are tremendous cedars around Israel. We can defend Jesus' botanical knowledge by pointing out that He says it is larger than the "herbs" (Greek *lachanon*). But He does call it a "tree" (Greek, *dendron*), too, and that is not accurate botanically.

The contrast between reality and Jesus' words is deliberate. By calling the mustard shrub a tree, He evokes several Old Testament passages. Ezekiel 17 is an allegory of exile and return, a "riddle" or "parable" that the Lord gives Ezekiel to tell the people of Israel. An eagle snatches the top of a cedar and takes it to another city, a city of traders, where the sprig of the cedar grows like a "low, spreading vine" beside the waters. Another eagle comes, and the vine turns its roots toward the new eagle, and in so doing pulls itself up from the soil and the waters and then withers. The Lord says this is an allegory of the Babylonian exile. The first eagle is Babylon, which takes the king and high-born nobles from Israel and plants them in a good land beside abundant water. The second eagle is Egypt, to which many in Judah are inclined. Babylon will bring prosperity, but Egypt will wither Judah. At the end of the story, the Lord promises to take a sprig from a cedar and plant it on the high mountain of Israel. Those who remain in Babylon, who seek the peace of the city, will be replanted in the land. The tree is going to become "a stately cedar. And birds of every kind will nest under it; they will nest in the shade of its branches" (Ezek. 17:23). Daniel 4 is another riddle about a tree where the birds of the air find refuge. Nebuchadnezzar is that tree. He is cut down, humbled, and driven from the world of men to become an animal for a time.

Jesus evokes all this by calling the mustard bush as a "tree" in which "birds of the air find nest." But what is most striking is the contrast between the plants. Ezekiel speaks of a cedar that spreads throughout the land; Nebuchadnezzar's tree is "great in height" (Dan. 4:10). By comparison, the mustard bush is pathetically small; to say that birds of the air find refuge in the branches of the bush – just like they do in a cedar or an imperial tree – sounds laughable. It is a "parody of itself."[6]

But that is Jesus' point. Israel was planted in the field of the world as a tiny seed, and when it grew up, it became – *TA DA!* – a bush! Even Jews looking at the "bush" of Israel were tempted to despise it. "We're supposed to be the great cedar! We're supposed to be the tallest mountain of them all!" Even Jews looking at the pathetic little bush are tempted to put their fortunes with the high and mighty cedars – to adopt the ways of Babylon and Egypt, of Greece and Rome. At least they look like *trees*!

---

[6] David Garland, *Reading Matthew: A Literary and Theological Commentary* (Macon, Ga.: Smyth and Helwys, 2001).

Jesus as Israel

Yet Israel is, despite appearances, the tree in which the birds of the air nest. It truly is the tree where the beasts of the field find shade, where the nations find refuge. Israel is the tree from which all living things eat (Daniel 4). When Israel rebuilt the temple after the exile, it seemed to be far less glorious than the temple of Solomon, and many of the Jews mourned the decline. But it was *not* a decline. Appearances deceived, and the smaller second temple was truly the house of prayer for all nations, just as the pathetic mustard "tree" – which is only a tree in quotation marks – is truly the imperial tree of all the earth. This is why the kingdom is a mystery. This is why some people cannot understand. The hidden meaning of Israel's history, the meaning that Jesus brings to fruition, is that the cosmic tree of the world is not the great, spreading imperial tree of Rome, but the small, despised, bushy-tree of Israel.

The leaven parable has a similar twist. Leaven is not, as some believe, always a symbol of corruption and evil influence. Israel ate *leavened* bread at Pentecost. Yet leaven is often a symbol of a dynamic evil that has to be purged. At the feast of unleavened bread, Israel was to put away old leaven. The feast of unleavened bread was a new beginning, as Israel put away the leaven of Egypt, the idolatrous attractions and desires that had permeated Israel and needed to be plucked out. No leaven was ever put on the altar, and Jesus in the gospels warns of the leaven of the scribes and Pharisees.

But God works like leaven. He uses despised things to overturn things that are honored. He uses the "unclean" and the apparently "corrupting" to leaven the lump of Israel. His prophets were leaven – considered unclean and dangerous, and subverting established ways of living and worshiping. Jesus is seen as a dangerously corrupting man, and He *is* corrupting Israel, if you are a Pharisee. He is spending all His time with tax gatherers and sinners. How can you build a kingdom from that?[7]

---

[7] Garland, *Reading Matthew*, 152. I am following Garland: "To compare the kingdom of heaven to leaven is to invert the common images of sacred and profane.... It would be like saying that the kingdom of heaven is like 'rust' or a

Yet Yahweh does. Israel is being leavened from the time of the exile by the prophets and others who are considered corrupting, but who are preparing the lump of dough to become bread. If we extend the metaphor, the goal is not just leavened dough, but bread. Israel is going to be bread for the world, but only after it has been thoroughly permeated by the "corruption" of the prophets and Jesus, and then tossed into the oven. Israel has to pass through fire before it is ready to be broken and given out to the nations.

These parables are allegories of Israel's history first of all, but they also show us patterns of God's work throughout the ages. As we absorb these parables, as they transform our hearts and imaginations, we begin to see similar patterns throughout the history of the church. One of the things we learn from all this is the centrality of faith. In these parables faith takes two forms. Faith means patience. Yahweh did not tear out the tares from Israel before the harvest; He planted a tiny seed and waited for it to grow. A lump of dough is not leavened immediately. God's kingdom comes slowly, and if we are going to keep in step with the King and His Spirit, we need to be patient.

Faith also means that we do not trust our senses. We trust God's word more than what we perceive. It looks as if the owner of the field is going to tolerate weeds forever; but He will not. There will be a harvest. It looks as if the "tree" of the kingdom is pretty tiny compared to the empires and nations of the world. That's false. The mustard bush is the central tree of the world. It looks as if corruption is working its way through the lump, but that apparent corruption is God's way of leavening the whole lump of dough, preparing it for baking. Jesus shows us that the ways of God's kingdom are not the ways of the kingdoms of this

---

'virus.' It is a rather iconoclastic image, but it accords with Jesus' assertion that the tax collectors and harlots enter into the kingdom of heaven before the chief priests and elders (21:32) and Matthew's conviction that one must believe that the kingdom has come in Jesus, the son of God who was crucified. The question is not: 'Can something so contemptibly small be representative of the work of God?' but 'Can something so contemptible be representative of the work of God?'"

world. God's kingdom comes slowly, silently, imperceptibly, and even when it comes it does not necessarily overwhelm us with its grandeur. That is not the kind of kingdom we expect or want, but it is the kind of kingdom we should expect from a King who brings His kingdom through a cross.

Seek the Kingdom
Matthew 13:44-58

[44] "The kingdom of heaven is like a treasure hidden in the field, which a man found and hid again; and from joy over it he goes and sells all that he has and buys that field. [45] Again, the kingdom of heaven is like a merchant seeking fine pearls, [46] and upon finding one pearl of great value, he went and sold all that he had and bought it. [47] Again, the kingdom of heaven is like a dragnet cast into the sea, and gathering fish of every kind; [48] and when it was filled, they drew it up on the beach; and they sat down and gathered the good fish into containers, but the bad they threw away. [49] So it will be at the end of the age; the angels will come forth and take out the wicked from among the righteous, [50] and will throw them into the furnace of fire; in that place there will be weeping and gnashing of teeth. [51] Have you understood all these things?" They said to Him, "Yes." [52] And Jesus said to them, "Therefore every scribe who has become a disciple of the kingdom of heaven is like a head of a household, who brings out of his treasure things new and old." [53] When Jesus had finished these parables, He departed from there. [54] He came to His hometown and began teaching them in their synagogue, so that they were astonished, and said, "Where did this man get this wisdom and these miraculous powers? [55] Is not this the carpenter's son? Is not His mother called Mary, and His brothers, James and Joseph and Simon and Judas? [56] And His sisters, are they not all with us? Where then did this man get all these things?" [57] And they took offense at Him But Jesus said to them, "A prophet is not without honor except in his hometown and in his own household." [58] And He did not do many miracles there because of their unbelief.

Jesus' parables are allegories of Israel's history, culminating in Jesus. The parable of the tares is about the devil sowing tares among the wheat of diaspora Israel. For centuries, tares and wheat have been growing together, but Jesus comes with a scythe in hand to begin the harvest and to separate wheat and weeds. The mustard seed was planted, and Israel has become – despite appearances to the contrary – the imperial tree where the birds of the air find nesting. Jesus is also commenting on His own ministry. His stories predict how things will play out in His own lifetime, and in the lifetime of His disciples. These dimensions of the parables correspond because Jesus is Israel.

Verses 44-58 mark the final section of the "day of parables" where Matthew presents Jesus as the new Solomon. The chapter is surrounded by references to Solomon and Solomonic wisdom. Rebuking the Pharisees when they ask for a sign, Jesus tells them that someone greater than Solomon has come. The Pharisees should imitate the Queen of Sheba, who came from the ends of the earth to hear the wisdom of Solomon (Matt. 12:42). At the end of Matthew 13, there is another reference to "wisdom" (v. 54), the wisdom that Jesus displays in His hometown but which the people reject.

The allusions to Solomon pinpoint where we are in Jesus' recapitulation of the history of Israel. Right after Solomon's reign, a large portion of Israel rejected Solomon, broke away from the house of David, and formed the kingdom of Israel from ten tribes to the north of Judah. In Solomon's case, the division occurred because of his own folly and sin. Yahweh raised up adversaries, including Jeroboam, and Solomon lost part of His kingdom. Jesus is without sin, and the opposition to Him is not a judgment for his own sin. But we see an analogy. Jesus comes as God's wisdom, announcing a kingdom, and the people do not want to hear the wisdom He speaks. They want another king, perhaps one, like Jeroboam, who has learned statecraft in Egypt and who knows how to design golden calves.

The intensity of the opposition is evident in Matthew 14. In Nazareth, the people take offense at Jesus, and He does not do many miracles. There is no immediate threat to Jesus' life, but Matthew inserts the story of John the Baptist's death, which foreshadows Jesus' future. If the people of Jesus' own hometown reject the new Solomon, then the Herods, already shown to be a murderous royal house (Matthew 2), will stop at nothing to remove Jesus.

In this last section as the Solomonic sage, Jesus sounds like Solomon in Proverbs, telling his son that wisdom is more valuable than anything (cf. Prov. 4:5-9; 8:11; 16:16; 23:23). The two brief parables about the treasure and the pearl are obviously companions (vv. 44-46), reiterating the Solomonic exhortation and applying them to the kingdom. Both describe the kingdom as something of such great value that one must "sell all that he has" to gain it. Both parables illustrate a point Jesus has made already in the sermon on the mount, namely, that we should seek the kingdom above all else. In Matthew 6, Jesus told His disciples not to be anxious for food, drink, clothing, or any other necessity. The Father provides liberally for His children, so there is nothing to fear. These two parables make the same point in a more symbolic form. A true disciple is willing to give up everything for the sake of the kingdom, willing to sell all in order to have the pearl.

There is a demand here. There is a radical call. But there is a promise attached. In both parables, the men give up everything they have, but in both cases they do it because they are receiving something of greater value. Again, Jesus has said something very similar in Matthew 6: If you give up all for the sake of the kingdom, the Father promises to give you whatever you need. Treasure on earth is corruptible; moth and rust destroy. Heavenly treasure is better, eternally durable. Jesus does not simply impose demands, but imposes demands and offers promises. That is why the men respond to the demand with joy. They do not drop everything to achieve the kingdom out of a grim sense of duty. They act in a frenzy of delight because the hidden things are things they have been wanting *forever*.

There is obvious commonality between the two parables, but there are differences between them. The kingdom comes to the man in the field as an unexpected surprise, while the merchant is already seeking pearls when he finds the pearl of the world. The treasure is found on land, associated with Israel, and the pearl is found in the sea, associated with Gentiles. Jesus may be contrasting the way the kingdom will come to Jews and Gentiles. Jews will stumble across the treasure hiding in plain sight, right there in the land, wherever the itinerant Nazarene rabbi teaches and heals. Gentiles find the kingdom after long, fruitless searching in the depths of the sea.

Jesus tells parables that are allegories of Israel's history. Can we find something similar at work here?

Commentators commonly question the first man's sanity and honesty. He finds a treasure and hides it in the *same* field, then arranges to purchase the field so he can have the treasure. That means he found a treasure in someone *else's* field, and instead of informing the owner about the value of his property, he buys the field for himself. Clearly, he pays less for the field than he would have if the prior owner knew it contained a treasure. He low-balls, and he gets the field and treasure. Some commentators think the purchaser has acted immorally. It is as if he finds an oil reserve beneath the land, and buys it before the owner can do a geological survey.

There may be something to this. Elsewhere, Jesus tells the parable of a steward who wins friends by writing down their debts to his former master. The "unjust steward" steals from his former employer in order to gain access to someone else's service when he is cast out. Perhaps Jesus' parable presumes that the seller is responsible for knowing the value of what he sells, and it is not the purchaser's responsibility to explain why the price should be higher.

These considerations complicate the parable. It is not simply about the value of the kingdom. The whole implied storyline is the storyline of the kingdom. It is not only a story about a man who places a high value on the kingdom; it is about an owner who *does not* know the value of what he has. The owner is an Esau, who does not value his birthright as he should, who does not even know that it contains hidden treasure. And when we introduce the possibility that this is a parable about Israel (since, in contrast to the pearl story, it is a land-based parable), we can see that the parable is about Israel becoming Esau. Gentiles, or the faithful among Israel, or Jews other than the Jewish leaders, are stumbling on the treasure that the Jewish leaders own but do not value. When they discover the treasure, they do whatever they need to gain the field. Thus they prove themselves true sons of Jacob. In short, this parable foreshadows the parable of the vineyard, where the kingdom is taken from the tenants and given to others (Matthew 21).

Both parables indicate that the coming of the kingdom inverts and subverts the normal pattern of life. Both men act irrationally. What are these men going to do about the future? What about their hedge funds and pensions? What about saving up for the kids' college education? What about supporting their families? Are not they acting rashly? This is what the kingdom does. The kingdom is of such surpassing value that it overturns normal economic calculations, accepted standards of rational self-interest. The advent of the kingdom shatters the world, it shatters our expectations and ideas about the future, and if we are going to respond to the demand of the kingdom properly, we need to act in a radical way.

Jesus depicts this overturning of normal values in economic terms, but the transvaluation of values is broader. Jesus indicates that the proper response to the news of the kingdom is to throw off everything in order to seek the kingdom. Drop your projects, your plans, your purposes, and reorient them so that you are seeking the kingdom above all things. Gaining the kingdom means giving up other projects and possibilities. It means radically changing what we thought our life was about, directing all our energies along new paths.

It is not accidental that Jesus uses economic terminology to describe the proper response to the kingdom. Gaining the kingdom means having a certain attitude toward wealth; it means "selling all we have" to attain the kingdom. Jesus says elsewhere that it is easier for a camel to go through the eye of a needle than for a rich man to enter the kingdom. Rich men are attached not only to their wealth, but to the world that creates their wealth and the way their wealth creates its own world. Wealth brings so many comforts as well as protection. If you are rich, you can do anything legal, and if you do something illegal, you can hire the best lawyers to get you off. They are attached to the delusion that they can control the future, to standards of value that their riches communicate to them, to certain ways of behaving – assessing costs and benefits in coldly rational terms. This will not work for the kingdom. The kingdom has a different set of values. For an entrepreneur, no purchase is a final purchase. You buy in order to sell and buy again in order to sell again. Jesus is describing the end of selling, a *final* purchase. The man with the pearl is left with something that is of great value – but what can He do with it? Jesus clearly does not expect the man to sell the pearl that he has just purchased with everything he owns. The kingdom, Jesus says, is of surpassing value, and, in terms of the world's valuations, *completely useless*.

That is the crunch point. That is where we stumble. We have lots of ways of blunting the force of these demands. We point to all the rich men of the Old Testament – Abraham, Jacob, Job, David. We point out that everything God created is good and should be received with thanksgiving. All this is true, but do we point these things out because we want to be faithful to Jesus? Or do we point these things out because we do not like Jesus upsetting our plans? We do not want a Jesus who interferes with our aspirations, our version of the American dream. But that means we do not really want Jesus, because Jesus is the one who says we need to hazard *all* on one thing, on the kingdom of God.

The parable of the dragnet in Matthew 13 repeats some of the themes of the parable of the wheat and tares. Both are allegories of Israel's history, and both speak of gathering, separating good and bad, the "end of the age" (vv. 39, 49), angels (vv. 41, 49), a "furnace of fire" (vv. 42, 50), and "weeping and gnashing of teeth" (vv. 42, 50). Yet the settings are different: The parable of the wheat is a land-based story, while the dragnet is on the sea. Again, the contrast is between Yahweh's work with Israel (in the wheat and tare parable) and His work among the Gentiles (in the dragnet). Israel has been sown with false sons, Esaus who despise their birthright, and as Israel has netted adherents among the sea of nations, she has gathered some good and some bad (v. 48). With Jesus, the time has arrived to separate the good and bad fish. This fits also with Jesus' comparison of His disciples to "fishers of men." They too will net all sorts of fish, but the time will come when they have to sort through them all.

The disciples profess to understand Jesus (v. 51), and Jesus commends them as Israel's new scribes who have become disciples of the kingdom. Because the Twelve are scribes, they can bring old things out of their treasure; because they have become disciples, they can bring new things. Jesus does not envision any conflict between the new and the old. He is not a traditionalist, but He does not reject what is old either. Jesus is talking here about teachers, not about every disciple. And He contrasts the scribes discipled by the kingdom with the scribes who exist in Israel. The Pharisees also bring out treasure, but it is corrupted treasure (Matt. 12:35). The Twelve have understood Jesus' parables and His explanations of them, and so they are prepared to be teachers. Jesus has brought out things old and new from His own treasure, and He prepares the Twelve to do the same.

The key to bringing out old and new treasure is to be instructed by Jesus and to understand Him. The "old" probably refers here to the Old Covenant, or the Torah specifically. The "new" refers to Jesus' teaching and the coming of the new. The order is intriguing, putting "new" before "old." They will not be able to bring out the old treasures unless they have received the new.

Jesus has declared Himself the climax of Israel's history. He starts the harvest. He brings the final sowing that will produce fruit. He announces the kingdom of such worth that we should sell all in order to follow Him. This is not a message calculated to leave people lukewarm. He demands total commitment, and those who refuse are condemned as tares, as bad fish that are going to be tossed into the fire. He is a scandal, and we find at the end of Matthew 13 an example of a faithless response to Jesus.

Matthew describes Jesus' new family, made up of those who do the Father's will (Matt. 12:46-50). After a series of parables in Matthew 13, Matthew returns to this family theme and shows Jesus' hometown rejecting Him. They are first astonished (Matt. 13:54) but eventually "stumble" at Him because He is too familiar (Matt. 13:57). The people of Nazareth enact Jesus' parable of the sower; He comes to sow seed, but it does not take root in His hometown.

According to Davies and Allison,[8] Matthew organizes the incident at Nazareth in Matt. 13:54-58 as a chiasm:

A. Jesus comes to his *patris* and teaches in the synagogue
   B. People are amazed
      C. Where did he come from? Do not we know his family?
   B'. People are scandalized
A'. Jesus speaks about His *patris* and does not do miracles

This little narrative shows the movement from amazement to scandal that has characterized Israel's reaction to Jesus. Nazareth is a microcosm of Jesus' "fatherland." His people object to Jesus' familiarity: Who does he think he is? He is just a craftsman's son; how dare He come in here and put on airs as if he were something great? These questions raise the issue of the source of Jesus' power. How can he do these things? This is the same question the

---

8   W. D. Davies and Dale Allison, *Matthew*, ICC, 3 vols (London: T&T Clark, 2004).

Pharisees asked earlier, but they charged that Jesus' power came from the devil. The people of Nazareth do not have an answer, but they have the same source of scandal.

Jesus says that what He offers is more valuable than anything we have, so valuable that we should give up *everything* to find it. He comes telling about things hidden from the foundation of the world, and we can know and acquire these hidden things if we sell everything and follow Him. Are we going to do it? Or do we, like Jesus' own family, find Him a little extreme; have we become so familiar with Jesus that we blunt the force of His demands? Are we offended by Jesus when He makes these absolute demands? Or do we recognize the value of what He gives and sell what we have out of the sheer joy of finding hidden treasure?

Two Feasts, Two Kingdoms
Matthew 14:1-36

[1] At that time Herod the tetrarch heard the news about Jesus, [2] and said to his servants, "This is John the Baptist; he has risen from the dead, and that is why miraculous powers are at work in him." [3] For when Herod had John arrested, he bound him and put him in prison because of Herodias, the wife of his brother Philip. [4] For John had been saying to him, "It is not lawful for you to have her." [5] Although Herod wanted to put him to death, he feared the crowd, because they regarded John as a prophet. [6] But when Herod's birthday came, the daughter of Herodias danced before them and pleased Herod, [7] so much that he promised with an oath to give her whatever she asked. [8] Having been prompted by her mother, she said, "Give me here on a platter the head of John the Baptist." [9] Although he was grieved, the king commanded it to be given because of his oaths, and because of his dinner guests. [10] He sent and had John beheaded in the prison. [11] And his head was brought on a platter and given to the girl, and she brought it to her mother. [12] His disciples came and took away the body and buried it; and they went and reported to Jesus. [13] Now when Jesus heard about John, He withdrew from there in a boat to a

secluded place by Himself; and when the people heard of this, they followed Him on foot from the cities. [14] When He went ashore, He saw a large crowd, and felt compassion for them and healed their sick. [15] When it was evening, the disciples came to Him and said, "This place is desolate and the hour is already late; so send the crowds away, that they may go into the villages and buy food for themselves." [16] But Jesus said to them, "They do not need to go away; you give them something to eat!" [17] They said to Him, "We have here only five loaves and two fish." [18] And He said, "Bring them here to Me." [19] Ordering the people to sit down on the grass, He took the five loaves and the two fish, and looking up toward heaven, He blessed the food, and breaking the loaves He gave them to the disciples, and the disciples gave them to the crowds, [20] and they all ate and were satisfied. They picked up what was left over of the broken pieces, twelve full baskets. [21] There were about five thousand men who ate, besides women and children. [22] Immediately he made the disciples get into the boat and go before him to the other side, while he dismissed the crowds. [23] And after he had dismissed the crowds, he went up on the mountain by himself to pray. When evening came, he was there alone, [24] but the boat by this time was a long way from the land, beaten by the waves, for the wind was against them. [25] And in the fourth watch of the night he came to them, walking on the sea. [26] But when the disciples saw him walking on the sea, they were terrified, and said, "It is a ghost!" and they cried out in fear. [27] But immediately Jesus spoke to them, saying, "Take heart; it is I. Do not be afraid." [28] And Peter answered him, "Lord, if it is you, command me to come to you on the water." [29] He said, "Come." So Peter got out of the boat and walked on the water and came to Jesus. [30] But when he saw the wind, he was afraid, and beginning to sink he cried out, "Lord, save me." [31] Jesus immediately reached out his hand and took hold of him, saying to him, "O you of little faith, why did you doubt?"[32] And when they got into the boat, the wind ceased. [33] And those in the boat worshiped him, saying, "Truly you are the Son of God." [34] And when they had crossed over, they came to land at Gennesaret. [35] And when the men of that place recognized him, they sent around to all that region and brought to him all who were sick [36] and implored him that they might only touch the fringe of his garment. And as many as touched it were made well.

Jesus preaches in parables, according to Matt. 13:14-15, to fulfill the prophecy of Isaiah concerning Israel. That prophecy describes how Israel, blind and deaf because of her own sins, will be further blinded and made deaf by the Lord speaking things they do not understand. Parables intensify judgment against Israel. Parables fill Israel with strange, obscure speech, as if they were already being invaded. According to Isaiah 6, this judgment will continue until the land is made desolate, until the people are driven into exile. Because of Israel's rejection of Jesus, the threat of a Roman invasion hangs over them.

But Isaiah's prophecy is not without hope. For example, Isa. 6:13 says, "But yet a tenth will be in it, and will return and be for consuming, as a terebinth tree or as an oak, whose stump remains when it is cut down. So the holy seed shall be its stump." The great tree of Israel will be cut down, and not much will remain. But there *will* be a stump, and from that stump will grow a branch that will be the restoration of Israel. Just a few chapters later, in Isaiah 11, the prophet returns to the image of a cut tree that comes back to life: "Then a shoot will spring from the stem of Jesse, and a branch from his roots will bear fruit. The Spirit of the Lord will rest on Him, the spirit of wisdom and understanding, the spirit of counsel and strength, the spirit of knowledge and the fear of the Lord." Isaiah 6, which Jesus cites in Matthew 13, is not just a prophecy of judgment and destruction. It contains a promise of renewal and restoration. The people will be driven out and the land made desolate, but Yahweh promises that a holy seed will remain. Despite the judgment, the Lord will not abandon Israel, and from the remnant of Israel, Yahweh promises to raise up a Spirit-filled servant.[9]

---

9   Isaiah 6 connects Matthew 13 and 14, but the two chapters are linked in another way as well. Matthew 13 ends with a story of Jesus' rejection in Nazareth. In Matthew 14, unbelief intensifies. Unbelieving Herod does not just refuse to listen to John, but tries to silence him, permanently. And this, of course, foreshadows what will happen to Jesus. If Herod puts John to death, he will not scruple at putting Jesus to death.

As we have seen repeatedly, Matthew shows us that Yahweh comes back to Israel, no matter what Israel tries to do to reject Him. Yahweh keeps sending servants, but Israel keeps harassing them, beating them, sending them away. So Yahweh comes in the flesh, and Israel kills Him. Even then, He does not quit. He comes back from the grave, passionate to save His people.

This divine relentlessness is good news for us, but it is not good news for everyone. For the Herods of the world, a resurrected prophet is the worst possible news. A God who keeps coming back is a God who will save; He is also a God who might take vengeance.

Matthew 14 starts out with Herod Antipas thinking about resurrection, the return of a servant of Yahweh, and for Herod it is a terrifying possibility. He cut down a tree, and he is afraid because it seems that a branch has sprung up out of a dead stump. Herod hears about Jesus, and thinks that Jesus is John restored from the grave.

The hope that Matthew holds out for Israel is the same as the hope of Isaiah. Israel cannot survive as a whole if she rejects Jesus, and she is rejecting Jesus. Israel cannot avoid judgment. But once the tree of Israel is cut down, the stump will come to life. God will raise Israel from the dead. And Jesus is already preparing for that by forming the core of a new Israel in the midst of Israel. The hope of Israel is that the Lord will form the core of what will become the "remnant," the remainder of Israel that will persevere through the judgment and form a new Israel.

This is the hope that sustained the faithful during the divided kingdom period in Israel's history, and especially during the period of the dynasty of Omri and Ahab. With Matthew 14, we enter a "divided kingdom period" in the ministry of Jesus. Jesus has spoken in parables like a new Solomon, announcing and describing the kingdom He brings. But the day of parables ends with the people of Nazareth rejecting their king, and then Herod intensifies that rejection by killing John. More specifically, with Matthew 14, the story of Jesus overlaps with the history of the dynasty of Ahab, the time of Elijah and Elisha. John is described as Elijah in the New Testament, and this chapter shows us how Elijah-like he was. Like Elijah, John confronts a wicked king. Like Elijah, John also has to deal with an apparently powerful and manipulative queen. Like Elijah, John is admired and feared by the king, but hated by the king's court. Like Elijah, John is threatened by the king. Unlike Elijah, John is actually killed by the king. John is an Elijah who does not ascend to heaven in a fiery chariot.[10]

If John is Elijah, then Jesus is a new Elisha. Even Jesus' name is like "Elisha's": both are built from the Hebrew verb for "save." Jesus' relation to John is like that of Elisha to Elijah. Elisha received the spirit of Elijah and was able to perform some of the same miracles that Elijah had done. Elisha got a *double* portion of Elijah's spirit, the portion of the firstborn, and became the "chief prophet" over a community of sons of the prophets. As soon as John is executed, Jesus withdraws from Israel, and we see Him

---

10 There are echoes of the book of Esther, at least in Mark's version of John's execution. Matthew tells us that when the daughter of Herodias danced before Herod, he promised with an oath to give her whatever she asked. Mark records Herod's words somewhat differently: He promises not just to give what she asks, but promises to give up to half his kingdom (Mark 6:22-23). This is the same promise that Ahasuerus gives to Esther when she says she has a request for him (Est. 5:3, 6). In both passages, we have a woman, a queen, requesting something from a king. In both stories, we have a king promising half his kingdom. We might even say that both Esther and Herodias are asking for someone's head. Esther knows that Haman is plotting to kill all the Jews, and she is asking for his life in order to protect the Jews. There the similarities end. Esther appeals to the king to save the faithful in Israel, while the daughter of Herodias is instructed to ask for the head of a faithful man, albeit a troubler of Herod's kingdom, a prophet who has made life difficult for Herod because of his faithfulness. Instead of being like the protective Ahasuerus in Esther, Herod is more like Haman, seeking to wipe out the true Israel.

Deeper in the background is the story of Jacob and Esau. Because Jacob took the birthright from his brother, Esau sought to kill him, and Jacob had to flee. Herod is an Edomite, an Idumean, descended from Esau, but he is in a sense a successful Esau, an Esau who gets his victim. Herod will later play a role in taking the life of the true Jacob, the true Israel, Jesus. But this victory of Esau is, of course, only temporary and only apparent. It will be swallowed up in the victory of Jacob's resurrection on the third day. The Jacob-Esau framework of Matthew 14 fits neatly with our reading of the parable of the field above, in which we saw the owner of the field as an Esau and the purchaser as a sly Jacob.

perform a sign that reminds us of a sign Elisha performed: feeding a multitude with a few loaves of bread. Jesus mimics Elisha, but something greater than Elisha is here; Jesus does not feed one hundred men with twenty barley loaves, but five thousand men, plus women and children, with five loaves and two fish. Elisha did more miracles than Elijah, and Jesus does more than John. Above all, like Elisha, Jesus forms the core of a future remnant within Israel. He preserves the stump that will spring forth with new life after the judgment comes.

John is like a sacrificial victim, a Passover lamb, innocently slaughtered. In the next pericope, Jesus performs a food miracle, the first such miracle in Matthew. It is a Passover meal, as well as a meal in the wilderness. Following the meal, Jesus' disciples get into a boat to cross the sea, but begin to founder. They are "afflicted," a word that connotes "torture," but Jesus appears and brings them to safety. This is clearly an Exodus story. Jesus comes in the "fourth watch of the night," that is, in Roman time reckoning, toward daybreak (Matt. 14:25), just as Yahweh confused Pharaoh's chariots and divided the sea in front of Israel in the "morning watch" (Exod. 14:24). While the disciples struggle with the waves, Jesus is on a mountain, alone, as Moses went to the mountain alone to pray. Jesus reinforces the exodus theme by His words: When He appears on the sea, He assures His disciples by saying, "it is I" (Matt. 14:27). Several times in Isaiah's "new exodus" section, the Lord assures Israel that they will survive the judgments to come by saying, "It is I" (Isa. 41:4; 43:10). The sentence is a variation on Yahweh, the name revealed to Moses on Sinai. Yahweh is the one who is with Israel, the "I am." In short, as Jesus-Elisha begins to shape His disciples in the core of a new Israel, given Israel's rejection, He leads them through a Passover and Exodus.

Jesus is the true prophet, like Elisha, but He is also an alternative king, king of a second kingdom within Israel. Pleased with the dance of Herodias' daughter at his birthday feast, Herod swears to give her whatever she asks, and eventually gives her John the Baptist's head, on a platter. John's head is the dessert course at Herod's banquet, who is another in a long line of cannibal kings who devour prophets. Mark calls Herod Antipas a "king" for thematic reasons, and perhaps because Herod was considered a "king" in a loose sense in his own time. We know from other sources that Caligula exiled Herod Antipas when he petitioned for the title "King." Matthew is more precise with his term "tetrarch," a term that originally referred to a ruler of a quarter of a kingdom but by the first century had come to mean a petty ruler who ruled a dependent state. Matthew's term is dismissive. Herod the Great gained the title "king of the Jews" from the Romans, and Antipas might fancy himself a king. He is no king; he is a mere "tetrarch," and his behavior is anything but royal.

Herod Antipas, the third Herod to appear in Matthew (cf. 2:1-18, 22), is as murderous as the others. Every time we hear Herod's name in Matthew, some innocent gets slaughtered. Herod the Great appears in Matthew 2, threatening to kill Jesus and actually killing the infants around Bethlehem. The name Herod does not appear again until Matthew 14, where Herod Antipas kills John. Herod does not appear again in Matthew, but the "Herodians" do, and they are trying to trap Jesus so that they can deliver him over to death. We know from Luke that Herod Antipas also plays a role in the death of Jesus.

We can see Herod's murderous character in his dealings with John, but we see it also in the contrast with the ministry of Jesus. Herod rules a kingdom of death, while Jesus brings life and healing (Matt. 14:13-15, 34-36). King Jesus demonstrates the nature of true kingship in the second episode in this passage. He is a king like King Yahweh. In a desolate place far from the palace, Jesus heals the sick (v. 14). When the people need food, Jesus provides it (vv. 15-20), like manna in the wilderness. Herod devours his people; Jesus feeds His people. The five thousand are a new Israel, following the greater Moses in a new Exodus. Jesus tells the multitudes to recline on the grass (v. 19), as the Good Shepherd-King, who brings His people to green pastures (Psalm 23). In Matthew 14 as throughout Scripture, the numbers are significant. After everyone is satisfied, the disciples gather up twelve baskets

(v. 20), a sign of future provision for the twelve tribes. In feeding the five thousand, Jesus goes through the actions of the Last Supper: He takes bread, blesses it, breaks it, and distributes it (v. 19; cf. 26:26-29). Just as John's death foreshadows Jesus', so Jesus' feeding of the five thousand anticipates the perpetual feast of the Eucharist.

Let us take some time to think more about the sea-crossing, in the light of the Old Testament teaching that Yahweh and Yahweh alone has power over the sea. Especially to a land-based people like Israel, the sea is threatening and tumultuous. The sea represents the surging flood of Gentiles that needs to be held back from the land. Israel depended on Yahweh to do the holding back. And so we have numerous passages in the Old Testament that speak of Yahweh striding on the sea, walking on the sea as if it were land (Job 9:8; Psalm 77:19; 107:23-30; Isa. 43:19; Hab. 3:16). Jesus is Yahweh in human flesh, with the same power over the waves, the same authority to walk on the sea and to calm them, the same power to save those who are drowning.

For the first time, Peter takes a lead role in a story about Jesus. He becomes the leading apostle, representative and spokesman for the rest. As Jesus is presented as the new Elisha, Peter is often presented as a Gehazi, the ambiguous servant of Elisha. Some think Peter acted presumptuously by jumping out of the boat before Jesus got there. His doubt, it is said, is the doubt that Jesus will reach them in time. I do not think so. Peter *can* walk on the sea. He does not get very far, and he is frightened by the waves and storm, but for a few moments He shares in Jesus' mastery of the sea. Even though he has only a "little faith," Peter is capable of doing what Jesus did, of moving mountains and tossing them into the sea. What will happen when his faith grows? Look at Acts, and you will know the rest of the story.

The episode shows us what we can expect when we climb into the boat of the church. As we follow the orders of Jesus and push off from shore, we will face storms and Jesus will not be there (or will not appear to be there) to help. We will have to endure the challenges of following Jesus *without* Him, as Adam faced the serpent without the Creator. But the storms will be calmed when Jesus comes. In the meantime, there is nothing to fear. Jesus is master of the wind and waves, and He can calm the storm with a word. He is that "manner of man," the Son of God.

And not only that: We can expect to share in the power of Jesus. Jesus is God's only Son, and He can walk on the waves because He is God. He can calm the sea because He created the sea. But Peter gives us a foretaste of what we can expect – that by faith in Jesus' power, we share in Jesus' power, and we will stride the waves just as He does.

Herod has just killed John, and the storm that the disciples face is a storm that will involve persecution, being delivered to kings to be tried, being threatened with death. Since Cain, the world has been full of Herods, those so hungry for power that they eat anyone who opposes them. And the Herods often seem to be winning. They are able to silence prophets, cut down the trees of God's kingdom, destroy the fruit. Herods stir up the sea of nations, and the little boat of the church seems in danger of overturning, and we fear we will drown. There is *nothing* to fear. Sooner or later, Jesus will come to us, draw us up as we sink into the waves, climb into the boat, and calm the storm. God is never finished, and when Herods dominate the land, He always has a kingdom of His own. He always is leading His people to green pastures and spreading a table in the wilderness.

Herod is thinking about resurrection. He thinks Jesus is John revived. That is *almost* true. Much of what happens to John here later happens to Jesus. Elijah's fate points to the fate of Elisha.

As presented in Matthew, John's ministry prepares for Jesus' work, and John's death foreshadows the cross. Both are seized and bound (14:3; cf. 26:4, 48, 50, 55, 57; 27:2). Herod fears the people because they think John is a prophet (14:5), just as the Jewish leaders fear the people's enthusiasm for Jesus (21:46). Herod hesitates to kill John (14:9), as Pilate tries to get out of killing Jesus (27:1-26). Herodias, Herod's wife, figures into the story (14:3, 8, 11), and so does Pilate's wife (27:19).

John's death foreshadows Jesus' death, and the aftermath of John's death also foreshadows the aftermath of the death of Jesus. Jesus instituted the Supper before His death, but the disciples celebrated it as a memorial after His death and resurrection. John's death is followed by a feast; so is Jesus' death. And after Jesus' resurrection he compels the Twelve to go out to the world, to the Gentile sea, to make disciples of the nations.

Following the meal, Jesus' disciples get into a boat to cross the sea but begin to founder. They are "afflicted," a word that connotes "torture," but Jesus appears and brings them to safety. Subsequent to the Passover feast, this is clearly an Exodus story. Jesus comes in the "fourth watch of the night" – in Roman time reckoning, toward daybreak (v. 25), just as Yahweh confused Pharaoh's chariots and divided the sea in front of Israel in the "morning watch" (Exod. 14:24). While the disciples struggle with the waves, Jesus is on a mountain, alone, as Moses went to the mountain alone to pray. Jesus reinforces the exodus theme by His words: When He appears on the sea, He assures His disciples with "it is I" (v. 27). Several times in Isaiah's "new exodus" section, the Lord assures Israel that they will survive the judgments to come by saying "It is I" (Isa. 41:4; 43:10). The sentence is a variation on Yahweh, the name revealed to Moses on Sinai. Yahweh is the one who is with Israel, the I am. As Jesus-Elisha begins to shape His disciples in the core of a new Israel, given Israel's rejection, He leads them through a Passover and Exodus.

The Old Testament teaches that Yahweh and Yahweh alone has power over the sea. Especially to a land-based people like Israel, the sea is threatening and tumultuous. It represents the surging flood of Gentiles that needs to be held back from the land. Israel depended on Yahweh to do the holding back. Numerous passages speak of Yahweh striding on the sea, walking on the sea as if it were land (Job 9:8; Psa. 77:19; 107:23-30; Isa. 43:19; Hab. 3:16). Jesus is Yahweh in human flesh, with the same power over the waves, the same authority to walk on the sea and to calm them, the same power to save those who are drowning.

But something else is happening here too. For the first time, Peter takes a lead role in a story about Jesus. He becomes the lead apostle, representative and spokesman for the rest. As Jesus is presented as the new Elisha, Peter is often presented as a Gehazi, the ambiguous servant of Elisha. Some think Peter is presumptuous for jumping out of the boat before Jesus got there. His doubt, it is said, is the doubt that Jesus will reach them in time. I do not agree. Peter can walk on the sea. He does not get very far, and he is frightened by the waves and storm, but for a few moments He shares in Jesus' mastery of the sea. Even though he has only a "little faith," Peter is capable of doing what Jesus did, of moving mountains and tossing them into the sea. What will happen when his faith grows? Look at Acts, and you will hear the rest of the story.

The episode shows us what we can expect when we climb into the boat of the church. As we follow the orders of Jesus and push off from shore, we will face storms and Jesus will not be there (or will not appear to be there) to help. We will have to endure the challenges of following Jesus without Jesus, as Adam faced the serpent without the Creator. But the storms will be calmed when Jesus arrives. In the meantime, there is nothing to fear. Jesus is master of the wind and waves, and He can calm the storm with a word. He is that "manner of man," the Son of God. To us, as to the Twelve, Jesus says through the storm: "Take courage; it is I. Do not be afraid." And when Jesus climbs into the boat, we get safely across, and find there a crowd eagerly waiting to hear the good news of the Kingdom.

And not only that: We can expect to share in the power of Jesus. Jesus is God's only Son, and He can walk on the waves because He is God in human flesh. He can calm the sea because He created the sea. But Peter gives us a foretaste of what we can expect – that by faith in Jesus' power, we share in Jesus' power and stride the waves just as He does. Jesus the King of nations gives His church mastery over the nations, so that the surging sea becomes as dry land beneath our feet.

Defilement
Matthew 15:1-20

Then some Pharisees and scribes came to Jesus from Jerusalem and said, ² "Why do Your disciples break the tradition of the elders? For they do not wash their hands when they eat bread." ³ And He answered and said to them, "Why do you yourselves transgress the commandment of God for the sake of your tradition? ⁴ For God said, 'HONOR YOUR FATHER AND MOTHER,' and, 'HE WHO SPEAKS EVIL OF FATHER OR MOTHER IS TO BE PUT TO DEATH.' ⁵ But you say, 'Whoever says to his father or mother, "Whatever I have that would help you has been given to God," ⁶ he is not to honor his father or his mother.' And by this you invalidated the word of God for the sake of your tradition. ⁷ You hypocrites, rightly did Isaiah prophesy of you:
⁸ 'THIS PEOPLE HONORS ME WITH THEIR LIPS,
BUT THEIR HEART IS FAR AWAY FROM ME.
⁹ 'BUT IN VAIN DO THEY WORSHIP ME,
TEACHING AS DOCTRINES THE PRECEPTS OF MEN.'"
¹⁰ After Jesus called the crowd to Him, He said to them, "Hear and understand. ¹¹ It is not what enters into the mouth that defiles the man, but what proceeds out of the mouth, this defiles the man."
¹² Then the disciples came and said to Him, "Do You know that the Pharisees were offended when they heard this statement?" ¹³ But He answered and said, "Every plant which My heavenly Father did not plant shall be uprooted. ¹⁴ Let them alone; they are blind guides of the blind. And if a blind man guides a blind man, both will fall into a pit."
¹⁵ Peter said to Him, "Explain the parable to us." ¹⁶ Jesus said, "Are you still lacking in understanding also? ¹⁷ Do you not understand that everything that goes into the mouth passes into the stomach, and is eliminated? ¹⁸ But the things that proceed out of the mouth come from the heart, and those defile the man. ¹⁹ For out of the heart come evil thoughts, murders,

adulteries, fornications, thefts, false witness, slanders. [20] These are the things which defile the man; but to eat with unwashed hands does not defile the man."

Fear of defilement and uncleanness seems so foreign to us, so primitive. We think we have outgrown these fears, and think that the Pharisees are childish in their obsession with ceremonial purity.

In one respect, "childish" is just the right word. The Law was given as a schoolmaster to lead to Christ (Gal. 3:24), a guardian and protector of Israel during Israel's minority, until the time when Israel came to maturity (Gal. 4:1-7). During that period, Paul says, Israel was the heir, the seed of Abraham, but was under managers to such an extent that their sonship took the form of a kind of slavery. There is something childish about the rules of defilement. They are rules for children.

But merely dismissing these rules as childish misses a couple of important things. Paul's image of a "schoolmaster" is an important one. A pedagogue conducts children to maturity, until they are able to conduct themselves. And Paul says this was the purpose of the law. The law actually prepares Israel for Christ's arrival. If kept faithfully, the law has a maturing effect. In particular, the purity laws of the Old Testament developed certain instincts in Israel toward life and God and the world. The prohibition against drinking blood, for instance, taught Israel that life belongs to God and should be returned to Him; it taught Israel that life comes from Yahweh and from no other. Purity laws taught Israel the protocols of addressing and entering the presence of a holy God. Purity is "simply the protocol for entry into the palace of the King. The priestly people is privileged to have his residence in their midst, and must consequently comport themselves in accordance with the prescribed etiquette."[11] Israel was being trained in the proper reception to the coming of the king.

---

11 Hyam Maccoby, *Ritual and Morality: The Ritual Purity System and Its Place in Judaism* (Cambridge: Cambridge University Press, 1999), 206.

Dismissing purity regulations as childish also misses the ways people today are still motivated by purity concerns. These come to most obvious expression in non-Western societies, like India, where "untouchable" is still a very live religious and social category. But more than we like to think, our behavior is still shaped by visceral fear of pollution. How do you react when a homeless person walks up to you on the street and asks for a dollar? What kinds of emotions do you experience? You might be fearful, and in some cases fearful of your safety. But often our reaction is revulsion and fear of something other than physical attack. Our first thought is "Ick, get away," and we want to avoid touching. How many of us would be willing to hold the hand of an AIDS patient or a leper? We are decades beyond Jim Crow laws, but it's not ancient history. What motivated separate toilets and water fountains and lunch counters? Racism, yes, but racism took the form of a fear of contamination. Why do some people react so strongly to mixed-race marriages? Is it because such a marriage might be unwise, or is it because some continue to have a revulsion to what we think are abominable mixtures?

We moderns like to think we've outgrown all these primitive taboos, but modern society, philosophy, and culture is motivated in many ways by a drive for purity. The goal of much modern philosophy has been to isolate an area of pure reason, uncontaminated by the uncertainties of language, history, religion. Modern politics is built on the imperative to avoid "mixtures" of religion and politics, church and state. Modern urban design pursues geometric clarity and cleanness, and resists the organic messiness of medieval cities. We sequester sick and dying people in hospitals, even when they aren't contagious: Why do we do that?

Mary Douglas has said that purity concerns are concerns for order and normalcy. Clean things and persons and animals conform to a norm and fit nearly into their classes. When things deviate from the norm, we are repelled by them, and classify them as unclean, impure, polluted. Israel put people with skin disease into quarantine; we put many people whom we classify as mentally ill in quarantine. This is not the same, but the analogy is too close for comfort.

Perhaps the question is not whether a culture will have standards of purity and defilement, but what those standards will be.

We might put issues of purity and defilement out of mind, but concerns about defilement were at the heart of much Jewish piety, especially among the Pharisees. Defilement is a biblical category. Scripture gives elaborate rules describing various forms of defilement, uncleanness, or pollution. When a woman had a baby, she was in a state of uncleanness or defilement for forty or eighty days, depending on the sex of the child (Lev. 12). Eating unclean meat made you unclean, and touching the carcass of an unclean animal also made you unclean (Lev. 11). Skin disease, the outbreak of flaking on the skin or the flesh showing through the skin, made a man unclean (Lev. 13). Various forms of emissions and flows from the genitals also made a person unclean (Lev. 15).

In some cases, these forms of uncleanness were contagious. If you touched someone who was unclean, you became unclean; if they touched you, you became unclean. At times, a particular form of uncleanness could make an inanimate object unclean, which would then become a communicator of further uncleanness. A man with an emission from his genitals was unclean, and if he spat on anyone he communicated uncleanness. If he sat on a saddle or a bed in this state of uncleanness, the saddle became unclean and passed on its uncleanness to anyone else who touched the saddle (Lev. 15:1-12). During her monthly period, a woman was also a communicator of uncleanness, and everything she sat on would become a communicator of uncleanness. Under the law, uncleanness was not only a danger, but a *spreading* danger.

Some defilements required elaborate rites of purification. After a person with skin disease got over his skin disease, he had to go through a ritual that resembled the rite of priestly ordination (Lev. 14), and if someone touched a dead body, he had to go through a rite that lasted for seven days (Num. 19). Most forms of uncleanness were handled much more easily. A person who touched a man with a genital flow, or his bed or saddle, had only to wash himself and his clothes, and by the evening he was clean. Anyone who touched a menstruating woman had to wash himself and his clothes and wait until evening. When a couple had sex, they had only to wash and they would be clean at the evening sacrifice (Lev. 15).

These laws of purity and defilement became relevant when Yahweh came to dwell in Israel in the tabernacle and later in the temple. There were purity regulations before that, but they were much less elaborate. When Yahweh came to live among Israel, when He was present with them in greater intensity, they had to maintain a higher level of purity. Within Israel, some had to maintain a higher level of purity still. The priests were under the same regulations as all Israel, but in addition they had to maintain a level of purity beyond that of the rest of Israel (Lev. 21-22). The closer you were to the sanctuary, the closer to the presence of God, the more concerned you had to be about purity and impurity.

The whole Pharisaical program was an effort to extend the purity of the priesthood to the entirety of Israel. They advocated for a "priesthood of all believers," and believed all Israel should maintain a rigorous observance of purity and a thorough shunning of defilement. If Israel would observe this kind of purity, Yahweh would be pleased to come to redeem His people from the Romans and restore them to their land. If all Israel would not go along with the Pharisaical program, at least the Pharisees would be clean. When Yahweh came to redeem, when He drew near to take His place in His sanctuary, they would be the ones who could draw near, because they were the clean ones. Blessed are the clean, for they shall be saved.

This is the background to the Pharisaical practice of washing before meals. There is no Old Testament requirement for washing before meals, but Pharisees did it in order to maintain this higher level of purity. After all, if a Pharisee went walking about town, at the market or in the synagogue, he had no idea what kinds of defilement he might have contracted. He might have accidentally sat in a chair a menstruating woman had occupied, or touched the hand of man with a genital flow. If he ate in this state of uncleanness, he would suffer deeper defilement. To be safe, to protect themselves from contagion, Pharisees washed before meals. They know that Jesus and His disciples don't, and they come demanding an explanation.

At first, Jesus doesn't answer their question directly, but instead offers several indirect responses. Instead of answering their question, Jesus turns the tables and charges them with nullifying God's law with their own tradition. The law requires that children honor their parents, and this means children must provide for their aged parents who are incapable of providing for themselves. The Pharisees, Jesus says, don't use their money to honor their parents, as the law requires (v. 4; cf. Exod. 20:12; 21:17), but devote those savings to God.

This doesn't directly address the Pharisaical question, but it addresses it at a general level. The Pharisaical practices concerning washing look pious – no, they look super-pious. Anyone who sees a Pharisee at work will think that he's deeply committed to obeying God's commandments. But the concern with purity leads them to ignore or downplay the central purposes of the law. Their concern for purity makes them uncharitable. Obsessed with purity, they ignore justice, mercy, and faithfulness, the weightier matters of the law.

Analogously, their use of their money for gifts to God instead of gifts to parents looks pious, but it is disobedience. In the very act of "worshiping" God with their offering, they are flouting His commandments. They offer lip-worship, but their hearts are far from God. True worship is obedience to God's commands. The fact that this is tradition doesn't help. Every faith and culture has a tradition. There's nothing wrong with Israel having a tradition. The question is, is the tradition consistent with Scripture, the origin of tradition? Or does the tradition nullify the Scriptures? Jesus charges that the Pharisaical purity tradition has taken so many twists and turns that it is no longer connected with the source.

Before He answers the question, Jesus also takes a moment to speak about the Pharisees, and how the disciples should regard them. They are not planted by the Father (v. 13), and therefore are sons of the evil one, who sowed Israel with weeds (13:36-43). As Jesus explained in the parable of the tares and wheat, the Lord will uproot the weeds, and the disciples are called to "let them alone" (v. 14) until the Father roots them out. Importantly, Jesus later acknowledges the Pharisees "have seated themselves in the chair of Moses" and urges the disciples to "do and observe" all that the Pharisees of Israel teach them (23:1-2). They give accurate enough teaching concerning the law, but their conduct doesn't match that, and so Jesus warns the disciples sternly not to imitate the lives of Pharisees. There are some teachers in Israel that we should honor as teachers and listen to as teachers, but refuse to follow their example. Though they think of themselves as "guides to the blind" (cf. Rom. 2:19), they are blind guides and will inevitably mislead.

After turning the interrogation back on the Pharisees and describing the Pharisees themselves, Jesus answers their question: The law does not require washing hands. No one is defiled by eating with unwashed hands (vv. 10-11, 20). Jesus does answer the question, but it's not just important to see that He answers it, but to see how He answers it.

Jesus could have made this point simply by pointing out that the law doesn't require washing before meals. Instead, he makes a much larger and broader point. Under the law, Israel was to maintain purity regulations, but these were intended as object-lessons about a broader notion of purity. The lesson of the purity laws themselves is that nothing that goes into the mouth defiles, because it simply passes through the intestines and doesn't touch the heart (vv. 17-18). Instead, what defiles are evils that come from within (v. 19). This is precisely what the purity laws taught. Most forms of uncleanness result from emissions from inside the body (Lev. 12; 15), or flesh breaking through the skin (Lev. 13). There were impurities that came from without – touching a dead body, eating unclean foods – but these were all lesser forms of impurity that could be taken care of by simple washing. The impurities that required more elaborate, sacrificial cleansing rites were the ones that defiled from within.

Jesus deepens the point by saying that defilement does not come from the physical flesh but from the murderous and adulterous and false thoughts, words, and actions that arise from the heart. This is what the purity laws taught. If they were paying attention to the law, the Pharisees would have learned their insides were boiling with defilement. The Pharisees, in fact, are guilty of every evil that Jesus describes here (9:4, 34; 12:7, 38; 26:60-61). They think of themselves as the pure ones; in reality, they are deeply polluted. And they deeply pollute others. This is the irony Jesus highlights: The pure ones, the Pharisees obsessed with cleanness, cause pollution. They are whitewashed tombs, which look clean but inwardly are full of dead men's bones.

Many readers think Jesus renounced all concern with purity. Purity is an old category that no longer pertains to the disciples of Jesus. That's not what Jesus says. Jesus was as concerned with purity and defilement as the Pharisees. He was just as strict about avoiding defilement and maintaining and recovering purity. What has changed is not the role of purity but its content. What defiles? What is purity? It doesn't involve concern for foods, or bodily emissions, or touching dead bodies. Instead, it has to do with what flows out of the heart.

Once we make that transposition, we can see that all the purity rules of Israel still have direct relevance. Someone who is defiled with murders, adulteries, slanders is a communicator of defilement, as much as a menstruous woman communicated defilement under the law. If you want to avoid defilement, avoid angry and lustful people. We should react with the same revulsion to people defiled by these evils as a Pharisee would do around a person who had a flow of blood or skin disease. If you have become defiled with these things, you are unclean, and you *do* need to be cleansed – not with washing the hands, but with confession and the blood of Jesus. Jesus makes it clear that the defilements that should fill us with revulsion are the ones that come from within us. We should be repelled by our own sin, use all strategies we know to avoid it, purge it. Defilements from the heart are far more virulent than anything that might come from outside. Kill it before it kills you.

The change that Jesus ultimately brings is actually more radical. It's not just a matter of the nature and direction of defilement. The change is at the heart of the gospel: The power of impurity has been neutralized. Think of Jesus: He regularly touches the ceremonially unclean, and is a friend of tax gatherers and sinners. Yet Jesus was not defiled. On the contrary, He cleanses by His touch. He purifies by His presence.

The Pharisees thought that defilement was a power, force, or contagion that threatened them from without. They put up their defenses, cleansed themselves regularly, avoided defiling people and circumstances, because there might be defilement around every corner. Of course, we can come under the influence of someone or something, and it can take root in our hearts. But spending time with a murderer does not defile us; being around an adulterer doesn't defile us. We are defiled when the evil in our own hearts expresses itself in murder, adultery, fornication, theft, and slander. Jesus is not instructing us to avoid people who may defile us. He's telling us to guard our own hearts so that they don't defile us. And, having purged our hearts, Jesus sends us out to mix and mingle with the unclean, in order to spread His purifying power.

The Pharisaical idea of purity leads to a lifestyle of fear, fear of defilement and contagion, fear of others, fear of the spreading of death. It was a lifestyle of avoidance – avoidance of Gentiles, of less than pure Jews, of places and people and circumstances that might potentially defile us. Jesus does not live in fear, and He calls us to follow Him, without fear. We are not called to huddle up in our clean enclaves so that we can maintain our small but oh-so-pure purity. We are to be like Jesus and enter into the defiled world, a world defiled by evil thoughts, murders, adulteries, fornications, thefts, false witness, slanders. We are called to be

Jesus as Israel

like Jesus, entering a polluted world to bring the message of the kingdom in the power of the *Holy* Spirit, to bring cleansing and renewal.

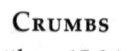

Crumbs
Matthew 15:21-39

21 Jesus went away from there, and withdrew into the district of Tyre and Sidon. 22 And a Canaanite woman from that region came out and began to cry out, saying, "Have mercy on me, Lord, Son of David; my daughter is cruelly demon-possessed." 23 But He did not answer her a word. And His disciples came and implored Him, saying, "Send her away, because she keeps shouting at us." 24 But He answered and said, "I was sent only to the lost sheep of the house of Israel." 25 But she came and began to bow down before Him, saying, "Lord, help me!" 26 And He answered and said, "It is not good to take the children's bread and throw it to the dogs." 27 But she said, "Yes, Lord; but even the dogs feed on the crumbs which fall from their masters' table." 28 Then Jesus said to her, "O woman, your faith is great; it shall be done for you as you wish." And her daughter was healed at once. 29 Departing from there, Jesus went along by the Sea of Galilee, and having gone up on the mountain, He was sitting there. 30 And large crowds came to Him, bringing with them those who were lame, crippled, blind, mute, and many others, and they laid them down at His feet; and He healed them. 31 So the crowd marveled as they saw the mute speaking, the crippled restored, and the lame walking, and the blind seeing; and they glorified the God of Israel. 32 And Jesus called His disciples to Him, and said, "I feel compassion for the people, because they have remained with Me now three days and have nothing to eat; and I do not want to send them away hungry, for they might faint on the way." 33 The disciples said to Him, "Where would we get so many loaves in this desolate place to satisfy such a large crowd?" 34 And Jesus said to them, "How many loaves do you have?" And they said, "Seven, and a few small fish." 35 And He directed the people to sit down on the ground; 36 and He took the seven loaves and the fish; and giving thanks, He broke them and started giving them to the disciples, and the

disciples gave them to the people. ³⁷ And they all ate and were satisfied, and they picked up what was left over of the broken pieces, seven large baskets full. ³⁸ And those who ate were four thousand men, besides women and children. ³⁹ And sending away the crowds, Jesus got into the boat and came to the region of Magadan.

This section of Matthew 15 begins with a notice that Jesus "withdrew" (v. 21). This is not the first time Jesus has withdrawn. Jesus withdraws regularly when conflicts with the Jews get heated up. After He heals the man with the withered hand on the Sabbath, the Pharisees gathered together to decide what they could do to get rid of Jesus, so He "withdrew from there" (Matt. 12:15). After the death of John the Baptist, we hear that Jesus "withdrew from there in a boat" (Matt. 14:13). This is not an act of cowardice, but an act of wisdom and prudence. Jesus is being wise as a serpent. He knows there is a climactic confrontation coming when He gets to Jerusalem, but He also knows that the time has not yet come. He withdraws and waits. This time, He withdraws farther than before. He goes not only out of the land but, we might say, into enemy territory, the region around Tyre and Sidon. Sidon was the first-born son of Canaan (Gen. 10:15), and so Jesus/Joshua is entering the territory of the Canaanites. This is also the region to which Elijah retreated when Jezebel was trying to kill him. It was in fact the region from which Jezebel came, since she was a Sidonian princess who married into the royal family of Israel. It was the region where Elijah met the starving widow and provided for her.

Matthew has taken us into a "divided kingdom" period of Jesus' history, and so it is appropriate that Jesus is following in the footsteps of Elijah and Elisha. Like Elijah and Elisha, Jesus is confronted by a woman who needs help for a child. Elijah raised the widow's son from the dead, and Elisha performed a similar miracle for another woman whose child died. Here, a Canaanite woman comes to Him seeking help for a daughter who is possessed by a demon. What follows is an extremely subtle story about Jesus' vocation, the meaning of faith, and the ultimate hope of the Gentiles.

In Matthew 15, Jesus and the woman have three exchanges: First, he ignores her (v. 23), then He says that His ministry is limited to Israel (v. 24), and then he denies her request by assigning Canaanites the status of scavenger dogs (v. 26). Like the mission of the Twelve, Jesus' mission is limited to the "lost tribes" (v. 23; cf. 10:5-6).

The role of the disciples in this exchange is important to notice. They call on Jesus to respond to the woman, and their request is often seen as a request for Jesus to simply dismiss her. But that does not make any sense. Jesus responds to the Twelve by reminding them that He is sent to the lost sheep of Israel. If they had wanted Him to send the woman away without healing, Jesus' response would have been nonsense. The disciples do not want to send the woman away; they want Jesus to respond to her appeal by healing her daughter. That is the way to get rid of a nuisance.

Part of the story, then, is a confrontation between two different ways of pursuing ministry and mission. The disciples want to respond to the immediate cry, whatever that cry is and wherever it comes from. In the earlier part of this chapter, they took Jesus aside and told Him that the Pharisees were offended at His words, as if this were reason for Jesus to back off or retract. The disciples seem to think that Jesus can pursue His mission faithfully without ever upsetting religious authorities and by responding to every cry from everyone all the time. Ministry means doing what people want and expect; ministry does not make waves. This is *not* Jesus' conception of His work. Jesus responds by reminding the Twelve of His vocation, the reason for His sending. For Jesus, the question is not "Who is clamoring for My attention?" but "Why am I here in the first place? What did God send me to do?" Jesus knows that His mission, His sending, is to the lost sheep of Israel, and that mission overrides even extreme need from elsewhere. What is most offensive about this story to us is that Jesus shows He has a higher standard of action than human need. He comes to address our needs, to deliver us from sin and death. That is all true. But Jesus is *not* first of all responsive to need but to the will of His Father. He is first of all responsive to the One who sent Him. He will not let genuine human need, even misery, distract Him from the thing He has come to do. He is God-centered, not a humanitarian. Ultimately, Jesus does respond to her but only after it becomes clear that her importunity fits with His mission. He does love the woman, but that love is an overflow of His love for His Father, His obedience to the first and greatest commandment.

Matthew often arranges things in threes. Back in Matthew 8-9, he told three miracle stories and then recorded something Jesus taught about discipleship. Then he tells three more miracle stories before recording the call of Matthew. Three more miracles stories, and then the Twelve are sent out to continue His mission. Matthew is so fond of telling stories in triads that we anticipate the story of the Canaanite woman is over after three episodes. But the story of the Canaanite woman has a surprise ending. Jesus ignores her, Jesus dismisses the disciples' request, Jesus responds to her with an insulting statement about her status as a Gentile and Canaanite. Three strikes and she's out. That should be the end of the story, we think. If Matthew followed his normal rhythm, he would be telling us a story about a Jewish Messiah. The woman will not let things rest. After three strikes, she will not leave the place. Even after Jesus has ignored her, responded negatively to the disciples, and dismissed her rather harshly, she keeps coming back. And so the story does not end with three encounters but goes beyond the third encounter into a fourth exchange. She is as persistent as Yahweh, who comes and comes again, even after His people kill Him. The story does not end on the third day but bursts through into a new day *after* the third day.

The surprise twist in the structure points to both the redemptive-historical and the personal application of the story. In terms of redemptive history, the Canaanite woman is a Gentile bride seeking help from the Jewish "Son of David," from the "Lord" Jesus (vv. 22, 27). Though she is a Canaanite, she knows how to give good gifts to her daughter.[12] If the Gentiles have the persistent faith of the Canaanite woman, they will gain a share of the children's bread.

The personal application has to do with the nature of faith, and the woman's faith is "great" in several respects. It is great because it is focused on Jesus, the Son of David. She knows that she has no other hope for her daughter. True faith is trust in the Lord Jesus, the one who rules — the King. Her faith is also humble. She prostrates herself before Jesus, pleading with Him. When Jesus describes her as a dog, she immediately accepts the designation, and yet she persists in asking for help from Jesus. Her faith is great, above all, in its persistence. She cries out to Jesus, and He ignores her and does not answer her at all. She does not stop. The disciples take up her cause, but Jesus dismisses them too. Still, she does not stop. Finally, she has a chance to appeal to Jesus directly. She bows to Him in honor, calls Him Lord, and cries out in desperation for help. He calls her a dog. Still, she does not quit. She turns Jesus' insult back in her favor, "catching" Jesus, as it were, in His own words. As a result, her daughter is healed, and Jesus commends her great faith – a contrast to the "little faith" of the Twelve – and then says that because of her faith "let it be done for you as you wish."

The next episode in Matthew 15 is the feeding of the four thousand, but we should not ignore verses 29-31. They are not filler but set the context for the feeding of the four thousand. Jesus moves back from the region of Tyre and Sidon to the sea of Galilee, climbs a mountain, and sits down. He has been on mountains a number of times already. Most recently, he ascended to a mountain to pray as the Twelve went across the sea in their boat and had to be rescued from a storm. Here Jesus goes to a mountain and sits, and the only other time He has ascended a mountain and taken a seat is at the beginning of the sermon on the mount. Sitting is the posture of authoritative teaching.

---

12   Daniel Patte, *The Gospel According to Matthew: A Structural Commentary on Matthew's Faith* (Minneapolis, Minn.: Fortress, 1986). See Patte's commentary on this passage.

Sitting on the mountain, Jesus is Moses, or Yahweh, delivering the law to Israel. Once Jesus sits down on the mountain, people swarm around Him, many of them with ailments that need to be healed. Matthew mentions four categories: lame, crippled, blind, dumb. Jesus heals all of these, so the dumb speak, the crippled are healthy, the lame walk, and the blind see. The number four is significant in itself, because it is associated with the corners of the earth. A four-fold healing covers the four corners of the earth.

After Jesus heals, "they glorified the God of Israel" (15:31). The people are restored so that they can worship. Under the law, many of these deformities would have prevented someone from being a priest. Jesus comes to heal them and transform them into a priestly people who glorify God. Once we see how the healings lead to worship, we can see the whole passage is organized like a worship service. Jesus ascends to a mountain, going nearer to the presence of God. He sits down and presumably teaches them. Jesus heals the multitudes so they are filled with praise to God, and then He feeds them before dismissing them.

This is what is happening every time the church comes together for worship. We assemble on earth, perhaps in a home or a place even less comfortable, but we are really on the mountain, the heavenly Zion. Jesus is here, and He is here to teach us, to heal us, to loose our tongues in praise, to open our eyes to see, and to restore our limbs so we can walk. And Jesus invites us to His table, where He seats us, as children, around His table, and feeds us.

At the climax of this worship service in Matthew 15, Jesus feeds four thousand. The feeding of the four thousand is like the feeding of the five thousand. Again, Jesus goes to a mountain (15:29; cf. 14:23). Again, Jesus heals (15:30-31; cf. 14:14). Again, Jesus feels compassion and instructs the disciples to feed the crowd (15:32; cf. 14:15-16), who again wonder where they are going to get enough food (15:33; cf. 14:15, 17). Jesus again anticipates the actions of the Last Supper (15:36; cf. 14:19). Both events are associated with the sea (15:29; cf. 14:13, 22), and both are followed by a sea-crossing (15:39; cf. 14:22-33). Jesus is again re-enacting a Passover-exodus sequence.

One of the key differences has to do with location. According to Mark, this second feeding took place in the Decapolis, a predominantly Gentile region (Mark 8:31). That fits the context of the previous story. Jesus has just responded to the request of a Gentile, Canaanite woman, and healed her daughter. Jesus has exorcised a Gentile girl and given bread to dogs. Now, in the Decapolis, surrounded by four thousand men, Jesus gives more bread to dogs: He is sent to the lost sheep of the house of Israel, but He feeds Gentile multitudes.

The number of loaves, people, and baskets of leftovers are all significant, but to get the point we need to read the two miraculous meals together. Jesus uses five loaves to feed five thousand men, and there are twelve baskets of leftovers (Matt. 14:17, 21). Twelve is obviously the number of Israel, but the number five also links with Israel, who left Egypt "five in a rank" (Exod. 13:18). The number four is often a numerical symbol of the earth as a whole, and so the four thousand represent the nations that spread to the four corners. The two stories of feeding show that Jesus has come to give bread to the children *and* to the dogs. The fact that there are five thousand Jews and only four thousand Gentiles shows the priority of Israel. The miracle for Israel is the greater miracle, the provision a greater provision. Gentiles will receive bread, but Jesus' ministry to the lost sheep of the house of Israel still retains priority. Symbolically, though not literally, the two stories show that the twelve baskets left over from feeding Israel feed the Gentiles, crumbs from Israel's table taken to the Gentiles. Once Israel has been fed, the remainder is taken to the Gentiles, who also are fed.

But we also need to notice what Jesus does with the twelve loaves. In the two incidents together, Jesus has broken twelve loaves and fed nine thousand. The symbolism goes back to the tabernacle and temple, where twelve loaves of showbread were placed on the table of showbread, with the light of God's eyes shining from the lampstand on the other side. Jesus breaks them before distributing them. As Jesus later says, the loaf that He breaks is His own body, broken for the sake of His people, distributed as food. Here there are twelve loaves, and that means that Jesus' body is the body of Israel. On the one hand, Jesus takes Israel herself and breaks her in pieces. This was always Israel's calling. She was always called to be a priestly people and to offer herself in sacrifice for the nations. She never existed for herself but always as the loaves of bread for the world. On the other hand, Jesus Himself is the true Israel, whose broken body feeds the world. Jesus is the twelve loaves. Israel must be blessed and broken before the Gentiles can be saved, before the crumbs can fall from the master's table. But it takes the incarnate Yahweh to become Israel and break her into fragments so that she can feed the nations.

We began by noting that Jesus "withdrew," but that is the last time He withdraws. In the middle of the next chapter, He begins a journey toward Jerusalem, and He begins to tell His disciples that He is going to have to suffer and die and rise again on the third day. Jesus will fulfill in His own body the symbolism of these two meals; He will give the loaf of His own body on the cross, He will break the twelve loaves of the true Israel, so that both Israel and the nations will eat from the Lord's table.

Food Test
Matthew 16:1-12

¹ The Pharisees and Sadducees came up, and testing Jesus, they asked Him to show them a sign from heaven. ² But He replied to them, "When it is evening, you say, 'It will be fair weather, for the sky is red.' ³ And in the morning, 'There will be a storm today, for the sky is red and threatening.' Do you know how to discern the appearance of the sky, but cannot discern the signs of the times? ⁴ An evil and adulterous generation seeks after a sign; and a sign will not be given it, except the sign of Jonah." And He left them and went away.

⁵ And the disciples came to the other side of the sea, but they had forgotten to bring any bread. ⁶ And Jesus said to them, "Watch out and beware of the leaven of the Pharisees and Sadducees." ⁷ They began to discuss this among themselves, saying, "He said that because we did not bring any bread." ⁸ But Jesus, aware of this, said, "You men of little faith, why do you discuss among yourselves that you have no bread? ⁹ Do you not yet understand or remember the five loaves of the five thousand, and how many baskets full you picked up? ¹⁰ Or the seven loaves of the four thousand, and how many large baskets full you picked up? ¹¹ How is it that you do not understand that I did not speak to you concerning bread? But beware of the leaven of the Pharisees and Sadducees." ¹² Then they understood that He did not say to beware of the leaven of bread, but of the teaching of the Pharisees and Sadducees.

From the beginning, food has always been a test. Adam was given a food test: You can have every tree of the garden, including the tree of life, but you cannot eat the fruit of the tree of knowledge. In the wilderness, Israel also was tested by food. Yahweh gave manna to Israel to see whether they would follow His instructions and commandments, to know what was on their hearts (Deuteronomy 8). Food tests are like the jealousy test of Numbers 5: Will the food prove Israel to be an unfaithful or a faithful bride of Yahweh? Like Adam, Israel failed the test. They kept some of the manna till the next day, fearing that there would not be enough manna; they did not trust Yahweh for their daily bread. Worse, instead of passing the test, Israel put Yahweh to the test. Instead of submitting to His trial, they try to put Him on trial, grumbling and quarreling and demanding a different menu.

As the true Israel, Jesus goes through the history of Israel again. Israel also is running through her whole history again. Twice in the past several chapters of Matthew, we have read that Jesus fed a large crowd of people. After Herod murders John, Jesus withdraws to a lonely place by himself, but the crowds follow Him and He feeds five thousand men, besides women and children. After He goes to a mountain near the Sea of Galilee, the crowds gather again, and He offers food to four thousand men, plus women and children, in a desolate place. Jesus is Yahweh incarnate, and like Yahweh, He provides bread in the wilderness. He gives Israel food in desolate places.

But, like Yahweh in the wilderness, He also puts Israel to the test. Like the Israelites in the days of Moses, the Jews of Jesus' day try to turn the tables and put their Lord to the test. The Israelites in the wilderness wanted a sign that Yahweh was among them. The place where Moses struck the rock was called "Massah and Meribah," "Testing" and "Quarrel," because "they tested Yahweh, saying, 'Is Yahweh among us, or not?'" The Pharisees and Sadducees raise the same question. After Jesus has fed thousands (Matt. 15:32-39), the Pharisees and Sadducees are not satisfied. They still grumble and doubt. With Yahweh incarnate standing before them, they demand to know, "Is Yahweh among us or not?" They come to Jesus demanding a "sign from heaven" (Matt. 16:1).

Pharisees and Sadducees are not natural allies. They are divided by a number of theological issues, but mainly on the question of resurrection. Pharisees believe in resurrection but Sadducees do not, and the tensions are strong enough that Paul was able to start a riot by siding with the Pharisees in his trial before the Sanhedrin (Acts 23:7-8). Pharisees and Sadducees also differ in their assessment of Rome: Pharisees think the Roman occupation defiles the holy land, while Sadducees generally cooperated with the empire. As N. T. Wright has noted, the political stances of the two groups are related to their theological positions. Believing in resurrection means believing that things can be turned upside down. The line dividing the living and the dead is the most obvious, permanent, and apparently impermeable line there is. It is a fixed boundary within humanity, between one group (the dead) and another (the living). If that line can be breached from the side of the dead, then other boundaries that divide humanity can also be breached. To believe in resurrection is to believe the world can be turned upside down.

The Pharisees *want* the world turned upside down. They do not want the Romans to remain in the land, dominating Israel and defiling the land. They do not want Israel to remain the doormat of the Middle East. They want the Lord to rise in His might and take down the Romans, like He took down Egypt and Aram and Philistia and Babylon and all the other nations that oppressed Israel in the past. Sadducees do not like the prospects of disruption. They are comfortable at the top of Israelite society, enjoying the privileges of priesthood and the benefits of being in good standing with the Romans.

The Pharisees and Sadducees are right: Belief in resurrection is belief in the possibility the world can be turned upside down. Christians might forget this. We act like Sadducees, who believe the world will go on and on as it has always been, even though we confess the resurrection of Jesus. Resurrection is not just a religious confession; it is a confession about the dynamics of political history.

What is important in Matt. 16:1, though, is that these two groups, at odds in many ways, unite against Jesus. The last time the Jews asked for a sign, it was the "Pharisees and scribes" (Matt. 12:38). Now the *Sadducees* join with the Pharisees to "test" Jesus, "testing" Him as Satan tested Him in the wilderness (Matt. 16:1; cf. 4:1). Jesus unites His people, but He also unites His enemies. He always does. Jesus still unites enemies. During the first century, Jews who hated the Romans still called on the Romans to assist them in suppressing the church. Romans and Jews – unnatural allies if there ever were unnatural allies – cooperated to stop Jesus. They became co-Satans in attacking Jesus and His people. This is almost a litmus test of persecution: it is real persecution if your opponents have nothing in common except their common hatred for you.

It is ironic, of course, that the Pharisees and Sadducees demand a "sign from heaven" (Matt. 16:1) to prove Jesus is the "son of David" (cf. Matt. 15:22), when they are surrounded by signs, when it is clear to everyone who has eyes to see that Jesus is, if nothing else, a wonder-worker. Jesus rebukes them. They are able to read the weather-signs in "heaven" (Matt. 16:2-3; in Greek, *ouranos* can be translated as "sky" or "heaven"), but are not able to see obvious signs of the times. He marvels at their ability to read the "face of the sky," and yet to miss what is going on all around them. Where it really counts, they are blind, unable to judge the signs of the times, blind to the fact that they are living in the fullness of times, the climax of the ages.

Jesus again calls them an "evil and *adulterous* generation" (cf. Matt. 12:54) whose search for a sign is actually a search for a new husband. Israel in the wilderness had her Husband in her midst; He provided faithfully for her, bread and water and protection. But Israel was not satisfied with these signs of husbandly favor: "Is Yahweh among us, or not?" So too the Pharisees and Sadducees claim to want confirmation of Jesus' claims, but in fact they are looking for an excuse to reject Him. He comes as the divine Husband, yet the Jews refuse to listen to Him, honor Him, love Him, embrace Him.

Jesus does promise to give them a sign, the sign of Jonah (Matt. 16:4). This is not a sign from heaven but a sign from the sea. The sign of Jonah involves death and resurrection, but it is also related to the theme of adultery that Jesus has just brought up. The principle behind the story of Jonah is the principle given in Deuteronomy 32: Yahweh predicts a time when Israel will turn away from Him and seek out other gods. They will provoke Him to "jealousy," a marital term. In response, Yahweh says He will turn to other nations, and set His affection on another bride. Israel provokes Him to jealousy by what is not God; He will provoke them to jealousy by what is not a bride. In Jonah's time, Israel has turned to idols as they had done since the founding of the Northern Kingdom, worshiping golden calves at Dan and Bethel. Israel has provoked the Lord to jealousy with what is not God, and when Yahweh sends Jonah off to Nineveh to preach to the Assyrians, He is provoking Israel to jealousy by sending his prophet to a nation that is not a people. Jonah's generation was adulterous, so Yahweh looked to the Gentiles.

Jesus warns that the same thing is happening again. The sign of Jonah is His death and resurrection, which fulfills the sign of Jonah's death and resurrection in the sea. But the sign of Jonah is also the sign of the Lord's turning to Gentiles, the sign that He is provoking Israel to jealousy by offering the gospel to the nations. This is how Paul uses the phrase "provoke to jealousy" in Romans: it is an explanation of his own ministry to the Gentiles. Paul preaches the gospel to the Gentiles in the hope that Israel will be provoked to jealousy and return to her husband. With a similar attitude toward Israel, Jesus foreshadows the "sign of Jonah" by "leaving them and going away" (Matt. 16:4).

The only time in Matthew that Jesus promises a "sign from heaven" is in Matthew 24, where He describes the destruction of Jerusalem by the Romans. The Jews will someday see the threatening "sign of the Son of Man in heaven" (Matt. 24:30). There are close links between these two signs. In Matthew 16, the Pharisees and Sadducees "come to" Jesus asking Him to "show" a "sign"; at the beginning of Matthew 24, the disciples "come to" Jesus and "show" Him the temple buildings and then ask for a "sign" of the end of the age. Jesus refuses to give a sign to the Pharisees and Sadducees, but He does explain signs to the Twelve. Matthew 24 is an elaboration of the "sign of Jonah," the sign of the Son of Man's resurrection and reign, the sign that the good news has gone to the Gentiles and raised up Gentiles against the unfaithful covenant people, to provoke the Jews to repent and return.

As Jesus leaves, He issues a warning to the disciples to beware of the teaching of the Pharisees and Sadducees. Jesus, as He often does, talks past the disciples. Jesus does not say up front that leaven equals teaching. In fact, He never says that. That is a conclusion the disciples later come to realize (Matt. 16:12). Jesus just keeps talking about bread and leaven, all the while making the point that He is not talking about bread and leaven but about something else. If someone said "be careful of that person's bread," what would you think? That you should not eat with them? That you should not take a loan from them? You would probably not think of teaching, and neither do the disciples. They have forgotten bread and think Jesus is unhappy with them because they do not have any food.

Jesus tells the disciples to beware of the leaven of the scribes and Pharisees. We are reminded of the Passover, when Israel left Egypt in such haste that they ate bread before it was leavened. That meant that they left Egypt without taking the "leaven" of Egypt with them. They left that leaven behind and had to start a new leaven when they got into the wilderness, because they needed leavened bread for the celebration of Pentecost. The Feast of Unleavened Bread was an annual commemoration of this event, as Israel purged the old leaven and began a new leaven for the coming year.

It becomes clear by the end of this exchange that Jesus is talking about teaching. Leaven is like teaching because of the way it slips in and quietly permeates our lives. When Jesus uses the image of leaven earlier in the gospel, in the parables of the kingdom in Matthew 13, Jesus is talking about the power of leaven to transform the world. The kingdom is like three measures of leaven put into a lump of dough, which goes into the leaven until the whole lump is leavened. Because teaching is so powerful, we need to be careful about whom we listen to. We are taught all the time, and things imperceptibly enter us and begin to leaven us. We listen to advertisements that tell us what the good life is like. We are taught by movies and TV shows to desire certain things. Our friends teach us. If we are not alert, we will let things leaven us, and begin to grow in us, that will corrupt us.

Jesus is not telling the disciples to refuse to listen. The commands can be translated as "see" and "pay attention to" the leaven of the Pharisees and Sadducees. Jesus wants them to take a close look, to scrutinize, to devote themselves to that teaching. But He warns them not to accept all that they say. Disciples need to be selective, judging what is good and true and rejecting what is evil.

The Exodus symbolism points to another connection of teaching and leaven. Leaven is not the same as yeast. The Jews did not make bread by heading down to the corner market and picking up a packet of yeast. Leaven came from a previous loaf of bread. Leaven is fermenting bread. An ancient baker would pull off a bit of a leavened loaf and insert that into a new batch of dough, so that the leaven from the earlier loaf could permeate the new loaf, and when the new dough was leavened, the baker would pull off a bit of that dough for the next loaf and so on. This is behind the Feast of Unleavened Bread. Once a year, the Jews would expel all leaven from their homes, eat unleavened bread for a week, and then start over with new leaven. (They got the new leaven by letting some dough sit out; it would pick up airborne spores and begin to ferment.) The leaven would be passed on for a year, and then another Feast would come around and they would have to start all over. The annual feast pointed to the great Passover, the final Feast of Unleavened Bread, when the old leaven would be cut off finally and a new leaven would begin.

In short, leaven is a symbol of continuity; unleavened bread is a symbol of endings and new beginnings. At the first Passover, Israel removed the old leaven, the leaven of Egypt, from their homes, so they could begin a new leaven. At the last Passover, Jesus cuts off the leaven and begins anew. Teaching is like leaven in this sense too, especially the teaching of Pharisees and Sadducees and others like them. The Pharisees especially are experts in oral tradition. They pass on leaven from one loaf to another, from century to century. Jesus warns His disciples to beware of the tradition of the scribes and Pharisees, to see and pay attention to what is being passed down, and not to accept it. Over the centuries, the leaven passed from hand to hand can become corrupted. It needs to be cut off and begun again (as, for instance, at the Reformation).

Jesus' series of questions fits in here. The Pharisees and Sadducees have a teaching, a tradition, that needs to be handled carefully and critically. Jesus warns the disciples not to accept everything the Pharisees and Sadducees teach and do. But Jesus also has a bread and a leaven. His bread is new bread, however, a new teaching, a teaching with authority that surpasses the teaching of the scribes and Pharisees. His bread does not depend on the leaven of the Pharisees and Sadducees. He comes to bring in the final Passover, the climactic feast of Unleavened Bread, which cuts off the old leaven not of Egypt but of corrupted Israel, the leaven of the Pharisees and Sadducees.

What is Jesus up to with his questions about the numbers of loaves and the numbers of baskets of leftovers? He expects the disciples to learn a lesson, but what is the lesson? It cannot simply be that Jesus provides more than enough, though that is true. Jesus could make that point without highlighting the numbers. He must be making a numerological point, but it is as hard for us to grasp as it is for the disciples. Austin Farrer suggests this solution, which is vastly better than most: Jesus uses five loaves for five thousand, with twelve baskets left over; then four loaves for four thousand, with seven baskets left over. The sequence of numbers leaves us expecting another feast of three loaves for three thousand: to reach a total of twelve loaves and twelve thousand fed. Yet there is no third feast, no "feeding of the three thousand" in Matthew. Farrer concludes:

> ..there are indeed three thousands still to be fed, but the Lord does not make a separate eucharist for them. They are to be conceived as late guests still destined to appear and to feed on the broken pieces of the second eucharist. Their three loaves have already been broken.

Farrer argues that the first "Eucharistic" feeding is for Jews, the second for Gentiles, which means that "there are still more of the nations to come." When they come, though, there will not be "any new eucharistic covenant" but simply "more guests to the table on which the seven loaves [the leavings from the second feast] have already been laid."[13] It may not be accidental that exactly three thousands are brought into the Eucharistic communion at Pentecost.

---

13   Austin Marsden Farrer, *A Study in Mark* (London: Dacre, 1951) 296-7.

If leaven is teaching, the pupil is the dough. Pharisees and Sadducees insert their leaven into their disciples, but their leaven is not healthy. It does not produce nourishing bread. The kingdom is different. Jesus inserts leaven into His people, so that we can become bread, so that we can be broken and distributed to feed the world. Or, to change the image slightly, Jesus gives bread to the church, gives it abundantly and lavishly, and leaves enough remaining to feed others.

On This Rock
Matthew 16:13-28

[13] Now when Jesus came into the district of Caesarea Philippi, He was asking His disciples, "Who do people say that the Son of Man is?" [14] And they said, "Some say John the Baptist; and others, Elijah; but still others, Jeremiah, or one of the prophets." [15] He said to them, "But who do you say that I am?" [16] Simon Peter answered, "You are the Christ, the Son of the living God." [17] And Jesus said to him, "Blessed are you, Simon Barjona, because flesh and blood did not reveal this to you, but My Father who is in heaven. [18] I also say to you that you are Peter, and upon this rock I will build My church; and the gates of Hades will not overpower it. [19] I will give you the keys of the kingdom of heaven; and whatever you bind on earth shall have been bound in heaven, and whatever you loose on earth shall have been loosed in heaven." [20] Then He warned the disciples that they should tell no one that He was the Christ. [21] From that time Jesus began to show His disciples that He must go to Jerusalem, and suffer many things from the elders and chief priests and scribes, and be killed, and be raised up on the third day. [22] Peter took Him aside and began to rebuke Him, saying, "God forbid it, Lord! This shall never happen to You." [23] But He turned and said to Peter, "Get behind Me, Satan! You are a stumbling block to Me; for you are not setting your mind on God's interests, but man's." [24] Then Jesus said to His disciples, "If anyone wishes to come after Me, he must deny himself, and take up his cross and follow Me. [25] For whoever wishes to save his life will lose it; but whoever loses his life for My sake will find it. [26] For what

will it profit a man if he gains the whole world and forfeits his soul? Or what will a man give in exchange for his soul? [27] For the Son of Man is going to come in the glory of His Father with His angels, and will then repay every man according to his deeds. [28] Truly I say to you, there are some of those who are standing here who will not taste death until they see the Son of Man coming in His kingdom."

Jesus and His disciples come to the district of Caesarea Philippi. Caesarea Philippi is the farthest north Jesus goes in Matthew's gospel, some one hundred and twenty miles north of Jerusalem, twenty miles to the north of the sea of Galilee. As always, the setting is important. As the name suggests, Caesarea Philippi was a Romanized city, but it was an ancient city, known as "Baal-Hermon" in the time of the judges (Judg. 3:3). Herod the Great built a temple there dedicated to Augustus, and later his son Philip enlarged the city and gave it the name that Matthew uses, the new name a nod to both Tiberius Caesar, who was ruling in Rome at the time, and to himself as the second founder of the city.

It is a city devoted to the cult of the emperor, an outpost of imperial ideology at the northern border of the land of Israel. This place name is a reminder that Jesus comes into a world dominated by the Roman empire, a world in which the Jews are a subject people. In this Roman city, a city named for Caesar and containing a temple devoted to Augustus Caesar, Jesus speaks of a different kingdom, a different empire, a different power in the world. The political dimension of this event is hinted at by the phrase Jesus uses to describe Himself, "Son of Man." "Son of Man" means "son of Adam," and designates Jesus as Last Adam, the true Son of the first man. But the phrase is prominently used in Daniel 7, where Daniel sees four beasts come from the sea and dominate the world for a time. Rome is the last of the four great monarchies envisioned by Daniel, but then all the authority and dominion of those empires is handed over to a figure that Daniel describes as "one like a Son of Man." After the bestial empires comes the beast tamer, the new Adam, the final world emperor, the Son of Man.

In Daniel's vision, the authority of the bestial empires is shared with the people of the Son of Man. Daniel says that "the sovereignty, the dominion, and the greatness of all the kingdoms under the whole heaven will be given to the people of the saints of the Highest One" (Dan. 7:27). Jesus comes as the "Son of Man" who takes the authority of those empires, and then *shares* that authority with His people. That is crucial for what happens here at Caesarea Philippi, because Jesus is not merely announcing that He is building His kingdom. He also confers authority on Peter, one of the "people of the saints of the Highest One."

Undoubtedly, Jesus singles out Peter. Given the history of interpretation, we need to clarify exactly how Jesus singles Peter out. Is Jesus establishing a permanent Petrine office in the church, the Papacy? No. Several things make it clear that Jesus is not establishing Peter as the beginning of a succession of Popes. The powers Jesus gives to Peter are not exclusively for Peter. Jesus tells Peter that whatever he binds on earth will be bound in heaven (v. 19), but in the same passage Jesus promises all the apostles (or even the whole church) the power to bind and loose: "Whatever you shall bind on earth shall be bound in heaven; and whatever you loose on earth shall be loosed in heaven" (Matt. 18:18-29). In John's account of the first Easter, Jesus breathes the Spirit on the *apostles* and says, "If you forgive the sins of any, their sins have been forgiven them; if you retain the sins of any, they have been retained" (John 20:19-23). Jesus is not granting exclusive privileges and powers to Peter. Peter's authority is shared by the rest of the apostles, who all have authority to bind and loose. Peter is first among the apostles, but his powers are the powers of the apostolate.

Acts shows that Peter was not permanent head of the church even in the first-century. Around the middle of Matthew's gospel Peter begins to take on prominence as the lead apostle. He alone walks on the water, poses questions to Jesus when the other apostles are silent, confesses Jesus and later denies Jesus. This preeminence continues into the book of Acts. After the Spirit comes, Peter preaches the sermon at Pentecost. He and John are dragged before the Sanhedrin, and Peter testifies to Jesus there. Peter visits Cornelius in Caesarea (another Caesarea, on the northern coast of Israel) and sees the Spirit fall on a Gentile household. Peter is imprisoned and delivered. Then, in the middle of Acts, Peter nearly drops from the story. He is present at the council of Jerusalem, but he is not in charge of the proceedings (Acts 15). He simply disappears. His name is used nearly sixty times in the first twelve chapters of Acts, but only once in the remainder of the book (Acts 15:7). After he is imprisoned, miraculously released, appears to women, is mistaken for a ghost, he departs – like Jesus. One might say that Peter has successors. After all, he is the initial leader of the Jewish church in Jerusalem, and then James takes over by the time of the Jerusalem council. Peter is the leading figure in the whole church during the first phase of her history, but then Paul takes more prominence. But there is no hint in Acts that the church as a whole continues to be under Petrine authority, even in the first century, much less throughout her history. The church moves from a Petrine phase to a Pauline phase within the first decades of her existence.

Acts also records a transition in the power to "bind and loose." Scholars debate about what the phrase means. In Jewish writings at the time, it refers to the authority to make authoritative declarations about what is permitted and what is not permitted, binding declarations about practice and teaching. We see Peter himself make a binding decision in Acts, when he encounters Cornelius, a Gentile whose house receives the Spirit. Peter defends himself against those who complain that he ate with uncircumcised men by telling them how the Spirit fell on Cornelius and his house, thus opening the way for the Gentile mission. The decision of the council of Jerusalem is made by the "apostles and the elders" (Acts 15:22). Peter is at Jerusalem, and he speaks, but he is not alone in making the decision. The apostles and elders are binding and loosing, making authoritative decisions about Christian practice.

Finally, there is nothing in the New Testament that links Peter with Rome. At the end of 1 Peter, Peter says, "She who is in Babylon, chosen together with you, sends you greetings" (1 Pet. 5:13), and this reference to "Babylon" is often taken as a veiled reference to Rome. It is much more likely that it refers to Jerusalem. Peter, after all, is the leader of the church in Jerusalem at the beginning of Acts, and in 1 Peter he addresses Christian Jews who were dispersed from Jerusalem after the stoning of Stephen. Peter is passing on greetings to the diaspora Christians from the home church. Besides, "Babylon" in the New Testament, especially in Revelation, refers to Jerusalem, not Rome. The "great city" that crashes to the ground in Revelation 17-18 is the harlot city of Jerusalem, the "great city" where Jesus was crucified (Rev. 11:8).

In short, none of the elements of the Papal doctrine are found in the New Testament. Peter's authority was not exclusive; even if it was exclusive, there is no sign of a continuing Petrine office lodged in a single person; Peter's leading role does not even last through the books of Acts; and even if it did, there is no sign that Peter was linked to Rome. In fact, the appeal to Peter's authority is not even witnessed in the earliest documents of the church at Rome. The tradition that Peter preached and died in Rome is fairly early and seems reliable, but the first lists of bishops of Rome from the later second century say that Peter and Paul jointly founded the Roman church, and they do not list Peter as the first bishop. Only in the third century is Peter listed as the first bishop, and only in the mid-third century do we find records that say Peter passed on his seat to Clement. Stephen I is the first to claim primacy based on this Petrine succession.[14]

---

14   Recent Catholic theologians (Joseph Ratzinger, e.g.) have admitted that the full Papal doctrine cannot be derived from the New Testament or from the earliest post-apostolic writings of the church fathers. Instead, they claim that certain seeds planted by Jesus grow up over time into Papal theology. Like all doctrine, they argue, the Papal doctrine undergoes a process of development.

Some Protestants, reacting to Roman Catholics, go to absurd lengths to deny that Peter is singled out here. They claim that Jesus founded His church on Peter's confession rather than Peter as a person, or that Jesus is calling Himself the rock on which the church is built. The first option mistakes the nature of the church; it is not an ideological group founded on ideas but a nation, founded on people. These people speak words and have ideas, but people form the foundation. And the church is built not only on Jesus but also on the people who were associated with Him. Jesus calls Himself the *"chief* cornerstone" (Matt. 21:42), but that implies that there are *other* cornerstones, which combine to form the foundation of the church (cf. Eph. 2:20).

The text makes it clear that Jesus is speaking to Peter. Peter gives Jesus a title "Christ"; Jesus in return gives Peter a title, *petros*, rock. Then He goes on to say that He will build His church on the *petra*. Jesus' pun identifies Peter himself as foundational to the church (Matt. 16:18). Of course, it is the Peter-who-confesses-Jesus who is the rock. Of course, Jesus is *the* Rock, the chief cornerstone of the church. But there is no reason to deny that Jesus is calling Peter a foundation stone of the church, a leading foundation stone of the church. There is every reason to think this is exactly what He is saying.

The imagery is architectural. Jesus is talking about building, and He says that Peter will be a rock, a stone at the foundation of the building. Paul picks up this same image when he describes the church as a building founded on the apostles and prophets (Eph. 2:20). When the new Jerusalem comes from heaven, its foundation stones are inscribed with the names of the twelve apostles (Rev. 21:14). Jesus is the chief cornerstone, and Peter and James and John form the other cornerstones of the house (cf. Matt. 17:1). Once the foundation is laid, more building has to take place, but you do not keep laying the foundation. The apostolate was as unique, as once-for-all, as Jesus' cross, resurrection, ascension, and the gift of the Spirit at Pentecost. It is not repeated any more than the cross is repeated. This is inherent in the apostolate, since the apostles were those who were eyewitnesses of Jesus in His resurrection especially. The church remains apostolic, and the authority to bind and loose continues to be exercised, but the specific role of the apostles does not carry on past the first generation, since no one after the first generation could qualify as an apostle.

What does Jesus intend to build on the foundation of Peter and the other apostles? He describes the authority of Peter with the image of "keys." The keys allude to Isaiah 22, where the Lord warns that the steward of David's house, Shebna, will be taken away into exile and replaced by a new steward, Eliakim, son of Hilkiah (Isaiah 22). Peter has confessed that Jesus is the Davidic "Son of the living God," the anointed "Christ," the new David. Jesus tells Peter that, on the basis of that confession, he will become the chief steward of that house. Peter, as the chief of the apostles, will have the authority to open and shut the doors, to keep people in and out, and so will the other apostles as well as those who follow the apostles as the stewards of David's house. Jesus is building a royal house, and the apostles are the doorkeepers and overseers of His house.

Jesus also describes this building as a "church" (Gr. *ekklesia*). We are so used to the word "church," and to thinking about the church in a certain way, that we miss the sense of the Greek word. The church is a group of people, not a building. What kind of group is it? In ancient Greek, an *ekklesia* is the decision-making citizen assembly of a city state. Citizens gathered as the *ekklesia* to deliberate about the needs of the city, make decisions, and pass judgments. An *ekklesia* is not a private club, but a public and political assembly. Jesus is establishing a decision-making body, His own *ekklesia*. When a church is planted in a city, it sets up its own citizen-assembly, distinct from that of the city. When Jesus' *ekklesia* is planted in a city, that assembly begins to determine the future direction of the city as a whole.

The church opposes Hades. Hades is primarily the place of the dead, the Greek equivalent of the Hebrew *sheol*. It specifically describes the condition of those who are cut off in the midst of life. The only reference to "gate of *sheol*" in the Old Testament is in Isaiah 38, where Hezekiah describes his mortal sickness and the Lord's deliverance. Jesus says the gates of death will not hold out against the church. The church proclaims the gospel of life and will make declarations of life from the dead, and the gates of death will not be able to prevent it. Death will not swallow up the church. Houses built on sand will fall, but the house built on Jesus the Rock, and on Peter the Rock, will never fall.

Gates are places of entry and exit to a city, and therefore they are a place of judgment and decision. Elders gather in the gates and make decisions about who belongs inside and who has to be cast out. The decisions of the gates of Hades will not prevail against the decisions and declarations of the *ekklesia* of Jesus. Peter and the apostles will make binding declarations, guided by heaven ("will have been bound"), and these decisions will stand against the declarations and decisions of death and hell.

Jesus, as it were, contrasts two patterns of human life, that of the *ekklesia* and that of the Satanic city of death. Once Peter makes his confession, Jesus begins to disclose that His mission requires Him to suffer and die in Jerusalem and to be raised on the third day. This is a significant turning point in Jesus' ministry. He has warned the disciples they would face persecution and even the cross, but this is the first time he has mentioned His own death on a cross. The fact that this comes on the heels of the confession of Jesus as Christ is confusing; it is certainly confusing to Peter. As Christ, Jesus is a king, but what kind of king talks about suffering and dying? Peter cannot grasp it, and he rebukes Him. But Jesus condemns Peter's rebuke as a Satanic stumbling block. Peter tempts Jesus to seize the kingdom without the cross, just as Satan had done (Matthew 4). Peter has grasped that Jesus is the Christ, but He does not yet know what being Christ means. He knows that Jesus is Son of God, but he does not really know what kind of God he is serving. "God's interests" involve self-giving in death, while man's interest is in self-preservation. God's way of life is to deny Himself and take up a cross. God's way is to give Himself. Jesus' cross is not a contradiction of His divine nature but a revelation of it. While the cross looks like a way of death – a way of Hades – it is the opposite: It is the only way to life.

Jesus' *ekklesia*, His kingdom, is one in which all follow Jesus. Jesus Himself goes God's way, and He calls all of us to do the same. He calls all of us to pursue God's interests. He calls all of us to deny ourselves, our own interests and plans, our own programs and ideas. And He does this with the assurance that we will not lose our lives but save them. We have this assurance because the Son of Man will come to judge, and He will vindicate, and He will reward. This is what will characterize the empire of Jesus, whose founding is declared in this city of Caesar, this outpost of Rome, this outpost of the empire of *superbia* and *libido dominandi*.

Jesus says all this in a city named for Caesar, in the shadow of Mount Hermon, which looms over Caesarea Philippi at the headwaters of the Jordan. Psalm 133 is talking about this region when it compares the oil on Aaron's head that flows down to the skirts of his garments to the dew of Hermon. All Israel shares in the priestly anointing of Aaron that flows down from the head to the hem of his robe, as the waters that descend on Hermon flow down the Jordan to water the entire land of Israel. Hermon is an Eden, the source of rivers that flow to the four corners of the land.

This setting adds one final dimension to Jesus' words here. Jesus is establishing a new Eden, a city built on a Rock. That description, of course, goes back to Old Testament passages that describe Yahweh as the Rock of Israel, the Rock that is struck and gives water in the wilderness. Peter also is a rock, called to be like Yahweh, not only part of the foundation of a building but a source of life and refreshment to the people of God. Like Jesus, Peter will become that life-giving rock only by being struck, by taking up his cross to follow Jesus. Like Jesus, the whole church bears the cross in order to become a new Eden, flowing with living water to the whole earth.

Death and Glory
Matthew 17:1-13

¹ Six days later Jesus took with Him Peter and James and John his brother, and led them up on a high mountain by themselves. ² And He was transfigured before them; and His face shone like the sun, and His garments became as white as light. ³ And behold, Moses and Elijah appeared to them, talking with Him. ⁴ Peter said to Jesus, "Lord, it is good for us to be here; if You wish, I will make three tabernacles here, one for You, and one for Moses, and one for Elijah." ⁵ While he was still speaking, a bright cloud overshadowed them, and behold, a voice out of the cloud said, "This is My beloved Son, with whom I am well-pleased; listen to Him!" ⁶ When the disciples heard this, they fell face down to the ground and were terrified. ⁷ And Jesus came to them and touched them and said, "Get up, and do not be afraid." ⁸ And lifting up their eyes, they saw no one except Jesus Himself alone. ⁹ As they were coming down from the mountain, Jesus commanded them, saying, "Tell the vision to no one until the Son of Man has risen from the dead." ¹⁰ And His disciples asked Him, "Why then do the scribes say that Elijah must come first?" ¹¹ And He answered and said, "Elijah is coming and will restore all things; ¹² but I say to you that Elijah already came, and they did not recognize him, but did to him whatever they wished. So also the Son of Man is going to suffer at their hands." ¹³ Then the disciples understood that He had spoken to them about John the Baptist.

Death has shadowed Jesus from His infancy, when Herod slaughtered the children of Bethlehem.[15] Death shadows Him when He warns His disciples that the bridegroom will be taken and they will mourn. Death shadows Him and His disciples when He gives them their missionary commission, telling them to expect opposition, persecution, arrest, imprisonment and death. Death shadows Jesus when the Pharisees plot to destroy Him,

---

15 Garland, *Reading Matthew*.

and death stalks Jesus when Herod beheads His forerunner, John. Jesus is a Man of Sorrows and acquainted with death. His entire life is a journey through the valley of the shadow of death.

At the middle of Matthew's gospel story, Jesus becomes preoccupied with His own death in a way that He has not before. As soon as Peter confesses that He is the Christ, Jesus says Peter will receive the keys of the kingdom and then immediately begins to "show His disciples that he must go to Jerusalem, and suffer many things from the elders and chief priests and scribes, and be killed, and be raised up on the third day" (Matt. 16:21).

This is a crucial turning point in the gospel. At the beginning of Matthew, we are told Jesus "began" His ministry with an announcement of the kingdom. Here, Jesus begins anew with a new message that is not really a new message. Jesus "began" to say that he would suffer and die in Jerusalem and be raised. After Jesus "began" His ministry, we have been hearing stories about miraculous works and astonishing teaching. True, there has been opposition, but His work has been focused on healing and exorcism and raising the dead. Earlier, Matthew stopped the action of the story to summarize Jesus' ministry of healing, casting out demons, proclaiming the kingdom, expressions of Jesus' power as He brings in the kingdom of the Father (cf. Matt. 4:23-25). After the midpoint of the gospel, those summary statements are replaced by Jesus' own words. Jesus is still summarizing His ministry, but the accent is different. He does not talk about His work primarily as a work of exorcism, healing, preaching. Instead, He speaks of His work as His death (Matt. 17:22-23; 20:17-19; 26:1-2). It looks as if Jesus' message has suddenly changed. He looks like a different kind of Messiah. The first half of the gospel focuses on the triumphant message of the coming of the kingdom. The second half seems to turn tragic, as Jesus speaks of the depressing future of suffering and death. His focus on death is softened somewhat by His repeated promises of resurrection, but the disciples are puzzled by that and never grasp what Jesus is saying. But they understand what it means for Jesus to die, and they mourn over His words.

Jesus is not the only one who will bear a cross. Jesus says He is going to Jerusalem to be handed over to the priests and scribes, and to suffer, and to die, and to be raised. When Peter rebukes Him, Jesus says that the disciples are going to have to share in that death. If they want to be disciples, they must take up the cross and follow Him. To Jesus, this way of self-denial and the cross is not the way of death but the way of life. We can enter into life only if we deny ourselves and take up the cross and follow Jesus. Peter does not want Jesus to take this way, but Peter's suggested way is the way of Satan. By wanting to avoid self-denial and the cross, Peter is setting his thoughts on man and not on God. God's way is the way of self-denial and the cross, and we as disciples of Jesus gain life only by being willing to give up our own interests for God's. Though this is paradoxical, the paradox is softened by what Jesus adds in Matt. 17:27-28. Those who lose their lives in devotion to Jesus can be sure that they will eventually be vindicated and rewarded. Even if they are defeated for a time, the Son of Man will eventually come to "recompense every man according to his doing" (Matt. 16:27; cf. Psalm 62:12). Jesus assures the disciples that this vindication will come within the lifetime of some of the disciples (Matt. 16:28).

That means the disciples who take up the cross and follow Jesus will eventually be delivered from their oppressors. The balance of power will be reversed. The disciples who have been crushed will be raised up and their persecutors will be cast down. Jesus will deal to everyone according to His deeds – to everyone who is faithful in the midst of trial, He will give rewards, and they will enter life; the oppressors will be delivered to wrath and indignation.

The reference to the Son of Man coming in glory and dealing out judgment is linked to the vision of Daniel 7. As we saw above, Daniel sees four beasts come from the sea and take dominion over the land. These are four Gentile powers, Gentile empires, arising from the sea of nations and taking possession of the land of Israel – Babylon, Persia, Greece, and Rome. After the last of the beasts has taken his place, one like the Son of Man ascends to take his throne and is given all the dominion and power of all the kingdoms of the earth. The Son of Man is the Son of Adam, the Last Adam, who will exercise dominion over the beasts once and for all. Jesus identifies Himself with this Son of Man, who will have authority over heaven and earth. That is the assurance Jesus' disciples can have in the midst of persecution and self-denial and cross-bearing. We can be sure that whatever injustice and affliction we endure, the Son of Man will take the throne and will deal out retribution and will judge all the nations in perfect righteousness. He will come to vindicate His people.

This is what the resurrection is all about, too. Jesus Himself will be raised and vindicated. His murderers will be put down, and He will be exalted. When Jesus says that we have to bear the cross along with Him, He is not saying this because the torture of the cross is good in itself. He means that faithfulness to the death will actually lead to life, because on the other side of the humiliation of the cross is the glory of resurrection, the glory of the coming of the Son of Man.

Matthew 16 ends with Jesus' promise to come in glory within the lifetime of His disciples, and Matthew 17 reveals the glory of Jesus. Given this context, some have thought the Son of Man's coming in glory took place "six days later" at the mount of transfiguration (v. 1). That does not work. When Jesus says that "some will not taste death," the clear implication is that some *will* taste death. Matt. 16:28 assumes that time will pass and some of the apostles will die before the coming of the Son of Man. But no one dies in the six days between Jesus' exchange with Peter at Caesarea Philippi and His transfiguration on a high mountain. Still, the transfiguration is connected with Jesus' prediction. It anticipates the resurrection appearances of Jesus (17:9) and reveals the glory of His own vindication in the resurrection. But that is not all. The transfiguration is a preview of the glory of the Son of Man, the glory He will show at His coming.

That is how Peter later understood the transfiguration. In 2 Peter 1, he reminds his readers of the promise of Jesus' coming and says that this is no fable or myth. The promise of Jesus' coming is not some cleverly devised tale but was confirmed by the preview of Jesus' majesty on the "holy mountain" (2 Pet. 1:16-18).[16] This implies that the transfiguration is not primarily a display of Jesus' divine nature. Many have thought that here, for a brief moment, the glory of Jesus' divinity shines through the cloak of His humanity. Here, for a brief moment, three of the disciples at least see Jesus for what he truly is, the eternal Son of the Father. It is true that the descriptions of Jesus' glory pick up images from Old Testament descriptions of Yahweh. Psalm 104 says the Lord clothes Himself with light, and elsewhere we learn that the Lord is a Sun and shield to His people. Jesus *does* display divine attributes on the mount of Transfiguration. It is also true that whatever glory human beings have comes from God. But Scripture says that human beings do share in that glory. The song of Deborah also says that "those who love Yahweh will be like the rising of the sun in its might" (Judg. 5:31). Daniel says that the righteous will shine like stars in the heaven, fulfilling the Abrahamic promise that his children will be like the stars. "I am the light of the world," Jesus says; but elsewhere He says, "You are the light of the world." Even if we say that the glory of transfiguration is divine glory, it is mediated through the man Jesus.

But Matthew is not mainly talking about Jesus' divine nature at all. That does not fit the context. Jesus has been talking about the *Son of Man* coming in the glory of the Father, and then He is transfigured before His disciples. The glory that is displayed on the high mountain is the glory of the Father, but it is Jesus as *Son of Man* who is glorified with the glory of the Father. The glory is the glory that the eternal Son shared from the foundation of the earth, but here that glory is shared with Jesus the God-Man, the Son of Man; His humanity is caught up into the glory of the Father and Son. This does display the inherent glory of the Son of God; the transfiguration shows the Son of Man sharing in the glory of the Father.

---

16 See my *The Promise of His Appearing: An Exposition of Second Peter* (Moscow, ID: Canon Press, 2004).

The typology of the passage confirms this reading. This passage is a knot of intertwined and overlapping types from the Old Testament. The mount of Transfiguration is analogous to the mountain of Eden, the mountain where God planted a garden and created Adam. Jesus is glorified on the "sixth day," as Adam was created on the sixth day. The cloud overshadows Jesus and the Twelve on the mountain, as the Spirit overshadowed and hovered over the creation in the beginning. After the cloud leaves and the disciples see Jesus alone, they speak of the restoration of all things, the new creation. Jesus is glorified as the New Adam, showing the glory that Adam was destined to receive. The mount of Transfiguration is also Sinai, and Jesus is not only Adam but also Moses. Moses enters the cloud of Yahweh's presence, and He returns with his face shining so brightly that Israel cannot bear to look at him. Moses actually appears on the mount of Transfiguration, and at the center of the event the Father tells the three disciples to "hear" this new Moses, who comes to teach the fulfilled law. In keeping with this exodus typology, Peter wants to build tabernacles for Jesus, Moses, and Elijah, just as Israel built the tabernacle at the foot of Sinai when Moses came down with his shining face.

On the mount of Transfiguration, Jesus is also the new high priest in the temple. The tabernacle and temple were architectural mountains, and so the priest entering the most holy place ascended to the highest peak of the mountain of God. As priests ministered in the temple, they wore garments of glory and beauty, clothes that sparkled with precious stones and flashed with golden thread. When they went into the most holy place on the Day of Atonement, they wore a simple white garment. Jesus is the true High Priest. On the mount of Transfiguration, Jesus is the great prophet. He enters into the cloud of the Father's glory, as Moses and Elijah both ascended Horeb to appear before Yahweh. Moses is the paradigmatic prophet of the Old Testament, and Elijah marks the beginning of the prophetic movement. Both are figures for a future prophet that the Lord promises in Deuteronomy and Malachi. As the new prophet, Jesus will speak God's words, and the Father tells the disciples to listen.

All these typologies and more are clustered here, and each one points in one direction: Jesus is the man who ascends and shares in the glory of Yahweh. What the transfiguration shows is not that the divinity of Jesus is seeping through the veil of His humanity. Instead, Jesus reveals the destiny of humanity, to be conformed to the glory of God and filled with that glory. The writer of a great Transfiguration hymn gets the point exactly right: "O Wondrous Might, O Vision Fair, of glory *that the church shall share.*"

When we recognize this aspect of the Transfiguration, we begin to see what the event tells us not only about Jesus, the Son of Man who will come to vindicate His people, but also about God: He is the God who shares glory. We often think of glory as a zero-sum game. God is glorious, and we are not. The more we glorify God, the more we have to empty ourselves of glory. Emptying ourselves of glory is the way of disciples; we are to deny ourselves and not to scrape up glory for ourselves. If we want God to be glorious, we need to become correspondingly *un*-glorious. But that thinking misses an important dimension of God's attributes: His glory is infinite, and He is glorious because He gives glory freely, and calls us to do the same. We also think of glory as a zero-sum game in human life. There is only so much praise, honor, and glory to go around, and so we become rivals. We speak and act to glorify ourselves and to deprive others of glory. Children compete for the approval of their parents. Parents sometimes act as if they can receive due honor only by dishonoring their children; they can get the glory they deserve only if the children are robbed of glory, only if they keep their children down. So parents talk about their children's faults and failures and never talk about their accomplishments and gifts. Parents nit-pick at the smallest fault. Parents feel superior, glorious, weighty, so long as they make their children seem small and inferior. Husbands think they can receive honor and glory only by humiliating and abusing their wives. At work, we think that we can be elevated and glorified only by belittling other employees. In social gatherings, we compete to be the center of attention, glorifying ourselves with stories of our triumphs and making sure everyone around us looks small and mean by comparison. We might think that glory in the church requires us to compete for attention and authority.

All this rests on a basic mistake about God. God is not selfish. God is not envious. God is not a miser. God displays His glory by *bestowing* glory. God is glorified not by keeping the glory all bottled up in Himself but by sharing it, generously, lavishly, excessively. He gives the glory of His Spirit to His Son eternally, and He gives glory to His created sons. God glorifies Himself not by making a world that lacks glory, but by creating a world that manifests His glory, a world that is so beauteous that people may end up worshiping the creature rather than Creator.

God's generosity in giving glory sets the pattern for us. Parents do not become glorious by stomping down their children, by grinding them down. Fathers are glorified by glorifying their sons, and mothers are glorified by glorifying daughters. Parents are glorified as parents by raising up their children so they can become glorious; parents become glorious and receive honor by giving honor, by words that glorify their children instead of putting them down. Brothers do not become glorious by putting down sisters but by glorifying and honoring their sisters. Employers do not become glorious by keeping their employees at minimum wage and low skill; employers become glorious by raising their employees to glory. This is the pattern of God's life, and it is the pattern that we are to imitate.

God never runs out of glory to give. When He has bestowed glory so that all is glorious, He still has infinite resources of glory left to bestow. Glory is not a zero-sum game but an infinite sum game. God's light is light because we are lights; God is a sun, and glorified as Sun, when we shine like suns. This is the Father of Jesus Christ: the God who glorifies by giving glory, the God who has infinite glory to give. You are the people of this God. Freely you have received glory; go and freely give.

Down from the Mountain
Matthew 17:9-27

⁹As they were coming down from the mountain, Jesus commanded them, saying, "Tell the vision to no one until the Son of Man has risen from the dead." ¹⁰ And His disciples asked Him, "Why then do the scribes say that Elijah must come first?" ¹¹ And He answered and said, "Elijah is coming and will restore all things; ¹² but I say to you that Elijah already came, and they did not recognize him, but did to him whatever they wished. So also the Son of Man is going to suffer at their hands." ¹³ Then the disciples understood that He had spoken to them about John the Baptist. ¹⁴ When they came to the crowd, a man came up to Jesus, falling on his knees before Him and saying, ¹⁵ "Lord, have mercy on my son, for he is a lunatic and is very ill; for he often falls into the fire and often into the water. ¹⁶ I brought him to Your disciples, and they could not cure him." ¹⁷ And Jesus answered and said, "You unbelieving and perverted generation, how long shall I be with you? How long shall I put up with you? Bring him here to Me." ¹⁸ And Jesus rebuked him, and the demon came out of him, and the boy was cured at once. ¹⁹ Then the disciples came to Jesus privately and said, "Why could we not drive it out?" ²⁰ And He said to them, "Because of the littleness of your faith; for truly I say to you, if you have faith the size of a mustard seed, you will say to this mountain, Move from here to there, and it will move; and nothing will be impossible to you. ²¹ [But this kind does not go out except by prayer and fasting.]" ²² And while they were gathering together in Galilee, Jesus said to them, "The Son of Man is going to be delivered into the hands of men; ²³ and they will kill Him, and He will be raised on the third day." And they were deeply grieved. ²⁴ When they came to Capernaum, those who collected the two-drachma tax came to Peter and said, "Does your teacher not pay the two-drachma tax?" ²⁵ He said, "Yes." And when he came into the house, Jesus spoke to him first, saying, "What do you think, Simon? From whom do the kings of the earth collect customs or poll-tax, from their sons or from strangers?" ²⁶ When Peter

said, "From strangers," Jesus said to him, "Then the sons are exempt. ²⁷ However, so that we do not offend them, go to the sea and throw in a hook, and take the first fish that comes up; and when you open its mouth, you will find a shekel. Take that and give it to them for you and Me."

Jesus will not let His disciples relax. Just when you think He has reached a high point, just when you think He has reached a point of mastery and victory, He starts on again about death, suffering, the cross. It already happened at Caesarea Philippi. Finally, at long last, one of the disciples says what he should say about Jesus. Peter finally comes to the realization that Jesus is the Christ, the Son of the living God. Finally, someone has disclosed this truth. But no sooner has Peter made that confession than Jesus starts talking about going to Jerusalem, suffering, dying, rising the third day. What a depressing fellow to be around!

It happens again after the transfiguration. Jesus is transfigured before the three disciples, His face shining like the sun and His garment flashing like light. Peter wants to stay there to erect permanent shrines for Jesus, Moses, and Elijah, and just stay there on the holy mountain forever and ever. But Jesus returns to His normal self, and as they walk down the mountain, Jesus and His disciples discuss Elijah. Jesus returns to the theme of suffering: "Elijah has come and they did to him whatever they wished." The same will be true of the Son of Man (v. 12). He too will suffer at their hands. Jesus casts out a demon. He gains a victory over Satan that His disciples were impotent to gain. But then He is back to talking about His death. "The Son of Man is going to be delivered into the hands of men, and they will kill Him, and He will be raised on the third day." Jesus cannot leave this subject alone, and He cannot leave it alone not only because it is in the immediate future for Him and His disciples. He cannot leave it alone because it is the story of Christian living. He cannot leave it alone because the Christian life is always a life of following the Christ who was crucified.

When you enter church, you are on the mountain peak. You are here in the house of God with the people of God. For a couple of hours, you can put your troubles behind you. Perhaps you can put those troubles behind you for the whole of this Lord's day. You are no sooner down from the mountain when the fight you were having before you arrived at church comes screaming back. Then Monday inevitably comes along, and you have to face everything again. Maybe even before Monday. If you are having marriage troubles, as soon as you leave church you face the demons again. The Lord has arranged the world, and the life of the church, so that the transfigurations are not yet permanent. We might be on the mountain for a time, seeing the flashing glory of Jesus. But there are still demon-possessed boys at the foot of the mountain, and we need to descend into hell to minister to them. We can find some peace and calm on the mountain peak, but we are called to travel to Jerusalem bearing the cross.

This is not defeatism. In the very moment that Jesus is being attacked and assaulted by the world, He is also overcoming the world. And it is the same for us: in all our afflictions, we are more than conquerors through Jesus Christ our Lord.

We can see that for Jesus it is not defeatism from the way He describes it. Throughout this section, He is talking about the suffering of the Son of Man. "So also the Son of Man is going to suffer at their hands" (v. 12). And then, "The Son of Man is going to be delivered into the hands of men" (v. 22). I will say it again: This phrase means "Son of Adam" or "last Adam," but the most immediate background is in Daniel 7, when Daniel sees a vision of beastly empires that are going to protect, but eventually trample, Israel. Finally, he sees one like the Son of Man lifted up so that He can tame the beasts and take His throne and take all dominion and authority. The Son of Man is going to be raised up in order to judge. Jesus has referred to the Son of Man dealing out judgment according to their deeds (Matt. 16:27), and I think Jesus is referring specifically to the coming judgment on Jerusalem and the *oikoumene* in AD 70. But we should not miss the other dimension of this. The judgment of men for their deeds does not begin *after* Jesus is raised and exalted. Instead, the judgment of men for their deeds begins on the cross. "*Now* is the judgment of this world," Jesus says, speaking of His death, "Now is the Prince of this world cast out."

We need to enrich our idea of what it means for Jesus to judge the world. He judges by rewarding the faithful and condemning the unfaithful. There is a final judgment to come. But the Son of Man's judgment takes a more paradoxical form as well. The judgment rendered by the Son of Man looks like the judgment *of* the Son of Man. When Jesus is on the cross, it looks as if He is the one condemned, but the reality is that the world has condemned itself by putting Him there. That is how we participate in Jesus' judgment of the world. We often think that we participate in Jesus' judgment of the world when we take mastery, when we are elevated and when we can stomp on those who have stomped on us. Retribution is real, and good. God is a God of justice. But we should not think that is the beginning of our sharing in Jesus' judgment. When we bear the cross, when we are persecuted by people hostile to Jesus, we are sharing in Jesus' judgment of the world. The world is condemning itself. When we are persecuted, we are also prosecuting the persecutors.

So when you go back to the foot of the mountain, expect to participate in Jesus' paradoxical judgment of the world. That oppressive boss, who is just looking out for an opportunity to screw you, he is the world to you; and if you suffer his injustices with patience and faithfulness, doing good in return to evil, you are judging the world by hanging with Jesus on the cross. That overbearing husband or nagging wife, who has grown to hate the sight of you, he or she is the world to you; if you turn the other cheek and return good for evil, you are judging the world by hanging with Jesus on the cross. Whatever faults Constantine had, he had at least this insight: the cross is a sign of Christ's victory not a sign of His defeat. We are witnesses, martyrs, when we suffer faithfully with Jesus.

Matthew is retelling the story of Israel. Jesus is the true Israel who takes on the roles of various Old Testament leaders. He comes as Moses the law-giver, as Joshua the conqueror, as Solomon the sage, and here in this section He comes as a prophet like Elisha. One indication that we are in a "divided kingdom" portion of Matthew is the prominence of Elijah. Elijah's name is used six times in Matthew 16–17, five in Matthew 17 alone. Otherwise, his name appears only three times in Matthew. Elijah himself appears on the mount of transfiguration, and as they leave the mountain Jesus and His disciples talk about Elijah again. The scene at the foot of the mountain is also reminiscent of this period of Israel's history. Jesus is Moses on the mountain, His face horned with the glory of God; and like Moses He descends to find His followers going astray. Moses came down from the mountain to discover that Aaron had built a golden calf for that faithless and crooked generation; Jesus comes down to find that the disciples are part of the faithless and crooked generation, lacking the faith to cast out a demon.

Jesus is also like Elisha. Elisha is the great wonder-working prophet of the Old Testament. He receives a double portion of the spirit of Elijah, the portion of the firstborn, and also twice as much spirit. Endowed with this double portion, Elisha does twice as many signs and miracles. But Elisha also has a disciple, Gehazi, who is often faithless and ineffective in his ministry. As Jesus and His three disciples descend from the mountain, they find the other disciples struggling to help a demon-possessed boy. The disciples fail. Jesus is the greater Elisha, and His disciples are like Elisha's bumbling sidekick, Gehazi.

Not only does the story link with Elijah and Elisha, but the topic of Jesus' conversation puts us in the divided kingdom period. As they descend from the mountain, Jesus warns them to keep quiet about the Transfiguration (cf. Matt. 8:4; 9:30; 12:16). Only after His death and resurrection will the meaning of the Transfiguration become clear, and then the three disciples will become unique witnesses to the Transfiguration. When He mentions the resurrection, the disciples are puzzled. They have learned from the scribes that there is a timetable for prophecy, which includes an appearance by Elijah. This Jewish eschatology is rooted in the Old Testament. Elijah is associated with resurrection because he raised the dead (1 Kings 17:17-24) and because of prophecies that his "return" would begin the restoration of Israel (Mal. 4:4-6). Jesus does not disagree with the eschatology of the scribes, except in the point of timing. Jesus says that Elijah *has* come in John and the restoration has already begun. Even here, however, Jesus cannot help turning the disciples' attention back to His imminent suffering. The Jews oppose Elijah-John, and the Son of Man will face the same opposition (Matt. 17:12).

The nine disciples are unsuccessful, but they need not have been. Even the smallest faith, if it is true faith in Jesus and the Father of Jesus, is virtually omnipotent: "Nothing shall be impossible to you" (Matt. 17:20). But there is a puzzle here. How can Jesus rebuke the disciples for "little faith," and then tell them that "little faith" is all they need to perform everything? Is their faith even *smaller* than a mustard seed? Or is Jesus talking about different sorts of faith? They have enough faith to stick with Jesus, to confess Jesus, to know that Jesus is very, very special. But they are called to greater faith, a different quality of faith. This greater faith depends on getting the insight that Jesus teaches them as they descend from the mountain. They have to have faith that Elijah has come and is restoring all things, faith that the Son of Man will restore all things through His cross and resurrection on the third day.

When Jesus later tells the disciples their faith can move mountains to the sea, He is looking at Jerusalem and its mountains (Matt. 21:18-22). Here the point is more general. He talks about moving "this mountain," but it is not specifically the mountain of Jerusalem. Elsewhere, the Lord moves mountains, and the moving of mountains is associated with the un-creating of the world, an un-creating that prepares for a new creation (cf. Jer. 4:23-25; Zech 14:4-8; Rev. 6:12-14). Faith to move mountains is faith to take the world apart, to undo the most solid thing in God's world, to tear down a world in preparation for building up. This fits the context.

In the context, the thing that will not be impossible for the disciples is the restoration of all things already begun by John, brought to a completion by Jesus, and then fulfilled in all its glorious reality by the disciples.

The disciples are mistaken about the timetable of that restoration. They think, apparently, that the resurrection will happen at the very end. But they are right about the character of the Messiah's work, prepared for by Elijah. They know it is a "restoration of all things." That is the aim of Jesus. He comes to restore all things. In Malachi, the specific focus is on restoring generations. Elijah will come – Elijah *has* come – to restore the hearts of fathers to children and the hearts of children to fathers. But Jesus says Elijah comes to restore all things and to prepare the way for the restoration of everything. This is Jesus' mission, following upon Elijah-John. He comes to restore generations, to restore husbands to wives and wives to husbands, to restore servants to masters and masters to servants, to restore lunatics to sanity and to deliver demon-possessed boys from Satan's power. He comes to put hearts back together when they are broken; He comes to raise up those who have been trampled by mud; He comes to raise the poor who have had their faces ground down by the rich, and He raises the poor from the garbage dump and seats them in seats of nobles.

And it does not matter how broken things are, how shattered your life has become. Your life may be broken into a million little pieces through your sin and folly, or through the abuse of others, or because of some illness. Can God put it back together? Of course He can. For a God who created a world from nothing, it is easy to gather together the fragments of your life, of your mind, of your marriage, of your job, of the church, of the broken and warring nations, of the effects of oppression and persecution and injustice.

This is not only Jesus' *eventual* goal. The disciples expect all that to happen at the end. But Elijah has already come and restored all things. The Jews refused to accept Him, and they did to him what they wished. They will do the same to the Son of

Man. But that does not stop the program; that does not mean the restoration will be delayed. John's death and Jesus' cross become the paradoxical means toward the restoration of all things. This is how it is going to happen.

It is happening, and that is the goal and ministry to which we are called. We are called to a faith that reorders creation and puts it back together in new ways. We are called to faith in Christ the Lord of all, and by faith we are called to participate in that restoration. Your life may look small, but if you are living with faith in Jesus in every area of your life, you are part of the biggest story there can be, part of the biggest reclamation project in history, a participant in the recreation of God's damaged world.

5

Toward the Temple

Greatest in the Kingdom
Matthew 17:24-18:14

24 When they came to Capernaum, those who collected the two-drachma tax came to Peter and said, "Does your teacher not pay the two-drachma tax?" **25** He said, "Yes." And when he came into the house, Jesus spoke to him first, saying, "What do you think, Simon? From whom do the kings of the earth collect customs or poll-tax, from their sons or from strangers?" **26** When Peter said, "From strangers," Jesus said to him, "Then the sons are exempt. **27** However, so that we do not offend them, go to the sea and throw in a hook, and take the first fish that comes up; and when you open its mouth, you will find a shekel. Take that and give it to them for you and Me." **18:1** At that time the disciples came to Jesus and said, "Who then is greatest in the kingdom of heaven?" **2** And He called a child to Himself and set him before them, **3** and said, "Truly I say to you, unless you are converted and become like children, you will not enter the kingdom of heaven. **4** Whoever then humbles himself as this child, he is the greatest in the kingdom of heaven. **5** And whoever receives one such child in

My name receives Me; [6] but whoever causes one of these little ones who believe in Me to stumble, it would be better for him to have a heavy millstone hung around his neck, and to be drowned in the depth of the sea. [7] Woe to the world because of its stumbling blocks! For it is inevitable that stumbling blocks come; but woe to that man through whom the stumbling block comes! [8] If your hand or your foot causes you to stumble, cut it off and throw it from you; it is better for you to enter life crippled or lame, than to have two hands or two feet and be cast into the eternal fire. [9] If your eye causes you to stumble, pluck it out and throw it from you. It is better for you to enter life with one eye, than to have two eyes and be cast into the fiery hell. [10] See that you do not despise one of these little ones, for I say to you that their angels in heaven continually see the face of My Father who is in heaven. [11] For the Son of Man has come to save that which was lost. [12] What do you think? If any man has a hundred sheep, and one of them has gone astray, does he not leave the ninety-nine on the mountains and go and search for the one that is straying? [13] If it turns out that he finds it, truly I say to you, he rejoices over it more than over the ninety-nine which have not gone astray. [14] So it is not the will of your Father who is in heaven that one of these little ones perish."

An offense is an obstacle, a trap, a barrier. It is the word Yahweh uses in Leviticus to warn Israel not to set a "stumbling block" in the way of the blind man (Lev. 19:14). Metaphorically, a stumbling block is something we do or say that makes it harder for people to believe us or to follow us. Specifically, it is something we do or say that makes it more difficult for people to believe the gospel. A preacher who preaches against pornography and yet indulges himself privately sets up a stumbling block because of his hypocrisy. Pharisees make it difficult for people to be obedient to Torah by adding extra laws. When Presbyterians hate Methodists, and Anglicans hate Catholics, and Christians are at war with each other, we all become a stumbling block and a rock of offense.

Jesus is more than willing to give offense, to set traps, and to put stumbling blocks in the way of the Jews. Jesus speaks in parables because the hearts of the Jews are closed, their ears deaf, their eyes blinded. Instead of trying to explain things more clearly, Jesus turns to obscure and parabolic riddles. He makes it more difficult for them to understand, not less. They are blind, and Jesus – apparently in violation of the law – puts a stumbling block in the way of the blind. When Jesus visits His hometown and people are offended, Jesus does not try to soften the offense but observes that "A prophet is not without honor except in his own home town, and in his own household" (Matt. 13:57). The disciples tell Jesus that the Pharisees were offended by Jesus' teaching about defilement, but Jesus answers with a "who cares?" and gives more offense. He says the Pharisees are like plants that the Father did not plant, associating them with the tares that were planted by the devil, and says they are "blind guides of the blind" (Matt. 15:12-14). Paul goes so far as to say Jesus *is* an offense, a stumbling block, set up by Yahweh, over which the Jews have stumbled (Rom. 9:31-33).

Jesus is not afraid of giving offense; He scandalizes; He sets up obstacles and stones of stumbling. But here Jesus pays a tax that He says He does not owe because He does not want to give offense. Why the difference? Why is Jesus willing to give offense in one case and not in another? The question in debate is payment of the temple tax, a custom rooted in the "atonement money" collected by Moses from Israelite men going to war (Exod. 30:11-16). Later in Israel's history, this Mosaic tax was the basis for a regular temple assessment (2 Kings 12:4), which provided for the repair and maintenance of the temple. 2 Chronicles 24 tells us this with explicit reference to the Mosaic law as the basis for Joash's tax (2 Chron. 24:5-7). By the first century, this had become a permanent tax that paid for sacrificial animals that were not brought by worshipers.

When asked whether Jesus pays the tax, Peter answers "Yes," and Jesus eventually affirms that answer. But "in the house," in private, among His disciples, He gives His reasons. In a temple context, the sons are those who are members of the house, who have access to the king. In short, the sons are priests. Strangers are the "unauthorized" who are not permitted in the house. By describing Himself and Peter as "sons," Jesus claims access to the Father, hinting at the coming of a new temple with a reorganized priesthood. Though free from the tax because of His sonship, Jesus is willing to pay to support the temple's operation. He is not obligated, but He gives the tax anyway. Thus, He stakes a position on what appears to be a debate among Jews of the first century concerning the legitimacy of the temple leadership and the legitimacy of the tax. His reasoning indicates that He is free to pay or not, but He ends up affirming Peter's initial answer – Yes, the teacher does pay the tax.

Why does Jesus get the tax money from a fish? The incident is prophetic. The sea and the fish of the sea are common images of Gentiles. Money transferred from a fish to the temple is the wealth of nations transferred to the house of God. This fishing expedition links to various prophecies about the Gentiles bringing their treasures to the temple. Peter is a fisher of men, and the men he reels in will give up their treasures to Jesus' temple.

Against this background, we can get an idea of why Jesus avoids offense here when He is willing to give offense elsewhere. The first reason has to do with timing. Eventually, the temple will be destroyed and the whole system will be dismantled. Christians will not need to pine for a new temple either. They will have their temple (Jesus) among them; and they will *be* a temple. That time has not come yet. Even into the book of Acts, the apostles continue to frequent the temple and to worship there. Scandalizing is a matter of right timing; sometimes it is time to start speaking in riddles, sometimes it is time to make flagrant displays of opposition to the temple – as Jesus will do at the beginning of the Passion Week. But not yet.

The other reason has to do with what is at stake. Jesus has a carefree attitude toward money and wealth. He tells us not to worry about money, clothing, food, shelter. We are not supposed to be anxious but instead observe the birds and the grass and see how well the Father takes care of them. And we are not supposed to draw battles lines over issues of money.

This is part of the message of Peter's fishing expedition. It answers certain questions, such as how can disciples of Jesus willingly give up their freedoms, pay money they do not owe? Will not that leave them bankrupt? This is the same question that arises from Jesus' teaching in the Sermon on the Mount: if we have to give up our cloak, will not we end up naked? Jesus demonstrates to Peter that he has nothing to fear from paying an unnecessary and even oppressive tax. Peter may be defrauded, but he will still have all he needs from the Father who makes fish cough up coins.

At the heart of Jesus' answer to the question is His willingness to give up rights and freedoms for the sake of others. He does not want to offend the people collecting the temple tax even though they are mainly opposed to Him. Jesus does not scandalize by clinging to His rights and privileges. We do not need to cling to our rights, our freedoms, because we know that there are fish in the sea who can provide every coin we need.

The issue of scandal continues into Matthew 18. English translations sometimes obscure this, but the verb for "give offense" in Matt. 17:27 is *skandalizo*, and the word for stumbling block throughout Matthew 18 is *skandalon*. Jesus is talking about stumbling blocks, offenses, scandals throughout this section. In Matt. 18:1, this question arises from the question the disciples pose — Who is the greatest?

The question that begins Matthew 18 seems to arise from nowhere. But it does fit with the previous section. Jesus has just described Himself as the Son of the royal house, the Son of the great king of Israel, and He has described His disciples as sons rather than strangers. They are princes, and they suddenly feel the grandeur of their status. The disciples are operating by the common assumptions of the ancient world that life is competition for honors, greatness, and glory: there is only so much glory to go around, and so we have to seek honor, gain it, and preserve it with all our energies.

Jesus undermines this whole system by placing a child in the midst of the disciples and urging them to emulate the child. Jesus does not reject the desire for greatness. He redefines greatness. Greatness is found by being like a child. Children were not role models in the ancient world. Children and women did not have access to the honor game that the disciples are playing. They typically did not have voice or status. Yet Jesus wants the disciples to be like them.

What is it about the child that the disciples should emulate? First, becoming a child means checking out of the competitive game of honor. Children are weak and dependent, and Jesus says that the subjects of His kingdom must recognize their vulnerability and need. Instead of competing for status, as both Jews and Greeks were in the habit of doing, they must recognize they have no status. Instead of scratching and fighting for recognition, Jesus says we should simply leave the game, cash in our chips and become children, outsiders to the competition.

Jesus specifically says that the disciples must become like children in their humility: "whoever humbles himself, he is the greatest in the kingdom of heaven." Jesus is not talking about attitude and behavior so much as station. If you want to be great, take a particular position; take the position of being the servant of all. In Matt. 18:5, Jesus goes further. We are not only to become like children but to *receive* children in Jesus' name, recognizing Jesus in them. If you are playing the status game, you receive people of high status. You do favors for great people so they will do favors back. You receive honorable people to enhance your honor. But Jesus tells us to act differently: receive children and invite people who have no status to your table. And trust your Father to reward you.

What does it mean to receive children? Jesus shows us: He lays hands on them, prays for them. He takes them in His arms and blesses them, according to Mark 10. This is not a sentimental childism. Jesus is not telling us that children are innocent, angelic. The scene is reminiscent of the scene at the end of Genesis, where

Jacob blesses his children and lays hands on them. But Jesus takes, holds, lays His hands on, blesses, and prays for little children because they constitute the new Israel.

Is that the way we treat children? Do we receive them? Or are we more like the disciples, who want to chase the children away because Jesus does not have the time for them? Do we find little children an annoyance? Or do we receive them for Jesus' sake? Children are not symbols of something else. Our spiritual condition is evident in the way we treat children.

It is important to see that Jesus *does* answer the question about greatness. He is telling them the way to greatness. But the way to greatness is counterintuitive, because Jesus tell the disciples to leave the field where greatness is achieved. From verse 6, Jesus changes His terminology. He no longer refers to "children" but to "little ones," a broader category. He is not simply talking about literal children, though they are included, but about any of those who are small, microscopic, in the eyes of the world. Jesus is talking about the way to greatness, and He subverts the ancient and modern presumptions about greatness.

Our treatment of insignificant members of the church is the standard by which we will be judged (Matt. 18:5; cf. 25:40). He tells His disciples to attend to the least of those who believe, and He warns that if they ignore or cause little ones to fall, they are in danger of hell. Whoever sets up a stumbling block might as well have a block, a stone, hung around his neck and be cast into the sea. In Revelation 18, this is what will happen to the harlot Babylon, the city that opposes the saints and causes many to apostatize and fall. She will be cast like a millstone into the sea, the city of God, Jerusalem, will be plunged into the nations. This is what God will do to us if we set up obstacles to the little ones who believe in Him.

How do we avoid giving offense? How do we avoid leading others into sin or discouraging them? Jesus has already showed us at the end of Matthew 17. He avoids giving offense by giving up freedoms that He has. As a Prince, He is exempt from the tax, but to avoid leading others away He gives up this freedom and pays the tax. If we want to avoid giving offense, to avoid causing one of the little ones of the church to stumble, we need to be willing to give up privileges, rights, freedoms that we have. Jesus also repeats some teaching that He gave in the Sermon on the Mount.

Matt. 18:8-9 repeat almost word-for-word Jesus' instructions dealing with adultery. In the context here, cutting off the hand, plucking out your eye, removing your foot has to do with avoiding offense. We deal radically with our own sin in order to avoid causing one of the little ones to stumble and fall, to sin or become discouraged. Finally, we avoid offense by following the example of the shepherd in Jesus' parable. We do not let the single straying sheep go away. Elsewhere, Jesus tells this parable (18:10-14) as a condemnation of the behavior of the Pharisees (Luke 15:5-7). Here, Jesus is setting up a government for His own community. He warns the Twelve not to ignore the smallest member of the church who wanders away. God is not willing that any should perish; a ninety-nine percent success rate is not good enough.

Ultimately, avoiding offenses and becoming like a child are the same thing. If we are going to avoid setting up stumbling blocks that bring ruin to others, we must follow Jesus' instruction to humble ourselves and become like children. We must follow Jesus' example; He is the most childlike of all, the eternal Child of the Father, who humbled Himself, took a lower position, gave Himself to death rather than offend the least little one who believes in Him. And having humbled Himself, the Father exalted Him above every name. That is the pattern of our lives as well: Humble yourself, take the position of a servant to all, check out of the honor game, and trust the Father to care for you and exalt you. Then you will be among the greatest in the kingdom of heaven.

Brothers
Matthew 18:15-20

¹⁵ "If your brother sins, go and show him his fault in private; if he listens to you, you have won your brother. ¹⁶ But if he does not listen to you, take one or two more with you, so that by the mouth of two or three witnesses every fact may be confirmed. ¹⁷ If he refuses to listen to them, tell it to the church; and if he refuses to listen even to the church, let him be to you as a Gentile and a tax collector. ¹⁸ Truly I say to you, whatever you bind on earth shall have been bound in heaven; and whatever you loose on earth shall have been loosed in heaven. ¹⁹ Again I say to you, that if two of you agree on earth about anything that they may ask, it shall be done for them by My Father who is in heaven. ²⁰ For where two or three have gathered together in My name, I am there in their midst."

This is *the* chapter on church discipline in the New Testament. Talk about "church discipline" can sound ominous, evoking visions of the Inquisition and the Star Chamber. We think of the rack and thumb screws and people losing their civil rights because of offense against the church. We imagine oppressive and angry bishops, meddling ministers, and generally a very disagreeable process. To counter these impressions, we need first to notice the context and the language that Jesus uses.

Throughout this section, Jesus and others refer to believers in familial terms. "If your brother sins...you have won your brother... how often shall my brother sin?" All this is linked to the fact that disciples of Jesus have a "heavenly Father" (v. 35) who is Father to all, and have a heavenly Son (17:25-26) who is Brother to them all. Because we all have the same Father, and all have the same Brother, we are all brothers together. Earlier in Matthew, Jesus said of His disciples, "Behold my mother, and my brothers, and my sisters" (12:48-50).

This points us in the right direction as we think about church discipline. Church discipline is not about lords with authority controlling peons or serfs. It is not even about hierarchy in the first instance. It is about *brotherhood*, about dealing with fellow believers as family members, as people who share the same baptismal name.

This is a central theme in the Gospels. One of the most immediate effects of sin was conflict among brothers: Cain and Abel, Jacob and Esau, Joseph and his brothers, the sons of David, Israel and Judah, and so on and on. The history of the Old Testament is a history of fratricide and brother-brother conflict. Jesus comes to establish a universal brotherhood; the fact that liberals also say this does not make it untrue. But it is also important to notice that brotherhood does not mean universal toleration, toleration of everything and anything our brothers might do or say or think. Brothers are to love one another and to cover sin with love. Brothers also confront one another. That is the brotherly thing to do when your brother is in sin.

This brotherhood challenges our attitude toward Christians in churches that are unfaithful. Are members of PCUSA churches, or ECUSA churches, or Roman Catholic churches brothers? If we answer, "Yes," then many will take that to mean we are accepting everything in those churches. We are not. We may still have strong objections to some teaching and practice in those churches. But they *are* brothers. When we confront them, and seek to correct them, we do it as brothers. That is *why* we confront them, precisely *because* they are brothers. It also means that if we are going to have any real effect on such churches, we cannot simply withdraw from contact with them. If you never talk to your brother and then try to confront him with his sin, he will not be inclined to listen to you. If you stand at a distance, observe that ECUSA cannot make up its mind about homosexuality, and then try to correct them, you will not get much of a hearing.

The context of Matthew 18 indicates something about the character, tone, and goals of church discipline. Just before Jesus brings up the issue of discipline, He exhorts His disciples to become children and He warns about setting up stumbling blocks in the way of the little ones. We are to become like children by assuming a lowly position in relation to others, by becoming their servants. That is what church discipline is about. Those who exercise discipline sometimes assume the position of lords, and they turn church discipline into something heavy-handed and brutal. That is an abuse of Jesus' commandments. Church discipline is not lording it over brothers but serving them. Discipline itself is a service. We should exercise discipline with the attitude of children. We should not be naïve or weak. But we should be lowly, and pursue discipline as a service to our brother, as a way of helping him. This is one of the ways we become servants to servants.

More immediately, Jesus brings up church discipline in the context of the parable of the lost sheep (vv. 12-13). Confronting a brother with his sin is a way of bringing a straying sheep back to the fold. The goal of church discipline is always to "win your brother" (v. 15). At the end of Matthew 18, Jesus instructs Peter to forgive a brother seventy times seven times, and tells a parable about the necessity of forgiveness. Church discipline is supposed to take place within a community where everyone is full of mercy and compassion, eager to forgive brothers.

The section on discipline is organized as a series of four "if" statements: if your brother sins . . . if he does not listen to you . . . if he refuses to listen . . . if he refuses to listen." Each "if" statement takes the matter to another level of seriousness. The first level is self-policing (v. 15). When a brother sins, you are not first to tell someone else, or tell the elders, or start spreading rumors. The first step is to take the matter to your brother in private, and call him to repentance. One-anothering is a common theme in the New Testament (Rom. 15:14; Col. 3:15; Heb. 10:24-25). All of these passages and more encourage us to be consistent in admonishing, correcting, encouraging one another in faithfulness. This is not just exhortation to spend time in fellowship, to enjoy one another's company. We are called to be involved in one another's lives like brothers. If a matter ends at this level, it should go no further. It is between your brother and you, and no one ever needs to know what happened. If it is edifying to the church, then tell it. If the church knows that two brothers are at odds, their reconciliation is a matter for celebration. But once the brother is gained, the matter should not be spread around. Paul emphasizes that we should do this in humility, mindful of our own sins (Gal. 6:1). Even at this private level, there is a temptation to lord it over one another, to become overbearing. Paul tells us to correct gently, but we are still called to correct.

Even the second step of discipline is fairly private. Jesus quotes a legal rule from Deut. 19:15 and tells the offended brother to take others with him. The witnesses need not be witnesses to the original sin, but they are representatives of the church and become witnesses to the sinning brother's impenitence.

The final step is to take the matter to the church as a whole (Matt. 18:17). This does not mean that the offended brother starts circulating reports of his brother's bad behavior. Jesus does not explicitly mention leaders or elders, but it is likely that He is simply assuming their existence. Jewish communities were led by elders and the early church communities were too. Reporting the matter to the church follows proper channels, through those gifted and ordained to lead the church (cf. 1 Cor. 12:28; Heb. 13:17). At times, a sin might be publicly announced and a church member publicly rebuked, publicly censured, but the orderly way to do that is not to start sending emails, or whispering to one another, or standing up during a church meeting and accusing someone. Everything should be done in order, and at this level, the leaders of the church have responsibility for correction.

What happens to a brother who refuses to listen to the church? What if he still refuses to repent after being publicly censured by the elders? Jesus says, he is no longer a brother but an outsider, a "Gentile" and "publican" (Matt. 18:17). Throughout Matthew's Gospel, Jesus has been generous and kind toward tax collectors and Gentiles. One of the main accusations against Jesus was His willingness to spend time with undesirable people, to eat with them, to help them. That should be our pattern, too. We are called to be with the publicans and Gentiles, as Jesus was, including publicans and Gentiles who used to be brothers.

There are two sides to what Jesus says. First, the brother who refuses to listen to the church should be treated as an object for evangelism. As long as he is in the church, you can appeal to him as a believer: "You are a Christian, and Christians are not supposed to behave this way. Be faithful to who you are." Once he is outside, the appeal changes: "Jesus will save you if you repent and seek Him." Second, by refusing to listen to the church, the brother forfeits various privileges. Specifically, he loses the privilege and blessing of being confronted by other brothers.

In fact, Jesus has a lot to say about how we treat brothers. If you are offering something on the altar and remember that your brother has something against you, go and settle it first (Matthew 5). That is something we do with *brothers*. If we know that some pagan has something against us, there is no requirement to be reconciled. Enemies can be implacable, and we have no command from Jesus to try to win over implacable enemies before we offer sacrifice. When you see a speck in your brother's eye, you help him to take it out, but first by removing the log from your own eye (Matthew 7). But what if you see a speck in a Gentile's eye? Are you obligated to try to remove it? Depending on the circumstances, it might be an occasion for evangelism. But you do not have the same obligation to help someone outside the family.

In Matthew 18, Jesus says that we should reprove brothers in private for sins. What if someone sins, and it is not a brother? We can attempt to work it out; we can attempt to pursue some sort of peace. But we cannot hope for reconciliation on the same scale in the same way. It is a privilege to be reproved and corrected, and those who persistently refuse to listen to the church no longer enjoy that privilege. As brothers, we are Jesus' representatives: Whoever does things to the least of the brothers does it to me (Matt. 25:40). Gentiles do not represent Jesus.

Paul says a few things that fill this out more. In 1 Cor. 5:11, he warns that we should not "associate with any so-called brother if he is an immoral person, or covetous, or an idolater, or a reviler, or a drunkard, or a swindler--not even to eat with such a one" (cf. 2 Thess. 3:14-15). When Paul says that we should not "associate" with such people, he is not saying that we should cut off all contact. Clearly, we are to have enough contact with the brother in 2 Thessalonians 3 to admonish him. He is warning us not to have intimate fellowship with such people. The "eating" in 1 Corinthians 5 is a reference, I think, to the Supper; we do not share in the fellowship meal with him or her. Table fellowship is a privilege of brotherhood.

We have a hard time seeing the effect of discipline when we are not actually living as brothers day to day. If we are not living like a family in the first place, then disciplining someone so that he is no longer a brother does not mean much. If we already treat brothers like publicans and Gentiles, then being excluded from the family does not have much weight.

Jesus' final words here are part of the same instruction about church discipline. Jesus does not change the subject. He teaches about prayer, but He does so in the context of church discipline. Of course, it is true that Jesus is with us when we gather for worship, but the setting Jesus envisions here is a decision of the church to exclude an impenitent brother. That is the request that the Father will answer. And this heightens the weight of church discipline. All institutions have some mechanisms of discipline. All institutions have rules that have to be followed. But the church has a unique promise and a unique authority. Jesus does not say to any other earthly authorities that it bears the authority of heaven. When the church *agrees* together, they have God's backing.

Among other things, this means that ignoring the church's decisions and pronouncements is tantamount to ignoring God. The church's decisions are not infallible; God renders the final judgment. But He has given judgment to the Son, who shares it with His church. Ignoring the church's authority is perilous. On the other hand, receiving the church's authority and responding to its correction is enriching both for the brother who sins and for the church.

The word "gain" has an important nuance. "What does it profit a man if he gain the whole world and lose his soul?" Jesus asks. Gain connotes possession. Obviously, the brother who is "gained" does not become our possession in a strict sense. We do not acquire a gained brother as personal property or a slave. But the word points to something important about the nature of the brotherhood that Jesus calls us to. We are called to a kind of mutual possession, which mimics the mutual possession of the Father, Son and Spirit. As Paul unpacks this in his letters, he talks about the gifts that we are given by the Spirit for the mutual edification of the body. We each have gifts, and though they are ours, they are also a common property. We have gifts so that we can use them for the benefit of others.

This is what brotherhood should look like. When a brother sins and goes astray, we no longer enjoy this mutual possession. We do not "possess" him and his gifts, and he does not have the benefit of ours. Gaining the brother enriches the whole body. Gaining the brother folds him back into the communion of the church, in which each member benefits all the others. This is one of the leading goals of church discipline. It is not to control and oppress. Church discipline, done with faithfulness, childlike humility, patience, is part of God's program for forming His new humanity, the communion, the brotherhood, the mutual possession that is the church.

SEVENTY TIMES SEVEN
Matthew 18:21-35

[21] Then Peter came and said to Him, "Lord, how often shall my brother sin against me and I forgive him? Up to seven times?" [22] Jesus said to him, "I do not say to you, up to seven times, but up to seventy times seven. [23] For this reason the kingdom of heaven may be compared to a king who wished

to settle accounts with his slaves. [24] When he had begun to settle them, one who owed him ten thousand talents was brought to him. [25] But since he did not have the means to repay, his lord commanded him to be sold, along with his wife and children and all that he had, and repayment to be made. [26] So the slave fell to the ground and prostrated himself before him, saying, 'Have patience with me and I will repay you everything.' [27] And the lord of that slave felt compassion and released him and forgave him the debt. [28] But that slave went out and found one of his fellow slaves who owed him a hundred denarii; and he seized him and began to choke him, saying, 'Pay back what you owe.' [29] So his fellow slave fell to the ground and began to plead with him, saying, 'Have patience with me and I will repay you.' [30] But he was unwilling and went and threw him in prison until he should pay back what was owed. [31] So when his fellow slaves saw what had happened, they were deeply grieved and came and reported to their lord all that had happened. [32] Then summoning him, his lord said to him, 'You wicked slave, I forgave you all that debt because you pleaded with me. [33] Should you not also have had mercy on your fellow slave, in the same way that I had mercy on you?' [34] And his lord, moved with anger, handed him over to the torturers until he should repay all that was owed him. [35] My heavenly Father will also do the same to you, if each of you does not forgive his brother from your heart."

In the first year of Darius, Daniel was studying the book of Jeremiah's prophecies when he came upon the prophecy that Israel would be released from captivity after seventy years. The seventieth year of exile was coming, and so Daniel began fasting in sackcloth and ashes. He began confessing the sins of Israel and pleading with the Lord to hear and restore Israel. While he was praying, Gabriel appeared and told him that the Lord had decreed "seventy weeks." Another period of seventy was going to follow the seventy years of exile in Babylon, and, Gabriel told Daniel, at the end of that seventy-week period, that period of seventy times seven, the Lord would finally take care of sin. After seventy times seven, the Lord would "finish transgression, make an end of sin, make atonement for iniquity, bring in everlasting righteousness, seal of vision and prophecy, anoint the most holy" (Dan. 9:24).

By the time of Jesus, this prophecy was an obsession for many Jews. It told them when the Messiah would come: from Daniel to the Messiah, there would be seventy times seven, or four hundred and ninety years. It told them what the Lord would do: at the end of seventy times seven, the Lord would deal with Israel's transgressions once and for all. At the end of the seventy times seven period, there would be a great Jubilee, a release from debt, a manumission of slaves, a return to the land. This would be the fulfillment of the hopes of all faithful Israelites. Yahweh promised that Abraham and his children, the family of Abraham, would be Yahweh's covenant partner in redeeming the world and bringing blessing to the Gentiles. Because of Israel's sins, she was under a curse. Because of the curse, the promises and program of God through Abraham have been blocked by Israel's sin and the curse on Israel's sin. Daniel's prophecy assured them that after seventy times seven years, the Lord will finally act and will remove that obstacle. This will be good news not only for Israel but for the world. God's program to restore the world through Israel, the covenant with Abraham, depends on the forgiveness of sin. The nations will come to know the Lord only if Israel is released from sin, for salvation is from the Jews. And Jesus, the true Israelite, has come to accomplish that, to release Israel from sin and curse.

Peter said it at Pentecost: Repent, believe, receive forgiveness, that you may receive the Spirit. The Spirit is the great promise given to Abraham (Galatians 3). But the Spirit is, as it were, bottled up unless Israel can be released from the curse, because the Spirit will come to the nations through Israel. Only after God removes Israel's sin will the promise be fulfilled.

When Peter asks Jesus how often he should forgive his brother, Jesus answers with an allusion to this passage: Forgive him seventy times seven times. And by this, Jesus is informing Peter and the rest of the disciples that the seventy times seven of Daniel's prophecy is reaching its climax. The Lord is acting through Jesus to bring the forgiveness of sins, with all that this means for Israel and for the nations. This is why forgiveness of sins is so central to the gospel story. Yes, it is about the pardon of individual sinners. But it is not just that. The gospel story is about the forgiveness of Israel's sins, which means that the promises to Abraham can, at long last, come to fulfillment. This is the context for much of what the New Testament says about forgiveness of sins.

At the birth of John the Baptist, Zecharias blesses God for raising up the Christ, the savior, who will "give His people the knowledge of salvation by the forgiveness of their sins" (Luke 1:77) and John comes "preaching a baptism of repentance for the forgiveness of sins" (Luke 3:3). It is the forgiveness of the *people* that Zecharias celebrates. After His resurrection, Jesus teaches His disciples that He has fulfilled all that Moses and the prophets had predicted, and He sums up the teaching of the Scriptures with: "Thus it is written, that the Christ would suffer and rise again from the dead the third day, and that repentance for forgiveness of sins would be proclaimed in His name to all the nations, beginning from Jerusalem" (Luke 24). The fulfillment is that forgiveness will be proclaimed to the nations, first in Jerusalem.

This is a constant theme of the apostles' preaching. "Repent and be baptized in the name of Christ for the forgiveness of your sins, and you will receive the Holy Spirit," Peter says at Pentecost. Before the Sanhedrin, Peter says that Jesus has been exalted "as a Prince and a Savior, to grant repentance to Israel, and forgiveness of sins" (Acts 5:31). When the Spirit falls on the members of the house of Cornelius the Gentile, Peter acknowledges that God is not a respecter of persons, and says that all the prophets bear witness that "everyone who believes in [Jesus] receives forgiveness of sins" (Acts 10:43). In his first sermon, Paul tells the story of Abraham and David and Jesus, and concludes by saying "let it be known to you brethren that through Him forgiveness of sins is proclaimed to you," adding that through Jesus believers are justified from things that the Law could not resolve (Acts 13:38-39).

The message is that through Jesus, God has acted to deal with sin once and for all, and especially to deal with Israel's sin, to deal with it in a way that the Law could not, to release Israel from the curse by the forgiveness of sins, so that the blessing of Abraham, the Spirit, can flow through Israel to the nations.

Jesus comes preaching the gospel of the kingdom. God is going to take His throne. He is going to assert His Lordship over creation, in heaven and on earth. In Christ, humanity is being exalted to share in that rule. And when the Lord ascends to the throne of His kingdom, He will show clemency and release people from sins and debts. His kingdom comes in His death, as He dies for Israel's redemption, and through Israel He dies for the redemption of the nations.

Through His death, Jesus forms a new kind of community, a new kind of human family. The numerology points to this, too. He not only alludes to the climax of God's dealings with Israel that Daniel prophesied; He also alluded to Lamech, who threatened to avenge himself "seventy-sevenfold" (Gen. 4:22-23). Lamech was a descendant of Cain, the first fratricide. His brother did him no wrong, but instead of confessing his sin to his brother and seeking reconciliation, he killed his brother. He established a city founded on the blood of an innocent brother. Lamech is in this tradition, and he takes the Cainite legacy and expands it. Genesis 4 tell us, "Lamech said to his wives, 'Adah and Zillah, listen to my voice, you wives of Lamech, give heed to my speech, for I have killed a man for wounding me; and a boy for striking me; If Cain is avenged sevenfold, then Lamech seventy-sevenfold." He makes vengeance the ruling principle of civilization. He establishes a city of vengeance.

Blood vengeance is a fundamental principle of civilization throughout history. The blood feud is the way order is maintained in antique Greece (see Aeschylus, Oresteian Trilogy); it is still there in the Renaissance (Hamlet); it is there in early America (Hatfields and McCoys). It persists because it seems effective: you can keep things relatively peaceful through threats of vengeance. If everyone is ready to respond to violence with massive counter-violence, then everyone will think twice about wronging each other. Mutually Assured Destruction. But once a wrong is done, then it cannot be stopped. Once a wrong is done, then the blood continues to flow until there is no one left with a beating heart and flowing blood.

We are fooling ourselves if we think that we have outgrown the instinct to be Lamechs. We all want to lash out at people that wrong us. When your wife or husband embarrasses you, you want to get him back. When your parents are too demanding, you want to make them pay seventy-sevenfold for wounding you; and much of our discipline of our children is vengeance against them for the shame and embarrassment they cause us. At work, in school, in social life, Lamech is very much alive.

Jesus' allusion to Genesis 4, though, indicates that He is establishing a new kind of city. His city, His kingdom, His brotherhood, is not characterized by vengeance but by forgiveness. It will be characterized not by settling scores to even things out; in Jesus' city, things are evened out by canceling debt and releasing obligations. Forgiveness is the opposite of vengeance, and the city of Jesus is not a Cainite city of vengeance but a city of expiations.

This also gives us a hint about what forgiveness actually is in practice, what forgiveness requires. Peter is to be the opposite of Lamech, forgiving seventy times seven instead of taking seventy-sevenfold vengeance. Forgiveness is the determination to put aside vengeance, and to be reconciled to a brother. Forgiveness is not mainly about our feelings. It is not a matter of having kindly feelings for a person who wronged us. We should have compassion and kind feelings for those who wrong us, but this is not what forgiveness is. Those feelings are products of forgiveness, but it is a product that may come long after we have granted forgiveness. We may well struggle with all kinds of ill feelings even after we have forgiven someone. From the perspective of Genesis 4, forgiveness is about putting aside vengeance. Someone treats you badly; you could do something to equalize that – treating them badly, slandering them, spreading the story of their mistreatment, looking for opportunities or creating opportunities to do something that hurts them as much as they hurt you, or hurts them more. Forgiveness means giving up all that. It means laying aside all plans to even the score. It means suffering the second slap instead of slapping back. It means ceasing to be a Lamech.

Forgiveness is not, as it were, an end in itself. Forgiveness is for the purpose of restored communion, for the purpose of reconciliation. Forgiveness is for the purpose of brotherhood, of restoring broken brotherhood. Peace reigns supreme where brothers confess their sins to brothers, where brothers confront brothers, where brothers forgive brothers. We might even say that forgiveness *is* brotherhood, the form that brotherly communion takes in a sinful world.

Forgiveness is the ground of brotherhood in another way as well. Lamech's life is determined by his past. Communities founded on blood feud can never do anything new. They just keep doing the same thing over and over and over again, in identical repetition. A city of vengeance is a city of repetitive cycles, a city without any possibility for renewal. But that is not Jesus' new brotherhood. Jesus' brotherhood is a new creation and a source of new creation. A community of forgiveness is a community whose life is not determined by the past, by what has happened. It is a community with a future, that embodies the possibility of new creation.

We can fill out this picture further by looking at what the Bible says about God's forgiveness of sinners. That is the analogy that Jesus draws in the parable. The servant is supposed to forgive as his king forgave him; we are to forgive as God forgives. How does God forgive us? Psalm 103:6-14 answers that question. The Lord is not quick to anger but slow to anger. He does not take offense easily. He does not snap and lash out at every small infraction. He is not quick on the trigger. This patience is part of what is supposed to characterize the brotherhood of Jesus, where pardon reigns supreme. It is supposed to be a city, a community where anger is held in check, where everyone is slow to anger. The Lord is slow to anger because He pities us and remembers our weakness. This also should characterize the brotherhood of Jesus.

Forgiveness means that the Lord ceases to strive with us and puts aside His anger when He does get angry. The Lord gets angry, and it is righteous anger. He strives with us, and His striving is perfectly right. But He does not strive forever, and He does not hold His anger forever. If someone sins against you, you can strive with them forever. You can keep stoking anger by meditating on the wrong, by holding it, nurturing it, enjoying its bitter sweetness. You can keep making the wrong a point of contention, something to fight over. Forgiveness means deciding and determining to stop striving. Forgiveness means regarding the one who wronged us in a certain way. The Lord removes our transgressions from us. When He looks at us, He does not regard our sin. Our sin does not become the colored lens through which He sees us. Instead, He removes that sin, and He regards us as friends, as His children, as family. Forgiveness means determining to look on our sinning brother in a certain way, not as stained by the sin, but as cleansed.

Forgiveness is not only a promise, but a demand. That is the point of Jesus' parable. Forgiveness is not a character trait – some people are more easy-going than others. Forgiveness is hard, and it is meant to be. Forgiveness is costly; it requires death. It requires us to die to our own desires for vengeance and to leave things in the Lord's hands; it requires us to die to the past. According to Psalm 103, the Lord does not respond to us according to sin. Forgiveness means that we *do not* equalize things. We *do not* try to make everything even. It means we accept inequity. It does not mean ignoring the fact that sins have taken place; it does not mean pretending it never happened. Forgiveness requires truthfulness about sin and wrong. But forgiveness means we do not react as the sin deserves. In effect, forgiveness means that the *wronged* party bears the wrong.

Forgiveness does not mean taking the easy path. Anyone who has been deeply wronged knows that this is not the case. Forgiveness is always costly and always involves bearing burdens that someone else put on us. Forgiving someone who has wronged us is sharing in the cross of Jesus, bearing in ourselves the burdens of another's sin.

Since forgiveness can be so difficult, Jesus reinforces the demand with a frightening parable. In Jesus' parable, the servant owes ten million working days wages to his king. He will never repay, yet when he pleads for mercy and says he will repay the king forgives the debt (Matt. 18:23-27). Yet, the servant immediately demands payment of a much smaller debt from another servant and throws him in prison when he cannot pay (vv. 28-30). Jesus teaches that our enjoyment of God's forgiveness is dependent on our forgiveness of our brothers. "Forgive our debts as we forgive our debtors," we pray, and God hears and answers that prayer. The most disturbing part of this parable is the threat that the king re-imposes the debt that he had previously forgiven (v. 34). This is not an extraneous bit of the story, because Jesus says that "My heavenly Father [shall] also do to you, if each of you does not forgive his brother from the heart" (v. 35). God will turn from mercy to wrath if we do not forgive one another. He removes burdens, but He will put it back if we do not remove the burdens of others.

Jesus is not joking around. He is not using dramatic hyperbole to make a point. "So will my heavenly Father do to you, if you do not forgive your brother." Do you want to end up with the torturers? Do you want to end up paying the last penny? Then by all means keep your vengeance. Hold your grudge. Keep striving. Hold on to your anger. Seek opportunities for seventy-sevenfold vengeance. Look for a chance to pay back in full. That is the path to the torturers, the path not only to a hellish life but ultimately the path to hell.

Karl Barth said that the heart of original sin is our desire to be judge. Forgiveness requires us to die to this desire, this Satanic desire to play God. It leaves room for God to be God, to be the Judge, to settle and sort. Forgiveness is a confession that vengeance belongs to the Lord. When we forgive, we are not saying justice does not matter. We are not saying that it is all OK, and he did not mean it anyway. We are not denying responsibility. We are saying that we are not going to play God, but we are going to let God sort things out, because He is the judge of all the earth.

At the same time, forgiveness gives us an opportunity to play God in the deepest way we can. "Who is this man, that he forgives sins?" the Pharisees ask about Jesus. "Who can forgive sins, but God alone?" And they are right. How *dare* anyone but God forgive sins? God is the offended party; who dares to speak for Him and declare sins absolved? Throughout the Old Testament, we never hear a human being say to another, "I forgive you." That authority is withheld until the Messiah comes, until the Spirit comes, until the 70 weeks have been fulfilled. This is part of the Lord's final act of dealing with sin and removing it: He gives men the power to forgive sins. In His kingdom, He shares His royal authority to forgive. He makes us kings and orders us to show clemency.

This is the message of Jesus' parable: The King has pardoned you and brought you into a brotherhood where pardon is supreme. Do not end up with the torturers. Act like the king, and forgive your brother his debt.

Marriage from the Beginning
Matthew 19:1-15

¹ When Jesus had finished these words, He departed from Galilee and came into the region of Judea beyond the Jordan; ² and large crowds followed Him, and He healed them there. ³ Some Pharisees came to Jesus, testing Him and asking, "Is it lawful for a man to divorce his wife for any reason at all?" ⁴ And He answered and said, "Have you not read that He who created them from the beginning made them male and female, ⁵ and said, for this reason a man shall leave his father and mother and be joined to his wife, and the two shall become one flesh? ⁶ So they are no longer two, but one flesh. What therefore God has joined together, let no man separate." ⁷ They said to Him, "Why then did Moses command to give her a certificate of divorce and send her away?" ⁸ He said to them, "Because of your hardness of heart Moses permitted you to

divorce your wives; but from the beginning it has not been this way. ⁹ And I say to you, whoever divorces his wife, except for immorality, and marries another woman commits adultery." ¹⁰ The disciples said to Him, "If the relationship of the man with his wife is like this, it is better not to marry." ¹¹ But He said to them, "Not all men can accept this statement, but only those to whom it has been given. ¹² For there are eunuchs who were born that way from their mother's womb; and there are eunuchs who were made eunuchs by men; and there are also eunuchs who made themselves eunuchs for the sake of the kingdom of heaven. He who is able to accept this, let him accept it." ¹³ Then some children were brought to Him so that He might lay His hands on them and pray; and the disciples rebuked them. ¹⁴ But Jesus said, "Let the children alone, and do not hinder them from coming to Me; for the kingdom of heaven belongs to such as these." ¹⁵ After laying His hands on them, He departed from there.

Jesus was born in Bethlehem of Judea, in the days of Herod the king, and He was baptized for His ministry by John in the Jordan River. As soon as Jesus hears about John's arrest, however, He withdraws into Galilee. From Matthew 4 until Matthew 19, Matthew never mentions Judea, and Jesus is never in Judea. Now, at long last, Jesus returns to Judea and is in the region beyond the Jordan where John baptized Him. When Jesus was young, Judea was a threatening place for Him to be. He was in Judea, in Bethlehem, when the wise men visited looking for the king of the Jews; He was in Judea, in Bethlehem, when Herod gave the order to kill all the children two years and younger in the area around Bethlehem. Joseph, of course, took Jesus and Mary and fled to Egypt, and that was the last time that Jesus was in Judea.

Along the way back toward Judea, He has prophesied several times that He is heading to Jerusalem to be delivered to the chief priests and elders and that He will be tried and killed and rise again on the third day. As in His original manifestation in Judea, He will be manifested again as the suffering, threatened, oppressed, persecuted, crucified Messiah. As He enters the territory of Judea, He comes under threat, and that threat will follow Him all the way to Golgotha. Whenever He is in Judea, He is threatened with death. Judea is the country that kills prophets, and Jerusalem is its capital.

His arrival in Judea is also a return to temptation and testing. Early in the gospel, Jesus went into the wilderness of the Jordan to be tempted by the devil. Back in Judea, He is tempted again, tested not directly by Satan but by the Pharisees who come to Him to "test" Him (in Greek, the same word as "tempt") concerning the law. Jesus is a new Moses here. When He was last in Judea, a king was trying to kill Him, just as Pharaoh tried to kill Moses both as a child and as an adult man. When Jesus was last in Judea, He had to flee from the Pharaoh-like Herod into Egypt, where He sojourned until Herod died, just as Moses fled to Midian until the Lord sent him back to deliver His people. Jesus' return to Judea, then, is like Moses' return to Egypt. Jesus returns to Judea to confront the Pharaoh and the magicians (chief priests and elders) who had tried to kill him. He is heading to Pharaoh's court in order to announce plagues on Jerusalem.

Jesus is also the greater Joshua, crossing the Jordan to enter the land and bring it under His dominion. Before the end of the next chapter, He will pass through Jericho, site of Joshua's great victory. But Jesus is heading for another, greater city, Jerusalem itself. A Mosaic typology is threaded through the whole gospel, but, as we have seen, the Gospel follows the history of Israel, and with Jesus' arrival in Judea, we enter a new phase of Jesus' recapitulation of that history. He has spent most of the Gospel in the Northern regions of Palestine, in Galilee, in territory that once belonged to the Northern Kingdom. In the last several chapters, He has been an Elisha. He feeds four thousand and then five thousand, heals the daughter of a Syro-Phoenician woman, gives instruction to His disciples. On the mount of Transfiguration, Elijah appears alongside Moses, and Jesus is glorified as the prophet greater than Elijah, the new Elisha. As Jesus enters Judea again, the focus changes. He is no longer like a prophet in the North during the divided kingdom but like a prophet in Judea and Jerusalem, a prophet of the last days of Judah. He is no longer a greater Elisha, but one greater than Jeremiah, announcing the end of the temple and city of Jerusalem, the threat from a new Babylonian empire, the Romans.

It is fitting that this Jeremiah section of Matthew is introduced by a dispute concerning divorce. Jeremiah, after all, was the prophet who delivered the writ of divorce to Israel, alluding to Deut. 24:1-4, the very passage that is under dispute in Jesus' debate with the Pharisees (Jer. 3:6-10). The entire section of Matthew, from Matthew 19 through Matthew 25, is overshadowed by the Lord's threat to send away His bride.

The specific issue at stake in Jesus' debate is whether divorce is legitimate under any and all circumstances (Matt. 19:3). The Pharisees are hoping to put Jesus in a corner, to get Him to stumble or offend someone. There were differences of opinion among Jews about divorce. Some were rigorous law keepers who believed a man should have cause to divorce, but the dominant view seems to have been close to "no-fault" divorce. The question posted to Jesus presumes the lax view of marriage and divorce widely held among Jews (v. 3: "any cause at all"). The Pharisees hope to get Jesus entangled in an intramural dispute, which will discredit Him with one or another faction of the Pharisees.

Jesus surprises them by taking them back to fundamentals. He quotes from the Torah, not the divorce provision of Deut. 24:1 but the creation of marriage in Genesis (Matt 19:4 with Gen. 1:27; Matt. 19:5 with Gen. 2:24). Jesus' remarks in Matthew 19 echo the creation account, which establishes the pattern for marriage as a lifelong union between one man and one woman. Man and wife become "one flesh" (vv. 5-6), yoked together (v. 6) in labor and service. If God has joined them, men ought not separate (v. 6). If man and woman are one flesh, divorce would be a kind of death. Since He comes to bring in a new creation and the overcome death, Jesus calls His disciples to follow God's original design for marriage. Jesus does not ignore Torah, but He shows the Pharisees that the passage concerning divorce has to be seen in the context of God's original created design for marriage. To start talking about marriage and divorce at Deuteronomy 24 is to get things backward. To grasp what Torah says about marriage and divorce, we have to start at the beginning.

The Pharisees have a comeback: Moses "commanded" divorce. Is Jesus saying that this is contrary to God's original design? Is there a contradiction in the law? Does Moses contradict himself? Or does he contradict God? In response, Jesus speaks of "permission" rather than command (v. 8), and He goes on to state both a rationale for the law and an interpretation of it. Divorce is a concession to hardness of heart (v. 8). God's original design was lifelong union, but He made adjustments to sin. Torah assumes Adam's fall; its provisions do not necessarily express God's ideal but His will for a hard-hearted people.[17]

Jesus still permits divorce in cases of *porneia* (v. 9), which refers to adultery and other sexual sins. Sexual union is the "sacrament" of marriage, the physical sign of the covenant bond between man and wife. If that sacrament is polluted by adultery, then the marriage itself is null. Jesus' exception clause applies both to the divorce and the remarriage. A man can divorce his wife, and a wife her husband, for *porneia*, for sexual unfaithfulness. And if he has divorced her for this reason, he may remarry. On the other hand, a man may separate from his wife for other reasons, but if he remarries he commits adultery, since the first marriage still exists before God (v. 9).

The Pharisees disappear, silenced by Jesus' skill with Torah and His rebuke of their hardness of heart. But the disciples protest that such stringent requirements for marriage make it unbearable (v. 10). The disciples think: If we have to stay married to a woman who burns our breakfast, who is an incompetent housekeeper, who is moody and crabby and harsh, who is overly critical, who suffers monthly PMS, who is sexually frigid – if those things are not grounds for divorce, it is better just to avoid marriage. Better to be a "eunuch," renouncing marriage and children altogether.

---

17 Note that Jesus implicitly accuses the Jews of Pharaoh's sin – hardheartedness (cf. Exod. 4:21; 7:3).

Jesus seems to change the subject in answering the question, but He is addressing the question. His saying about "eunuchs" is an answer to their question about marriage and divorce. The disciples basically suggest that the best option is giving up marriage because it will save a lot of hassle and difficulty. Jesus acknowledges that there are some who give up marriage – the "eunuch," the castrated male gives up the possibilities and pleasures of marriage. But Jesus rebukes the disciples for their attitudes and reasons to become eunuchs. Some cannot marry for natural reasons, some because they have been castrated (slaves and defeated enemies were often castrated in the ancient world). And there are voluntary eunuchs, who renounce family life willingly, but not for the selfish reasons that the disciples think. The eunuch for the kingdom is one who has renounced the common pleasures of family life for the sake of God's kingdom.

Eunuchs appear most frequently in the book of Esther, as attendants to the king and queen. They are eunuchs for the kingdom of Persia, and eunuchs in Jesus' kingdom have a similar vocation to serve in the house of Christ and His bride. But there is another dimension to this as well. Eunuchs did not merely give up family life. They gave up manhood. Manhood in many ancient civilizations was expressed in violent acts on the battlefield, in vengeance and retaliation for wrongs, in defending honor, in self-defense in public *fora*. It was also expressed in sexual dominance. A man was a man only if he was sexually dominant over a woman or many women or boys. For the ancients and even into the early modern period, many regarded a promiscuous man not as macho and highly masculine, but feminized, since he was under the control of women. For Jews, manhood has to do with ancestry. The future is secured by having children who will carry on the family name. The symbol of all this – of violence and defense of honor, of sexual mastery, of descendants – was the male sexual organ, and a man who lacked these organs was literally and symbolically deprived of these marks of manhood.[18]

---

18   See J. D. Hester, "Eunuchs and the Postgender Jesus," *Journal for the Study of the New Testament* 28.1 (2005) 21-22: "Generally, [eunuchs] were

Jesus says some will give up their manhood – physically and symbolically – for the sake of the kingdom. In saying this, Jesus is preeminently talking about Himself. He is not literally a eunuch, of course, but as He moves toward the cross, He becomes the eunuch for the kingdom, as He gives up everything that the ancient world counted as manhood for the sake of establishing His kingdom. He turns the other cheek instead of retaliating. He loves his enemies. He submits Himself to torture and humiliating mockery. He is silent when He is charged in court. He gives Himself voluntarily over to a shameful death on the cross. He gives up all the comforts and glories of family life, does not marry, does not have children, does not enjoy the comforts of a home, because He is pursuing the kingdom of His Father. By all ancient standards, Jesus is unmanned. By all ancient standards, Jesus might as well be a eunuch.[19]

This, I think, is behind the disciples' objection to people bringing small children to Jesus. Taking care of nursing children is not a man's work for the disciples, or for most ancient men. It is a woman's work, and the disciples think it is inappropriate to bring them to Jesus. When the children get older, when they are ready to enter the public world of men, then Jesus can attend to

---

viewed as soft (*mollis, eviratus*), effeminate (*semivir, semimas, effeminatus*), sexually passive, unkind, immodest (*impudieitia*), 'changeable,' 'light-skinned,' weak, impotent, deceitful, cowardly and incapable of virtue. Popular novels depicted them as power-seeking, unscrupulous, greedy, untrustworthy and undependable. Achreia attributed to Diogenes had him commenting upon an inscription over the door of a house of an 'evil eunuch' that said, 'Let nothing evil enter' by responding, 'How can the owner then enter?' Dream interpretation, popular sayings, fables, even popular superstitions, all viewed the eunuch as an object of scorn, bad luck and deception. The eunuch, by definition, was not (could not) be a morally upright and virtuous figure, but was always suspicious."

19 In the full biblical story, Jesus is unmanned in the cross in order to assume the new Adamic manhood of the resurrection. As the Risen One, the eunuch for the kingdom becomes the Bridegroom of the church. Jesus becomes the fruitful eunuch. In that movement from death to resurrection, Jesus subverts ancient conceptions of masculinity; He remakes and redefines manhood.

them. Not in their infancy. Keep them where they belong, with the women. But Jesus, the eunuch for the kingdom, does woman's work; He gathers the children to Him and blesses them.

Isaiah prophesies of the coming kingdom in which eunuchs, who had been excluded from the assembly of God and the priesthood (Lev. 21:20; Deut. 23:1), will be fruitful in the Lord's service (Isa. 56:2-5). Elsewhere, Isaiah urges Jerusalem to rejoice as a barren woman rejoices over children (Isaiah 54), and the fruitful eunuch is the male counterpart to the virgin mother, the barren mother. In the kingdom of heaven, the eunuch will bear fruit; the dry tree will have many children. This is the other side to the scene with the children. Immediately after speaking of eunuchs, Jesus is shown surrounded by His children, blessing them like Jacob blessed his children at his death. In this, we have a picture of the entire promise of the gospel: life from the dead, loss and recovery, renunciation and restoration. It is the good news of virgin mothers and fruitful eunuchs.

Last and First
Matthew 19:16-20:16

[16] And someone came to Him and said, "Teacher, what good thing shall I do that I may obtain eternal life?" [17] And He said to him, "Why are you asking Me about what is good? There is only One who is good; but if you wish to enter into life, keep the commandments." [18] Then he said to Him, "Which ones?" And Jesus said, "You shall not commit murder; you shall not commit adultery; you shall not steal; you shall not bear false witness; [19] honor your father and mother; and you shall love your neighbor as yourself." [20] The young man said to Him, "All these things I have kept; what am I still lacking?" [21] Jesus said to him, "If you wish to be complete, go and sell your possessions and give to the poor, and you will have treasure in heaven; and come, follow Me." [22] But when the young man heard this statement, he went away grieving; for he was one who owned much property. [23] And Jesus said to His disciples, "Truly I say to you, it is hard for a rich man to enter the

kingdom of heaven. ²⁴ Again I say to you, it is easier for a camel to go through the eye of a needle, than for a rich man to enter the kingdom of God." ²⁵ When the disciples heard this, they were very astonished and said, "Then who can be saved?" ²⁶ And looking at them Jesus said to them, "With people this is impossible, but with God all things are possible." ²⁷ Then Peter said to Him, "Behold, we have left everything and followed You; what then will there be for us?" ²⁸ And Jesus said to them, "Truly I say to you, that you who have followed Me, in the regeneration when the Son of Man will sit on His glorious throne, you also shall sit upon twelve thrones, judging the twelve tribes of Israel. ²⁹ And everyone who has left houses or brothers or sisters or father or mother or children or farms for My name's sake, will receive many times as much, and will inherit eternal life. ³⁰ But many who are first will be last; and the last, first. ²⁰:¹ For the kingdom of heaven is like a landowner who went out early in the morning to hire laborers for his vineyard. ² When he had agreed with the laborers for a denarius for the day, he sent them into his vineyard. ³ And he went out about the third hour and saw others standing idle in the market place; ⁴ and to those he said, 'You also go into the vineyard, and whatever is right I will give you.' And so they went. ⁵ Again he went out about the sixth and the ninth hour, and did the same thing. ⁶ And about the eleventh hour he went out and found others standing around; and he said to them, 'Why have you been standing here idle all day long?' ⁷ They said to him, 'Because no one hired us.' He said to them, 'You go into the vineyard too.' ⁸ When evening came, the owner of the vineyard said to his foreman, 'Call the laborers and pay them their wages, beginning with the last group to the first.' ⁹ When those hired about the eleventh hour came, each one received a denarius. ¹⁰ When those hired first came, they thought that they would receive more; but each of them also received a denarius. ¹¹ When they received it, they grumbled at the landowner, ¹² saying, 'These last men have worked only one hour, and you have made them equal to us who have borne the burden and the scorching heat of the day.' ¹³ But he answered and said to one of them, 'Friend, I am doing you no wrong; did you not agree with me for a denarius? ¹⁴ Take what is yours and go, but I wish to give to this last man the same as to you. ¹⁵

> Is it not lawful for me to do what I wish with what is my own?
> Or is your eye envious because I am generous? [16] So the last
> shall be first, and the first last.'"

Since the patristic period, the parable of the laborers in the vineyard (20:1-16) has been detached from its context and read as a separate story. It has been given a number of different interpretations. In the second century, Irenaeus said that the parable had to do with redemptive history, Jews and Gentiles. The vineyard is the Lord's own vineyard, His kingdom or land. The owner's visits to the marketplace represent different stages of history, and each time He brings a few more laborers into the vineyard. Throughout the centuries, most of the laborers have been Jews, but now the eleventh hour has come, Gentiles are also being gathered in, and they are receiving the same reward as the Jews who have labored through the scorching heat of the day. Jews grumble, thinking that they should get more because they have been there longer and had to endure more. In the following century, Origen took it as a parable about individual conversion. Some people are saved early in life, in childhood; some in adolescence, some as adults, some in old age. But all receive the same payment, the gift of eternal life.

There are both possible applications of the story, though the first works better than the second. Irenaus' interpretation makes sense of the grumbling, and suggests links between this parable and the parable of the prodigal son (Luke 15), where we have a grumbling older brother who does not appreciate the favor his father lavishes on his wayward brother. Origen's interpretation does not make sense of this, and this is the climax of the parable.

In Matthew's gospel, the parable itself is set in a discussion about wealth, sparked by the exchange with the rich young man (19:16-22). This is evident when we follow the sequence of discussion that begins in verse 16. First, the man, whom we later learn is young, comes to Jesus and asks him what he has to do to have eternal life. Jesus responds in a way that leaves him grieved, and he goes away. Jesus comments on the incident by talking about the difficulty of rich men entering the kingdom, and the conversation continues with Peter. At the end of Matthew 19, Jesus, abruptly, says that the "first will be last and the last first," and this introduces and concludes the parable (Matt. 20:16). The first/last statement is part of the same discourse, and so there is a seamless movement from the rich ruler to the parable.

In addition, there is a literary frame around the last half of Matthew 19. The young man asks about "eternal life" (v. 16), and Jesus says that the climactic inheritance of His disciples will be "eternal life" (v. 29). Plus, Matt. 19:30 and Matt. 20:16 match neatly, though they are themselves reversed (first/last/last/first in 19:30; last/first/first/last in 20:16). So, the passage divides into two sections, 19:16-29 and 19:30-20:16. The first is about wealth and rewards and "eternal life," and the second is about the reversal of first/last, last/first. Yet the whole is also framed by important themes. The young man asks what "good" he must do to enter life, and Jesus answers by talking about the good: "Why do you ask me concerning the good? There is One who is good," implicitly God (19:16-17). The passage ends with the lord of the vineyard saying "Is it not lawful for me to do what I wish with what is my own? Or is your eye evil because I am good?" The owner of the vineyard, who represents God, is the "One who is good," and the parable displays His goodness.

The parable about the first and last is still part of the answer to the question that the rich young man asks, the question about entering into life. Further, the parable that talks about first and last is about wealth. How so? To grasp how these things are connected, we have to start at the beginning of the passage and work through.

As Jesus enters Judea, He is again tested and tempted, and it will become even more intense after he enters Jerusalem, the heart of the "Egypt" that Israel has become. But the young man who comes asking about how to have life seems sincere. Jesus' answer is equally sincere. He is not toying with the man, nor is He preaching the "law" as a preparation to the gospel. That is how the passage is often interpreted: Jesus is setting up the young man, telling him he needs to obey the law to have life. But Jesus does not really *want* the young man to obey. He wants to teach him that he does not have to obey to receive eternal life. He is hoping to drive the man to despair so that Jesus can then spring the gospel on him: "Just kidding; you do not have to *do* anything to inherit life. Believe in me, and it is all fine." Jesus does set a trap, but it is not a law-gospel trap. As much as the young man, Jesus believes and teaches that obedience is necessary for entry into life. The issue is, What is the standard of obedience? The young man's second question is the right one: *Which* commandments?

Jesus affirms the Torah, and again He does it sincerely. He teaches everywhere that no one enters into life without keeping these commandments. He quotes from several of the Ten Words, all having to do with the so-called "Second Table," the relations we have with other people: No murder, no adultery, no theft, no false witness, honor to parents, and love for neighbors. Jesus is saying, in all sincerity, that no one can enter life who impenitently and persistently violates these commands. Paul makes the same point: "the unrighteous shall not inherit the kingdom of God," and he includes under the heading of "unrighteous" these categories: "fornicators, nor idolaters, nor adulterers, nor effeminate, nor homosexuals, nor thieves, nor the covetous, nor drunkards, nor revilers, nor swindlers" (1 Cor. 6:9-11). This is the consistent testimony of the New Testament. Obedience is necessary for entry into the kingdom, entry into life. That obedience is *entirely* a gift of God, *entirely* a work of the Spirit. And there is no one-to-one correspondence between the gift and the work – no correspondence between the work that we do and the reward we receive. But God does call us to *do* something, and if we do not do it, we will not enter life.

The trap is not that Jesus makes the man think he has to obey, when he does not really have to obey. The trick has to do with the contrast between the righteousness and obedience that Jesus demands of His disciples and the obedience and righteousness of the scribes and Pharisees. This section of Matthew contains a number of references to the sermon on the mount. Jesus' exhortation to be "perfect" (v. 21) reminds us of His exhortation at the end of Matthew 5: "Be perfect, as your Father in heaven is perfect." In Matthew 18, Jesus deals with marriage and divorce, another topic of the Sermon. Jesus talks about wealth in the sermon, and the phrase "evil eye" (Matt. 20:15) is found in that discussion of wealth (Matt. 6:23).

Linking this to the Sermon on the Mount is the key to understanding what Jesus tells the young man. The young man has the righteousness of the scribes, but Jesus requires His disciples to live out a righteousness that exceeds the righteousness of the scribes and Pharisees, a righteousness that is not confined to refraining from evil but expresses itself in doing excessive, redeeming good. Jesus calls His disciples to a "redemptive righteousness," a righteousness that not only avoids evil but reverses evil and positively establishes justice. Jesus' own righteousness is a redemptive righteousness, and He invites us to share in that righteousness. It is not just that we refrain from striking back when we are struck; we turn the other cheek, absorb the shame, take the returned blow in ourselves, and thus diffuse the cycle of insult and dishonor that feeds hatred. It is not just that we avoid litigation, but we make *friends* on the way. It is not just that we tolerate or avoid enemies, but we love them, returning good for evil rather than evil for evil, heaping coals on their heads so that they become Pentecostal human altars.

This is what Jesus wants from the young man. The young man might refrain from theft, but Jesus calls Him to give His wealth to the poor. The young man might refrain from murder; but Jesus calls him to refrain from hatred and become an agent for reconciliation. The young man might have refrained from false witness, but Jesus says his "Yes" should be "Yes" and his "No" should be "No." Above all, the young man might keep "all these things," and yet not be a disciple of Jesus. That is the absolute bottom line to entering into life. That is the essence of the greater righteousness that Jesus demands of the scribes and Pharisees: Jesus is the new Torah, and following the commandments means, fundamentally, following Him. Specifically, Jesus says that for the young man the redemptive, generous righteousness is giving to the poor. Jesus wants goodness, the kind of goodness that His heavenly Father manifests, which is illustrated by the parable. There is One who is good, and the young man should model that goodness.

But we are getting ahead of ourselves. Jesus calls the man to give up all his wealth, distribute it to the poor, and become a disciple. Saint Francis heard this parable and did just what Jesus commanded the young man to do: he gave up his considerable family inheritance and took a vow of poverty. I do not think Jesus literally wants every believer to do this, and I do not think that the Spiritual Franciscans were right to think poverty represented a more spiritual way of life. Throughout the New Testament, Christians own things, without reproach or qualms of conscience. Zachaeus gives away *half* his wealth to the people he defrauded, and Jesus commends him for that. Jesus calls the young man to absolute renunciation because the man is wealthy, and this is the place where his idolatry is most manifest. This is the thing *he* must renounce to enter life, because this is the idol that he must demolish.

But we cannot leave things at that. The discussion with the disciples that follows shows that Jesus is making a more general point. If we want to be perfect as our Father is perfect, that has to be manifest in the way we use our wealth. Wealth is highly seductive, and it is seductive because it can appear to be all-powerful. If you have got enough money, you can buy almost anything – cars and food and houses and vacations and justice and loyalty and people. You cannot buy love, but you can buy sex, and not just from prostitutes. Rich men are tempted to trust wealth because wealth can seem omnipotent. It is hard for a rich man to enter the kingdom. Jesus does not say that it is impossible, but that it is difficult. He compares it to the impossibility of putting a camel through the eye of a needle. This has been softened by saying that there is a "needle gate" in Jerusalem, too narrow for a camel. That is not right: Jesus uses an *impossible* entry – the largest Palestinian animal (the camel) going through the smallest opening (the eye of a needle). It is an entry that is only possible with God.

Jesus' command to the young man applies to all of us. We are not all called to sell all our possessions and give the proceeds to the poor. But we are all called to use our possessions for the benefit of the poor. This does not mean only that we should donate to charities. In our day to day use of money, we should be asking: Am I helping those in need or am I using my wealth to fill out my portfolio? What do we invest in? Do we invest in the businesses that will give us the biggest return? Or do we invest in the businesses that will bring the greatest blessing to poor people, even if we have to take a lower return? When we do our daily shopping, do we consider how our decisions might affect the poor? Those effects are very complicated; I am not offering a simple formula. But our purchasing decisions should be affected by concern for the poor. Faced with a choice between a new car that will cost us fifty-thousand dollars, and a cheaper used car that leaves us more to donate to charities, we should ask: What would Jesus have us do?

Jesus promises rewards to His disciples, and this is what prompts the parable. Renunciation is never the end of the story. Giving up what we have for the sake of the poor is not just for the sake of the poor. Jesus promises authority (19:28) and exponential returns on our investments (19:29). Jesus promises wealth *and* eternal life in the "regeneration," the new age of the kingdom. But the only way to achieve both is the way of self-denial and the cross. If we renounce the kingdom and cling to earthly treasures, we will lose both earth and heaven.

Jesus' statement that the "first will be last, and the last first" (19:30; cf. 20:16) applies to the rich and the disciples. The parable illustrates the saying about first and last in a couple of ways. Most obviously, the owner of the vineyard pays the last workers first (20:8). This seems an incidental detail, but the fact that the first/last language is used only here within the parable means that it is worth attending to. This sets up a situation where the first workers watch as everyone else gets their payment, and meanwhile their expectations keep rising – if everyone else got a denarius, we will get more, right? But there is a reversal of expectation, not only of the first workers but for readers. We sympathize with them. They *did* work through the scorching heat of the day, and these eleventh-hour workers have only done an hour's work. But they are paid according to their contract, not according to their expectations. It is not a *complete* reversal. They do get what they contracted for, and the eleventh-hour men receive only a denarius, a day's wage. But it is a reversal. The last workers should appear to be last on the pay scale; the first workers first on the pay scale. That is not what happens.

Jesus tells the story in such a way that we sympathize with the first-hour workers. All the owner has said to the later worker is "whatever is just I will give you." It is a surprise when we get to Matt. 20:9, and he starts handing out a denarius – the equivalent of a day's wage – to workers who worked only an hour. When the first men get their pay, we think they are right to grumble. How is it just to give the same payment to those who worked the whole day and those who worked only an hour? That does not seem fair.

Who are the "first" and "last"? There are several layers to the answer. Jesus is still talking about rich and poor, and the first and last have to do with wealth. The young man looks like a first man; the disciples who have left everything look like last men. In social standing, the disciples are lower and lesser and last. Yet, in the end, the first will be last and the last first. When the owner comes to distribute payment, "many who are first" in society and economy will be last. The kingdom brings a reversal of social order and expectations. In context, Jesus has also made a distinction between the disciples who have been following Him, and who will endure the scorching heat of the assaults of the Pharisees, the trial of Jesus, the cross, and the persecutions that follow, and the "everyone else" who come later. The disciples are the first-hour men, and they should not resent later laborers who are sent out into the vineyard later on. The rich young man operates by the standards of the old age. He has achieved a righteousness in the law, the righteousness of the scribes and Pharisees. The disciples and their followers are Johnny-come-latelies. But the first shall be last and the last first, and the disciples will enter the kingdom first. At another level, the first and last are, as Irenaeus said, Jews and Gentiles. All will receive the same gift from their Father, and the Jews who started earlier should not grumble against Gentiles who come late to the vineyard.

The punch-line of the parable is the owner's defense of himself. We are sympathetic with the first-hour men until the owner speaks. He has done no injustice. He gives the first-hour workers what they contracted for. Instead of cheating anyone, he has shown kindness and generosity to the other workers, paying them *more* than they deserved. All the while the first-hour men waited to be paid, they were thinking either "We'll get paid even more" or "What's he doing? Giving those guys the same money he gave us?" Instead, they should have been thinking, "What a generous employer! He is taking a big loss today, by paying far more labor cost than is necessary. He could be saving money."

The owner goes on to rebuke the first-hour men for their grumbling. The owner asks the first-hour men if their eyes are evil, and Jesus is posing the same question to us. In Matt. 6:23, the "evil eye" is associated with greed, with mistaking the value of earthly possessions. Eyes are organs of valuation and judgment, and an evil eye places value on the wrong things or too much value on less valuable things. Deut. 15:9 uses the phrase "hostile eye" to describe a man who refuses to give to a poor brother because the year of release is coming, and he does not want to be generous. The opposite of an evil eye is an "open hand." Jesus is posing the question to us, who have sympathized with the first-hour men: Is your eye evil? Do you resent the open-handed goodness of God? When your friend gets a promotion, or a higher score on a test, or more points in the game, or rises to fame that you think you deserve, what do you think? Do you rejoice with him? Or is your eye evil because God is good? When a far younger man exceeds your success, a success you have labored for over decades, do you resent him?

We need our eyes opened so that we can see God's goodness. That is the overarching theme of this section: "What good thing shall I do?" the man asks. Jesus answers, "There is One who is good." Then He tells a parable about the goodness of the owner of Israel's vineyard. What good thing shall I do? Rejoice in the goodness of the owner and imitate that goodness by following Jesus. Then you shall enter into life.

Servant of All
Matthew 20:17-34

[17] As Jesus was about to go up to Jerusalem, He took the twelve disciples aside by themselves, and on the way He said to them, [18] "Behold, we are going up to Jerusalem; and the Son of Man will be delivered to the chief priests and scribes, and they will condemn Him to death, [19] and will hand Him over to the Gentiles to mock and scourge and crucify Him, and on the third day He will be raised up." [20] Then the mother of the sons of Zebedee came to Jesus with her sons, bowing down and making a request of Him. [21] And He said to her, "What do you wish?" She said to Him, "Command that in Your kingdom these two sons of mine may sit one on Your right and one on Your left." [22] But Jesus answered, "You do not know what you are asking. Are you able to drink the cup that I am about to drink?" They said to Him, "We are able." [23] He said to them, "My cup you shall drink; but to sit on My right and on My left, this is not Mine to give, but it is for those for whom it has been prepared by My Father." [24] And hearing this, the ten became indignant with the two brothers. [25] But Jesus called them to Himself and said, "You know that the rulers of the Gentiles lord it over them, and their great men exercise authority over them. [26] It is not this way among you, but whoever wishes to become great among you shall be your servant, [27] and whoever wishes to be first among you shall be your slave; [28] just as the Son of Man did not come to be served, but to serve, and to give His life a ransom for many." [29] As they were leaving Jericho, a large crowd followed Him. [30] And two blind men sitting by the road, hearing that Jesus was passing by, cried out, "Lord, have mercy on us, Son of David!" [31] The

crowd sternly told them to be quiet, but they cried out all the more, "Lord, Son of David, have mercy on us!" [32] And Jesus stopped and called them, and said, "What do you want Me to do for you?" [33] They said to Him, "Lord, we want our eyes to be opened." [34] Moved with compassion, Jesus touched their eyes; and immediately they regained their sight and followed Him.

Jesus is on the way to Jerusalem, which is always an ascent. Matthew tells us that Jesus was "about to go up" to Jerusalem, and then Jesus says "We are going up to Jerusalem." Literally, Jerusalem was in high country, so a walk to Jerusalem was a climb up mountains. This literal fact translated into a theological point: Jerusalem was the high place, the house of Yahweh was on a mountaintop, the earthly place that was closest to the heavens, the chief of the mountains. To go up to Jerusalem was to "ascend" into the presence of the Lord. As Israel approached Jerusalem for festivals, they sang "Psalms of ascent." The ascent to Jerusalem is a royal ascent, an ascent to a throne. Jerusalem is the city of the Great King, King Yahweh, and the capital city of David's kingdom, the city of the temple and palace of Solomon. An ascent to Jerusalem is an ascent to a throne. Jesus is traveling to Jerusalem, it appears, to come into His kingdom.

The passage begins with a reference to this ascent, and it also begins with a reference to the "way." Verse 17 says that Jesus spoke to the disciples on "the way" to Jerusalem and at the end of the passage, when Jesus is leaving Jericho, He finds two blind men sitting by the way (20:30). After He heals them, they join the crowds that follow Jesus as He makes His way to Jerusalem. The opening verses set up the question of this passage: What is the way of ascent? What is the path to kingship? If the last shall be first, how do they become first?

As He ascends, excitement builds. Jesus is not alone with the twelve. The "great multitudes" that followed Him from Galilee have built up again and are following Him to the city. In the next chapter, multitudes hail Him as the Son of David who comes in the name of the Lord. The excitement is understandable. For generations, Israel has had no Davidic king in Jerusalem. For a generation, the king of the Jews has not been an Israelite at all but a Herod, an Idumean convert to Judaism. But the Jews have not lost hope. They believe Jeremiah's prophecy that a son of David will return to the throne (cf. Jer. 23:5-6; 33:14-17), and Ezekiel's promise that after the Lord had scattered the false shepherds, He would set David over His people (Ezek. 34:23-26). The Jews also hope that Yahweh Himself will return. The coming of the Messianic, the anointed David, was part and parcel of the reconciliation of Israel with Yahweh, her estranged husband. This is the good news that Isaiah promised would be proclaimed to Israel, that Zion would see the Lord assume the throne: "How beautiful upon the mountains are the feet of the messenger who announces peace, and brings good news, who announces salvation, who says to Zion, Your God reigns" (Isa. 52:7).

According to N.T. Wright, the return of Yahweh would involve the coming of a new covenant: "It would be the betrothal of YHWH and Israel, after their apparent divorce. It would be the real forgiveness of sins; Israel's god would pour out his holy spirit, so that she would be able to keep Torah properly, from the heart. It would be the circumcision of the heart of which Deuteronomy and Jeremiah had spoken. And, in a phrase pregnant with meaning for both Jews and Christians, it would above all be the 'kingdom of god.' Israel's God would be come in reality what he was already believed to be. He would be King of the whole world."[20] These are the expectations and hopes that electrify the crowd that accompanies Jesus on His way of ascent to Jerusalem.

Jesus does not muzzle these expectations. He fans them. In the following chapter, He deliberately constructs a scene to fulfill the prophecy of Zechariah: "Say to Daughter Zion, Behold your King is coming, gentle, and mounted on a donkey." Jesus does not deny that He is king. He does not deny that His ascent to Jerusalem is an ascent to a throne. He does not silence the blind men when they call out to Him as the "son of David," and He does

---

20 Wright, *The New Testament and the People of God* (Minneapolis: Fortress, 1992), 300-301.

not silence the crowds and children who hail Him with Hosannas. He is in fact ascending to His throne, coming into His kingdom in the royal city of Jerusalem.

For Jesus, the issue is not whether or not He is on the way of ascent. The issue is the quality of that way. And He makes abundantly clear that this way is a way of suffering. He tells the Twelve, though not yet the crowds, that the way of His ascent is the way of rejection, mockery, and a cross. This is Jesus' most elaborate passion prophecy yet, and it sets out the plot for the final chapters of Matthew's gospel. He gives a few more details than He has before. For the first time, He tells them that He will be handed to the Gentiles. For the first time, He tells the disciples that His death will be preceded by humiliating mockery and scourging.

Jesus applies to Himself the message of the parable that opened this chapter. The point of the parable, He said, was that "the last shall be first, and the first last." That is the history of Jesus: He is made last, the lowest, and yet He will be made the first. Crucifixion was not only physically excruciating; it was humiliating and degrading. It was the form of execution for slaves and rebels. Those who tried to "lift themselves up" by leading rebellions were "lifted up" on crosses. For the Romans, the message of the cross is: This is what happens to people who try to ascend too high. It was a form of execution reserved for the lowest classes, and yet Jesus says that the last shall be first and the first last. He says that He will be given over to the Gentiles and executed shamefully on a cross, but that in the great reversal of resurrection, He will be exalted to the first place, so that He might be preeminent in everything.

Jesus discloses this future, this way, to the twelve by themselves, but the disciples do not understand. They are blinded by the Messianic enthusiasm of the crowds. As the king approaches, people start jockeying for power, trying to slip into places close to the king. The wife of Zebedee comes with a request for her sons, but her sons are right there with her (v. 20). They have just heard Jesus tell them that He goes to Jerusalem to suffer and die, but they cannot get Jesus' earlier words out of their heads. Jesus has promised that the Twelve will sit on thrones in the regeneration (19:28), and that is what James and John remember. They have missed Jesus' teaching about the way to those thrones, about the way of the cross. Their mother asks that the two brothers will sit at the right and left of Jesus when He enters His kingdom. For these brothers, it is not enough to sit on thrones; they want to sit on the thrones right next to Jesus.

"Right" and "left" in the kingdom may refer to sitting on the thrones to the right and left of Jesus. But the picture could also be a royal feast, with the brothers on either side of Jesus at the head of the table. When Jesus asks if they can drink the cup that He drinks, he re-envisions their request as a request for places of honor at a banquet. Kings have cups. Joseph was a cup bearer to Pharaoh, and Nehemiah served Artaxerxes in the same capacity. A king with a cup of wine in His hand is a king who has defeated His enemies and can take His rest. Kings do not drink before battle, but after victory. The Bible sometimes describes the cup as a weapon. As Judge, Yahweh has a cup in His hand, filled with wrath and judgment (Psalm 75:6-8). He pours it on the nations, they drink it, and some become drunk and fall. The ones who do not drink the cup of wrath stand and are exalted. Jeremiah 25 uses this imagery very elaborately. Yahweh has a cup that He pours out on various nations, which get drunk, stumble, and fall. Revelation has the same imagery in the vision of the bowls, filled with the wine-wrath, the blood of the saints (Revelation 16). These bowls are poured out on the city, Babylon or Jerusalem, and the city staggers and falls.

Jesus is a King, so He also has a cup. But as Jesus talks about it, it is not a cup that He pours out on His enemies. Not at first. Someday, as Revelation shows, Jesus will send His angels to pour out the cups of wrath against the rebellious city, but first He drinks the cup Himself. He takes the cup of the wine-wrath of God Himself, drinks it, and absorbs it. Even the cups that the angels pour out are cups of martyr-blood. Matthew's Gospel bears out Jesus' words. He says that the ones on the right and left have to drink the cup with Him – that is, they will share His sufferings with Him. That is what happens within the Gospel. The language of their request – one on the right hand and one on the left – reappears in Matt. 27:38: "At that time two robbers were crucified with Him, one on the right and one on the left." To be on the right and left of Jesus is to drink down the royal cup of suffering.

The other ten disciples become indignant. Are they indignant because the two brothers are being self-centered and seeking their own glory? Or are they indignant because the two brothers beat them to the punch? It seems that the latter is the more likely. After all, these are the same twelve who have been wondering about greatness in the kingdom of heaven (18:1) and arguing about who is going to be the greatest apostle.

In response, Jesus says that the way to greatness and primacy is the way of Jesus. This diverges from the Gentile way to greatness and primacy among the Gentiles, which is the way of lording and domination. He probably has the Romans in mind, but His statement applies to Jews insofar as they have adopted Roman and Gentile patterns of life. Romans gained authority and prestige by superior birth or superior achievements in battle or in government. Upper class Romans bolstered their reputation by hiring an entourage to announce them in the streets wherever they went. Romans lorded it over one another by doing favors. If I do you a favor, I put you in my debt, and I can call on that debt of gratitude any time I like. In Roman practice, "benefaction" laid oppressive burdens on the beneficiaries.

That is not the way to greatness in God's kingdom. Rather, the way of ascent, the way to primacy, is the way of service: the last shall be first and the first last. Jesus does not say there is no such thing as greatness; He does not say that all in His kingdom are equal. But he radically challenges the disciples' preconceptions about the way to greatness.

Jesus uses two different words for service here, neither of which is particularly attractive. The first is the Greek word that is the basis for "deacon," and it refers to menial service such as waiting on tables. Matt. 20:27 is even stronger: If you want to be first, become a *slave*. A slave does not own himself, his time, or his labor. His energies and life are completely at the beck and call of his master. That is what Jesus does among the Twelve. That is the life that Jesus adopts. When the Lord comes among His people, He comes as a slave.

In the course of this exhortation, Jesus describes for the first time what His death is going to accomplish. He calls it a "ransom," and the word is used to describe payments and redemptions of various kinds. After the exodus, Yahweh claimed all the firstborn of Israel's animals. Unclean animals like donkeys could not be sacrificed, but they could be useful work animals. A donkey could be "redeemed" or ransomed by substituting a lamb (Exod. 13:13). A kinsman who bought his brother from slavery also paid a "ransom." Jesus says that His death will be a liberating death, a substitution for those who are condemned to die. He will drink the cup for those who deserve to drink it and so give His own life as a ransom for many.

Two disciples ask for glory at the right and left hand of Jesus, and the passage ends with two other men, a pair of blind men. The juxtaposition is significant: the disciples are themselves blind men who need Jesus to heal them. The request of the mother of John and James, and the indignation of the other ten, show that the disciples have what Jesus calls "evil eyes" (Matt. 20:15). Eyes are organs of judgment and valuation, and evil eyes are eyes that value things wrongly. Evil eyes are greedy eyes, eyes that value earthly riches and status too much. The disciples have such evil eyes.

Jesus does not condemn the desire to be in places of honor. He *promises* places of honor. The issue is the *way* to honor. James and John do not see what they are asking for because they do not see the path that leads to primacy in Jesus' kingdom, and the ten are blind when they become indignant at the two brothers. All the disciples need to have their eyes healed and opened. They need new eyes to see things rightly.

And not only the Twelve. When the two blind men cry out for mercy from the Son of David, the crowd attempts to silence them (Matt. 20:31). They are a royal entourage; they are part of the procession of the Great King as He ascends to His throne in the royal city. But the multitudes are as blind as the Twelve to the nature of Jesus' kingdom. He is the Son of David, and as Son of David, He has compassion on the blind. He is the Servant of Yahweh, come to serve and give His life, who has come to bear the infirmities and weakness of His people, to open the eyes of the blind, to open the ears of the deaf and loose the tongues of the blind, to make the lame run.

When Jesus stops, they ask Him to open their eyes (Matt. 20:33). Once their eyes are open, they will be able to see and judge clearly. When their eyes are open, they will see the way of Jesus, and they will be able to see what path leads to ascent to the kingdom. When their eyes are open, they can share in Jesus' kingdom, sitting on thrones judging the twelve tribes. But they will see these things *only* if their eyes are open. So long as we are blind, we will believe that the way to greatness and primacy is the way of the Gentiles, the way of jockeying for power and lording it over others. The way of service and sacrifice and suffering looks like the way of descent, not the way of ascent. Only those who have their eyes opened by partaking of Jesus, the tree of knowledge, will follow Him in the way of His ascent into His kingdom, which is the way of compassion and of the cross.

The King and His House
Matthew 21:1-17

[1] When they had approached Jerusalem and had come to Bethphage, at the Mount of Olives, then Jesus sent two disciples, [2] saying to them, "Go into the village opposite you, and immediately you will find a donkey tied there and a colt with her; untie them and bring them to Me. [3] If anyone says anything to you, you shall say, 'The Lord has need of them,' and immediately he will send them." [4] This took place to fulfill

what was spoken through the prophet: [5] "Say to the daughter of Zion, Behold your King is coming to you, gentle, and mounted on a donkey, even on a colt, the foal of a beast of burden." [6] The disciples went and did just as Jesus had instructed them, [7] and brought the donkey and the colt, and laid their coats on them; and He sat on the coats. [8] Most of the crowd spread their coats in the road, and others were cutting branches from the trees and spreading them in the road. [9] The crowds going ahead of Him, and those who followed, were shouting, "Hosanna to the Son of David; blessed is He who comes in the Name of the Lord; Hosanna in the highest!" [10] When He had entered Jerusalem, all the city was stirred, saying, "Who is this?" [11] And the crowds were saying, "This is the prophet Jesus, from Nazareth in Galilee." [12] And Jesus entered the temple and drove out all those who were buying and selling in the temple, and overturned the tables of the money changers and the seats of those who were selling doves. [13] And He said to them, "It is written, My house shall be called a house of prayer; but you are making it a robbers' den." [14] And the blind and the lame came to Him in the temple, and He healed them. [15] But when the chief priests and the scribes saw the wonderful things that He had done, and the children who were shouting in the temple, "Hosanna to the Son of David," they became indignant [16] and said to Him, "Do You hear what these children are saying?" And Jesus said to them, "Yes; have you never read, 'out of the mouth of infants and nursing babies you have prepared praise' for yourself?" [17] And He left them and went out of the city to Bethany, and spent the night there.

Jesus is the living, eternal Word of the Father (John 1:1-3). Just as we reveal the deepest things about ourselves in our words, so God reveals Himself in the living Word that is with God and is God. Just as we act on the world and on other people through our words – issuing commands, making requests, expressing wishes – so God acts in the world through His living Word, enfleshed as Jesus. Just as we make imaginary worlds through words, so God makes and remakes the real world through His living Word. Jesus is the living Word, and as the living Word, He is the Word that gives meaning to all the words that God has spoken. After His resurrection, Jesus told His disciples that everything in the whole of the Old Testament speaks of Him (Luke 24). He is the reality about which the whole Bible speaks. Scripture consists of written words that reveal the living Word. As the writer to the Hebrews says, in the past God spoke in many portions and in many ways, but in the last days He spoke in His Son.

That is the theology behind Matthew's teaching concerning fulfillment. Jesus, Matthew says, fulfills the prophetic Scriptures in His life and ministry. Much of the time, this is a matter of providential orchestration. Jesus does not arrange for Herod to kill the babies of Bethlehem or arrange His move to Nazareth, but Matthew tells us in both cases that these events in the life of Jesus fulfill things spoken by the prophets. At other times, Jesus consciously fulfills prophecy. He speaks in parables in fulfillment of Psalm 78's words about speaking in riddles and dark sayings. He heals, conscious that in healing He is acting as the Servant of Yahweh who bears the infirmities of His people. Especially as He enters Jerusalem, He fulfills prophecy, and He does it deliberately. He plans to fulfill prophecy by requisitioning a donkey and by making a scene in the temple.

Jesus is acting out a conscious strategy. Throughout His ministry, He has been avoiding confrontation. When John is arrested, Jesus withdraws from Judea into Galilee. He warns the people He heals not to make Him known. He stays in the shadows and keeps His Messianic claims secret. Now, as He enters Jerusalem, He deliberately constructs a series of scenes that cannot help but provoke an angry response from the scribes and Pharisees. He arranges to ride into the capital city on a donkey, surrounded by adoring crowds hailing Him as the son of David, the one who comes in the Name of the Lord. As soon as He is in the city, He makes His way to the temple. If we read the narrative literally, there is no break at all. He almost seems to ride the donkey into the temple. We read of the street theatrics of His entry into Jerusalem, and then the overturning of the tables of money-changers and the interruption of buying and selling in the temple.

Jesus *chooses* this moment as the moment of confrontation. The time for silence and withdrawal and hiding has ended, and Jesus shows Himself. It is strategy, the wisdom of Jesus' perfect timing. But it is not entirely strategy. It is also conscious fulfillment of the Scriptures. And it is the most Scripture-saturated event in Matthew's gospel since Jesus' infancy. By His actions at His entry to Jerusalem, Jesus makes a series of claims, about Himself and His ministry. By deliberating arranging things to fulfill prophetic Scriptures, He is saying something about Himself. What is He saying?

As the prophecy from Zechariah indicates, Jesus is making a claim to kingship. The whole scene bespeaks Jesus' kingship. Matthew gives an inordinate amount of space to Jesus' instructions about securing the donkey. Three verses are devoted to this, while Jesus' entry itself is told in only four verses. Jesus intends to allude to Jacob's blessing to his son Judah designated him as the royal tribe, the tribe of the scepter and the ruler's staff, and then he adds, "He ties his foal to the vine, and his donkey's colt to the choice vine; He washes his garments in wine, and his robes in the blood of grapes" (Gen. 49:8-12). When Jesus' disciples find a donkey tied, they know that they are finding it for the seed of Judah, the king, the one with the scepter. The donkey itself is a sign of kingship. Donkeys are not highly regarded today, but donkeys and mules were royal animals in ancient Israel (cf. Judg. 10:4; 12:14; 1 Sam. 9:1-5; 2 Sam. 18:9; 1 Kings 1:32-40). Horses were associated with war, but a king on a donkey was a king of peace. Donkeys are unclean animals, representing Gentiles; Jesus rides into the city of the Jews with a symbolic demonstration that He is the master also of the nations.

Jesus moves from the Mount of Olives, across the Kidron Valley, into the city, reversing the path that David took when he fled from Jerusalem during the rebellion of Absalom. David left weeping and was given two donkeys to carry his household (2 Sam. 16:1); Jesus comes amidst a rejoicing crowd, with two donkeys. His return is the return of the Davidic kingdom, and the people appropriately hail Him as the son of David. (Jesus' death will be more reminiscent of David's son, Absalom, than they realize – Jesus too will be hung on a tree.) The carpet of garments that are laid in the road for Jesus are also a royal symbol, a sign of royal welcome, the "red carpet" laid out for the visiting king. By throwing their garments before Jesus, the people are symbolically throwing themselves before Him, laying themselves down in acknowledgment that Jesus has conquered. More specifically, Jesus is like Jehu, the king anointed over Israel in order to take vengeance against the house of Ahab. Like Jehu, Jesus rides on a carpet of garments (2 Kings 9:13), and like Jehu he heads to a temple that will be destroyed (2 Kings 10:18-28).

When Matthew tells us that Jesus fulfills Scripture, it is usually fulfillment with a twist. According to Matthew 2, Jesus fulfills Hosea's prophecy about an exodus, but He fulfills it not by leading people out of Egypt but by escaping from Israel to Egypt. In Matthew, Israel has itself become an Egypt, ruled by a king who murders infants, and Jesus' exodus is an escape from Israel's Pharaoh. That same typology is operating here in Matthew 21 as well. Jesus comes with two donkeys and is hailed as both king and prophet (v. 11). The scene is reminiscent of Exod. 4:19-20, the story of Moses' return from Midian to Egypt. Moses comes with his wife and son, and both they and he sit on donkeys. Jesus is the prophet like Moses who comes with two donkeys to confront "Pharaoh" in the "Egypt" of Judea.

The crowd's acclamation (Matt. 21:5) combines Isa. 62:11, which promises that salvation will come to Daughter Zion, and Zech. 9:9, which portrays the arrival of a conquering king. But there is another twist in Jesus' fulfillment of Zechariah 9. To grasp the irony and power of this quotation, we have to see the whole of Zechariah 9. The king enters Jerusalem at the climax of a procession of conquest. Tyre and Sidon are going to be dispossessed (Zech. 9:4). The Philistine city of Ashkelon will not be inhabited, and the king of another Philistine city, Gaza, will perish (Zech. 9:5). In Zech. 9:10, we learn that Yahweh, through His king, will "cut off the chariot from Ephraim and the horse from Jerusalem; and the bow of war will be cut off. And He will speak peace to the nations; and His dominion will be from sea to sea, and from the River to the ends of the earth." Zechariah's king brings peace, but it is a peace that comes at the end of a war of conquest, a war that cuts off all the weapons by which anyone will continue warfare. Likewise, Jesus comes to Jerusalem from a lengthy war of conquest over Satan, sin, the curse, all the plagues that kept Israel in bondage.

If Jesus fulfills Zechariah 9, He must be a conqueror. Yet, Matthew leaves out the lines of Zech. 9:9 that would speak directly of conquest, and instead emphasizes Jesus' meekness (Matt. 21:5). Is Jesus a conqueror or not? The answer is Yes, but He is a conqueror with a twist, a conqueror who conquers not by superior firepower but in some other way. We know from the rest of the story how that happens. He is a conqueror, who eventually has all authority in heaven and on earth. But He does not take that authority by the sword or spear. He gains that authority by offering Himself on the cross. He conquers, but He gives the conquest a distinctive, cruciform imprint. He is a conqueror, but He is a meek conqueror. He conquers in the way He instructs His disciples to conquer, gains the earth in the way He tells His disciples to gain the earth: "Blessed are the meek, for they shall inherit the earth" (Matt. 5:5).

Rumors of a new king always throw the capital city into turmoil. When the magi visited Jerusalem, the city was stirred (Matt. 2:3), and it happens again when Jesus enters (Matt. 21:10). No wonder the scribes, Pharisees, and priests are disturbed. When a king arrives, He begins to set things in order. When the king arrives, He will review the performance of His officials. The Pharisees already know how Jesus will assess them.

Jesus arranges a fulfillment of Scripture to confront Jerusalem with His claim to be the king, the son of David; the greater Jehu, avenger of Yahweh; the greater Moses, the prophet of the exodus; the true son of Judah, the scion of the royal tribe. But He does more. He moves from the streets of Jerusalem to the greatest symbol of Judaism, the temple, and stirs things up there. When He enters, Jesus casts out the buyers and sellers and overturns the tables of the money-changers. He is not condemning cheating by the sellers in the temple; if He were doing that why would he throw out the buyers? Nor is He displeased with the fact that there is a market for sacrificial animals in the temple; that was a natural product of temple worship (cf. Deut. 14:22-27). The economic transactions of the temple are necessary to keep the liturgical transactions going, and interrupting the buying and settling literally interrupts the sacrificial worship.

As N. T. Wright has argued, Jesus pre-enacts the destruction of the temple, warning the people, in the words of Jeremiah, that the Lord would destroy their "robbers' den" (Matt. 21:13; cf. Jer. 7:11), the place where robbers retreat for safety. Jeremiah specifically warned the people that they could not escape into the temple after abusing one another, committing injustice, oppressing the orphan and widow and the innocent (Jer. 7:5-11). The Jews are brigands, Jesus says, who rape and pillage and commit violence and oppress, and then retreat to the temple and sacrifice and think they can get away with it. They cannot. They cannot act like brigands outside the temple and then find safety in the temple. Jeremiah goes on to say that the temple in Jerusalem will go the same way as the tabernacle at Shiloh, destroyed by the Philistines during the time of Eli the high priest. Jesus is announcing the same doom on Herod's temple. Shiloh will happen yet again.

Quoting Isaiah, Jesus says that the temple should be a "house of prayer" (Matt. 21:13). It is interesting, then, that Jesus does not actually pray in the temple. Instead, He spends His time in the temple healing the blind and lame who come to Him. But this is consistent with Jesus' teaching and example elsewhere. Compassion for the blind and lame is true prayer, true sacrifice. It is what the temple is for. Instead of being a haven for brigands who prey on the weak, it is a haven for the weak, where they can be strengthened and restored to wholeness. As Jesus said elsewhere, echoing Samuel and Hosea, "I desire mercy, and not sacrifice."

Jesus' actions in the temple continue His claim to kingship. Solomon built the first temple, and Davidic kings after Solomon maintained and rebuilt the temple. But Jesus is aiming at something more radical. He claims authority to expel certain residents of the temple and welcome others, authority to inspect the operations of the temple and to order the temple according to His own purposes. In other words, He is claiming to be Yahweh Himself. His entry into Jerusalem fulfills the hope of Israel for a Davidic king. More profoundly, it fulfills their yearning for Yahweh's own return. When Jesus comes from the east, from the Mount of Olives, across the Kidron Valley, into Jerusalem, He reverses the path of David's exit from the city; He also reverses Yahweh's path of exit (Ezek. 8-11). His entry into Jerusalem is Yahweh's *parousia*.

The chief priests and scribes are indignant at Jesus' actions (Matt. 21:15; cf. 20:24), especially at the praise Jesus receives from children. Like the disciples, the scribes and Pharisees do not want the children around; they do not want to give children voice. Jesus, though, identifies children as the ones who render proper praise to Him. He is referring to the actual children who praise Him in the temple, but there is more going on as well. In the last several chapters of Matthew, He has used children as object lessons for discipleship several times. When the disciples argue about who is the greatest, Jesus puts a child in their midst and tells them to be like the child. When the disciples turn away little children from Jesus, Jesus welcomes them and blesses them (cf. Matt. 18:1-5; 19:13-15). Now, in the temple, Jesus identifies the children who represent true discipleship as the ones who give the Lord fitting praise. The priests are very serious and very adult, and they do not want to join the children's choir of Jesus' kingdom. Jesus turns their seriousness upside down: infants and nursing babies are the true priests of Jesus' temple (Matt. 21:16). If you are not willing to join the children's choir, you do not belong in the temple at all.

Jesus quotes from Psalm 8, and that gives an additional dimension to His response. The Psalm begins and ends as a celebration of the excellence of the Lord's name in creation. He sets His glory above the heavens. The central thrust of the Psalm is about the Lord's gracious care for the "sons of men." They are a little lower than the angels, so insignificant in themselves that the Psalmist is surprised that God pays them any mind at all. But the Psalm goes on to celebrate the glory of man: Yahweh "crowns Him with glory and majesty" and "makes him to rule over the words of Your hands." This is the context for the declaration that Yahweh will cause praise to come from the mouths of infants and nursing babes. He takes babes and makes them strong. He takes insignificant men and crowns them as Adamic kings of the creation.

While priests of the temple have turned into brigands hiding in their den, the children are true priests and temple servants. They are the true Adams, with dominion and rule. And they are joined by the weak and broken. The lame and blind gather to Jesus, helpless as children; He heals them and fills their mouths with praise and their hands with strength. Jesus assembles a children's choir, gives children voice, and it is the voice of victory.

Jesus arrives in the city fulfilling Scripture, but He fulfills it with a cruciform twist. He conquers by the cross, not the sword. His disciples have to follow His lead. The new Adamic race does not consist of the strong or the wealthy or the well-born. The new Adamic race is made up of the lame and blind who are healed by Jesus; the true priests are the childlike disciples who sing His praises. He comes to inherit the earth and to gain all authority in heaven and earth as the son of David and son of God, and He comes to share that authority and kingship with us. For Jesus and for us, the pattern of inheritance is the pattern Jesus enunciated in the Beatitudes: Blessed are the meek, for they shall inherit the earth.

Toward the Temple

The Fig Tree and the Vineyard
Matthew 21:18-46

[18] Now in the morning, when He was returning to the city, He became hungry. [19] Seeing a lone fig tree by the road, He came to it and found nothing on it except leaves only; and He said to it, "No longer shall there ever be any fruit from you." And at once the fig tree withered. [20] Seeing this, the disciples were amazed and asked, "How did the fig tree wither all at once?" [21] And Jesus answered and said to them, "Truly I say to you, if you have faith and do not doubt, you will not only do what was done to the fig tree, but even if you say to this mountain, 'Be taken up and cast into the sea,' it will happen. [22] And all things you ask in prayer, believing, you will receive." [23] When He entered the temple, the chief priests and the elders of the people came to Him while He was teaching, and said, "By what authority are You doing these things, and who gave You this authority?" [24] Jesus said to them, "I will also ask you one thing, which if you tell Me, I will also tell you by what authority I do these things. [25] The baptism of John was from what source, from heaven or from men?" And they began reasoning among themselves, saying, "If we say, 'From heaven,' He will say to us, 'Then why did you not believe him?' [26] But if we say, 'From men,' we fear the people; for they all regard John as a prophet." [27] And answering Jesus, they said, "We do not know." He also said to them, "Neither will I tell you by what authority I do these things. [28] But what do you think? A man had two sons, and he came to the first and said, 'Son, go work today in the vineyard.' [29] And he answered, 'I will not,' but afterward he regretted it and went. [30] The man came to the second and said the same thing; and he answered, 'I will, sir,' but he did not go. [31] Which of the two did the will of his father?" They said, "The first." Jesus said to them, "Truly I say to you that the tax collectors and prostitutes will get into the kingdom of God before you. [32] For John came to you in the way of righteousness and you did not believe him; but the tax collectors and prostitutes did believe him; and you, seeing this, did not even feel remorse afterward so as to believe him. [33] Listen to another parable. There was a landowner who planted

a vineyard and put a wall around it and dug a wine press in it, and built a tower, and rented it out to vine-growers and went on a journey. ³⁴ When the harvest time approached, he sent his slaves to the vine-growers to receive his produce. ³⁵ The vine-growers took his slaves and beat one, and killed another, and stoned a third. ³⁶ Again he sent another group of slaves larger than the first; and they did the same thing to them. ³⁷ But afterward he sent his son to them, saying, They will respect my son. ³⁸ But when the vine-growers saw the son, they said among themselves, 'This is the heir; come, let us kill him and seize his inheritance.' ³⁹ They took him, and threw him out of the vineyard and killed him. ⁴⁰ Therefore when the owner of the vineyard comes, what will he do to those vine-growers?" ⁴¹ They said to Him, "He will bring those wretches to a wretched end, and will rent out the vineyard to other vine-growers who will pay him the proceeds at the proper seasons." ⁴² Jesus said to them, "Did you never read in the Scriptures, 'The stone which the builders rejected, this became the chief cornerstone, this came about from the Lord, and it is marvelous in our eyes?' ⁴³ Therefore I say to you, the kingdom of God will be taken away from you and given to a people, producing the fruit of it. ⁴⁴ And he who falls on this stone will be broken to pieces; but on whomever it falls, it will scatter him like dust." ⁴⁵ When the chief priests and the Pharisees heard His parables, they understood that He was speaking about them. ⁴⁶ When they sought to seize Him, they feared the people, because they considered Him to be a prophet.

Jesus arrives in Jerusalem and heads directly to the temple. He has come to the control center of Judaism. He is at the heart of the land, the heart of the people of God. The temple is the great symbol of Jewish election and Jewish history. The temple declares to the world, to the Gentiles, that Yahweh, the Creator of heaven and earth, has chosen this small, backwater people to dwell with, to make His own, to use as His instrument to put everything right. It declares to the world the history of the exodus, the glories of Solomon, the reality of the restoration from Babylonian exile.

Jesus comes to this temple and starts throwing around the furniture. He declares it a den of brigands, a retreat for petty criminals and Mafiosos. It would be as if he rode into DC on a donkey, went to the steps of the Lincoln Memorial, burned a flag on the steps, and then started tossing around the souvenir booths on the Mall. He would be arrested and would instantly be attacked from both Republicans and Democrats as a dangerous and un-American rabble-rouser.

Jesus is doing something more than making a scene, though. He is enacting the future of the temple. It is a den of brigands, as Solomon's temple was during the days of Jeremiah, and like Jeremiah, Jesus warns that the den will be destroyed, its sacrifices interrupted. Jesus says, "You see me turn over the tables? You should wait and see what the Romans can do with these! They will not leave a single stone on another that will not be torn down." But Jesus is doing even more than this. He is a prophet of doom, but He is also a prophetic founder. Moses was a prophet who received God's revelation on the mountain and then delivered it to the people; he was the prophetic founder of Israel. Jesus is the new Moses. He is not just tearing apart the golden calves and the Baals; He is been on the mountain, and He comes with a new blueprint for the temple. He comes to tear down but also to build up. He comes not only as the temple-destroyer but as the architect of a new temple, a temple of healing for the lame and the blind, a temple of teaching. In His first visit to the temple, He both warns and promises. He warns the Jews that they need to change course; then He sets up His own temple service to show them what repentance will look like – what it will look like when the house of the Lord becomes the house of prayer for all nations.

The rest of Matthew 21 and all of Matthew 22-23 take place in the temple. Jesus enters the temple in Matt. 21:23 and does not leave again until Matt. 24:1. In between, we see the reaction of the Jewish leaders to Jesus' challenge. It is not pretty. It is not repentance. First, they challenge His authority. Jesus responds with questions, proverbs, riddles, and parables. Then the Pharisees and Sadducees alternately try to trap Jesus, and He turns all their traps against them. Finally, in Matthew 23, He speaks directly to the people and the disciples, pronouncing woes against the Pharisees and scribes, ending with the warning that

Jerusalem has not turned and so her house will be left desolate. He comes once calling for repentance, and then the next time He comes to announce judgment. It is a small-scale recapitulation of Jesus' entire ministry, from the call to receive the kingdom to the warning that God will judge.

By Matthew's account, this all takes place over the course of two days. The first day is the day of Jesus' arrival in Jerusalem; the next day begins at Matt. 21:18 and ends with Jesus walking away from the temple, the glory departing. Two days, and the doom of the Jewish leaders is sealed. This seems awfully abrupt. What happened to the long-suffering God? What happened to the God who is slow to anger? God is indeed long-suffering, patient, merciful, slow to anger. He leaves time for repentance. Jesus has given the Jews three years to repent. Once the time comes, when the fullness of time arrives, things move in a hurry.

This is a pattern for Israel and for us. You might go years stumbling along with some sin, some habit that you are not serious enough to break. God keeps working with you, calling you, teaching you. Then some disaster breaks in, your sin is exposed, and you have got only a moment to decide whether to repent or cover and shift blame. Your decision had better be the right one, or Jesus will walk away, leaving your house desolate.

The incident with the fig tree shows where things are headed. In Mark, the story of the fig tree frames Jesus' action in the temple (Mark 11:12-24). Jesus speaks to the fig tree, then goes into Jerusalem and condemns the temple, and then comes back and His disciples see that the fig tree has withered. That structure indicates that the fig tree and the temple incident are mutually interpreting – they throw light on one another. Similarly, the withering of the fig tree in Matthew is a foreshadowing of the future of the temple and of Israel. The fig tree is desolated, and the temple will be as well.

Fig trees are signs of Israel's peace and prosperity. The Lord brings Israel into a land of vineyards and groves and fig trees. The land that flows with milk and honey is a land of fig trees. During the height of Israel's prosperity, each Israelite had his own vineyard and his own fig tree (1 Kings 4). Israel lived under the sign of plenty and peace. Picking up on this Solomonic imagery, the prophets often describe the desolation of Israel as the withering of the vine and the fig tree (cf. Deut. 8:8; 1 Kings 4:25; Jer. 5:17; 8:13), a curse falling on Solomonic peace. Jesus is the Lord of the land, the Lord of Israel. Israel has the land only by His favor, and they owe Him fruit. When He comes to collect fruit, there is none. Israel has become a fruitless people, capable only of producing Adamic fig leaves (Gen. 3:7). Jesus curses the fig tree as He will curse the Jewish leaders (Matthew 23).

His disciples are amazed at the power of Jesus to cause this fig tree to wither. Jesus' response seems like a *non sequitur*. How did we get from fig trees to mountains? The key is to recognize that Jesus does not speak of mountains in general, but of *"this mountain"* (Matt. 21:21). He and His disciples are on the western slope of the Mount of Olives, overlooking the Kidron valley toward Jerusalem and Herod's magnificent, still unfinished temple. From that vantage point, He tells His disciples that they can move *this* mountain, the temple mount, and have it tossed into the sea of nations, if they ask in faith. Jesus confers on them the power to pass judgment on Jerusalem through prayer. They will sit on twelve thrones judging the twelve tribes of Israel.

It also seems like a *non sequitur*, because Jesus moves from commands to prayer, from imperatives to requests. He speaks directly to the fig tree, "No longer shall there ever be fruit from you" and He tells His disciples they can say, "be taken up and cast into the sea." These are not requests, petitions, but commands. But then He starts talking about prayer. The sequence is not accidental, and it gives a profound insight into the power of prayer. Jesus is saying that His disciples, when they speak in faith, will be able to declare judgments that will happen; what they say on earth shall be done in heaven. God is God, and not at our beck and call. Yet the prayer of faith shades over into a quasi-command that God promises to hear. Like Jesus, God the Father takes the form of a servant, His ear open, like a slave, to our prayerful "commands."

The fig tree episode is not an encouraging sign. We do not expect Jesus to find fruit in the temple. And the temple scene is made more ominous by the appearance of chief priests and elders (Matt. 21:23). Jesus confronted these leaders in His first appearance in the temple (Matt. 21:15), but prior to that He has not battled them. He has predicted that they would arrest Him, beat Him, and have Him put to death. He has already identified them as the villains of the story. Now the villains take the stage.

The chief priests and scribes are typical professionals, whether religious or other. They want to see some credentials. They want to know where Jesus gets the authority to do what He does in the temple – overturning the tables, setting up a healing ministry, teaching. It is a remarkable demand, coming from experts in the scriptures. Jesus has just quoted from Isaiah, saying that the house of Yahweh should be a house of prayer for all nations. He has quoted from the prophet Jeremiah, who condemns Solomon's temple because of the wickedness of the people of Judah. If nothing else, He has prophetic authority for His work. How could the Jewish leaders fail to recognize that the purpose of the house of Yahweh is to be a house of prayer for all nations? How could they object to healings in the temple? The fact that they ask for credentials shows that they do not have any idea of what the house is for. They have this great privilege of being the Creator's housekeepers, and they do not have the first clue about how to keep house.

They think they are setting a clever trap for Jesus. If he says He acts by human authority He will undermine Himself, but if He claims divine authority the priests will have grounds for acting against Him. Jesus responds to their question with a question of His own, setting a trap for the trappers (Matt. 21:24-26). The chief priests and elders know they are in a trap, and they fear the crowd too much to say what they really think. They are not only professionals, but they are politicians who check the opinion polls to find out how to respond to questions from the press. Jesus is not merely setting a trap. He does answer their question, since His authorization to act in the temple comes from His baptism by John.

At His baptism, the Spirit descends on Jesus and Father declares Him to be the beloved Son, the heir of His Father's kingdom and house (Matt. 3:17). John's baptism, which is a heavenly baptism, qualifies Jesus to put the temple in order.

Jesus' parable of two brothers (Matt. 21:28-29) is puzzling on several levels. It is a continuation of the discussion of John (21:32), and of various reactions to John. But there are several interpretive challenges. There is a major textual variant; the NKJV, following one tradition, puts the defiant-but-remorseful brother first and the NASB puts the compliant-but-disobedient brother first. We can address the textual question, I think, when we have figured out the other puzzle: What is Jesus getting at? How does the parable fit into the discussion of John's ministry, Pharisees, tax collectors and prostitutes, the kingdom of God?

Israel is a vineyard (Psalm 80; Isaiah 5), and both John and Jesus call people to a life of service in the vineyard of God. Our instinct is to match the two brothers with the two groups that Jesus mentions (disobedient son = scribes and priests; obedient son = tax gatherers and sinners), but it is hard to make them match. If the context is John's ministry (Matt. 21:32), then the parable implies that the "sinners" originally refused and the Pharisees initially accepted John. That is not the way Matthew tells the story; the only time John speaks to Pharisees, he denounces them as a brood of vipers (Matt. 3:1-12), and there is no indication that outcasts initially greeted John with skepticism. It rather seems that the Pharisees initially refused and *continued* to disobey, while the tax gatherers and prostitutes initially accepted and persisted in faith.

That is the key to the parable: the options of total disobedience and total obedience are excluded.[21] Jesus is setting a trap, as He did with His question about John's baptism and as He does later with the parable of the vineyard. *Neither* brother is truly obedient. A son who refuses his father to his face has broken the fifth commandment and has all but "cursed" him - taking him

---

21 Wendell Langley, "The Parable of the Two Sons (Matthew 21:28-32) Against its Semitic and Rabbinic Backdrop," *Catholic Biblical Quarterly*, 58.2 (1996), 228-243.

"lightly" (*qalal*) instead of taking him and his words weightily (*kabed*; cf. Exod. 21:15-17). The first son's behavior would have been shocking. Yet the other son clearly did not do his father's will either. He does not curse him to his face, but he certainly does not put any weight on his father's words either.

This is the trap: The Pharisees cannot say that either son was fully obedient, fully honoring his father. But they take the bait and offer a choice, and this leaves Jesus with an opening for a *qal wahomer* ("how much more") argument. As Wendell Langley says, "Jesus presents a situation in which each son is partly obedient, partly disobedient, and neither is totally obedient, totally disobedient. Thus Jesus grounds his use of the *qal wahomer*, for if we admit that, by implication, either son failed to do the will of the father (though each is obedient on one of two accounts), how much more so a son who is disobedient on both accounts. Jesus is left free to dog his adversaries, whichever way they jump." If they admit that the compliant-but-disobedient son was right, then Jesus can say, "Why didn't you accept John?" If they say that the defiant-but-remorseful brother was right, then Jesus can ask, as He does, "Why didn't you feel any remorse? If he was the righteous son, why did you not repent eventually?" (21:32). Either way, Jesus can say, "You should have been more like that son, then. But in fact, you both refused to your father's face and also persisted in disobedience. How much more disobedient then are you than they." They could reject the choice by arguing that John is not speaking for the Father, but that would put them back in the same dilemma they were in earlier (21:24-27).

Meanwhile, the tax gatherers and sinners took John as a prophet from the beginning (21:26) and have listened to Jesus as well. If the Pharisees say, "Neither son was obedient. An obedient son both agrees to work and also does the work," they will be implicitly endorsing the behavior of the tax gatherers and sinners. Which is just what they *do not* want to do. The Pharisees, it seems, are more like the defiant brother; Jesus treats them as such in verse 32, but says they are even worse because they did not become remorseful and go to work. When they endorse the behavior of the defiant-but-obedient brother, they are condemning themselves, because they did not turn from their initial refusal in order to follow John, which would mean following Jesus.

The second parable of the vineyard moves from the response of the Pharisees, chief priests, and elders to John and begins to address their response to Jesus. He is also setting another trap. Like the prophet Nathan before David, Jesus tells a story that the Pharisees do not recognize; they condemn characters in the story, and then realize too late that they have condemned themselves. Here the vineyard is explicitly Israel. Jesus quotes some phrases from Isaiah 5, where Yahweh describes His beloved as a vineyard. What Jesus adds is that the vineyard yields only wild, useless grapes, because of the tenants who are renting the vineyard. They have grapes, but they refuse to let the owner receive benefit from the vineyard. The owner sends one servant after another, and they beat, kill, and stone them. Finally, they kill the son. The problem is not that the vineyard produces nothing but that the tenants in the vineyard want the vineyard for their own.[22]

Jesus tells the story of Israel, and the Pharisees recognize that it is the story of Israel. But they do not recognize themselves in it. When Jesus asks how the owner is going to treat the vine growers, they pile up the judgment: They are evil and will come to evil; they will be driven from the vineyard; others will have the vineyard. Not until verse 43 does Jesus tell them that they

---

[22] This is possibly a parable specifically about the temple, the vineyard of the Lord, and the tenants are specifically the priests who take care of the vineyard, vineyard growers. In Jesus' telling, Yahweh lent Israel a kingdom and a land, and expected Israel's leaders to produce fruit in it. But when Yahweh sent servants, the prophets, to collect the fruit, the tenants of the vineyard refused and abused the servants. When the son, Jesus, arrives, the tenants – the leaders of Israel – plan to kill Him. The result is that the kingdom/vineyard is taken from the leaders of Israel and given to another nation, the church (21:43). When Jesus asks what the vineyard owner should do, the listeners stretch their imaginations to think of appropriate tortures. It is not enough to bring the vineyard owners to an end; the vineyard will be taken and given to another people. It is another parabolic trap, as Jesus, like Nathan before David, leads them to judge themselves (21:41). The Jewish leaders go away and ironically fulfill the parable by making plans to seize Jesus, but they still fear the crowd (21:46; cf. v. 26).

are the husbandmen of the vineyard and that the kingdom, the vineyard, is going to be taken from them and given to another nation. Instead of the Pharisees, scribes, and chief priests, Jesus implies, the vineyard will be ruled by the Twelve, who will sit on twelve thrones judging the twelve tribes of Israel.

In both of these parables, the kingdom is being compared to a vineyard, which is obviously a source of blessing, food, and especially of wine. The kingdom is a place of joy and abundance. But it is also a place of labor. This is the vineyard that has been taken from the Pharisees and priests and given to the apostles, and given to us. For us as for Israel, this is both a blessing and a task. To enter the kingdom is not just to enter into life and blessing, the joy of the wine of the new covenant; at the same time we are called to produce fruit. To enter the kingdom is to be placed, like Adam, into a garden, to dress and keep it. God comes to us too to collect; He comes seeking fruit. Jesus' warnings apply equally to us: Have we brought forth the fruit of repentance? Are we the truly obedient sons who both agree to obey and actually obey?

Caesar's Coin
Matthew 22:1-22

¹ Jesus spoke to them again in parables, saying, ² "The kingdom of heaven may be compared to a king who gave a wedding feast for his son. ³ And he sent out his slaves to call those who had been invited to the wedding feast, and they were unwilling to come. ⁴ Again he sent out other slaves saying, 'Tell those who have been invited, "Behold, I have prepared my dinner; my oxen and my fattened livestock are all butchered and everything is ready; come to the wedding feast."' ⁵ But they paid no attention and went their way, one to his own farm, another to his business, ⁶ and the rest seized his slaves and mistreated them and killed them. ⁷ But the king was enraged, and he sent his armies and destroyed those murderers and set their city on fire. ⁸ Then he said to his slaves, 'The wedding is ready, but those who were invited were not worthy. ⁹ Go therefore to the main highways, and as

many as you find there, invite to the wedding feast.' ¹⁰ Those slaves went out into the streets and gathered together all they found, both evil and good; and the wedding hall was filled with dinner guests. ¹¹ But when the king came in to look over the dinner guests, he saw a man there who was not dressed in wedding clothes, ¹² and he said to him, 'Friend, how did you come in here without wedding clothes?' And the man was speechless. ¹³ Then the king said to the servants, 'Bind him hand and foot, and throw him into the outer darkness; in that place there will be weeping and gnashing of teeth.' ¹⁴ For many are called, but few are chosen." ¹⁵ Then the Pharisees went and plotted together how they might trap Him in what He said. ¹⁶ And they sent their disciples to Him, along with the Herodians, saying, "Teacher, we know that You are truthful and teach the way of God in truth, and defer to no one; for You are not partial to any. ¹⁷ Tell us then, what do You think? Is it lawful to give a poll-tax to Caesar, or not?" ¹⁸ But Jesus perceived their malice, and said, "Why are you testing Me, you hypocrites? ¹⁹ Show Me the coin used for the poll-tax." And they brought Him a denarius. ²⁰ And He said to them, "Whose likeness and inscription is this?" ²¹ They said to Him, "Caesar's." Then He said to them, "Then render to Caesar the things that are Caesar's; and to God the things that are God's." ²² And hearing this, they were amazed, and leaving Him, they went away.

We often think that Jesus was above it all. He enters a world of conflict and political strife and terrorism. During his youth, Judas the Galilean led a tax revolt, first persuading the Jews to refuse to pay the tax and then mounting an armed insurrection that was bloodily suppressed by the Romans. Periodically, Romans and Jews clashed in Jerusalem over some provocative action of the Roman administrators. It was not just Jew vs. Roman; it was also Jew vs. Jew. During the middle of the first century, radical Jews known as the Sicarii, dagger-men, first-century Jewish jihadi, roamed the streets of the cities, assassinating their targets and then lamenting over the corpse to hide themselves.

Jesus as Israel

According to most readings of the Gospels, Jesus just ignores all this. He does not express any political opinion, and He urges His disciples to ignore it all too. They should be concerned with interpersonal ethics, like loving their neighbors or giving clothing to the poor. They should let Caesar and the Jews fight it out.

As an historical matter, this is not plausible. For the Jews of the first century, all discussions of the law, of resurrection, of holiness and purity, were politically fraught. When Jesus taught about giving a coat to the one who asks for an outer garment, or going two miles with the one who asks you to go one, He was talking about how to treat the Romans. When Jesus taught about loving enemies, the Romans would have been among the enemies that His disciples would think of. Especially in this final day of Jesus' final confrontation with the Jewish leaders, everything is politically charged.

That is explicit in the story of the tribute money, but it frames the whole discussion. Jesus' entry and takeover of the temple is precisely the kind of thing a Jewish Messianic figure would do; it is precisely the kind of thing that would perk up Roman ears. Such activities were usually followed by a rousing call to arms. The Jews and Romans were not wrong to interpret Jesus' activism as political activism. This entire conflict in the temple is about Jesus' authority, His kingdom, not in some heavenly spiritualized sense, but in the sense of His kingship over Israel.

The passage is framed by concern for Jesus' authority. "Who gave you authority to do these things?" (Matt. 21:23) is the question that initiates the action, and the series of confrontations ends with Jesus raising a question about the Christ as David's "Lord" or master (Matt. 22:41-46). After that, the Jewish leaders are silent and speak to Jesus only at His trial. Within this frame there are two sequences of three. In response to the question about his authority, Jesus tells three parables: the two sons in the vineyard, the tenants of the vineyard, and the wedding feast. These describe Israel's history of rebellion from various angles. Yahweh's relation is Father-son, and the kingdom is a place of labor; Yahweh's relation is Landowner-tenants, and the kingdom is a place that is to bear fruit; Yahweh's relation to Israel is, finally, that of a King and his guests, and the kingdom is a wedding feast. The three parables are followed by three temptations, about tribute to Caesar, the resurrection, and the greatest commandment, representing Israel's chief conflicts in the period - relation to Rome, eschatology, and the law.

The parables of the vineyard and of the wedding feast cover the same ground. In the first parable, as we have seen, Jesus charges the Jewish leaders with being rebellious sons who refuse to hear the Father's call to work in the vineyard. In the parables of the vineyard and wedding feast, Jesus charges that the behavior of the Jewish leaders is par for this course. Rejecting prophets and killing them is what Israel does and has always done.

The next parable again tells the story of Israel, this time using the image of a wedding feast. This parable is not as straightforward. It seems way over the top. The parable of the vineyard had some plausibility to it. Greedy tenants keep the vineyard for themselves. But what can we say about wedding guests who *kill* the messengers who invite them, a king who destroys a city because people refuse an invitation, and a man who gets thrown into "outer darkness" because he is not wearing a tux? The key is to recognize the political setting. This is not just a wedding and not just a royal banquet. It is the wedding of the king's son, the one who is going to inherit the kingdom, the successor of the current king. The response to the son's wedding is a political response because the event is a political event. The acts of the invitees are not just rude; they are rebellious. Killing the messengers is an act of insurrection, and the king does what kings do to rebels: he suppresses them. Likewise, the offense of the man without the proper clothing at the wedding feast is a political offense. This is the king's son's wedding, an occasion of state, and a lack of preparation is not just a social insult to the host but a political act of defiance. This is not to say that the story is completely plausible as a story of actual events, but it is more plausible when we recognize the political dimension.

The parable does not seem to fit the audience. The opening part of the story sounds like the ministry of John, Jesus, and the disciples. They go out calling people to a wedding feast, and the people refuse. Because of this, the king threatens to come to destroy their city. Most commentators see this as a reference to the destruction of Jerusalem in AD 70. That would be plausible if the story stopped there. But it does not. It goes on to describe a second set of invitations and climaxes with someone being cast into outer darkness out of the feast. This is usually taken as a warning to the church, but Jesus is not talking to the church. He is talking to the chief priests, elders, and Pharisees. How is this part of the parable relevant to them?

The initial invitation to the wedding feast is not the ministry of John or Jesus but reaches back earlier in Israel's history. Temple worship is, perhaps, the reality behind the image of the wedding feast; Yahweh invites Israel to share in the festivity of His son, but they instead reject the invitation and abuse and kill the messengers. The king's destruction of their city is not, as usually supposed, a prediction of AD 70, but a description of Nebuchadnezzar's destruction of Jerusalem. Jesus' ministry and that of the disciples thus begins in v. 8, when others are called from the streets and highways. The king's coming to inspect is the same event that Jesus describes in Matthew 13 and again in Matthew 25; it is the "end of the age" when the king is going to separate tares and wheat, good and bad fish, sheep and goats. The parable is about what is happening in the temple on the day that it is told. The temple is the site of the wedding feast of the Son. Jesus has invited lame and blind in. Some guests, though, are improperly dressed. The warning is to the priests and elders, those who wear the garb of temple ministry. Such clothing is not sufficient.

Clothing symbolizes many things in the New Testament (Rom. 13:12-14; Gal. 3:27; Eph. 4:22-24; Col. 3:9-11). The one that fits this parable best is the use of clothing as a symbol of righteous living. The fine linen worn by the bride at the wedding feast at the end of Revelation is described as the "righteous acts of the saints"

(Rev. 19:8). Both Revelation 19 and Matthew 22 are describing weddings, and the clothing means the same in both. The parable is a warning to the Jewish leaders who have not put on the righteous deeds that God demands. They have not walked humbly, done justice and mercy. They have turned the wedding hall into a den of brigands, and Jesus says they are going to be cast out.

The parable builds on the prophecy of Zeph. 1:2-8. Jesus describes the great "day of the Lord." He says that this day of crisis and judgment has arrived. It is the day of His own appearance and the coming day of the Lord's inspection and review of Israel. The Jewish leaders have been called, they have been gathered into the house of the king, they are there for the celebration of the Son's wedding. But they are rebels against the king, and they want to kill the king's son. They are not wearing the acts of righteousness that Yahweh requires.

The chief priests and scribes tried to trap Jesus and found themselves trapped (Matt. 21:23-32). Now the Pharisees and Sadducees step into the ring. They fare no better (Matt. 22:15-40). The Pharisees first attempt to trap Jesus politically. The tax issue had been a huge concern in Israel for a generation. Judas the Galilean, whom Gamaliel mentions in Acts 5:37, was a tax rebel, who convinced Jews to resist the tax by refusing to pay and eventually started a revolt. The Romans put it down bloodily. Taxation was both a religious and a political concern for the Jews. It was political because the tribute tax imposed by the Romans was an assertion of their authority and of Israel's subordination. It was a religious issue not only because many Jews did not think the Romans should be in the holy land. Coins themselves had religious significance. The coin here is probably the denarius issued by Tiberius, which asserted on one side that Tiberius himself was son of God and on the reverse side depicted his mother as the goddess victory. Even handling the denarius was an offense to some Jews.

The Pharisees think they have Jesus in a corner. Either Jesus will endorse tax revolt, which will get Him into trouble with the Romans, or He will endorse compliance with Rome, which will get Him into trouble with some of the Jews (Matt. 22:16-17). He will have to offend someone, and the Pharisees will exploit His answer to undermine his popularity.

Jesus' cryptic words leave his hearers mystified about Jesus' politics. "Render to Caesar" could mean "give Caesar what he deserves," or it could mean "pay your taxes." Jesus seems to sidestep the trap by saying something that both sides, and neither, can be happy with. But there is more going on in Jesus' words. The specific word here is not simply "give," but "give back." It refers to a return gift of something already given. "Give back to Caesar" means that Caesar has already given something to the Jews. Clearly, Caesar has given the Jews the coin, which they produce. Caesar has also, more generally, provided the order within which the Jews operate. The Jews do not like the Romans, but the Roman empire makes trade across the Mediterranean safe; the Romans protect Judea from traditional enemies to the East; the Romans provide a kind of stability and safety. Since the time of Nebuchadnezzar, the Jews were under a series of Gentile empires, and Jeremiah's instructions regarding Nebuchadnezzar were the instructions for Israel's relation to all of these empires: Seek the peace of the city; Yahweh has made the emperor the new Adam, so submit to him.

The basis for saying that the Jews should "give back" what Caesar gave them is that the coin bears Caesar's image. The logic holds for the second statement too. Again, the verb is "give back." Jesus does not merely tell them to "give" what belongs to God, but to "give back" what Yahweh had first given. Because we bear the divine image, we are to give back to God what He has given us, which is ourselves. Since we have nothing we have not received, we must "give back" everything that we have to God, the original Giver. "Give back" is particularly used in the Septuagint in liturgical contexts. Yahweh gave Israel the land, and they were to "give back" from what He gave us in worship.

Jesus aphorism has sometimes been taken to mean that Jesus sets up two spheres of life, sealed off from one another, with no overlap.[23] There is the realm of Caesar, which is the realm of submission to brute earthly power; then there is the realm of worship, the spiritual realm, the realm of the things of God, in which we give God His due. What Jesus says is far more complicated. If we give ourselves to God and give back only what Caesar gives, then Jesus is setting *limits* to our submission to Caesar. We give back what Caesar gives, and since we use Caesar's money to buy our cars, pay our mortgages, give loans, since we receive Caesar's money in our paycheck, we should gladly pay taxes, giving back what is his due.

But God has given us *everything*. Even what Caesar gives is ultimately what God gives. God's realm is not separate from Caesar's, not set off in a neatly bounded spiritual realm. God's realm encompasses Caesar's, envelops it completely, and we are called to give back to God in Caesar's realm as well as everywhere else. With regard to taxes, Jesus says that giving to God what is God's means giving to Caesar what is Caesar's. But Caesar's demands are not always compatible with God's, and there are times when giving back to God what is God's means we *cannot* give back to Caesar what it Caesar's.

Jesus is not being apolitical here. He avoids the trap, but in avoiding the trap, He is not avoiding the question. He answers the question, but in a way that splits the difference between competing Jewish parties. He is not a tax rebel; He is not a Zealot, and in fact Zealotry is one of the things He most opposes. But neither does He urge political compromise. He leaves His disciples a complex politics to follow, a politics that combines submission and resistance, a politics that recognizes that Caesar has given, and gives back to Caesar, but only what God allows. It is a politics of revolutionary subordination, submission to the powers that be as a means of resisting the powers that be. It is the politics of

---

23   Frederick Dale Bruner, *Matthew, A Commentary, Volume 2: The Churchbook, Matthew 13-28* (Grand Rapids: Eerdmans, 2007), 396-402. In what follows, I follow Bruner's work.

Jesus Himself, who submits Himself to a Roman cross in order to remake Rome, in order to make all kingdoms the kingdoms of our Lord and His Christ.

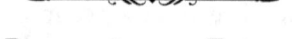

Battle for the Temple
Matthew 22:23-46

²³ On that day some Sadducees (who say there is no resurrection) came to Jesus and questioned Him, ²⁴ asking, "Teacher, Moses said, 'If a man dies having no children, his brother as next of kin shall marry his wife, and raise up children for his brother.' ²⁵ Now there were seven brothers with us; and the first married and died, and having no children left his wife to his brother; ²⁶ so also the second, and the third, down to the seventh. ²⁷ Last of all, the woman died. ²⁸ In the resurrection, therefore, whose wife of the seven will she be? For they all had married her." ²⁹ But Jesus answered and said to them, "You are mistaken, not understanding the Scriptures nor the power of God. ³⁰ For in the resurrection they neither marry nor are given in marriage, but are like angels in heaven. ³¹ But regarding the resurrection of the dead, have you not read what was spoken to you by God: ³² 'I am the God of Abraham, the God of Isaac, and the God of Jacob? He is not the God of the dead but of the living.'" ³³ When the crowds heard this, they were astonished at His teaching. ³⁴ But when the Pharisees heard that Jesus had silenced the Sadducees, they gathered themselves together. ³⁵ One of them, a lawyer, asked Him a question, testing Him, ³⁶ "Teacher, which is the great commandment in the Law?" ³⁷ And He said to him, "You shall love the Lord your God with all your heart, and with all your soul, and with all your mind. ³⁸ This is the great and foremost commandment. ³⁹ The second is like it, You shall love your neighbor as yourself. ⁴⁰ On these two commandments depend the whole Law and the Prophets." ⁴¹ Now while the Pharisees were gathered together, Jesus asked them a question: ⁴² "What do you think about the Christ, whose son is He?" They said to Him, "The son of David." ⁴³ He said to them, "Then how does David in the Spirit call Him Lord, saying, ⁴⁴ 'The Lord said to my Lord, Sit at My right hand, until I put your enemies beneath your feet?' ⁴⁵ If

David then calls Him Lord, how is He his son?" [46] No one was able to answer Him a word, nor did anyone dare from that day on to ask Him another question.

Jesus' life and ministry are coming to their climax, with a showdown in the temple. Jesus provokes the showdown. His time has come, and He is ready to confront Judaism at its heart. When He enters Jerusalem, the crowds celebrate Him as the king, the Son of David, who comes in the name of the Lord. That title, Son of David, spoken at the beginning of Matthew 21 is repeated again here at the end of Matthew 22, closing out the section. Jesus' time in the temple is framed by His claim to be the greater Solomon, the son of David, the temple-building king. As soon as Jesus arrives in the city, He goes directly to the temple, inspects it, and condemns the false worship of the Jews. They have turned the house of prayer into a den of brigands; rebels and tax protesters and murderers and wealthy elites all find refuge from their evil in the temple worship. Jesus turns over the tables and casts out the money-changers, an enacted sign of the judgment that will come on the city and temple in the near future. The chief priests and elders demand that He give an account of Himself: By whose authority are you doing these things? Jesus refuses to answer, but instead asks a question in return: What do you think of John's baptism? He tells a series of parables in which the Jewish leaders are villains – unfaithful sons, false tenants who end up as murderers, nobles who refuse the invitation of the king.

This is a public conflict. Jesus is in full view in the temple, and He is crying out against the priests, elders, Pharisees, scribes, and Sadducees. All of them feel the sting. They are losing the favor of the crowds; Jesus is becoming a folk hero, telling stories about the greedy tenants who are thinly disguised versions of the Pharisees themselves. They are shamed and defeated in public debate, and they need to shut Him up and shut Him down.

This is not only a battle in the temple, but a battle *for* the temple, a battle for leadership of Judaism. The Jewish leaders are worried that they are losing clout with the crowds. The day before, Jesus arrived in Jerusalem to the acclamation of the crowds – He is the son of David. In Matt. 22:33, Matthew reminds us that this is all taking place in public, before a crowd of people. Jesus wins them over, and so the Pharisees keep coming back hoping to regain the initiative, hoping to silence Him. The battle is about the identity of genuine Judaism: Who is going to guide Judaism? Which teacher is the teacher of the Law? What is the temple for? To whom are the crowds going to open their ears?

But when they try, nothing goes right for Jesus' opponents. They bring up all the hot issues of the day – Roman power and taxation, the resurrection, the law – and they cannot catch Jesus in His words. He is too shrewd, and His responses only leave them more bewildered and the crowds more supportive of Jesus. One by one, these leaders – Herodians, Sadducees, Pharisees (22:15-40) – approach Jesus to trap Him, and one by one they are put beneath the feet of the son of David (22:44).

The Pharisees came with a question about Roman taxation. Now, the other major group of Jewish leaders comes, with a theological question. Sadducees were the party of the priesthood (cf. Acts 4:1; 5:17), the aristocracy of Israel. Being the privileged class, they rejected the socially disruptive notion that dead people could live again. They wanted everyone to stay just where they were, since they were comfortably ensconced at the top of the heap. Sadducees were Torah-fundamentalists. They took the Torah as the central revelation of God, and rejected later revelation. Since many of the "proof texts" of resurrection came from the Psalms and prophets, the Sadducees were not convinced. Relying on Torah, they want to show that the resurrection is impossible.

They present to Jesus a scenario designed to expose the absurdity of belief in the resurrection. They cite the levirate law that requires a brother to marry the widow of his dead brother to raise up sons who will continue his legacy, inheritance, and name. As in Genesis 38, a woman can run through several husbands, and they all die. If the resurrection is true, then she would be married to all of them at once, which is ridiculous. More importantly, they are trying to show that the Torah actually contradicts belief in resurrection. Or, belief in resurrection creates inherent contradictions and anomalies in Scripture. Torah prescribes levirate marriage if a brother dies; but Torah proscribes polyandry, the practice of one woman marrying several men simultaneously. If all the brothers, and the woman, are all alive at the same time, in the resurrection, then the law is nullified in one way or another. Either the levirate law is annulled, or the prohibition of polyandry is annulled. If you believe in resurrection, you cannot believe in an eternal, inviolate Torah.

Jesus gives several answers to this line of argument. He rebukes the Sadducees for not understanding either the Scripture or the power of God. How are they misunderstanding these things? Where in the Scripture do they find teaching that would show them otherwise?

Let us start with the power of God, the focus of Matt. 22:30. The Sadducees can only conceive of a world organized by marriage, family, continuity through procreation. They cannot imagine a world where marriage has reached its climax in something else, something greater. But that is what Jesus says is the case. In the resurrection, marriage will come to an end. He is not simply saying that there will be no *new* marriages. The question has to do with existing marriages, and how they continue in the resurrection. Jesus' simple answer is, "They do not." We will not be like angels in every respect, but in this one respect we will be – no more marriage. This is consistent with the regular theme in the gospel, Jesus' relativization of family. The true family is the one that gathers around Jesus to do the will of the Father. If you do not hate father or mother, sister or brother, wife or children, for the sake of Jesus, you are not worthy to be His disciple. This does not mean that marriage and family are useless, merely that their use comes to an end at the resurrection. Whatever comes after will be greater, better, deeper, but it will not be marriage.

But they misunderstand the Scriptures as well. Jesus charges that they do not even understand the Scripture they have quoted. Matthew makes this point very subtly. The quotation from Deuteronomy 25 says that the levirate brother is supposed to "raise up seed" for his dead brother. The verb is the verbal form of "resurrection," the very same word that the Sadducees use in Matt. 22:28 in posing their conundrum and the word Jesus uses in Matt. 22:30-31. The very passage they quote hints that the Scriptures aim at "raising up" a dead man, by "raising up" seed. The implicit point is: If God gave Israel a law that gave hope of continuing life to a dying, childless man, hope that his name would live on, hope that he would have an heir, does not that mean God is a God of resurrection, the God of life after death?

They also misunderstand some of the more fundamental passages of the Old Testament. Jesus goes back to a founding text of Israel's history, Yahweh's appearance to Moses at the burning bush. There, God describes Himself as the "God of Abraham, Isaac, and Jacob." Jesus claims that God is not a God of graves and ghosts, but a God of the living. If He is God of Abraham, Isaac, and Jacob in the time of Moses, then they must be alive still today. "Resurrection" in the first century meant "bodily resurrection," but proving that Abraham was alive was sufficient to refute the Sadducees, who thought that a person simply passed from existence at death – no spiritual or bodily existence after death at all.

But there is still more. With the question about the levirate still echoing in the background, Jesus reminds the Sadducees that they claim to serve the God of Abraham, the God who gave Abraham a son when he was as good as dead, the God who did not have to rely on the levirate institution or human procreation to continue Abraham's seed, who literally, very literally, "raised up" a seed to Abraham from Abraham's dead body and Sarah's dead womb. In denying the resurrection, the Sadducees are denying their very confession, the confession that they were the children of Abraham.

The context of the quotation in Exodus 3 is important. This is Yahweh's first revelation to Moses, in which He promises Moses that He is heading down to Egypt to bring plagues on Pharaoh's house and to liberate Israel. The God of Israel is a God who brings His people out of slavery, also the slavery of death. Jesus is also implicitly announcing His own new Exodus, when He will bring judgment on the "Pharaohs" of Israel and lead out a new people to His promised land.

Ultimately, Jesus is making a point about God. What kind of God does Israel serve? Is He a God who binds Himself to Abraham, Isaac, and Jacob, but lets that bond go once death comes? Is He a God who is limited by the grave, whose faithfulness goes only so far and no further? Or, is He a God who is faithful unto death, and yet again faithful? What kind of God is it who will go to mortals, say that He is binding Himself to them, but never deal with the greatest obstacle to their final happiness, death? Truly the Sadducees do not understand the power, or the faithfulness, of God.

Seeing the Sadducees reduced to shamed silence, the Pharisees "gather" and plot one last test. The Pharisees "gather" again in verse 41. The last time the Pharisees gathered, they got together to figure out how to trap Jesus, and they have been plotting to kill Him for some time. Matthew intends us to hear an allusion to Psalm 2, where the nations gather together against the Lord and His anointed. Matthew puts the Jewish leaders, proud of their Jewishness, in the role of the rebellious Gentiles who will be broken by Israel's Messiah. The verb for "gather" is the verb form for "synagogue;" the Pharisees form a synagogue, a gathering, against Jesus. Sadducees and Pharisees were not always friendly toward one another. But here the Pharisees take up the cause against Jesus that the Sadducees failed in. They present a united front against this trouble-maker.

We know that this is a temptation because Matthew tells us (Matt. 22:35). But how are they trying to trap Him? The main trap seems to be that Jesus will say something that will offend some of the Jews, or some of the crowd. It is like asking an American politician, "What's the most important issue facing us today?" If he says "Health care," he makes the conservatives mad, since they think the main problem is international terrorism or illegal immigration. If he says "Abortion," he makes nearly everyone mad, and positions himself on what the mainstream thinks of as the lunatic religious fringe. You cannot answer that question, it seems, without starting a new argument. That is the kind of thing the Pharisees want. They want to trap Jesus in His words, trap Him so that He loses the support of at least some of the crowd.

Asked about the law, Jesus quotes the Torah itself (see Matt. 22:37 with Deut. 6:5; v. 39 with Lev. 19:18). Jesus does not dismiss the Torah, as some Christians today believe. He affirms the Torah, and says that what He teaches is what the Torah and prophets always aimed at. Jesus initially answers the question with a quotation from Deuteronomy 6. He says that love of God is the great and first commandment.

What does it mean to love God? Loving God is not a matter of meeting His needs or giving Him service that He cannot do without. Love of God means obedience. "If you love me, keep my commandments," Jesus says. Love means loyalty; when we love God, we are loyal to Him even if it means opposition, mockery, slander, threats, and ultimately death. Loving God means fearing Him. Loving God means walking in His ways. Loving God means listening to His voice. Loving God means desiring Him, desiring to please Him, desiring to be with Him, desiring to serve Him. Loving God means clinging to Him the way a helpless needy child clings to His father.

Jesus does not just say that we should make God the highest object of our love, loyalty, obedience, fear, devotion. He does not treat God as just one more thing that we have to love, just love it a bit more. Jesus says that we should love God in a way that appears to leave no room for love of anything else. We should love Yahweh with all heart, all soul, all mind. In the Hebrew, the word "strength" is added, and this includes possessions.

That is not the end of Jesus' answer. It cannot be. If loving God means walking in His statues and keeping His commandments, then other commandments come to the fore. Loving God with all we have *requires* us to love other things, other persons. Loving God with our whole heart and soul and mind means listening to Him, and He tells us we have to love neighbors, too. What looks like an exclusive, one-on-one devotion to God opens up into relations with others. Love for God expresses itself in devotion to our neighbors. Love for the God of the Bible includes love for all that this God loves.

Jesus has answered the question, but He has not yet answered the question. The question assumes a single "great commandment": Which is the "great commandment in the law"? Jesus does answer that question, but He complicated it by adding a "second" command that is "like" it. Instead of simply giving an example of the "great commandment" of the law, He gives a double commandment, twin commandments that cannot be separated.

The second is "like" the first in stressing love, and also in its importance or greatness. Love of God cannot be combined with hatred of neighbor; love of neighbor cannot be combined with hatred of God. They are "twin" commandments.

What does it mean to love your neighbor as yourself? The original context of Leviticus 19 includes a number of specific commandments concerning the neighbor. "You shall not oppress your neighbor, nor rob him. The wages of a hired man are not to remain with you all night until morning" (v. 13). You love your neighbor by paying people who work for you. "You are to judge your neighbor fairly" (v. 16). "You shall not hate your brother in your heart" (v. 17). You may reprove your neighbor, but you shall not incur sin. You shall not take vengeance, nor bear any grudge.

These are mostly negative, but Paul gives us the positive side to this. Paul gives us a clue when he talks about how a husband should love his wife as his own flesh (Ephesians 5). We never hate our own flesh; we nourish and cherish it, and so a husband should love his wife as himself. Loving ourselves means that we care for and nourish ourselves. When we are hungry, we look for food; Jesus says, be as quick to feed your neighbor. When we are thirsty, we get something to drink; Jesus says, give a cup of water to your neighbor. When we are cold, we grab a blanket or turn up the heat; be as quick to clothe your neighbor. When we are wronged, we want things to be put right; be as quick and diligent to defend your neighbor against injustice and abuse. We want to be told if we were lurching headlong to Hell – we would want to hear good news; so, tell the good news to your neighbor.

The interrogation ends, and Jesus turns the tables and poses a riddle to the Pharisees. He asks about the Messiah's lineage, and then quotes from Psalm 110: Yahweh said to my Lord. Jesus' argument is: David wrote the Psalm, and he was inspired by the Spirit in writing the Psalm; the Psalm is about the Messiah, who is David's son; yet David, against all natural logic, calls his own son his "lord." We know that Jesus is the son of David who will be exalted to the Father's right hand, and that He is also the eternal Son of God. But the Pharisees do not have the categories to answer the question. In raising this question, Jesus returns to the question that alarmed the Jewish leaders when Jesus first entered Jerusalem, His identity as "son of David" (cf. Matt. 21:9, 15). This has been the underlying question throughout the day of parables and traps: Who is Jesus? Jesus does not answer the question directly, but instead poses a question that the Pharisees cannot answer.

They give no answer, bringing the day of testing to an embarrassed end. In Matthew's Gospel, the Pharisees never speak to Jesus again (cf. Matt. 27:62). Jesus' long day of trial in the temple ends in victory. He is the son of David who is also David's Lord, and He is on His way to the right hand of the Father. It ends in the silence of the scribes and Pharisees. Jesus' silence is only momentary, for in the next chapter, on the same day, in the same public setting of the temple courts, Jesus begins to excoriate the leaders whom He has just humiliated in public debate.

For the leaders, their silence is not acceptance of victory, or of Jesus. Silence is a prelude to murder. They do not answer Him again because they cannot, but they still want to silence Him, and now want to take revenge for the public thrashing they have received. And they will silence Him. For the next several chapters, Jesus speaks in a monologue, without any response from His enemies. But then, Jesus is silenced. The Pharisees hope that His silence will be permanent. They are wrong. Jesus is silent as a lamb before shearers, but after they have quieted Him for a few days, He is back, and then His disciples cannot stop chattering about the resurrection.

6

Not One Stone

Woe to You
Matthew 22:41-23:12

⁴¹ Now while the Pharisees were gathered together, Jesus asked them a question: ⁴² "What do you think about the Christ, whose son is He?" They said to Him, "The son of David." ⁴³ He said to them, "Then how does David in the Spirit call Him Lord, saying, ⁴⁴ 'The Lord said to My Lord, Sit at My right hand, until I put Your enemies beneath your feet?' ⁴⁵ If David then calls Him Lord, how is He his son?" ⁴⁶ No one was able to answer Him a word, nor did anyone dare from that day on to ask Him another question.

¹ Then Jesus spoke to the crowds and to His disciples, ² saying: "The scribes and the Pharisees have seated themselves in the chair of Moses; ³ therefore all that they tell you, do and observe, but do not do according to their deeds; for they say things and do not do them. ⁴ They tie up heavy burdens and lay them on men's shoulders, but they themselves are unwilling to move them with so much as a finger. ⁵ But they do all their deeds to be noticed by men; for they broaden their phylacteries and lengthen the tassels of their garments. ⁶ They love the place of honor at banquets and the chief seats in the

synagogues, ⁷ and respectful greetings in the market places, and being called Rabbi by men. ⁸ But do not be called Rabbi; for One is your Teacher, and you are all brothers. ⁹ Do not call anyone on earth your father; for One is your Father, He who is in heaven. ¹⁰ Do not be called leaders; for One is your Leader, that is, Christ. ¹¹ But the greatest among you shall be your servant. ¹² Whoever exalts himself shall be humbled; and whoever humbles himself shall be exalted."

Jesus' day of interrogation in the temple ends on the same note on which it began. Jesus came into Jerusalem acclaimed as "Son of David," and the trial in the temple ends with a question about the "Son of David." This has been the underlying question throughout the day of parables and traps: Who is Jesus? Jesus never answers the question directly, but instead poses a puzzle that the Pharisees cannot solve. Psalm 110:1 says, "Yahweh said to my Lord (*adonai*)." Jesus' argument is: David wrote the Psalm; the Psalm is about the Messiah, who is David's son; yet David, against all natural logic, calls his own son his "lord." We know that Jesus is the son of David who will be exalted to the Father's right hand, and that He is also the eternal Son of God. But the Pharisees do not have the categories to answer the question. This is more than a failure of interpretation. They cannot make sense of Psalm 110, and that means they cannot make sense of what is been happening in the days since Jesus entered Jerusalem. This is the time of Israel's visitation, and they do not recognize it. They do not recognize that Jesus is the One who comes in the Name of the Lord. The Jewish leaders cannot tell time.

But Jesus is not only bringing up the issue of His identity as the Son of David. He also warns the Pharisees and scribes about what is coming, a warning that Jesus will fill out in the following chapters. As we have seen the "gathering" of the Pharisees in verses 34 and 41 recalls Psalm 2, the assembly of the nations in rebellion against Yahweh. Yahweh's response is to set up His Son as king on Zion, and to warn the kings that the Son is going to crush them with a rod of iron. In the Psalter, this warning early in the Psalms is completed in Psalm 110, another Psalm about the Messiah being given authority to rule and power to conquer enemies. Jesus quotes the Psalm's promise that enemies will fall under the feet of the one at Yahweh's right hand, and the Psalm ends with a description of a Samson-like hero: "The Lord *is* at Your right hand; He shall execute kings in the day of His wrath. He shall judge among the nations, He shall fill *the places* with dead bodies, He shall execute the heads of many countries. He shall drink of the brook by the wayside; therefore He shall lift up the head." The Pharisees and scribes have gathered; they are enemies of the King on Zion; and they will be judged like the other nations on the day of wrath, the day when the Messiah at the right hand will shatter kings and execute judgment on the nations.

By issuing this warning, Jesus turns the tables on the Pharisees and Sadducees and scribes and elders and priests. They fancy themselves clever prosecutors who can trip up the witness and force a confession on the stand. But they fail again and again, and Jesus turns their tricks back on them. Jesus begins enunciating a lawsuit, a set of charges, an indictment, against Israel's leaders. This is what prophets do: they are prosecutors who bring Yahweh's charges to a disobedient people.

After the Pharisees slink away, Jesus addresses the crowds and His disciples concerning the Jewish leaders. It is one of the most intense rhetorical displays in the New Testament, full of passionate scorn. It is a passage of condemnation, denunciation, disdainful censure; it is a diatribe, a frontal attack, a tirade, a rant. Jesus calls the Jewish leaders "hypocrites" and "blind guides" throughout this passage. He pronounces curses – "woes." Frequently used by prophets (over twenty times in Isaiah), "woe" can express pity, call attention to an evil, or imply a threat or curse. Here, it functions as a curse: *Cursed* are the scribes, Pharisees, hypocrites. Jesus makes fun of their religious pretensions: big phylacteries and long tassels and washing the outside of cups are all satiric. Jesus' satire is in earnest. He tells them that they are making their disciples "sons of hell," says that their insides are "full of dead men's bones," repeats John's description of the Pharisees and scribes as a "brood of vipers," children of the serpent, and warns them that they are heading to hell and to desolation. This is strong, blunt language. And if Jesus denounces the Pharisees and scribes in this way, we may, in imitation of Christ, adopt the same rhetoric of denunciation. It is the rhetoric of prophets, and of the great prophet Jesus. It is a rhetoric that the church may deploy.

But that immediately needs to be set in context. This tirade against the Pharisees and scribes occurs in Matthew 23. That is, it is late in the story, during the last week of Jesus' ministry, just after His combat with the Jewish leaders in the temple and just before they carry out their plot to arrest and murder Him. Jesus has warned the Jews before. He tells His disciples to shake the dust from their sandals against cities that refuse to accept them and the gospel they proclaim. He declares "woes" to the cities that the apostles visited and which rejected Him. He has warned against stumbling blocks and scandals in the church. But we have not had anything like this. Jesus has not attacked his opponents this sharply in the past. Jesus is the *new* Moses, the prophet of a new covenant, and He *begins* His teaching ministry offering an eight-fold beatitude to Israel (Matt. 5:1-12); His teaching ministry ends with an eight-fold woe against Jerusalem and a prophecy about the destruction of the temple (Matthew 23–25). Jesus' life with Israel recapitulates Israel's history, which begins in exodus and ends with exile. Woes come at the *end*. Prophets denounce a people when they fail to keep covenant, when they fail to respond to the preaching of repentance.[24]

The beatitudes and woes match numerically and in specific details. The first beatitude promises the "kingdom of heaven" to those who are poor in spirit, and the first woe condemns the Jewish teachers for shutting the kingdom off from men. The last beatitude pronounces a blessing on those who suffer like the prophets, who are persecuted for righteousness' sake. The last woe denounces the serpents who, Satan-like, bring accusations against the prophets and murder them.

---

24 John's ministry begins with "woe" because he is the last prophet of the old order, concluding a long history of rebellion and resistance.

Jesus' example shows us how the church's ministry is to be conducted. Jesus assaults the Jews when they have rejected Him. He does not assault them first. First He offers life, blessing, a way of righteousness and peace that surpasses the righteousness of scribes and of the Pharisees. Those blessings may turn to curses, beatitudes to woes, but we begin with an offer of blessing. Taking the whole of Matthew's Gospel, we can see that Jesus' rhetoric moves through three stages: He teaches the way of life; when the Jews resist, He begins teaching in parables; when they plot to kill Him, He denounces them with woes.

We should also notice how the chapter ends. After a chapter of vehement satire and blunt censure, Jesus addresses Jerusalem, the Jerusalem who kills prophets and stones those who are sent: "How often I wanted to gather your children together, the way a hen gathers her chicks under her wings, and you were unwilling" (Matt. 23:37). Jesus does not end with rebuke but with lament, with deep sorrow for Jerusalem's resistance.

This is the tone of Yahweh's denunciations of Israel throughout the Old Testament. Yahweh's wrath does not arise from hatred, but the opposite. Yahweh's wrath expresses His fierce, *loving* jealousy for Israel. He entered into a marital covenant with His people. He loves Israel with a perfect, holy passion. He loves her with a love that is loyal and faithful. He gives and gives Himself to Israel. Yet Israel turns away from Him and flutters her eyelids at other gods; she goes out looking for other husbands, men who can do nothing for her. Roused to jealousy, Yahweh acts in wrath. Wrath is not an expression of hatred, but an expression of unrequited love. That is true of Jesus' anger as well. His wrath against the scribes and Pharisees, who are planning to kill Him, is not hatred, but slighted love. These are the people He has come to save, to turn back to the way of life, but they refuse. These are the tenant owners who have had the privilege of working in the vineyard; instead of responding with grateful tribute, they look for an opportunity to kill the son and seize the vineyard.

Jesus and Yahweh's example provides the model for the church's prophetic witness to the world. Our witness – even the most severe witness – must not express hostility or hatred, but love. Sometimes we think we are being prophetic, when in fact we are just being hateful and proud.

Finally, notice that Jesus focuses His wrath on the leaders and teachers in Israel. He does not call the people in general a "brood of vipers," but the Pharisees and scribes. He does not charge the people in general of being "sons of hell," except insofar as they have become sons of hell by following the Pharisees and scribes. He does not think the people as a whole is a collection of white-washed tombs; He says that about the hypocritical leaders. They have greater condemnation because they have greater responsibility. He is severe as the prophets are severe, not with "sinners in general," and certainly not with sinners who sorrow over their sins. He is severe with the powerful, the leaders, those in high places, who use their power not to lift burdens but to impose burdens.

Interestingly, though, the audience for this diatribe is *not* the scribes and Pharisees themselves. They apparently disappeared after Matt. 22:46. Perhaps they are eavesdropping. But Matt. 23:1 says that Jesus is speaking directly to the crowds and the disciples. He attacks the leaders of Israel, but the attack is spoken to a third party, the people who are led by these hypocritical leaders. Why? The Pharisees and scribes are teachers in Israel, a community that values teaching. Pharisees and scribes claim to be teaching God's commandments to the people, but they use that position and that office to maintain their positions of domination and their status. They say, "You have to do this," and the people take it as the word of God. Like the prophets, Jesus' tirade is severe, but it is intended to be liberating. He is loosening the hold that the Pharisees and scribes have on the people. By holding the Pharisees and scribes up to ridicule, He is showing the crowds and His disciples that they do not have to fear these religious tyrants. By speaking plainly, by mocking these powerful men, Jesus shows that there is nothing to fear. Jesus is the new Moses, who speaks to free Israel from slavery.

Throughout the day, the Jewish leaders have been trying to trap Jesus. Jesus wants to make sure that everyone understands the stakes in these conflicts. They are not polite theological discussions; they are life-and-death struggles over the future of Israel. One path – the path of the scribes and Pharisees – leads to destruction. Jesus pronounces woes to warn the people not to follow that path.

Given that, His first words are surprising. He has earlier warned about the "leaven" of the Pharisees and Sadducees, and the disciples discern that He is talking about their teaching (16:5-12). Here He distinguishes between the teaching of the leaders and their behavior. They are in the seat of Moses, that is, they are the official interpreters of the law; as such, they deserve respect, and even obedience. When the Pharisees and scribes teach something, Jesus says that His disciples should observe and do them. Yet, if their teaching is relatively sound, their conduct is not. They sit in the seat of Moses, but their practice is the opposite of Moses'. This should be understood against the background of Jesus' earlier claim to be the Son of David: Jewish leaders may sit on Moses' seat; Jesus will sit on the throne at the right hand of Yahweh. The teachers of Israel have authority, but their authority is radically inferior to the authority of Jesus, *the* Teacher of Israel.

Jesus is severe because the Jewish leaders oppress the people. Jesus says that they "tie up heavy loads, and lay them on men's shoulders" (23:4). Yet they are not willing to give the slightest help to the people who are burdened. This is not Mosaic behavior. Moses came to bring Sabbath, to break the yoke of the burden and let the prisoner and slave go free. Jesus too comes to the weary and heavy-laden and offers rest. The Pharisees and scribes are small-town Pharaohs, forcing the people to make bricks without straw.

Jesus thinks that religious *teachers* can be oppressive. They "devour widows' houses," he says; they literally prey on the weak. But in verse 4, He is not talking about preying on the weak and vulnerable in that kind of explicit way. Their *teaching* is a burden; their doctrine and ethics are the ethics and doctrine of the slave-master. The Pharisees impose burdens on people by their rules about the Sabbath, their rules about tithing, their obsession with purity. The law is made for man, made to enrich human life, to encourage the flourishing of human life. The law is given to water the garden of Israel. The Pharisees turn the law into a blunt instrument to beat people up, whips to scourge them, poison to turn the garden into a desert.

They form a self-protective *class* of oppressors. They pursue the markers and signals that mark their status. They increase the size of their phylacteries so everyone can see just how much Scripture they have in their heads.[25] Every Israelite is required to wear a tassel (Numbers 5), but the teachers display their piety with double-length tassels. They strive to have the places of honor in the synagogue, and expect people to greet them with bows and shows of respect when they pass them in the marketplace. When Roman noblemen went out into the streets, they were accompanied by an entourage. Slaves shouted out their names, and commoners had to give way. Everyone who saw a nobleman would be impressed at his clothing, his bearing, the number of servants that surrounded him. This was his glory. Jesus charges that the scribes and Pharisees have turned Israel's faith into another version of the ancient honor game. They use the law and their status as teachers of the law to form a tightly-bounded "inner ring," an inner circle within Israel, a ring designed to exclude the majority of faithful Jews. They puff themselves up with honorific titles (Matt. 23:7-10).

---

25 Phylacteries were "Torah boxes," small containers with a scrap of the law inside, and many Jews wore them on their heads or on their hands. Phylacteries were a literal way of holding to Deuteronomy 6, which instructs Israel to write the law on their foreheads and their hands.

Jesus' saying about titles like "Rabbi" or "father" or "leader" has often been misconstrued. Jesus is not encouraging disrespect for religious leaders. Nor is He condemning all official titles. Paul insists on his right to be considered an "apostle," and calls himself such in many of his epistles. Besides, the New Testament says that some men in the church are teachers and pastors, and Paul more than once describes himself as a father to the congregations. Perhaps Jesus was saying that it is appropriate to call someone a "teacher" or "father" in third-person indirect discourse, but not to his face. We can talk about "Pastor Smith" but we have to call him "Charlie." If this is what Jesus meant, He is being uncharacteristically nit-picking, and this would be an especially odd stance for Him to adopt in a chapter condemning the Pharisees for focusing on minutiae rather than the weighty things of the law. If Jesus is simply making a distinction between direct address and indirect description, He is proving Himself every bit as much a tither-of-dill-and-cumin as any Pharisee. Whatever Jesus is saying, it is something big, something about justice and mercy and faithfulness.

Several things help us understand Jesus' point. The satiric tone of the passage has to be taken into account. This is a chapter of enlarged phylacteries (not a disease suffered by middle-aged men), lengthened tassels, competition for places and titles of honor. In such a passage, hyperbole feels quite at home, quite welcome. Jesus is clearly condemning the self-regard of the Pharisees for one another, their habit of greeting one another in the markets with high-sounding titles, their love for being called "rabbi" or "great one." Behind all this is a motivation to be seen by men, to be honored by their fellows. Their aim is to be honored by men. They do not seek the honor that God bestows.

Finally, Jesus gives a double theological rationale for His assault on honorific titles. On the one hand, no one is "my great one" (rabbi) because all are united in equality as brothers; no one is father because there is a single heavenly Father. On the other hand, greatness, honor, and exaltation in the church comes through service not through multiplying titles.

Put these together, and we get this: There is one Teacher, and the ones who teach in the church are only servants of this one Teacher. There is one Father, and the ones who (like Paul, comparing himself to Moses) are nursing fathers are no more than humble servants of the one Father. There is one Leader, and those who lead in the church are above all disciples of that leader, Christ.

That honor comes along a different path. Jesus is not saying that there is no honor. He is not denouncing the reality and role of teachers as such. He is not saying that we are all identically the same, and that seeking honor is wrong. In fact, He says that the Pharisees and scribes are aiming far too low, seeking the tarnished honor that comes from their fellow teachers rather than the glorious honor that comes from God Himself. This honor comes through service. As Jesus has emphasized before, true greatness is service (23:11), and those who exalt themselves are humbled (23:12). That is the dynamic of the "eschatological discourse" that follows this chapter, as the end of Matthew 25 makes plain. What brings a judgment on Jerusalem, what desolates Jerusalem so that not one stone is left on another, is the attempt to be great, the refusal of the path of service and humility.

Weighty Things of the Law
Matthew 23:13-28

[13] "But woe to you, scribes and Pharisees, hypocrites, because you shut off the kingdom of heaven from people; for you do not enter in yourselves, nor do you allow those who are entering to go in. [14] Woe to you, scribes and Pharisees, hypocrites, because you devour widows' houses, and for a pretense you make long prayers; therefore you will receive greater condemnation. [15] Woe to you, scribes and Pharisees, hypocrites, because you travel around on sea and land to make one proselyte; and when he becomes one, you make him twice as much a son of hell as yourselves. [16] Woe to you, blind guides, who say, 'Whoever swears by the temple, that is nothing; but whoever swears by the gold of the temple is obligated.'

[17] You fools and blind men! Which is more important, the gold or the temple that sanctified the gold? [18] And, 'Whoever swears by the altar, that is nothing, but whoever swears by the offering on it, he is obligated.' [19] You blind men, which is more important, the offering, or the altar that sanctifies the offering? [20] Therefore, whoever swears by the altar, swears both by the altar and by everything on it. [21] And whoever swears by the temple, swears both by the temple and by Him who dwells within it. [22] And whoever swears by heaven, swears both by the throne of God and by Him who sits upon it. [23] Woe to you, scribes and Pharisees, hypocrites! For you tithe mint and dill and cummin, and have neglected the weightier provisions of the law: justice and mercy and faithfulness; but these are the things you should have done without neglecting the others. [24] You blind guides, who strain out a gnat and swallow a camel! [25] Woe to you, scribes and Pharisees, hypocrites! For you clean the outside of the cup and of the dish, but inside they are full of robbery and self-indulgence. [26] You blind Pharisee, first clean the inside of the cup and of the dish, so that the outside of it may become clean also. [27] Woe to you, scribes and Pharisees, hypocrites! For you are like whitewashed tombs which on the outside appear beautiful, but inside they are full of dead men's bones and all uncleanness. [28] So you, too, outwardly appear righteous to men, but inwardly you are full of hypocrisy and lawlessness."

Jesus' woes to the Pharisees and scribes, the teachers of Torah, fall into four sections, three of which includes two or three woes:
1. Jesus condemns the teachers and scribes because of the effect that they have on their disciples, their followers (23:13-15; three woes).
2. Jesus condemns the teachers and scribes for nit-picking distinctions that undermine the true intent of the law (23:16-24; two woes).
3. Jesus condemns the teachers and scribes for concentrating on purity of the flesh and ignoring the purity of the heart (23:25-28; two woes).
4. Jesus condemns them for their treatment of the prophets (23:29-36; one woe).

The woes numerically match the macarisms at the beginning of the Sermon on the Mount. Jesus' ministry begins with an announcement of blessing for those who receive the kingdom He proclaims. His ministry ends with woes directed against those who resist the kingdom. The Jews stand exposed to the wrath of God, because to whom much is given much is required. Seven times Jesus attacks Jewish teachers as "hypocrites" (23:13, 14, 15, 23, 25, 27, 29). The Greek word comes from the theater, and its use here suggests religious play-acting. As hypocrites, the Pharisees and scribes have incorporated the covenant into a competitive honor game; they preen in prayer and worship to gain honor from men.

The first woe in Matt. 23:13 assumes that the mission of the teachers of the law is to open the kingdom of heaven. Entrusted with the treasures of Torah, they were supposed to be like the scribes that Jesus describes earlier in Matthew, scribes who bring from the storehouse things old and new. Instead, they guard their treasure like dragons. Yahweh gave the law so that Israel could enjoy the blessing of God's kingdom. But the Pharisees and scribes have turned the law into a locked door. They treat the kingdom of heaven as their own personal treasure house, their own possession, and they guard it jealously.

The second woe is like unto the first (23:14): Instead of inviting orphans and widows to enter the kingdom and enjoy the blessing of land and the bounty of God, they shut them out. In Mark and Luke, the curse of verse 14 links to the story of the widow and her mite (Mark 12:38-44; Luke 20:45-21:4). Though the widow gives her small gift out of sincere devotion, Jesus sees that she is driven to give her last bit of money because of pressure from greedy Jewish teachers.[26]

The law demands justice for widows. Virtually every time widows are mentioned in the Torah, God warns against ill treatment of widows. "Cursed is he who distorts justice due to an alien, orphan, and widow," Israel repeated from Mounts

---

26 Nicholas Perrin, *Jesus the Temple* (Grand Rapids: Baker, 2010).

Ebal and Gerazim (Deut. 27:19), a curse repeated in Cranmer's Ash Wednesday liturgy. Many passages show widows being fed by the righteous. At feasts, Israel was supposed to include the orphan and widow, the stranger and Levite, and everyone else who lacked land and money – they were all supposed to be invited and included in feasts (Deut. 14:29; 16:11, 14). Widows and orphans were allowed to glean in the fields and pick grapes at the corners of vineyards (cf. Lev. 19:9-10). When Boaz first meets Ruth, he invites her to share a meal with him (Ruth 2:14). Elijah provides an ongoing supply of bread to the widow of Zarephath (1 Kings 17:8-16). Widows are supposed to be fed, but Pharisees and scribes instead manipulate the law things so that they can feed *on* widows. Scribes and Pharisees were lawyers, specialists in Torah who had the opportunity to manage the estate of widows. Jesus accuses them of using up the estate for their own purposes, of "devouring" widows' houses. They offer prayers to earn a reputation for piety and honesty, to get opportunities for managing widows' estates and bilking them out of their money.[27]

In condemning the Pharisees for their treatment of widows, Jesus repeats what He said early in His ministry: He comes to fulfill rather than abolish the law.

Jesus condemns the Pharisees and scribes for their perverse zeal in evangelism. After the exile, the Jews were energetic in mission, but Jesus charges that the Pharisees' converts are even worse than they are (Matt. 23:15). They should be gathering converts into the kingdom, but they are preparing proselytes for hell.

The next two woes condemn the teachers for their distorted attention to minutiae. The key to Jesus' teaching is His claim that the Jewish teachers have neglected the weightier matters of the law, the things that the law fundamentally aimed at, are

---

27 J. Duncan M. Derrett, "Receptacles and Tombs," *Studies in the New Testament*, Volume 5: The Sea-Change of the Old Testament in the New (Leiden: Brill, 1989) 59-70. "Pretense" translates the Greek word *prophasis*, a pun on *prophetes* (Matt. 23:29-31, 34). True prophets defended the weak. These teachers are false prophets, prophets of pretense, who pray to cover their abuse of the weak.

"judgment, mercy, and faith" (23:23). Jesus wants His disciples to obey the details of the law: "these things you should have done" (23:23). But it is possible to respect details in order to avoid the primary demand of the commandment. In the first century, the scribes and Pharisees would distort the law by their a heavy emphasis on purity regulations. They said or implied: "You can enjoy the blessings of the kingdom, provided you follow our traditions. You can enter with us into the kingdom, provided you wash fifteen times an hour. You can enjoy God's bounty, provided you are not a Gentile, or a Jew who has too much contact with Gentiles, or a tax collector." They erect boundaries and barriers that keep people out of the kingdom, instead of recognizing that the law exists to give access to the bounty of God's kingdom. Torah is Yahweh's invitation, not a barrier. Jesus implies that the Jewish leaders do not understand the Torah they claim to specialize in.

The law prohibits perjury, and emphasizes the importance of truth-telling and honesty. So does Jesus, but He accuses the Pharisees and scribes of making fine distinctions between binding and non-binding vows. To be binding, a vow had to use a certain set of words, and be directly a vow to God. If you say, "I swear by heaven," that was not *quite* a vow in God's name and thus was less binding than swearing in God's name. Once again Jesus stands for Torah against Jewish Torah-breakers.

The specific examples have to do with votive gifts. The "gold of the temple" is probably the gold of the temple treasury. If you give gold, and declare it Korban, using that specific word – "it is Korban," a devoted gift – then you were obligated; but if you swear by the temple, and do not use that specific word, then you are not obligated to keep the promise. Similarly, if you swear by an offering, with the specific word Korban, it is obligatory; but if not, then it is not. These subterfuges allow the Pharisees and scribes to escape responsibility for their words. Jesus again claims that teachers do not understand the holiness system that they teach. Gold in itself is not holy, but is only sanctified, becomes *holy* gold, because God claims it. An animal becomes holy because holiness is communicated to it by the most holy altar on which it is offered, and the altar is most holy because it is the Lord's table.

Because holy things are God's things, you cannot swear by anything without implicitly swearing by God's name. If you swear by the gold of the temple, you are implicitly swearing by the temple that sanctifies the gold; and you are in turn swearing in the Name of Yahweh who inhabits the temple. You cannot swear by the food on the altar without swearing by the altar, and by the Lord whose food it is. Practically, Jesus demands that oaths be straightforward, clear promises, backed up by an appeal to God as witness. The Pharisees abuse the law by using it to open up gaps between their words and their own commitments. "Let your Yes be Yes, and your No be No," Jesus has said, demanding coherence between words and speakers.[28]

The law prescribes tithing, and the Pharisees and scribes at least conform to the overt demand of the law. God claimed ten percent of Israel's increase (Lev. 28:30-33; Num. 18:21-32; Deut. 14:22-29), and Pharisees gave 1/10 of even the smallest seeds. Careful tithing is intended to avoid sacrilege, misusing God's holy things. The tithe belongs to Yahweh, and the Pharisees did not want to consume the Lord's portion of their mint and dill and cumin. Jesus endorses their scrupulosity. Contrary to popular opinion, Jesus' motto is *not* "Do not sweat the small stuff." He says that the smallest jot or tittle of the law will not be annulled until heaven and earth pass away. He demands obedience in the smallest things. But we cannot pursue obedience in the small things in a way that nullifies weightier matters. We cannot be scrupulous in our tithing while we are devouring widows' houses. Ignoring the small things is one form of disobedience, but obeying in small matters while ignoring the weightier matters is an even worse form of disobedience. Tithing all the little seeds while ignoring mercy, justice, and truth is not true tithing. Mercy and justice are

---

28 Garland, *Reading Matthew*.

among the goals of tithing – the tithe supports orphans, widows, aliens and others who are not able to make a living on the land (Deut. 26:12-13).

Jesus again resorts to mockery and satire. The Pharisees are worried about swallowing an unclean gnat, eating the tiniest untithed seed. But they ignore the primary source of impurity, the unclean camel at the bottom of the chalice (Matt. 23:24). They excuse injustice and lack of compassion, which is far *more* defiling. Again Jesus charges that the teachers, for all their obsession with purity, do not understand how the purity system works. Specifically, they ignore the abominations that defile the land.[29]

That same charge is behind the third pair of woes, both of which focus on the distinction and connection of inner and outer. Jesus wants His disciples to be clean inside and out (23:26). The Pharisees' error is not their concern with outward purity, purity of action. Their error is that their purity is partial, and neglects the starting point for purity. They are like vessels that are shiny on the outside, but full of impurity and death on the inside (23:25). The law sometimes uses vessels as images of men. Adam was molded from the dust of the ground, from clay. If something unclean drops into a metal pot, it has to be scoured on the inside (Leviticus 11). When it is all scoured, it becomes clean again. A clay pot that becomes unclean on the inside has to be broken to pieces. Is God concerned about pots? No, Jesus says. He is concerned about people. People are vessels, with insides and outsides, and, as the law teaches, what makes us holy or not is not the outside but the inside. The Pharisees, foolishly, scour the outside of the pot, are very concerned with exterior cleanliness, but do not take the lesson of the purity laws, the purity laws that demand inward purity as much as outward purity.

---

[29] Jonathan Klawans, *Impurity and Sin in Ancient Judaism* (Oxford: Oxford University Press, 2000). Klawans distinguishes between "ritual" and "moral" defilements. Moral impurity results from incest, idolatry, and the shedding of innocent blood, and pollutes the land. Ritual defilement results from bodily processes (menstruation, skin disease) and registers in the sanctuary. In Klawans' terms, the Pharisees major on ritual defilement while excusing moral impurity.

Jesus' comparison of the Pharisees to whitewashed tombs makes the same point, but with an ironic twist. Jesus' image of the Pharisees as "white-washed graves" is multi-dimensional. There is the obvious contrast between the apparently pure outside (white) and the inside (bones and uncleanness). In context, the Pharisees are filled with corpses by devouring other Jews, because they are cannibals, insatiable as the grave. They are about to devour Jesus (cf. Psalm 5). As Duncan Derrett points out, tombs were whitewashed at Passover to enable pilgrims to avoid contamination caused by inadvertently stepping on a grave.[30] The Pharisees wear seasonal colors; they are especially concerned with purity in the time Jesus speaks to them because Passover is coming. But the extra shine they put on themselves for Passover is like the whitewash put on graves. The irony is: their hypocritical scrupulosity about outward purity marks them as *im*pure. Jesus says, in effect: "Do you want to know how to identify tomb-teachers, cannibal-shepherds? Look for the ones who have marked themselves as tombs. Look for the white markings. And avoid them." They are death-spreading tombs.

Throughout these woes, Jesus raises the question, What is true religion? What kind of life pleases God? The Pharisees thought they were pleasing to God because they made long prayers, because they were scrupulous about tithing, because they were very careful about maintaining ritual purity. They thought they could please God by being religious.

"What fools!" we scoff. "How could they be so blind, so stupid? How could anyone think that is true religion?" We scoff, but surely we have our own substitutes. God is pleased with me because I am a deacon, or a pastor, or an elder. How could he not be pleased? I am a leader in His church! True religion is reading Augustine and Thomas, Calvin and Turretin and Bavinck, or at least setting them impressively on the bookshelf. True religion is being able to defend preterism and being able to respond to an atheist with the transcendental argument. True religion is having

---

[30] Derrett, "Receptacles and Tombs," *Studies in the New Testament*.

a Sabbath meal every Sunday, or observing a Lenten fast, or being a member of a church that has a robust liturgy. If anything is clear from Jesus' ministry, it is that religious rituals can be dangerously abused, and that religious people of this sort are an especially egregious offense against God.

Jesus teaches that we please God by doing what God requires, by keeping His commandments, by acting out a righteousness that surpasses the righteousness of the scribes and Pharisees, by pursuing righteousness from a single heart, a heart devoted exclusively to our Lord.

Jesus' message is the same as that of the prophets. Isaiah too had his litany of woe: Woe to those who join house to house; they add field to field, till they dwell alone in the midst of the land! Woe to those who call evil good, and good evil! Woe to those who are wise in their own eyes! Woe to men mighty at drinking wine! So did Jeremiah, preaching, like Jesus, in the temple, to the priests and prophets who managed the temple: "you trust in lying words that cannot profit. Will you steal, murder, commit adultery, swear falsely, burn incense to Baal, and walk after other gods whom you do not know, and then come and stand before Me in this house which is called by My name, and say, 'We are delivered to do all these abominations'? Has this house, which is called by My name, become a den of thieves in your eyes? Behold, I, even I, have seen it" (Jeremiah 7).

So did Ezekiel. False prophets "have misled My people by saying, 'Peace!' when there is no peace. And when anyone builds a wall, behold, they plaster it over with whitewash; so tell those who plaster it over with whitewash, that it will fall. A flooding rain will come, and you, O hailstones, will fall; and a violent wind will break out.'" The shepherds have turned cannibal: "Woe to the shepherds of Israel who feed themselves! Should not the shepherds feed the flocks? You eat the fat and clothe yourselves with the wool; you slaughter the fatlings, but you do not feed the flock. The weak you have not strengthened, nor have you healed those who were sick, nor bound up the broken, nor brought back what was driven away, nor sought what was lost; but with force and cruelty you have ruled them."

The prophets, Jesus, and the apostles all speak with a united voice on this point. There is no tension or contradiction. Every last one of them says that no one is more hateful to God than religious hypocrites. Every last one says what James says: "*This* is pure and undefiled religion in the sight of God, to visit widows and orphans in their distress, and to keep oneself unstained by the world."

Jerusalem, Jerusalem
Matthew 23:29-24:2

²⁹ "Woe to you, scribes and Pharisees, hypocrites! For you build the tombs of the prophets and adorn the monuments of the righteous, ³⁰ and say, 'If we had been living in the days of our fathers, we would not have been partners with them in shedding the blood of the prophets.' ³¹ So you testify against yourselves, that you are sons of those who murdered the prophets. ³² Fill up, then, the measure of the guilt of your fathers. ³³ You serpents, you brood of vipers, how will you escape the sentence of hell? ³⁴ Therefore, behold, I am sending you prophets and wise men and scribes; some of them you will kill and crucify, and some of them you will scourge in your synagogues, and persecute from city to city, ³⁵ so that upon you may fall the guilt of all the righteous blood shed on earth, from the blood of righteous Abel to the blood of Zechariah, the son of Berechiah, whom you murdered between the temple and the altar. ³⁶ Truly I say to you, all these things will come upon this generation. ³⁷ Jerusalem, Jerusalem, who kills the prophets and stones those who are sent to her! How often I wanted to gather your children together, the way a hen gathers her chicks under her wings, and you were unwilling. ³⁸ Behold, your house is being left to you desolate! ³⁹ For I say to you, from now on you will not see Me until you say, 'Blessed is He who comes in the Name of the Lord!'"

> [1] Jesus came out from the temple and was going away when His disciples came up to point out the temple buildings to Him. [2] And He said to them, "Do you not see all these things? Truly I say to you, not one stone here will be left upon another, which will not be torn down."

Jesus' curses against the scribes and Pharisees come to a climax in a lament over the doomed city of Jerusalem. He has tried to gather her to Himself, but she has refused. Like Yahweh in the days of Ezekiel (Ezekiel 8-11), Jesus abandons the temple (Matt. 24:1). Under the law, a house could become leprous, stained with mildew or other mold. When the priest discovers that the mold is spreading and cannot be stopped, the house has to be torn down (Lev. 14:33-53, esp. v. 45). Throughout His time in the temple, Jesus has been an inspecting priest. He has discovered that the temple is full of defiling mold, the Pharisees, scribes, elders, and priests who contaminate the house and the land. There is no choice: The house must be dismantled until not one stone is left on another (Matt. 24:2).

Human history is the story of innocent blood. And for much of human history, it appears that it is the story of *un-avenged* innocent blood, the story of innocent blood forgotten as soon as it stains the ground. Adam and Eve were barely outside the garden when their sons fought over worship, and the blood of a man first stained the earth (Genesis 4). Abel's blood cried out for vengeance, but the prayer seemed to go unanswered. Cain received a mark and was sent to wander in the land of Nob. Cain is punished, but he lives on, long enough to build a city over the blood of his martyred brother. Did Abel's blood ever quiet down? Did anything silence that blood? While Abel's blood shrieks from the earth, more blood is added. The sons of God marry the daughters of men, and the earth is filled with violence. Lamech threatens to avenge himself seventy-sevenfold against anyone who harmed him, stating an ethic of vengeance that was characteristic of his time. Blood cries out again, and this time God does something: He bathes the whole earth, cleanses it of innocent blood, and starts afresh.

Then the new world starts filling with blood, the clean ground again goes incarnadine with innocent blood: The blood of the male babies of Israel, drowned in the Nile River and turning that river to blood. Israel stains Yahweh's land with blood, the blood of Abner and the blood of righteous Uriah and the blood of Amasa and the blood of Saul's son Ish-bosheth, and the blood of innocent Naboth, which the Lord saw in his vineyard near Jezreel, the blood of prophets slaughtered by Ahab and Jezebel, the blood shed by Manasseh that polluted Jerusalem, the blood of the prophet Zechariah, the son of Jehoiada the priest, whom Joash slew. Jesus uses the word "blood" four times. Four is the number of the winds of heaven, the points of the compass. The earth has four corners, and by Jesus' reckoning, the four corners of the earth are covered with blood, as much as the four corners of the altar are bloody with the blood of bulls and goats

All this blood cries out from the earth. Some of it is answered, but not all of it. Will it *ever* be answered?

Even that is not the end of it. Jesus says there will be more innocent blood. He will send prophets and wise men and scribes to challenge and replace the false prophets and scribes of Judaism, but the Jews will do what their fathers have done, making sure that these wise men and scribes join Jesus in scourgings and crosses (Matt. 23:34). More blood, more shrieks from the ground. Jesus acknowledges that the Pharisees and scribes try to distance themselves from the actions of their fathers: If we had been alive in the days of our fathers, we would not have joined with them in killing prophets. Though they erect shrines to the prophets and adorn their monuments, they are "sons" of the fathers who killed the prophets, and even acknowledge this.

Jesus traps the scribes and Pharisees in their own words. If we were in the days of our fathers . . . they say. Stop right there, Jesus says. Who are you talking about? "Our fathers, the ones who killed the prophets." So, Jesus says, you admit you are their sons. Jesus wants them to renounce their patrimony, give up their heritage, renounce their fathers, hate their parents for the sake of the kingdom. "We would not be sharers in the blood of the prophets," they go on. Stop right there, Jesus says. Do not you *want* to share in the blood of the prophets? Do not you want their blood to be coursing through your veins, and spilling out in self-sacrifice? Do not you want to be sons of the prophets instead of sons of the prophets' murderers? Jews are going to be implicated in the blood of the prophets one way or another. They can either share in the blood of the prophets by joining their "fathers," their "blood ancestors" in shedding the blood of the prophets; or they can become sons of the prophets, sharing prophetic blood by joining them in martyrdom. It is blood either way.

Jesus recognizes the inner connection between persecution and glorification of the persecuted. The scapegoat who is destroyed for the sake of the people is always honored and glorified by the same people who put him to death. It is part of the story, part of the drama of scapegoating, the last act of the play. Here's how it works: Prophets turn things upside down. Prophets disrupt. Prophets throw tables around in the temples, and they silence the religious leaders. If we are going to have peace and quiet, we have got to stop the prophets, have got to silence them. Prophets get killed, *always*, always for the sake of the people, always for the sake of the peace and harmony of the community. But then, a miracle! The community quiets down, harmony is restored, the prophet who was making everyone uncomfortable is quietly in his grave, and they can get on with their lives. And they realize that killing the scapegoat is what saved the city. The scapegoat turns out to be a savior. The man who was tearing the city down was actually keeping it from falling apart. So, in the last act, the very same people who put the scapegoat out and cry out for his blood, erect monuments to him.

Most basically, Jesus predicts that the scribes and Pharisees are going to do with the ones He sends just what their fathers did to earlier messengers. They might distance themselves from their fathers, but Jesus knows that they are like their fathers: like father, like son. They will have the same bloody response to the ones Jesus sends as they have to Jesus, the One who was sent. This is part of the dynamic of history: By killing the prophets that Jesus sends, they will "fill up the measure of the guilt of their fathers" (Matt. 23:30). They will top off the vat of blood that their fathers shed. In Revelation, the city of Jerusalem is pictured as a harlot, with a chalice in her hand, a chalice filled with the blood of the saints, and she is drunk on that blood (Revelation 17). At the time of Jesus, that chalice is not yet full, but it soon will be, when the blood of the martyrs is mingled with the blood of Jesus, then the harlot city will drink, get drunk, totter, and fall.

Jesus alludes to Gen. 15:16, where Yahweh promises the land to Abram, but tells him that his seed will inherit the land many centuries later, since the "sin of the Amorites is not yet full." In Abram's day, Yahweh gives the Amorites time to fill up their guilt, waiting until it is clear that they deserve judgment. Jesus says that the same will happen to Jerusalem. They have become Amorites, and the sons are filling up the sin of their fathers, until the cup overflows. They are like their father the devil; they are murderous Satans, vipers who spread their poison and kill. Blood will return on their own heads.

The earth shrieks with blood. Will anyone hear? Jesus says "Yes." Blood cries out, and the Blood Avenger hears. The God who made the ear hears. There is a God in heaven, a Judge of all the earth. Jesus says that all this blood, from the blood of Abel to the blood of Zechariah, the A to Z of Old Covenant blood, the Genesis to Revelation of Old Testament blood – this will all have its definitive answer. All the innocent blood shed during the old time, the old creation, will be avenged.

Our first thought may be that the answer to all this blood will be the blood of Jesus, that Jesus' death will wipe the earth clean. That is true in a sense, but that is not what Jesus says here. Instead, he says that all the blood will fall on the city of Jerusalem, on the generation that sees Jesus, hears Him, rejects Him, crucifies Him, and then does it all over again to His disciples and apostles. All the blood is going to have an answer, and the answer is the destruction of Jerusalem.[31]

---

31 That this is the topic of Jesus' discourse is clear from the context. Jesus laments over Jerusalem, leaves the temple, and takes His place on the Mount of

This seems entirely unfair, entirely unjust. Surely there are righteous men outside of Jerusalem, for which Jerusalem bears no responsibility. Jesus names one: Abel. Why is Abel's blood charged to Jerusalem? Why must Jerusalem suffer because of Cain's sin? They may be like Cain, even sons of Cain; but why do the sons suffer for the sins of their fathers? Besides, all the blood shed by Israelites throughout all the centuries is going to be charged to the single generation of residents of Jerusalem. Why? How is that fair? They may put Jesus to death, and they should suffer for that; they will kill Stephen and shed the innocent blood of others. Why should they be punished for Zechariah's blood?

We can answer the second question first: Why does *this generation* suffer for the sins of all generations of Israel? The answer has to do with the character of God. On Sinai, Yahweh reveals His glory to Moses, and proclaims before Moses, "The Lord, the Lord, compassionate and gracious, slow to anger and of great mercy, who forgives iniquity but will by no means clear the guilty." This is the glory, the innermost character of God. He is slow to anger, compassionate, patient. He displays this patience throughout history. He did not send the flood as soon as Adam sinned, but waited until the earth was filled with violence. He did not destroy the Northern kingdom as soon as Jeroboam set up golden calves, or even when Ahab built an altar to Baal in Samaria. He did not destroy Judah even after the sins of Manasseh. He waits, He is patient, He gives time for repentance, He sends His prophets again and again and again, calling Israel back to Himself. And only *then* does Judah suffer for the righteous blood. He does it again with Jerusalem in the first century. God does not destroy the city after the death of Jesus. The blood of the greater Abel is not the end. He lets Jerusalem drink down Jesus' blood, and then Stephen', and then James', and then hundreds of Christian martyrs. He lets the cup fill to the brim, and when it is full, He acts, and Jerusalem totters and falls.

Olives, where He tells His disciples that the temple will be dismantled stone-by-stone. Their questions arise from that comment, and Jesus' discourse answers those questions.

When the judgment finally falls, it is clear to everyone that Jerusalem deserves what they suffer. It is clear that the sin of the Amorite has matured. Until judgment falls, Jerusalem is busy preparing her own indictment.

The answer to the second question – why should *Israel* be punished for all the blood of every righteous man from Abel onward? – has to do with the role that Israel has had among the nations. Israel is the priestly nation. That means that they are the nation that keeps house for Yahweh. His house is in their midst, and they are His household servants. It also means that they are sin-bearers among the nations. To be a priest is to bear the burdens of others than yourself. The animals of the temple sacrifices were priestly, taking the burden of the worshiper's sin, and ascending to heaven in his place. The priests, especially the high priest, also bore the burdens of the sins of the people, bearing them away on the Day of Atonement. Part of Israel's housekeeping duty is to clean up God's house, and they clean up the house by taking the dirt on themselves. Jerusalem is the city of Yahweh, the "temple-city," the priestly center of the priestly nation, and it bears the sins not only of its predecessor generations but also the sins of all the nations.

God is going to send another flood, the flood of Roman armies, to destroy the world that then was, and to make way for a new world. Blood cries out from the ground, and Jesus says it will be answered. The fall of the city of Jerusalem is not a minor event in the corner of the Mediterranean. It is not a minor disaster for a small, albeit tenacious, Semitic people. It is the end of the accumulation of blood; as much as the flood, it wipes away innocent blood and cleanses the creation.

The fall of Jerusalem is, in short, God's answer to evil. For the Bible, the question of evil is not about God's existence but about God's justice, and His attention. Why are you far off, O Lord? Where are you in time of trouble? How can you stand by, silent, when the wicked prosper, and when they get drunk off the blood of the saints? Are you asleep? How long, O Lord, will You refrain from avenging our blood?

The destruction of Jerusalem is Yahweh's answer to that question, and it answers that question not only for the saints and martyrs of the Old age, but for you. How long will the Lord let the blood of unborn babies fill our land? We do not know because God is patient, but we can be sure that the God who avenged innocent blood in AD 70 will do the same again. How long will He allow Muslims to kill Christians, or grasping Christian leaders oppress His sheep? We do not know, but the end of Jerusalem is the great historical proof that He will not let it go on forever.

The same applies closer to home: How long will God let me suffer under the harsh treatment of my boss, my wife, my husband, my parents, my kids, my teachers, my friends, my enemies? How long will He let this injustice stand? We do not know, but we know that the God who destroyed His own city, His own beloved Zion, to avenge Himself against its wickedness, will not let innocent blood cry out forever. This is the good news of the end of Jerusalem: God hears, and He will answer. Be patient and endure, in hope for the coming of God's justice.

Not One Stone
Matthew 23:37-24:14

[37] "Jerusalem, Jerusalem, who kills the prophets and stones those who are sent to her! How often I wanted to gather your children together, the way a hen gathers her chicks under her wings, and you were unwilling. [38] Behold, your house is being left to you desolate! [39] For I say to you, from now on you will not see Me until you say, 'Blessed is He who comes in the Name of the Lord!'"

[1] Jesus came out from the temple and was going away when His disciples came up to point out the temple buildings to Him. [2] And He said to them, "Do you not see all these things? Truly I say to you, not one stone here will be left upon another, which will not be torn down." [3] As He was sitting on the Mount of Olives, the disciples came to Him privately, saying, "Tell us, when will these things happen, and what will be the sign of Your coming, and of the end of the age?"

⁴ And Jesus answered and said to them, "See to it that no one misleads you. ⁵ For many will come in My name, saying, I am the Christ, and will mislead many. ⁶ You will be hearing of wars and rumors of wars. See that you are not frightened, for those things must take place, but that is not yet the end. ⁷ For nation will rise against nation, and kingdom against kingdom, and in various places there will be famines and earthquakes. ⁸ But all these things are merely the beginning of birth pangs. ⁹ Then they will deliver you to tribulation, and will kill you, and you will be hated by all nations because of My name. ¹⁰ At that time many will fall away and will betray one another and hate one another. ¹¹ Many false prophets will arise and will mislead many. ¹² Because lawlessness is increased, most people's love will grow cold. ¹³ But the one who endures to the end, he will be saved. ¹⁴ This gospel of the kingdom shall be preached in the whole world as a testimony to all the nations, and then the end will come."

As Matthew presents His life and ministry, Jesus relives the history of Israel, assuming the personas of prominent leaders of Israel. On the mountain, He is a new Moses, leading His people toward a righteousness that surpasses the righteousness of the scribes and Pharisees. When He commissions His disciples to carry on His ministry to the lost sheep of the house of Israel, He is Moses commissioning Israel to conquer the land or Joshua leading the hosts of the Lord in conquest. Sitting in a boat near the shore of the Sea of Galilee, He teaches about His kingdom in parables, like the sage king Solomon. He gathers up a small band of disciples, like Elisha, and trains them to be an alternative Israel within Israel. Finally, as we come to the last great discourse of Matthew's gospel, Jesus plays the role of the great prophets of the end of Judah.

He plays the role of Jeremiah, proclaiming judgment against the corrupt priests of the temple and warning that the temple is going to be destroyed like Shiloh. He excoriates the scribes and Pharisees for their hypocrisy, and warns them that they are being left desolate. In a vision (Ezekiel 8-11), Ezekiel sees Yahweh's glory leave His house in the temple, and Jesus likewise leaves the temple, never to return. He shakes the dust from his sandals against the house, and moves to the Mount of Olives. Like Jeremiah, Jesus laments over the city that will be destroyed. He does not gloat but sorrows that it has come to this impasse.

Most of Matthew 23 is directed against the Jewish leaders who abuse the people and break the law, all the while claiming to keep and teach the law. At the end of the chapter, Jesus widens His condemnation. He addresses Jerusalem as a whole, calling it the city that kills prophets and stones those sent to her. Jesus has come as a protective mother hen, to hide the little ones of Jerusalem from the foxes, the scribes and Pharisees. Jerusalem prefers the foxes. The capital city, representative of the whole of Israel, rejects Jesus, and so she will be left desolate, a dusty desert instead of a garden. The city that stones prophets will be left with a temple in which there is not one stone on another.

Houses have been destroyed before. Gardens have been left desolate. Stone temples have been reduced to rubble. It happened to the tabernacle at Shiloh (1 Samuel 4-6). When Hophni and Phinehas turned the tabernacle into a brothel and stole the Lord's portion of the sacrificial meat, and when Eli their father failed to restrain them, Yahweh sent the Philistines to desolate the house of the Lord there. When the kings of Judah had turned the temple of Solomon into a house of idolatry, the source of oppression and false worship, Yahweh sent in the Babylonians to desolate the house. The same will happen to Herod's temple, not yet finished when Jesus is speaking to His disciples. Jerusalem will soon shed the blood of *the* prophet, and then will kill and persecute the apostles that Jesus sends to proclaim his resurrection. That blood will be avenged.

That is the *parousia* Jesus is talking about. Many Christians take this as a reference to the final coming of Jesus, the end of the history of the old heavens and earth and the beginning of the history of the new. But *parousia* does not mean "second coming." It means "arrival" or "appearance" or "presence." Specifically, it refers to the arrival or appearance of a king who has been absent for a time. At his *parousia*, the emperor inspects, passes judgment, distributes benefices and pronounces sentences, sets things in order. That is what Jesus promises to do in and to Jerusalem.

He says it will happen within the "generation" of the disciples (Matt. 24:34). This phrase is one of the keys to understanding what Jesus is talking about. Throughout Matthew, the phrase refers to the first-century Jews who were alive for the ministry of Jesus and John. Because the Jews refuse to listen to John and to Him, Jesus compares "this generation" to children sitting in the market who refuse to dance to the tune being played (11:16). When the Jews ask for a sign, Jesus condemns the "evil and adulterous generation" that asks for a sign, and warns that Nineveh and the queen of Sheba will stand up as witnesses against "this generation" (12:39, 41). When the disciples cannot cast a demon out of a boy, Jesus laments "You unbelieving and perverted generation, how long shall I be with you?" In all these passages, "this generation" is the generation of John and Jesus, of Mary Magdalene and Herod and Salome, of scribes and Pharisees who hear and reject what John and Jesus have to say. He is not talking about the Jews throughout the ages, but about the Jews of the early first century AD.

Jesus' warning to "this generation" is not a new theme. Both John and Jesus have prophesied about an approaching catastrophe. "The ax is laid at the root of the trees," John says to the serpentine scribes and Pharisees who come to him for baptism. At the end of the Sermon on the Mount, Jesus warns the Jews that their house is threatened. He tells a parable about two men building houses. One builds on a rock, and the house stands even though a flood and storm comes against it. That house is built on the teaching of Jesus Himself, on Jesus Himself. But the house built on the sand will not stand. The Jews reject the cornerstone, the rock that would found their house. Jesus says a storm is coming, a flood of Roman troops, that will remove the house once and for all. After the disciples return from their mission trip, Jesus warns the cities of Galilee that they face judgment for rejecting the gospel of the kingdom: "Woe to you, Chorazin, Bethsaida....it will be more tolerable for Tyre and Sidon in the day of judgment than for you

. . . it will be more tolerable for the land of Sodom in the day of judgment than for you." When Jesus first begins describing His arrest, trial, and death in Jerusalem, He also assures His disciples that He will return to put things right. The Son of Man will come in glory to reward each according to his works, and "there are some standing here who shall not taste death until they see the Son of Man coming in His kingdom." After the parable of the vineyard, He warns that "the kingdom of God will be taken from you and given to a nation bearing the fruits of it. Whoever falls on this stone will be broken; but on whomever it falls, it will grind him to powder."

When I preached through Matthew, I was accused – good-naturedly, and with only slight exaggeration – of mentioning AD 70 in every sermon. My defense is that I am simply following Matthew's lead. Announcement of judgment, imminent judgment, judgment within the generation, judgment on Jerusalem and its temple, is a central thrust of Jesus' ministry. And it comes to its climax in Matthew 24. If we get this wrong, we miss a central aspect of Jesus' preaching and ministry.

Jesus' disciples ask him to describe the signs that will help them know when He is coming to take vengeance against the house (v. 3). Jesus eventually answers that question (v. 15), but first he describes events that are *not* signs of His coming but only the "beginning of birth pangs" (v. 8). He wants His disciples to stay calm, to wait in patience. When things start falling apart, they will be tempted to overreact, to think that *now* is the end. But Jesus says it is not the end. Watch out for the Apocalypticists who say, "The Dow is down two thousand points, the end is near; the US is fighting eight wars at once, the world's almost over. Temperatures are sky-rocketing, and if Trump is re-elected (or the Democrats win back Congress) it will definitely be the end." These frantic messengers are false prophets.

False prophets appeared during the last days of Judah, before Nebuchadnezzar destroyed Solomon's Temple (cf. Jeremiah), and they will be back to mislead the disciples in the first century (Matt. 24:4-5, 11-12). False prophets and false Christs will mislead many, as Satan misled Eve in the beginning. False prophets will lead an apostasy, betrayal of one Christian by another Christian, lawlessness. Because of false prophets, love will grow cold. Persecution is not the greatest threat to the church. It never is. Christians have endured unimaginable persecution since the beginning. What destroys the church is the internal enemy, the false teachers and false Christs who mislead many, encourage lawlessness, and cool the love of the saints.

In the first century context, Jesus is talking mainly about within the church. These are the false prophets and teachers who lead disciples back to Judaism in a great apostasy that nearly threatens the elect. Judaizing is the great crisis in the early church. More broadly, Jesus warns about Jewish prophets who, like the false prophets of Jeremiah's day, will encourage rebellion against Rome, assuring the people of victory when God has determined that Israel will be defeated.

False prophets will be active, but this is *not* a sign of the end. Wars, especially conflicts among Christians and between Jews and Romans, will occur before Jesus returns, but these are *not* signs of the end (Matt. 24:6). Nor are famines and earthquakes (Matt. 24:7). All this will happen, but Jesus warns His disciples not to become agitated or impatient when they happen; the disciples are not to conclude from these events that the end is near. These are the things that Christians often cite as signs of the end – wars and rumors of wars, earthquakes, famines. Jesus says the opposite. These are only the *beginning* of birth pangs.

Before the end, Christians will be persecuted (24:9). This is what Jesus means when He speaks about the "Great Tribulation." The tribulation is not the suffering of the Jews at the hands of Romans, or to the horrific violence of the Roman destruction of Jerusalem, or some crisis in the future. The tribulation that Jesus talks about is the tribulation of His people; it refers to the sufferings of early Christians ("you," see 24:9; v. 21 speaks of the same tribulation). This tribulation will put pressure on disciples to renounce Christ, and many will fall away – there will be a great apostasy during the first century, many who play Judas and betray other Christians (24:10).³² Yet even that is not a sign of the end.

There *are* signs of the end. The end will come, Jesus says, when "the gospel of the kingdom" is preached throughout the "whole world" (*oikoumene*) as a witness for nations. In the New Testament, *oikoumene* does not mean "inhabited earth" in some general sense that includes China, India, and Chile; it refers to the imperial system that Yahweh set up during Israel's Babylonian exile (cf. Daniel 2, 7). In the first century, it refers specifically to the Roman world. Caesar Augustus decrees that "all the world (*oikoumene*) should be taxed" (Luke 2:1). In Acts, Agabus prophesies that there will be a famine throughout all the "world" in the days of Claudius (Acts 11:28). The apostles are accused of turning the "world" upside down, but they have only traveled to Asia Minor and Greece at that point (Acts 17:6). Paul is accused of being a leader of Jewish sedition throughout the "world" (Acts 24:5).

Jesus is not talking about an end that comes after the whole world has been discipled, after the great commission is completed. The scope of His prophecy is more limited. Before the end comes, Jesus' kingdom will be preached from one end of the Mediterranean to another. And that happens. By the end of the apostolic generation, the gospel has been preached throughout Judea, it has gone down to Roman Africa, it has spread west to Asia Minor, Greece, finally to Rome, and Paul aspires to get to

---

32 The tribulation is linked to the false prophets and false Christs. The gospel upsets people, especially Jews. Jews respond with vicious persecution, a persecution that intensifies after the temple is finally completed in AD 64, the same year Nero turns on the Christians in Rome and blames them for the fire that burned part of the city. Some Christians become fearful, and think it is safer to be a Jew; some Christians think their fellow Christians are being too belligerent and provocative, so they switch sides and start helping the Jews and Romans find troublesome Christians. False teachers – teachers who encourage a return to the old order – intensify persecution of faithful disciples.

the very end of the "world," to Spain. Before the end comes, God opens space for the church's witness to spread throughout the imperial world.

Jesus, I've said, is talking about a specific time and place, a specific set of historical events. But this does not mean that His prophecy is irrelevant to our circumstances. This sequence happens again and again in history. This is always how God ends one world and begins another. What Jesus predicts for His disciples is precisely what happens to Him: He was delivered up for tribulation; He was killed; He was hated by all; liars brought false accusations; He was abandoned by His closest companions in the greatest crisis of His life; love grew cold, and some did not endure to the end. For Jesus, those events were not signs of defeat, of death, or frustrations of His work. They were the beginning of birth pangs (the word "sorrows" means "pain of childbirth"), the birth pangs that came to a climax on the cross and that birthed a new creation.

When God dismantles a world and forms a new one, we can expect the same things. We can expect wars and rumors of wars, conflicts and chaos – but this is not the end; we can expect great tribulation, the hatred and enmity of all who want to protect the decaying old world directed against Christians who are hoping for a new world – but this is not the end; we can expect false prophets who will mislead many; we can expect that many will fall away because of the pressure, and that even the elect will endure only with great difficulty – but this is not the end; we can expect the opportunity to witness to the ends of our world before the end comes – and *then* the end comes. This may look like death, but it is not death. It may look like the final end, but it is not the end. Even the "end" is but a beginning. We who are in Christ are privileged to share those birth pangs because we have the Spirit of Jesus, the Jesus who birthed a new world through the labor of His cross.

Abomination of Desolation
Matthew 24:15-28

[15] "Therefore when you see the abomination of desolation which was spoken of through Daniel the prophet, standing in the holy place (let the reader understand), [16] then those who are in Judea must flee to the mountains. [17] Whoever is on the housetop must not go down to get the things out that are in his house. [18] Whoever is in the field must not turn back to get his cloak. [19] But woe to those who are pregnant and to those who are nursing babies in those days! [20] But pray that your flight will not be in the winter, or on a Sabbath. [21] For then there will be a great tribulation, such as has not occurred since the beginning of the world until now, nor ever will. [22] Unless those days had been cut short, no life would have been saved; but for the sake of the elect those days will be cut short. [23] Then if anyone says to you, 'Behold, here is the Christ,' or 'There He is,' do not believe him. [24] For false Christs and false prophets will arise and will show great signs and wonders, so as to mislead, if possible, even the elect. [25] Behold, I have told you in advance. [26] So if they say to you, 'Behold, He is in the wilderness,' do not go out, or, 'Behold, He is in the inner rooms,' do not believe them. [27] For just as the lightning comes from the east and flashes even to the west, so will the coming of the Son of Man be. [28] Wherever the corpse is, there the vultures will gather."

When Jesus' disciples ask him about the sign of His coming, He begins by telling them all sorts of things that are *not* signs. Wars and rumors of wars will occur – but these are not signs of the end. Earthquakes will happen – but this is not the end. Kingdom will rise against kingdom, famines will happen – these are just the beginnings of birth pangs. False Christs and false prophets will arise – but this is not the end. Union thugs will beat up people protesting Obama's health care reform, but this is not the end. The budget deficit will go through the roof, but "do not be frightened." Why are not these events signs of the end? In part, it is because these signs are not distinctive enough to be signs of anything. When has there been a time without "wars and rumors of wars" or "kingdom fighting kingdom"? These things might increase before the real crisis comes, but they happen too regularly to be signs.

But the more important reason these are not signs is because they misconstrue how history works. History is not driven by power. History is shaped and guided by a sovereign God, and this sovereign God responds to His people. When we focus all our attention on wars and rumors of wars, on nation against nation and kingdom against kingdom, or when we think that elections and lobbying determine the direction of the political world, we are in the grip of an idolatry of power.

Jesus does predict political events. He prophesies a major upheaval in the political order of the ancient world. But the political events that Jesus thinks are most fundamental, most important, most transforming are *not* the political events we tend to focus on. The jockeying for power that took place in the Roman Empire – these were not the most important political events. The military contests between rivals for the imperial throne were not the central political events. The most important events – the most important *political* events – were taking place in Judea, in Jerusalem, in the temple of Herod. If we keep our attention on the contests for power in Rome, we are going to miss the key events. The problem is not the focus on politics. The problem is that when we focus on wars and conflicts among nations and contests for power we are not focusing on the primary *political* issues. When we focus on the conflicts between nations and powerful men or women, we are misunderstanding politics.

This is a hugely important lesson for us. Our perceptions of what is happening in the world are shaped, even determined, by what we read in the newspapers and the Internet, what we see on TV or listen to on the radio. With almost no exceptions, these sources of information about what is happening in the world are obsessed with politics. Politics is the center of the media universe, and so political debates and political events are seen as the central shaping powers of the world. Trump's election, Trump's policies, Trump's popularity, Trump's collusion or non-collusion with Russia – these are world-shaking events for the media. The media believes these are signs of basic shifts in the world. I am not merely saying that the media distorts what is happening; I am not merely saying that the media indulges fake news. It does. I am not complaining about leftist media bias, though that is true, too. I am talking about a phenomenon that cuts across the political spectrum. What does Rush Limbaugh talk about all the time? Sean Hannity, Tucker Carlson, whoever? They are all obsessed with the petty politics of Washington D.C. And that means what they think are signs of the times *are not*.

Think about this: What was the most important *political* event of the first century AD? Far and away the most important event, the most important political event, was the birth, life, death, and resurrection of Christ. The destruction of the temple was vastly more significant for the future of Western civilization and Western politics than any of the petty struggles between emperors. Yet, not a single media outlet would have caught it – not the conservatives, not the liberals. They would not have thought these events were significant because all of them – right and left – are in the grip of the idolatry of power.

Suppose every church in the country decided to start singing Psalms every week in worship? Suppose they started praying imprecatory Psalms in defense of the unborn or to turn back statism? Would that register on the news? Perhaps; it would be a story about those crazies in the Christian church. No one in the media would see it as a major event in the history of America. But it would be. It would be far more potent, far more important for the future of America or any other nation than the next election, the next Supreme Court nominee, the next piece of abysmal legislation coming out of Congress. We need to be weaned from our infatuation with politics, from our idolatry of power, which sees the distribution of political power as the key to the real world and the main force of the future.

We have to keep this in mind as we think about what Jesus means when he warns His disciples of the "abomination of desolation." Beginning around Matt. 24:14, Jesus gives signs of the end. One of these signs is the growing intensity of persecution of Christians. Another is that the gospel will be preached throughout all the *oikoumene*, the entire Roman world (see above). And then, in Matt. 24:15, He gets to the heart of things: The sign that the end has come and that Jesus' disciples should flee the city is the "abomination of desolation" spoken of by Daniel.

What is the abomination of desolation? Many Christians think that this is a future event, something done by the Antichrist or the "man of lawlessness." The Antichrist is some future world leader who will, in Paul's words, "exalt himself above all that is called God or that is worshiped, so that he sits as God in the temple of God" (2 Thess. 2:3-4). That gets the timing wrong. Jesus is talking about events that will take place within the generation of the disciples, events of the first century, not events of the twenty-first century.

Even Christians who think that Jesus is predicting the end of Jerusalem get this wrong. They say that Jesus is predicting some political or military event – the siege of Jerusalem, the Roman army surrounding the city, the destruction of the Jewish city and the Jewish temple. Political and military events are not the hinges of history, not the center of Jesus' concerns. *Israel* is the center of ancient world, and the *church* is the center of the new history that follows. The abomination of desolation that marks the end of Jerusalem is something that happens in Israel, something Israel does. The very phrase suggests this. It can be expanded as "abomination that causes desolation." The abomination is not the act of destruction itself, but an act that provokes destruction, an act that leads to destruction. The abomination of desolation is not the destruction of Jerusalem per se, but must be something that leads to the desolation of the house.

The word "abomination" has a specific meaning, typically referring to Israel's idolatry. Solomon is tempted by his many wives to worship "detestable" or "abominable" idols like Milcom,

Chemosh, Molech (1 Kings 11:5, 7; 2 Kings 23:13, 24). Isaiah condemns the people of Judah because their worship has become corrupted, and they "delight in their abominations" (Isa .66:3). Jeremiah calls on Israel to return to Yahweh by putting away their "detestable" or "abominable" things (Jer. 4:1), and in his temple sermon Jeremiah condemns the Jews for the "detestable things" that have been put into the house (Jer. 7:30). Israel, the bride of Yahweh, has become a harlot, and the Lord sees their "abominations" (Jer. 13:27), and the Lord complains that Israel has put "abominable things" in His house. Ezekiel takes a visionary tour of the temple in Jerusalem and sees the sanctuary defiled by "detestable idols" (Ezek. 5:11) that have turned the beauty of the Lord's ornaments into "detestable things" (Ezek. 7:20). Because of their "detestable things," the Lord threatens to "bring their conduct down on their heads" (Ezek. 11:21). In all these cases, the abominations are connected with idolatry, idolatry that is committed by *Israel*. Israel commits abominations when they set up idols in God's own house, when they desecrate and defile His place.

And these abominations lead to the desolation of God's house. The destruction of Herod's temple was the last in a string of temple destructions. Each is preceded by an "abomination" that leads to the desolation. Eli's sons do abominable things in the tabernacle, and Yahweh sends Philistines to destroy it (1 Samuel 2-6). Eli's sons steal the Lord's portion of the sacrifices, eating their portion before serving at the Lord's table. They have sex with the holy women, the virgins, who serve as deaconesses at the tabernacle. Those sins provoke Yahweh so that He abandons His house; they are abominations that lead to the Lord's departure, and the tabernacle's desolation. A similar thing happens in the destruction of Solomon's temple. Israel fills the temple with abominable idols (Ezek. 5:9, 11; 6:9, 11; 7:3-9; 8:6-17) and as a result Yahweh leaves the house to be desolated by the Babylonians.

We have this recurring pattern: Israel, and particularly the priests, flagrantly commits idolatry in the presence of God, in His own house; as a result, Yahweh leaves the house; and the house without the Lord is vulnerable to Gentiles, whom the Lord sends to destroy it.

Jesus refers to a specific "abomination of desolation," the one spoken of by Daniel (Dan. 11:30-34). There are several characters in that passage. The "he" and "him" refers to the "king of the north," which is a reference to the Hellenized Syrian ruler Antiochus Epiphanes who was ruling in Syria in the early second century BC. Verse 30 tells us that he will become enraged against the holy covenant, but show favor to those Jews who forsake the covenant, who loose the marriage bonds that tie them to Yahweh. As Daniel prophesies, Antiochus favored the Hellenizing Jews who were vying to take over the priesthood at the time. He removed the faithful priest and replaced him with a Hellenizing priest named Joshua, who immediately Hellenized his name to Jason.

In addition to Antiochus, there are "forces" from Antiochus. The word is literally "arm" or "shoulder." Yahweh punished Egypt with an outstretched arm, and Antiochus is going to pour out his anger against the holy covenant through arms of his own. In Dan. 11:31, it is the arms that do everything – the arms defile the sanctuary, they remove daily sacrifices, and they give the abomination of desolation. The verbs here are all plural; *they* defile/curse the sanctuary fortress, *they* end the regular sacrifice, *they* give the abomination that brings desolation. Antiochus does not do this directly. Antiochus went into the temple and plundered it; but Daniel is not referring to that. Antiochus set up an altar to Olympian Zeus, but Daniel is not talking about that either. He is not talking about what Antiochus himself did, but about what his "arms" did. Antiochus encouraged the arms but did not do what the arms did.

Now the question is, who are the "arms" of Antiochus? The structure of Daniel 11 suggests that they are the "ones who forsake the holy covenant." Verse 30 talks about these apostate Jews, and verse 32 returns to these same apostates, calling them "those who act wicked toward the covenant," whom Antiochus turns to godlessness. These apostate Jews are the ones who change the worship of the temple, forsake the Lord while they still perform His sacrifices, turn away from the covenant. They are also the arms of Antiochus in attacking the faithful Jews who resist Antiochus and the apostasy.

Thus, in Daniel 11, the sequence is this: A Gentile ruler attacks the covenant, but does it by supporting apostate Jews. The apostate Jews defile the sanctuary and commit abominations that will eventually lead Yahweh to abandon His house, and at the same time they attack those Jews who remain faithful. These abominations desolate the house.[33]

Jesus is predicting an analogous event. What event? We get a hint of what Jesus is talking about by noting the connection with Matt. 23:38: "Your house is being left to you *desolate*." Jesus has been talking about the blood shed in the city (23:34-35) and the fact that Jerusalem rejects prophets and stones those sent to her (23:37). When the Jewish persecution of Christians becomes frenzied (24:9-10, 21), then the city is about to fall. We can grasp the dynamics of the situation if we imagine what Jews were thinking as they watched the Romans approaching to lay siege. They know that victory depends on God, and they want to please God. They think that the Christians in Jerusalem are a threat to their success, a defilement. They want to purify the city so they can win the battle; the Jews act like Phinehas (Numbers 25) and slaughter the people who brought the plague. Like Jesus Himself, His disciples will become a scapegoat. Jews think killing Jesus' disciples will protect them from the Romans; what they actually do is remove whatever protection they may have had. Yahweh would have spared Sodom if there had been ten righteous people;

---

33 In 1 Maccabees, the abomination is blamed on Antiochus, who offered a pig on the altar or the erection of an image of Zeus; 1 Maccabees refers to this passage in Daniel. But 1 Maccabees is blame-shifting; the apostate Jews committed the abomination, not the Gentile king. From the Old Testament itself, we can infer that the abomination of desolation is an idolatrous act by Jews, a defilement of the Lord's house, which leads the Lord to abandon His house and leave it to the Romans to devastate and destroy.

killing the few righteous people in Jerusalem was not a good way for the Jews to protect themselves. They commit an abomination that brings desolation. They kill Jesus' followers, thinking they are doing God service.

Once the disciples see that the sanctuary has been defiled by the blood of the saints, once they see the detestable acts committed by the apostate Jews who control the temple, when the Jews lay their hands on the true temple, the church, and begin to destroy it, then the disciples are supposed to flee. When the Lord sent fire from heaven onto Sodom, Lot escaped (Genesis 19). Jerusalem is the new Sodom (Rev. 11:8), and Christians are to be like Lot, fleeing from the city in a great new exodus to the mountains (Matt. 24:16). They are not to be like Lot's wife, who looked back to her old life (24:17-18). Flight during winter would be difficult, and Christians leaving the city on the Sabbath would be conspicuous (24:20). Persecution will be so intense that even the elect will be in danger, but the Lord will mercifully interrupt it (24:22-24). In short, the destruction of Jerusalem that follows the abominable slaughter of God's holy people is the manifestation of the Son of Man (24:27). By destroying Jerusalem, Jesus will prove that He is the Lord, enthroned in heaven, ready to avenge His bride. He will leave the corpse of the city for the Roman "vultures" to finish off (24:28).[34]

Shedding holy blood is the great defilement of the city, the abomination that brings desolation. Jews were strictly forbidden to eat blood, but in the first century the city had become a bloodthirsty harlot, drinking down the blood of the saints, laying hands on Yahweh's bride and His holy people and putting them to death.

---

34 In Revelation 14-16, John sees an angel with a scythe harvesting grapes from the vines, and the grapes are put into a wine press that presses them and produces blood. Seven angels then take the blood in seven bowls and pour out the blood on the city; the harlot city drinks down the blood, and then is destroyed. The passage does not refer to the death of Jews in the destruction of Jerusalem. Many Jews died, but Revelation is focused on what happens to the Church. The blood is the blood of Christians, and the harlot city falls when she becomes drunk with the blood of the saints.

You want to know the signs of the times: Do not take the news seriously; do not believe the pundits who tell you that the future of the world depends on who is in the White House. Keep your eyes on the Church. Watch how the nations treat the holy people of God. Keep your eye on the living temple of Jesus, and you will be wise.

Cosmic Collapse
Matthew 24:29-35

> [29] But immediately after the tribulation of those days the sun will be darkened, and the moon will not give its light, and the stars will fall from the sky, and the powers of the heavens will be shaken. [30] And then the sign of the Son of Man will appear in the sky, and then all the tribes of the earth will mourn, and they will see the Son of Man coming on the clouds of the sky with power and great glory. [31] And He will send forth His angels with a great trumpet and they will gather together His elect from the four winds, from one end of the sky to the other. [32] Now learn the parable from the fig tree: when its branch has already become tender and puts forth its leaves, you know that summer is near; [33] so, you too, when you see all these things, recognize that He is near, right at the door. [34] Truly I say to you, this generation will not pass away until all these things take place. [35] Heaven and earth will pass away, but My words will not pass away.

In Revelation 12, John sees a dragon in heaven standing before a woman in labor, waiting for her to give birth to a son. The dragon plans to devour the newborn. Instead, as soon as the son is born, he is swept up to heaven, where he rules with a rod of iron. After the child's ascent, "Michael" makes war on the dragon in the sky. Michael the chief angel triumphs and the dragon falls to the earth. There he attacks the woman who gave birth to the child, but the Lord protects the woman as she flees into the wilderness. In the following chapter, the dragon, Satan, calls up two beasts, one from the sea and one from the land. The sea beast is a Gentile beast, an imperial figure, and the land beast represents Jews who lend support to Rome. Together, the dragon and the two beasts form a counterfeit Trinity, and together they begin to attack the church. Prior to this, the Jews were the main persecutors of the church, but after this point, Romans and Jews work together to destroy the new Israel.

Over the following chapters, John sees visions of the persecution of Christians. In Revelation 14, "one like a son of man" comes on a cloud with a sickle to harvest the wheat. Another angel appears, also with a sickle, to gather the ripe grapes from the vines. The plants represent the saints, the people of grain and grapes, of bread and wine, being harvested into heavenly glory by shedding their blood. From a heavenly perspective, they are being caught up into heaven by the Son of Man; from an earthly perspective, they are being slaughtered and killed by the combined powers of apostate Jews and Romans.

At the end of Revelation 14, the grapes are put into a wine press, and the wine press presses the grapes, producing the wine of God's wrath. Then angels fill bowls with wrath-wine, which they pour out onto the earth, the sea, the rivers, and the throne of the beast. When we see the city of Jerusalem, the city Babylon, the great harlot (Revelation 17), she has a chalice in her hand, and she drinks the wrath-wine that had been poured out on the earth, which is the blood of the saints. John watches as the beast she rides on turns against her and destroys her. The harlot becomes drunk with the blood of the saints, and she stumbles and falls, while the saints who have been delivered from her and from the beasts rejoice.[35]

In Matthew 24, Jesus says that the great sign of His coming will be the "abomination of desolation spoken of through Daniel the prophet, standing in the holy place" (v. 15). This is the same series of events that John saw in the vision of revelation. That abomination is not the Roman siege of Jerusalem or the destruction of Jerusalem itself. It is the event that *leads* to the destruction of

---

35 For full discussion, see my *Revelation 12-22* (ITC; London: T&T Clark, 2018).

Jerusalem, the abominable act of Israel that causes the desolation of the city by the Romans. As we saw above, the abomination of desolation is a detestable act like the sins of Eli's sons before the destruction of the tabernacle at Shiloh; it is like the abominations of Manasseh that provoked the Lord to send the Babylonians to destroy Solomon's temple.

Daniel himself prophesies about Antiochus Epiphanes, a Hellenized ruler from Syria. But Antiochus does not himself set up or place the abomination of desolation. Rather, he allies with those who forsake and act wickedly toward the holy covenant, apostates within Judaism, who desecrate the sanctuary, end the regular sacrifice, and set up the abomination of desolation. Apostate Jews and a Gentile ruler ally in opposition to the faithful Jews who resist them: "Those who have insight among the people will give understanding to the many, yet they will fall by the sword and by flame, by captivity and by plunder, for many days" (Dan. 11:33). A great tribulation comes.

Jesus' prophecy and John's Revelation are telling the same story, the story of Judaism's abominations, the fall of the temple and the destruction of the city of Jerusalem, the story of a great tribulation for the saints that marks the way into a new world. It is a repetition of the events prophesied by Daniel. But Jesus is not just talking about Jerusalem. *After* the tribulation of those days, the great tribulation in which the saints are slaughtered, the sun is darkened, the moon does not give light, and stars fall from the sky. According to Jesus, it is not just Jerusalem that falls, but the whole universe. This is one of the places where Christians have difficulty understanding how this passage can be talking about the fall of Jerusalem. We still see the sun in the sky, the moon and stars are still there, and that must mean that Jesus' prophecy has not been fulfilled yet. We are still waiting.

One response to this is to notice again what Jesus says in Matt. 24:34: "All these things" will take place before the generation of the disciples passes away. Jesus uses the phrase "this generation" in a natural way, to mean "this generation." Before the time of the apostles is over, all that Jesus prophesies will happen, including the darkening of the sun, the darkening of the moon, and the fall of the stars. Even when Jesus starts prophesying about the collapse of the universe, He is still talking about events of the first century.

The heavenly bodies were created on the fourth day of the creation week to "rule" the day and the night, and to be "for signs, for seasons, for days and years" (Gen. 1:14-16). Two things are crucial here. Heavenly lights "rule" the day and the night, and because that is their function in nature they become natural symbols of kings and political powers generally. Kings are luminous, glorious, exalted. Kings through the centuries have worn robes adorned with stars to show that they are high and lifted up. Louis XIV was called the "Sun King." Even in the modern age, when we have largely forgotten this symbolism, heavenly bodies function as symbols of powers. Many, many of the world's flags have stars, a sun, or a moon. To say that the sun is darkened means that some king, some ruler, some nation is going to lose power. To say that the stars fall is to say that rulers are "falling" from their high position.

Heavenly lights are also placed for seasons, days, and years. They mark time. Especially before we learned to control electricity, days were marked by sunrise and sunset. Under the Old Covenant, Passover was the cornerstone of Israel's festival calendar, and the time of Passover was determined by the moon. Astronomical phenomenon function as clocks. When Jesus says that the sun is going to be dark, he is saying that someone's "day" is coming to an end; their time is over; their clock is stopped.

This symbolism is behind Old Testament prophecies that refer to sun, moon, and stars in precisely the same terms as Jesus does. Isaiah describes the fall of Babylon by saying that "stars of heaven and their constellations will not flash forth their light; the sun will be dark when it rises and the moon will not shed its light" (Isa. 13:9-10). In Ezekiel's lament over Egypt, the Lord says that He "covers the heavens and darkens the stars," that He will "cover the sun with a cloud and the moon will not give its light" and the shining lights in the heavens will go dark (Ezek. 32:7-8). Prophets talk about the end of a political power, the world of Babylon or the world of Egypt, as if it were the end of the world. This is metaphor, but it is also true: When Babylon fell, a world collapsed.

So Jesus is not talking about the collapse of the solar system, but the "eclipse" of a great power. The question is: Which great power? Fundamentally, the Olivet Discourse is about the fall of Jerusalem. But how can this event be described as the end of the world? Jesus prophesies a series of events that took place in a small corner of the Roman world. Herod's temple was magnificent, but there were spectacular temples elsewhere. Jerusalem was an ancient city, but it was not the center of the empire. Surely, the events of AD 70 in Judea do not warrant the kind of inflated language Jesus applies to them. The fall of Babylon was a major historical event; but talking about the fall of Jerusalem as if it were an event of the same magnitude seems to be nonsense.

We might think that Jesus is prophesying the shake-up of Rome in 68-69. He does have that in view, but Jesus sees the shakeup in Rome as an *aftershock* of a greater shakeup, the collapse of the universe, which was centered in Jerusalem. The epicenter of the earthquake was not Rome but Jerusalem. Jesus reflects the biblical perspective on the centrality of Jerusalem. According to Scripture, Jerusalem is a "great city" (Rev. 11:8; 16:19) that "reigns over the kings of the earth" (Rev. 17:18). Jerusalem is "Babylon the great" (Rev. 17:5), and her fall is like the collapse of the heavens. Jerusalem is the power that reigns over the world: "The scepter shall not depart from Judah" (Gen. 49:10; cf. Psalm 60:7, 108:8). She is the false "king of kings" whom Jesus overthrows (Rev. 17.18, 14).[36]

---

36 Thanks to my friend James R. Rogers for this suggestion. In a private communication, Jim writes, "To be sure, for most of [Jerusalem's] history this power was latent (or ceded away) because of her faithlessness – just like Adam ceded it, but that does not change her official (or latent) status as ruler of the world. Jerusalem's 'political' status as God's king on earth resolves into union with her liturgical setup and practice – the heavens are located in the temple in Jerusalem (or at least the firmament in which the stars are set and the angels fly). So Jerusalem's destruction is, as it were, the exemplary example of the whole sun & moon darkened/stars falling images – it all falls in Jerusalem; it is 'the' fall. After

But there is another dimension to this. Jesus predicts an earthquake that will reverberate across the Mediterranean world. By the time of Jesus and Paul, Jews were spread all over the Mediterranean world. They were not all in Palestine. When the Jewish War began in the mid-sixties in Judea and Jerusalem, Jews and Gentiles began fighting all over the Roman world. As Madden writes:

> As news of the violence in Jerusalem spread [in 66], the killing was mirrored across the region and then the empire.... Diaspora Jews sympathized with their coreligionists, but few would condone this sort of slaughter. And yet, in some places in the Middle East, Jews celebrated the massacre of Romans. Several cities with large Jewish populations saw open warfare between them and their Gentile neighbors....In places like Alexandria, Caesarea Maritima, Caesarea Philippi, Tyre, and Ascalon, the Jews had the worst of it, with many thousands killed. In other places like Sebaste, Gaza, Anthedon, Gaba, and the Decapolis it was the Jews who won out, massacring the Gentiles.

After six thousand Romans were killed in Caesarea Maritima, the citizens of Damascus "poured into the streets killing Jews wherever they could find them."[37]

More fundamentally, after the exile, Jerusalem and Judea were nestled within a larger imperial political structure, a succession of empires climaxing with Rome (cf. Daniel 2, 7). In Daniel 2, Daniel interprets Nebuchadnezzar's dream of a great statue made of four different metals. The metals represent empires: Nebuchadnezzar and Babylon are the head of gold, Persia the chest of silver, Greece the belly and thighs of bronze, and Rome the legs of iron. A stone cut without hands hits the statue and the statue collapses

---

all, if Israel is God's firmament-people – and v. 30 establishes that they are (in this argument, at least) – then the obvious 'place' where you'd gather a firmament-people when they're shaken out of their place and falling is on the 'winds from one end of heaven to the other.'"

37   Thomas F. Madden, *Empires of Trust: How Rome Built – And America Is Building – A New World* (London: Penguin, 2008) 273.

into dust, while the stone grows up into a mountain that fills the earth. Daniel 7 presents the same history as a sequence of four beasts, which are eventually tamed by a New Adam, the Son of Man, who ascends to the ancient of days to receive authority and dominion. Jerusalem was the ruler of the kings of the earth, the great city that led the world, but after the exile Jerusalem was, by God's design, set within an imperial structure that the Bible calls the *oikoumene*. When Jerusalem fell, that whole world fell with it. The entire geopolitical system collapsed. It is no accident that the city of Rome experienced a shake-up during the years leading up to the destruction of Jerusalem. The Julio-Claudian dynasty ended with the suicide of Nero (AD 68), after which Rome was engulfed with the chaos of the "Year of the Four Emperors" (AD 69). The Roman Empire continued for centuries to dominate the Mediterranean, but its role as protector of Judaism ended.

All this is a prelude to the coming of the Son of Man. There is no break in the text, no leap forward in Jesus' prophecy from the first century to the end of time. Jesus says that "all these things" will happen before the generation is over, and one of the things that happens before the generation ends is that the "sign of the Son of Man will appear in the sky" and angels will gather the elect from the four winds. To get verse 30 right, we have to notice an ambiguity, which appears in both Greek and English. The sign of the Son of Man in heaven could mean that the *sign* is in heaven, or it could mean that the sign is about the *Son of Man* being in heaven. Either reading works, but the latter is preferable. The quotation from Daniel 7 at the end of the verse does not refer to the Son of Man coming down from heaven, but the Son of Man ascending *to* heaven. Jesus prophesies that there will be a sign that the Son of Man has indeed ascended to receive all authority and power, that He is enthroned. The sign, I think, is the fall of Jerusalem itself. The destruction of the city and temple is the great demonstration that all authority and power has been given into the hands of the Son of Man. It is the vindication of the Christ.

Who is the Son of Man? Obviously, Jesus. The fall of Jerusalem is a sign that Jesus the Son of Man is enthroned in heaven (Matt. 24:30). The fall of Jerusalem proves that Jesus is a true prophet, since His prophecy about the fall of the city came true. It demonstrates that He has power to avenge Himself against the powers that oppose Him. But in Daniel the phrase "Son of Man" has a corporate meaning (cf. Dan. 7:13-14, 18, 22). The Son of Man is identical to, or linked with, the saints of the most high, who also receive authority and dominion. If the fall of Jerusalem is a vindication of Jesus, it is also a vindication of His people. It is proof that Jesus is enthroned; and it is proof that His people are enthroned with Him in heavenly places. This is one of the central lessons we learn from the fall of Jerusalem. It is a sign that Jesus is faithful to His Word, and faithful to His people.

It is a sign that exemplifies both the promise and demand of the gospel. The promise is that Jesus is trustworthy. The fall of Jerusalem proves that Jesus' words can be trusted. And, for us, it is a sign that Jesus intends to raise up His people to share in His rule. At the same time, it exemplifies the demand of the gospel. Jesus entered His rule by enduring the "great tribulation" of the cross. Jesus came to His glory through suffering, and Jesus is saying that the same is true for us. The humble will be exalted and the elect will be saved; but those who will be saved are those who endure, bearing the cross to the end.

Be on the Alert
Matthew 24:36-51

³⁶ "But of that day and hour no one knows, not even the angels of heaven, nor the Son, but the Father alone. ³⁷ For the coming of the Son of Man will be just like the days of Noah. ³⁸ For as in those days before the flood they were eating and drinking, marrying and giving in marriage, until the day that Noah entered the ark, ³⁹ and they did not understand until the flood came and took them all away; so will the coming of the Son of Man be. ⁴⁰ Then there will be two men in the field; one

will be taken and one will be left. [41] Two women will be grinding at the mill; one will be taken and one will be left. [42] Therefore be on the alert, for you do not know which day your Lord is coming. [43] But be sure of this, that if the head of the house had known at what time of the night the thief was coming, he would have been on the alert and would not have allowed his house to be broken into. [44] For this reason you also must be ready; for the Son of Man is coming at an hour when you do not think He will. [45] Who then is the faithful and sensible slave whom his master put in charge of his household to give them their food at the proper time? [46] Blessed is that slave whom his master finds so doing when he comes. [47] Truly I say to you that he will put him in charge of all his possessions. [48] But if that evil slave says in his heart, 'My master is not coming for a long time,' [49] and begins to beat his fellow slaves and eat and drink with drunkards; [50] the master of that slave will come on a day when he does not expect him and at an hour which he does not know, [51] and will cut him in pieces and assign him a place with the hypocrites; in that place there will be weeping and gnashing of teeth."

Evangelicals are often tedious when they talk about eschatology, sometimes downright silly. In trying to figure out what is going to happen and when, Bible students pore over the text of Scripture, scrutinizing details, paying close attention to numbers and dates, connecting one Scripture with another. You can find a lot of stuff in the Bible if you dig around in the right way. A video on YouTube tries to prove that Jesus named the Antichrist, and that his name is Baraq Bamah. In Luke 10, Jesus says that He saw Satan falling like lightning, and the word for "lightning" in Hebrew is *baraq*; Satan falls from heaven, which is a high place, and the word for high place is *bamah*. QED. I am not making this up, and the guy is not joking.

This and other sorts of speculations are easy to mock, and they are badly wrong in many ways. They get the text wrong; they ignore the historical context of the passages they are reading; they make all kinds of false assumptions – like the assumption that the Bible teaches that there is a single person that can be called

Antichrist with a capital A, as if it were a personal name. Worst of all, these types of speculations distract people from the central thrust of Jesus' teaching about eschatology.

But in criticizing these sorts of readings of the Bible, we can easily slip into errors ourselves. We can slip into the view that God is indifferent to specific details, and especially about details of time. We can slide into sloppiness. When we criticize people who want to figure out the prophetic timetable, we need to acknowledge that at times the Bible *does* give us a prophetic timetable.

When God appeared to Abram and confirmed the covenant with a sacrifice of animals and an appearance like a burning furnace, He told Abram that his people would be given a land after four hundred years of slavery. Abram was not supposed to say, "Well, it might be four hundred, it might be forty, it might be four thousand. The timeless God is not interested in numbers and chronologies." He was supposed to believe that it would be 400 years from the time Yahweh spoke to Abram and the time He brought Abram's descendants out of slavery in Egypt. And it was! When Jeremiah told the people of Judah that they would be in exile for seventy years, he meant seventy years. That is what Daniel assumes, and in Daniel 9, he has been studying Jeremiah, finds that prophecy, realizes that the seventy years is almost fulfilled, and begins getting ready for the return from exile. By the end of the chapter, Daniel has learned from Gabriel that the Lord is extending the exile another period of seventy, this time "seventy weeks," seventy weeks of years, or four hundred and ninety years. That number too was to be taken seriously, and the Jews did. Apocalyptic speculations went into high gear as the clocked ticked up to four hundred and ninety years from Daniel's time. Biblical prophecies sometimes names particular people, players in the future history of Israel. Isaiah names Cyrus as the "Anointed One" who will deliver Judah from exile, the new Solomon who will sponsor the building of the temple. The Gentile Emperor will be God's new agent. Isaiah expected the people to be looking for a real person named Cyrus.

C. S. Lewis once said that if God did not like things, He would not have made so many of them. We can say something similar here: If God did not care about details, why did He include so many? If he did not care about timing, why does the Bible have so many dates? The problem with prophecy fanatics is not attention to detail. The problem is that they get the details wrong.

We have one such detail in this text. Unlike passages in Genesis, Jeremiah, and Daniel, this detail does not give us a specific time period. It is the opposite. Jesus says that He is *not* going to tell His disciples the exact day and hour when all these things are going to happen, and He will not tell them because He does not know it. Other prophecies are similar. Daniel is told to "seal up the book" because the prophecies will not take place for a long time. When Jesus appears as the slain Lamb at the beginning of Revelation, He receives a sealed book and begins opening the seals. That means that the prophecies delivered to Daniel are about to come to pass.[38]

The main question has to do with the event Jesus has in view. Is He talking about the destruction of Jerusalem, or has the topic shifted? Some commentators believe that Jesus starts talking about a different event in Matt. 24:36. Up to this point, they say, Jesus prophesies events of the first century, the events surrounding the destruction of Jerusalem. Verse 34 is the cutoff. Everything up to verse 34 is about the destruction of Jerusalem and the events leading up to that event. Then Jesus shifts ground, and in verse 36, instead of talking about the first century, he turns His attention to the end of the world, the final coming of the Son of Man at the end of history.

---

38 How can Jesus, who is the incarnate Son of God, not know something that His Father knows? It seems to have something to do with His humble earthly state, since in Revelation Jesus the Lamb opens the book and unleashes its contents. There are complicated Christological mysteries here, but we should say at least this: The Son of God became true man, and real human beings do not know everything. Jesus' ignorance is the same problem as His weakness, neediness, fatigue, and all His other human experiences. Just as the Son of God really experienced all these things in the flesh, so the Son of God also experienced ignorance.

Commentators say this for several reasons, mainly because Jesus seems to contradict himself. On the one hand, Jesus gives a number of signs of the end. When the persecution of Christians intensifies, when the gospel of the kingdom reaches the end of the *oikoumene*, when the abomination of desolation appears – then the end comes. The disciples can predict the end because they have signs. Verse 36 seems to contradict that. Instead of saying that the disciples can know when the Son of Man is coming, Jesus says that they *cannot* know the day or hour, that even the Son does not know the day or hour. Either Jesus contradicts Himself, or He begins talking about a new event.

This is not, however, a contradiction. In the first section of the Olivet Discourse, Jesus tells His disciples what events will precede the end of Jerusalem, and He tells them that these events will take place within the generation of the apostles (v. 34). He gives them a general chronological context for His coming, and tells them the signs that will alert them that His coming is near. But He does not tell them the year or even the decade when they will occur (v. 36, 42, 44). If He told them an exact day and hour, they could have acted like college students, coasting along until that day and hour arrived and then scrambling to get ready. Jesus does not give them that luxury. He does not allow the disciples to relax until the mid-sixties; instead, He tells them to be *constantly* on the alert (v. 42).

In one sense, Jesus does change His focus a bit. The "coming" of the Son of Man in Matt. 24:30 is His coming up to heaven to receive authority and dominion (cf. Dan. 7:13). Jesus still uses the word *parousia* after Matt. 24:37, but this later arrival is a descent, not an ascent. Jesus does not talk about coming on clouds in verse 37, but about the Son of man coming as He came in the time of the flood, coming to select one man from the field and one woman from the mill and leaving others. Earlier, He came on clouds up to the ancient of days, but now He is coming like a thief in the night, to break into the homes of people on earth.

Jesus compares the situation preceding the coming of the Son of Man to two other historical events. It will be like the coming of the flood (cf. 2 Pet. 3:1-7). We know from Genesis that the world was full of violence before the flood, and that the flood came to destroy the violent and to renew the creation. That is not the kind of situation Jesus describes. Instead, He talks about people eating and drinking, marrying and giving in marriage. Life seems to be going on as normal, and people are not aware that anything unusual is coming until the day the flood comes and takes them all away. The flood came suddenly to such people, and the coming of the Son of Man, when it happens, will happen suddenly and catch many unawares. People did not *have* to be taken unawares by the flood. Noah was a "preacher of righteousness," calling people to repentance and spending a century building a boat (2 Pet. 2:5). They had plenty of warning, but they ignored the warnings and kept on as if everything was going to be fine, as if the world were in a steady-state from now until doomsday. The coming of the Son of Man is like the flood in *this* respect – both are sudden and surprising to the inattentive.

The comparison with the flood is remarkable. The flood was a worldwide catastrophe. It destroyed cities and civilizations; it wiped out fields and vineyards and olive groves; it killed the people who lived on earth, with only Noah and his family saved. It wiped out one world and brought in another, but Jesus says that His coming will be like this. The destruction of Jerusalem will be the end of the world that then was, and will lead to the formation of a new world.

The other event that Jesus refers to is the exile (Matt. 24:40-41). Many Christians believe that verses 40-41 are about the "rapture." Sometime close to the beginning of the millennium, it is believed, Christians will suddenly be sucked up from the earth into heaven. Christians differ on precisely when this happens – before the tribulation, during the tribulation, after the tribulation. The New Testament does talk about a kind of rapture. People will be "caught up in the air" and will ever be with the Lord. As we saw in our brief review of Revelation 12-18 above, the grain and grapes are "raptured" from the earth. In that case, the rapture is not a sudden ascension of the saints, but persecution and bloody death. *Martyrs* are caught up into the air to be with the Lord forever. That is the rapture, and it is the *same* as the tribulation.

When Christians today talk about the rapture, they think of it as an event in the future. That is not what Jesus is talking about. He draws on Old Testament descriptions of exile. When Nebuchadnezzar invaded Judah, he took many Jews to Babylon, but left some of the poorest in the land to keep the vineyards and fields (2 Kings 24:14; 25:12; Jer. 40:7; 52:16). In the first century, Jesus says, some men will be taken from their fields to serve as slaves; some women will be taken from their mills to "grind" for their captors (for "grinding" as a sexual metaphor, see Job 31:10). Jesus is talking about the capture of some who are in Israel at the time of the Roman invasion; He is talking about the death of some of the people who are alive at the time of His first-century *parousia*.

The New Testament frequently says that the Son of Man is coming like a thief (1 Thess. 5:2, 4; 2 Pet. 3:10; Rev. 3:3; 16:15). Thieves do not announce themselves beforehand, and only an alert homeowner will be ready when they come. In Joel, invading armies come like thieves (Joel 2:6), and Zechariah sees a vision of a curse that slips into the houses of the wicked like a thief (Zech. 5:4). As the angel of death slipped into Egyptian houses to slaughter firstborn sons, so the Son of Man will slip in to take one and leave another. The point is that the Son of Man will come unannounced, suddenly, surprisingly, for the people who do not listen to Jesus and take His warnings and predictions seriously. The disciples themselves should not be caught by surprise. They are to be prepared, because Jesus told them ahead of time.

Matthew 24 ends with the first of three parables about His coming, that lead up to the judgment scene in Matthew 25. Jesus does not tell His disciples when He is coming, and as it turned out, the coming of the Son of Man took place four decades after Jesus ascended. The parables address the problem of delay.

Forty years is a long time. Forty years ago, we were still living in the Seventies, still wearing bell-bottoms; forty years ago, Jimmy Carter was President, and Reagan was just a gleam in conservatives' eyes; forty years ago, many of you were not alive, and your parents were not married because they were still kids. Many alive today cannot remember anything from forty years ago. But it was forty years between the time Jesus spoke these words and the destruction of Jerusalem. Forty years is time for a generation to leave the stage, and a new generation to come. Forty years was the time that the Exodus generation died off in the wilderness, and a new generation took their place and began the conquest.

Here's the problem: How can the disciples maintain the intensity of their alertness over forty years? Jesus said, Be alert; I am coming like a thief. Jesus said, Persevere, because I will come to avenge your blood. But years passed, then decades passed, and there was no coming of the Son of man. Over the decades between the ascension of Jesus and the destruction of Jerusalem, Christians became impatient. "Where is the promise of His coming?" is the question Peter addresses in his second letter (2 Pet. 3:4). The "delay" tempted Christians to shrink back, and some reverted to Judaizing (cf. Hebrews).

Jesus is the master in His parable, who leaves His disciples in charge of His house during His absence (Matt. 24:45-51). He warns them not to mistreat their fellow servants, or to indulge themselves (Matt. 24:49). If they do, they will be among those who are taken by surprise when the thief comes. They should not use the apparent delay as an excuse to mistreat one another.

This parable is perennially relevant to the church because Jesus reigns; He rules over the rise and fall of powers, the increase and decrease of civilizations. He is the Word who brought this creation into existence, and He is the Word who tells the story of every world, the Alpha word who speaks the beginning of new world, and the Omega word who pronounces The End. He *does* come, again and again. He *does* judge, over and over throughout history. But He does not judge on *our* timeline, or according to our wishes. He judges rightly, always at the right time. And we must resist the temptation to complacency, the temptation to think that the Master is not coming back for a long time, the temptation to think we can get away with mistreating our brothers. We do not want to be taken by surprise when the Master comes, and we do not want to be sent to the place of hypocrites. The way to avoid that is to be diligent in good works, serving and not abusing others, alert, vigilant, waiting always for the righteous judgment of the righteous Judge who judges all the earth.

Parables of the Kingdom
Matthew 25:1-30

¹ "Then the kingdom of heaven will be comparable to ten virgins, who took their lamps and went out to meet the bridegroom. ² Five of them were foolish, and five were prudent. ³ For when the foolish took their lamps, they took no oil with them, ⁴ but the prudent took oil in flasks along with their lamps. ⁵ Now while the bridegroom was delaying, they all got drowsy and began to sleep. ⁶ But at midnight there was a shout, 'Behold, the bridegroom! Come out to meet him.' ⁷ Then all those virgins rose and trimmed their lamps. ⁸ The foolish said to the prudent, 'Give us some of your oil, for our lamps are going out.' ⁹ But the prudent answered, 'No, there will not be enough for us and you too; go instead to the dealers and buy some for yourselves.' ¹⁰ And while they were going away to make the purchase, the bridegroom came, and those who were ready went in with him to the wedding feast; and the door was shut. ¹¹ Later the other virgins also came, saying, 'Lord, lord, open up for us.' ¹² But he answered, 'Truly I say to you, I do not know you.' ¹³ Be on the alert then, for you do not know the day nor the hour.

¹⁴ For it is just like a man about to go on a journey, who called his own slaves and entrusted his possessions to them. ¹⁵ To one he gave five talents, to another, two, and to another, one, each according to his own ability; and he went on his journey. ¹⁶ Immediately the one who had received the five talents went and traded with them, and gained five more talents. ¹⁷ In the same manner the one who had received the two talents gained

two more. ¹⁸ But he who received the one talent went away, and dug a hole in the ground and hid his master's money. ¹⁹ Now after a long time the master of those slaves came and settled accounts with them. ²⁰ The one who had received the five talents came up and brought five more talents, saying, 'Master, you entrusted five talents to me. See, I have gained five more talents.' ²¹ His master said to him, 'Well done, good and faithful slave. You were faithful with a few things, I will put you in charge of many things; enter into the joy of your master.' ²² Also the one who had received the two talents came up and said, 'Master, you entrusted two talents to me. See, I have gained two more talents.' ²³ His master said to him, 'Well done, good and faithful slave. You were faithful with a few things, I will put you in charge of many things; enter into the joy of your master.' ²⁴ And the one also who had received the one talent came up and said, 'Master, I knew you to be a hard man, reaping where you did not sow and gathering where you scattered no seed. ²⁵ And I was afraid, and went away and hid your talent in the ground. See, you have what is yours.' ²⁶ But his master answered and said to him, 'You wicked, lazy slave, you knew that I reap where I did not sow and gather where I scattered no seed. ²⁷ Then you ought to have put my money in the bank, and on my arrival I would have received my money back with interest. ²⁸ Therefore take away the talent from him, and give it to the one who has the ten talents. ²⁹ For to everyone who has, more shall be given, and he will have an abundance; but from the one who does not have, even what he does have shall be taken away. ³⁰ Throw out the worthless slave into the outer darkness; in that place there will be weeping and gnashing of teeth.'

Jesus finishes His prophetic discourse with a series of three parables – the parable of the wicked slave (24:45-51), the parable of the ten virgins (25:1-13), and the parable of the talents (25:14-30). Each of these is about expectation, and each describes how wise and faithful disciples respond to their master's delay. Though these parables match as parables about the delay of the Master's coming, and the assessment that the Master will bring when He comes, they also form a sequence. Jesus moves from a story about household slaves or servants, to one about the virgin bridesmaids who await the coming of the bridegroom, to one about a master who gives goods into the hands of his servants to invest and use. In the first parable, the slaves are simply keeping house, preparing food at the proper time, keeping thing together. In the last they are called to use the goods that the Master gives them while He is gone on the journey. By the end of the sequence, they are no longer serving at the table, but they are putting the Master's goods to work in the world.

It is a progression from priestly to kingly work. The first parable is about household servants, and the "house" is a temple setting. Jesus' "house" is His temple, and the servants in the parable are implicitly priests. Their main work is to prepare food at the proper time; they are table servants, butchers, and bakers. That is essentially what the priests were, preparing food for the daily, weekly, and festival sacrifices, serving the house as Yahweh's household servants. Jesus warns His household servants that they need to be diligent in their household service. If they get drunk – something forbidden to priests (cf. Leviticus 10) – the Master is going to surprise them and cut them down. If they become like the rebellious son that Deuteronomy 21 talks about, they are going to suffer the consequences. If they fail to keep up their household service well, they will become sacrifices, cut in two by the Master.

The slaves in the final parable are not doing household work. They are given a huge amount of money. A talent is equivalent to six thousand denarii, or twenty years wages for a day laborer. Priests could be wealthy, but their wealth was in treasuries inside the house. In the Old Testament, money is mostly associated with kings in the Bible (cf. 2 Sam. 12:30; 1 Kings 9:14; 10:10, 14; etc.).

Jesus tells His disciples that they must serve faithfully as priests in His house, and faithfully work as kings in the world.

These parables are directed to the disciples of Jesus. He erects a new house, a new temple, and leaves His apostles and their followers in charge of the house. He gives His disciples the great privilege of being household servants of the Great King. He puts goods of enormous value into their hands, a gospel that is the priceless pearl. And in the time between His departure and His return, they are called to perform their priestly and royal responsibilities.

The parable of the virgins ends with a warning to "be on the alert" (25:13), which echoes the warning that Jesus gave in Matt. 24:42. That *inclusio* brings the parable of the virgins into the context of the prophecy about AD 70. This parable too is about the delay between Jesus' departure in the ascension and His "return" a generation later for the wedding feast (25:1; cf. Rev. 19:1-10).

Like the first parable, the symbolism of the parable suggests a temple setting. The temple was the "trysting place" of Yahweh and Israel. The temple was built on a threshing floor, and in Ruth the threshing floor is the place where Ruth and Boaz meet at night (cf. 2 Chron. 3:1 with Ruth 3). The temple is the meeting place for Yahweh the Husband with Israel His bride. Further, there were young women, virgins, at the tabernacle who assisted in the work of the priests. Exodus mentions that they donated mirrors to make the bronze altar (Exod. 38:8), and Jephthah's daughter ascended to the tabernacle to serve. Hophni and Phinehas, the sons of Eli, slept with the virgin women who served the tabernacle at Shiloh.

Passover provides another layer of background to the parable. The original Passover occurred at midnight, when the angel of death swept through Egypt to kill all the firstborn in the land, apart from those within houses on which blood had been shed. Earlier, Jacob had left the house of Laban, where he had been a virtual slave, in the middle of the night. The deliverance in the book of Esther also takes place at midnight, and several events in the book of Acts take place at midnight. As at Passover, the Bridegroom of the parable arrives at midnight (Matt. 25:6; Exod. 12:29; cf. Est. 6; Acts 16:25; 27:27-44). He comes as a deliverer. The coming of the Bridegroom, the Son of Man, is a Passover event; He will come as the angel of death to carry out His threat against Jerusalem, the new Egypt. He comes as the deliverer of His people, those who have kept themselves pure virgins in anticipation of His arrival.

The most important background to this parable comes from within Matthew's gospel itself. We can understand some of the important features of this parable when we see how it links back to the end of Matthew 7. In both passages, Jesus refers to a door that must be entered. In Matthew 7, He warns, "Enter by the narrow door; for the door is wide and the way is easy, that leads to destruction, and those who enter it are many. For the door is narrow and the way is hard, that leads to life, and those who find it are few." In Matthew 24-25, the door image reappears. On the day of the Bridegroom's arrival, Jesus will admit those properly prepared (25:10; 7:21). But then the door will be closed; the opportunity to enter will come to an end, and the foolish will find themselves standing outside.

Likewise in both passages, Jesus contrasts "wise" and "foolish," terms that appear together only in these passages in Matthew. In Matthew 7, Jesus contrasts wise and foolish builders; the wise builders are those who hear and act on His words, and their house stands. The foolish builders may hear Jesus' words, but they do not *do* them, and their house will fall. In Matthew 25, Jesus contrasts the wise and foolish virgins, the wise ones who have an extra supply of oil for the bridegroom's coming and the foolish who are unprepared. Matthew 7 and Matthew 25 both include the sentence "I never knew you," spoken first to those who performed signs but did not obey, then to the foolish virgins. At some point, the door closes, and the unprepared, foolish virgins are left outside. Near the beginning of the Sermon on the Mount, Jesus says that His disciples are the light of the world, like a lamp on a stand. The lamp and the light symbolize the good works that the disciples of Jesus should do so that men will see their works and glorify the Father. Lacking good works, the foolish virgins are left in the dark.

This helps us determine what distinguishes the wise and foolish virgins. They are supposed to have a continual supply of oil to keep their lamps lit; and Jesus earlier said that the disciples' good works are lights. The virgins without oil are the foolish builders, who listen to Jesus but do not do what He says. The difference between virgins who enter the wedding and those who are locked out is whether or not they do the works of Jesus, whether their light is shining before men. Jesus emphasizes that the virgins need to be *doing* something, like the servants in the other parables, but this is not a form of "works righteousness." Oil symbolizes the Spirit, which energizes us to do good works. Without the oil of the Spirit, the virgins have no light to shine, nor do we. What keeps our light shining is a continual fresh supply of the Spirit, whom the Father freely gives to those who ask.

The issue with this parable of the talent is not so much about what it means but when it happens: Is Jesus still talking about the time between His departure and the "settling of accounts" in AD 70? Or is He talking about the entire period between His ascension and the final judgment? There seem to be good reasons to think that Jesus changes topic and begins to talk about His final coming for the last judgment. First, as noted, Matt. 25:13 matches Matt. 24:42, and thus closes out the section about the "day and hour" that is coming within "this generation." Second, the master in this parable is gone for a "long time" (25:19). Jesus appears to be talking about the whole age between the ascension and the final judgment.

But these considerations are not decisive. There is an *inclusio* between Matt. 25:13 and Matt. 24:42, but there is *also* an *inclusio* in Matt. 24:51 and Matt. 25:30. Both of those verses speak of a place where worthless, rebellious slaves are sent, where there is "weeping and gnashing of teeth." That suggests that the parable of the household slaves is linked to the parable of the slaves with the talents, and that hints that the two parables are addressing the same topic. That *inclusio* also links the parable of the virgins to the parable of the talents; if the first is about the time before AD 70, the second should be as well. The "long time" could well be a description of the forty years between Jesus' ascension and the destruction of Jerusalem. A great deal can happen in forty years, and when something that you eagerly await is delayed for forty years, it is a *very* long time.

Besides, verse 14 does not seem to provide enough of a transition. Matt. 25:1 compares the kingdom of heaven to virgins with their lamps awaiting the coming of the bridegroom; the "kingdom of heaven will be comparable to ten virgins." Matt. 25:14, which introduces the next parable with "for just like a man to go on a journey," and that seems as if he is illustrating the same event with a different parable. The parable describes the situation of the disciples after the ascension. Jesus is going away on a journey, and He will return to assess how His slaves have been doing with the treasures He distributes. This means that the Son of Man's coming in AD 70 is not only a time for Him to judge and destroy apostate Israel, but also a crisis in the *church*, a time for judgment and sifting and assessment of His disciples.

The parable is familiar. The master deals out his treasures to his servants according to their abilities. Those who are productive and responsible and efficient get a lot of wealth to work with; the man who has not been very productive gets a single talent. The first two double their wealth during the master's long journey, but the third man simply buries his talent in the ground to preserve it.

Jesus is talking about the treasure that He gives His church, the treasure of the gospel and the ministry that we have in proclaiming, elaborating, and applying that gospel. This is not in the *first* instance about our abilities – whether we are good singers, or canny in business, or good with our hands. It is about what we do with the gospel. And the point is that the gospel, the pearl of great price, the kingdom of God, is given to us so that we can increase it, not so that we can keep it to ourselves.

There is a close connection between the servants' view of their master and their performance. We do not hear what the first two servants say about the Master, we do not know what they think. We can infer that they know that he has high expectations for them, and that they need to work. But the last servant expresses a particular view of his master. He offers a "theology proper": "I knew you to be a hard man, reaping where you did not sow, and gathering where you scattered no seed." He thinks of the master as a hard manager, even a dishonest one. He is the sovereign God of truncated Calvinism. But the Master is not that kind of Master. He is a generous master, a master who gives valuable gifts into the hands of his servants, a master who rewards faithful servants.

Jesus has given the disciples fair warning about what is coming over the next generation. They know some of the signs of Jesus' return as the triumphant Son of Man. But He also warns them that He may take a while, may delay, and that will tempt the disciples to various sins. As priests, the disciples will be tempted to give up their work in the house of the Lord, and instead abuse and mistreat their fellows; they will be tempted to join the drunkards, and to become part of the community that Jesus says He is coming to judge. As kings, they will be tempted to hoard their goods, to wrap them in a napkin and keep them safe, afraid of the Master's anger if they should lose anything. If they are going to gain the Master's approval, they have to be faithful priests and kings. And if we are going to be kings and priests to God, we too have to prepare in the same way that the disciples prepared, by serving faithfully, by keeping our lamps burning, by investing and increasing the great treasure that our Master has given into our hands.

The Least of These
Matthew 25:31-46

[31] "But when the Son of Man comes in His glory, and all the angels with Him, then He will sit on His glorious throne. [32] All the nations will be gathered before Him; and He will separate them from one another, as the shepherd separates the sheep from the goats; [33] and He will put the sheep on His right, and the goats on the left. [34] Then the King will say to those on His right, 'Come, you who are blessed of My Father, inherit the kingdom prepared for you from the foundation of the world. [35] For I was hungry, and you gave Me something to eat; I was thirsty, and you gave Me something to drink; I was a stranger, and you invited Me in; [36] naked, and you clothed Me; I was sick, and you visited Me; I was in prison, and you came to Me.' [37] Then the righteous will answer Him, 'Lord, when did we see

You hungry, and feed You, or thirsty, and give You something to drink? [38] And when did we see You a stranger, and invite You in, or naked, and clothe You? [39] When did we see You sick, or in prison, and come to You?' [40] The King will answer and say to them, 'Truly I say to you, to the extent that you did it to one of these brothers of Mine, even the least of them, you did it to Me.' [41] Then He will also say to those on His left, 'Depart from Me, accursed ones, into the eternal fire which has been prepared for the devil and his angels; [42] for I was hungry, and you gave Me nothing to eat; I was thirsty, and you gave Me nothing to drink; [43] I was a stranger, and you did not invite Me in; naked, and you did not clothe Me; sick, and in prison, and you did not visit Me.' [44] Then they themselves also will answer, 'Lord, when did we see You hungry, or thirsty, or a stranger, or naked, or sick, or in prison, and did not take care of You?' [45] Then He will answer them, 'Truly I say to you, to the extent that you did not do it to one of the least of these, you did not do it to Me.' [46] These will go away into eternal punishment, but the righteous into eternal life."

Jesus is the last and greatest of the Prophets. He is *the* Prophet that Moses predicted (Deuteronomy 18). That means He gives the final word, brings the blueprints for the final temple, speaks the final world into existence, and has complete and permanent access to the divine court, where He can offer a defense for His people. Everything prophets have done, Jesus does, and more. That has tremendous implications for understanding how to interpret the specific prophecies that Jesus spoke during His lifetime. If He is the Last Great Prophet of Israel, we should try to understand His prophecies in the way we understand the prophets of the Old Testament. Israel's prophets, in short, give us a pattern and a model for understanding Jesus' prophecies.

What we find in many of the Old Testament prophets is the reality of double fulfillment. There is often a double time frame operating in prophecies of the Old Testament. Jeremiah prophesies that a new covenant is coming for Israel, and he explicitly speaks of entry into the land, restoration from exile. "Days are coming, says the LORD, when I will make a new covenant with the house of Israel and with the house of Judah." It is a prophecy in the first instance that was fulfilled in the history of Israel in the Old Testament. It is about return from exile. A few verses earlier, Jeremiah said, "They shall again use this speech in the land of Judah and in its cities, when I bring back their captivity" and "I will sow the house of Israel and the house of Judah with the seed of man and the seed of beast." When we get to the New Testament, though, Hebrews quotes from this passage and applies it to the new covenant in Jesus. Jeremiah's prophecy was actually fulfilled in the restoration from exile, but there is a surplus that is not fulfilled until the coming of Jesus.

Isaiah prophesies about the coming of the Messiah. Isaiah also says that in the "last days" the mountain of the house of the Lord will become the chief mountain. Nations will stream to it, and they will beat their swords into ploughshares and their spears into pruning hooks. When was that fulfilled? It was fulfilled in the last days, the days after Israel returned from exile, and it was also fulfilled in the first advent of Jesus, and it is still being fulfilled today. Isaiah also talks about a Davidic king. He is going to be a Davidic king, and the government will be on his shoulders; His government and peace will increase; He will establish it with justice and righteousness forever. That is Jesus, and that was fulfilled in the first advent of Jesus. But the first advent of Jesus was just the beginning. There was much more to come.

This is what typology is about. Typology is a way of interpreting Scripture. It puts the work of Christ at the center, and interprets the Old Testament as a series of foreshadowings of Christ. More fundamentally, typology is a way of looking at *history*. When we read history typologically, we see recurring patterns, patterns that the Bible highlights for our instruction. There is not just one exodus, but many exoduses; there is not just one fall into sin, but many falls into sin; there is not just one man who moves from suffering to glory, but many. We find ourselves in the middle of a biblical story, and we can anticipate how it is going to turn out. And even more fundamentally than that, typology is about God. It assumes that God works in history in a consistent way. The Bible gives us clues to God's habits, and so we can anticipate what He is up to in our lives, and we can follow His lead faithfully. God is consistent. He does the same kinds of things over and over again.

All this is important for understanding the final section of the Olivet Discourse. I have been interpreting the Olivet Discourse throughout as a prophecy concerning the coming of the Son of Man to destroy Jerusalem and the temple in AD 70. Jesus tells us explicitly that these things will take place before the generation of the apostles passes away. Yet I've also emphasized that this passage applies, in a secondary way, to the church throughout all ages. Because God is consistent, because God does the same kinds of works again and again, we can find other times when some similar sequence of events occurred. When we get to the end of Matthew 25, we come to a passage that is almost universally understood as a passage about the final judgment. Even Bible students who think the rest of Matthew 24 is about AD 70 think that Jesus shifts here. And here the pattern of Old Testament prophecy becomes especially important.

There are clues that the text is connected to the events Jesus has been describing, that the judgment of the nations, the sifting of the nations into sheep and goats that He describes here, is connected to the first-century events that He has been describing. Jesus says that all this will happen when the Son of Man comes in glory with His angels (Matt. 25:31). Jesus has used almost this same phrase earlier in Matthew, when He warned that the Son of Man would come to "recompense every man according to His deeds" (Matt. 16:27). In that earlier passage, Jesus says that some of the disciples would live to see it (Matt. 16:28). The judgment scene in Matthew 25 takes place at the end of the Old Covenant.

The other clue is the phrase "glorious throne." That phrase is used only one other time in the book, in Matt. 19:28, where Jesus promises that "in the regeneration, when the Son of Man comes on the throne of His glory" the Twelve will sit on "twelve thrones judging the twelve tribes of Israel." The regeneration is not the end of the world, but the beginning of the new creation that was initiated in Jesus' ascension and the beginning of His reign over all things. Jesus is talking about the Twelve sharing in His assessment and judgment of Israel. That is part of the apostolic age, and it is when the Son of Man sits on His glorious throne.

The Olivet Discourse progresses from the judgment on Jerusalem (24:1-35) to parabolic warnings about Jesus' assessment of His own disciples (24:36-25:30) to a judgment on the nations (25:31-46). This section is about the Son of Man's judgment on the nations. The nations are going to be shaken by the coming of the Son of Man. Jesus has said that before the end comes, the gospel will be preached to the entire *oikoumene* (24:14). The Roman world from one end to the other will hear the good news of Jesus, as the apostles fulfill the commission that Jesus gives at the end of Matthew, the great commission. During that time, nations and cities are going to accept or reject the gospel. At the end of the age, Jesus is going to assess and judge the nations based on their treatment of these missionaries. Matthew 25, I think, describes the way that Jesus will assess nations on the basis of their treatment of the apostles and the early missionaries of the church. As Jerusalem will be judged by how it responds to the messengers Jesus sends, so will the nations.

The nations will be judged according to their treatment of Jesus' "brothers" (25:40, 45). The naked, hungry, sick, imprisoned in this passage are not, in the first instance, the poor and needy in general. They are the brothers of Jesus, and I think specifically the missionaries that Jesus sends out. Jesus earlier sent out the Twelve, and judged the cities of Samaria and Galilee based on their treatment of the missionaries (10:1-15; 11:20-24). The missionaries went out without anything, and the cities that received the gospels had to care for the missionaries as well. When the gospel moves to the Roman empire, the nations will be judged in the same way. In the first instance, the nations will be judged according to whether they received the traveling missionaries sent by Jesus (cf. 10:42).

We can put it this way: Jesus is the seed of Abraham, and His "brothers" are children of Abraham. Because of that, they are the bearers of the Abrahamic promise, and the Abrahamic promise is, "I will bless those who bless you and curse those who curse you."

That is one way, the main way, that the apostles will participate in the judgment of the nations and the judgment on the twelve tribes of Israel. They participate by bearing the Abrahamic promise. Whoever gives a cup of cold water to a prophet will receive a prophet's reward.

This begins with the dispersion of the Twelve with the great commission, but it does not end there. Throughout the history of the church, the nations are being judged by their response to the gospel, and their response to the bearers of the gospel. In this, the judgment of the nations is perfectly consistent with Jesus' judgment of the tribes of Israel. The Son of Man comes to destroy Israel because of the abomination of desolation, because the harlot Jerusalem drinks down the blood of the saints, and is ripe for desolation as a result. For Israel, that is not only a moral evil but a ceremonial evil, too. When other nations drink the blood of the saints, they put themselves in a similar danger. When the nations receive Jesus' messengers, clothe them, feed them, visit them, they are going to receive a reward from the Son of Man. But there are also hints here that Jesus is talking about something beyond AD 70, something even beyond the process of sifting and judgment that takes place throughout the church's history. There are signs in the text that Jesus is talking about a final judgment, which occurs at the end of all things.

Jesus' rewards and punishments are permanent. The King says to the sheep on the right that they are "blessed of the Father" and will "inherit the kingdom prepared for you from the foundation of the world." At the end, he says that the righteous enter into "eternal life." The goats, meanwhile, are sent off to "eternal fire that has been prepared for the devil and his angels." Those do not sound like historical judgments. He is not simply saying that these nations will collapse, or that they will be invaded by enemies, or that they will become poor. He is sending people to eternal life or death, to the kingdom or to hell. More generally, the end of the old covenant foreshadows the end of the new, just as Old Testament prophecies are frequently fulfilled in Jesus' ministry and more fully later. It is not surprising that the New Testament teaches that a final judgment will take place after the millennium (19:11-12), and that final judgment will also be a judgment "according to their deeds" (Rev. 19:12). Our entry to life or death will be determined by how we treat Jesus, as He shows Himself in His brothers.

We can draw two conclusions from this passage, the first theological and the second practical. The three parables in Jesus' Olivet Discourse all emphasize that Jesus assesses His disciples according to their performance. The judgment scene at the end of Matthew 25 makes the same point: The ones who enter life are the ones who have acted righteously toward the least of Jesus' brothers. It is not enough to be a household servant; how do you perform your responsibilities? Are you being a faithful priest, preparing food at the proper time, or are you drinking yourself drunk and beating your fellow servants? It is not enough to be part of the wedding party; are you a wise or a foolish virgin? Are you putting aside a reserve of oil, continually seeking a fresh outpouring of the oil of the Spirit to keep your lamp burning? It is not enough to be *given* a talent; the question is, what do you *do* with that talent?

The judgment at the end of Matthew 25 takes this even further. These people are not being judged by what they do, but, like the virgins, for what they *have not* done. They are being sent to eternal punishment or eternal life based on whether they have *actively* assisted the naked, the hungry, the sick, the imprisoned, whether or not they have sought out needy people and actually helped them, generously giving of their own things to help others.

Many Protestants minimize this kind of passage, and weaken it. Protestants insist that we are *not* saved by what we do; we are saved by what Jesus does. When we stand at the final judgment, Matthew 25 does not describe what is going to happen, many Protestants think. Jesus *will not* ask whether we have been generous to the needy, but whether we believe in justification by faith. We will not be judged by our righteousness, but by the imputed righteousness of Jesus.

These passages, and many others, show that we will be judged by what we *do*, according to our works. There are *no* passages in Scripture that say anything different. We are brought into the kingdom by God's grace and favor, but in the end we will be judged by our works. We have a standing as slaves of the house by the grace of God, but we are finally assessed based on our performance as slaves. Of course, we are saved by what Jesus does. But what Jesus does is to produce good works through His Spirit, make us faithful household servants, give us the wisdom to be faithful virgins, enable us to invest and gain an increase. That is Jesus working in us. If He is really working in us, He is going to produce fruit in us.

The practical point has to do with the basis for judgment. Think about the situation Jesus has been talking about. Judgment is coming on Jerusalem, and the nations are going to be shaken. What should the disciples do? They would be tempted to hoard their goods, stockpile weapons, hunker down for the tough times. Get a generator, for sure. That is what we are tempted to do. It *is* a temptation, and needs to be resisted. As the disciples await the judgment, they should be doing what Jesus has done: not hoarding, but *giving*; not stockpiling but serving; not hunkering down but clothing the naked, feeding the hungry. That is the way to prepare for disaster. I've said that in the first instance Jesus is talking about the treatment of His "brothers," those who are sent out on a mission to the nations. But Jesus is also judging based on our treatment of the poor and needy generally. He is not saying, "You need to provide for the poor, *if they are Christians*, but otherwise you can simply ignore them." We are judged based on whether we actively provide for those who needed food and clothing, by whether we visit the sick and imprisoned.

Jesus does not judge based on how well we know our catechisms, whether we know how to dot every "i." He does not judge based on whether we support the right kinds of candidates and causes. He does not judge us by our beauty, or our skill, or our intelligence. He does not judge based on whether we conform to middle class American expectations. He does not even judge us by how well we avoid sin, how well we avoid murder, anger, adultery, lust, envy, slander. He judges us by our *works*, and by whether or not we have actively done good, not whether we have simply avoided evil. He judges us based on whether we have produced the righteousness that surpasses the righteousness of the scribes. Jesus is sending people to hell because they failed to care for the needy.

In this too, Jesus is the final prophet. Many of the prophets addressed both Israel and the nations. When they addressed Israel, they condemned Israel for idolatry, for violations of the law. They condemned Israel for mistreatment of the poor, but that too was on the basis of the law. When they address the nations, the standard is different. Those who have the law are condemned by the law; but those without law are condemned on a different basis. They are judged based on whether or not they abuse the image of God, whether or not they mistreat the weak.

Jesus is a final prophet, but He has deepened this prophetic theme. Jesus identifies Himself with the hungry, thirsty, naked, sick, imprisoned, and strangers. That is nothing new. He has been doing that His whole life. Jesus spent much of His ministry associating with outcasts, tax gatherers and sinners (9:10-11; 11:19), feeding the hungry (15:32), calling prostitutes to repent (21:13), encouraging generosity to the poor (19:21), rescuing the helpless. Jesus focused His ministry on bringing the good news to the poor (11:5; cf. Luke 4:18), and He identifies Himself with them. Treatment of the needy is thus the basis for the judgment of the nations because these are the people that the Son of God has chosen to identify as His brothers.

Incarnation means that God the Son, the Eternal and Almighty God, takes flesh, every bit of it. He takes every bit of our condition to Himself. We are naked and ashamed; Jesus takes that to Himself, and calls the naked His brothers. We are hungry for the tree of life, thirsty for the water of the garden; Jesus takes that to Himself, too. We are sick, imprisoned, strangers – and Jesus assumes all that to Himself, makes that too His brother, becomes a stranger, takes our infirmities on Himself, allows Himself to be arrested and mistreated. He comes to be brother to the stranger, brother to the naked, brother to god-forsakenness, brother to despair, brother to death, brother to the cross, brother to every last sling and arrow that flesh is heir to.

"Where were you?" the goats ask. Jesus says, "I was there in front of you, in the beggar, in the homeless, in the drunk and the drug addict, in the mentally ill, in the unemployed." "Where were you?" they ask. "I showed the face of the Father in the broken image of humanity, and if you want to find Me, and serve Me, then you'll have to look there." "Where were you?" "I was right there," Jesus says, "and if you ministered to the least of these My brothers, you minister to Me."

The Christ Crucified

Delivered Up
Matthew 26:1-16

¹ When Jesus had finished all these words, He said to His disciples, ² "You know that after two days the Passover is coming, and the Son of Man is to be handed over for crucifixion." ³ Then the chief priests and the elders of the people were gathered together in the court of the high priest, named Caiaphas; ⁴ and they plotted together to seize Jesus by stealth and kill Him. ⁵ But they were saying, "Not during the festival, otherwise a riot might occur among the people." ⁶ Now when Jesus was in Bethany, at the home of Simon the leper, ⁷ a woman came to Him with an alabaster vial of very costly perfume, and she poured it on His head as He reclined at the table. ⁸ But the disciples were indignant when they saw this, and said, "Why this waste? ⁹ For this perfume might have been sold for a high price and the money given to the poor." ¹⁰ But Jesus, aware of this, said to them, "Why do you bother the woman? For she has done a good deed to Me. ¹¹ For you always have the poor with you; but you do not always have Me. ¹² For when she poured this perfume on My body, she did

it to prepare Me for burial. ¹³ Truly I say to you, wherever this gospel is preached in the whole world, what this woman has done will also be spoken of in memory of her." ¹⁴ Then one of the twelve, named Judas Iscariot, went to the chief priests ¹⁵ and said, "What are you willing to give me to betray Him to you?" And they weighed out thirty pieces of silver to him. ¹⁶ From then on he began looking for a good opportunity to betray Jesus. [39]

After the Olivet Discourse, Jesus "finished *all* these words." Matthew has used a similar phrase before (26:1; cf. 7:28; 11:1; 13:53; 19:1). Throughout the book, in fact, each time that Jesus finishes a long section of teaching, Matthew tells us that Jesus "finished these words." That does more than tell us that the discourse is over. We know the discourse is over because the red lettering stops, or the quotation marks close, or, in the original Greek, simply because Matthew goes on to begin telling us another episode. We know all this. Why does Matthew have to tell us?

Matthew is drawing on the language of the first chapters of Scripture. After God has created, Genesis 2 tells us that He "finished" His work. Yahweh is introduced to us in Scripture as a speaking and creating God, a God who creates by speaking, a God who speaks the worlds into existence. That is the same God who appears to Abraham. Abraham is a wanderer and has no secure place; the only security He has is the reliable word of God. He believes it, and Yahweh's word proves sure. Jesus is the incarnation of that creating God; through His words, he is speaking a new world into being, verbalizing a new Israel into existence.

Matthew has used similar phrases before, but this one is different. This time, Matthew does not simply say that Jesus "finished these words," but that "Jesus finished *all* these words." That "all" is a hint that we are entering a new phase of Jesus' ministry. His words are ended, all of them. Jesus is finished speaking to Israel. Matthew is also alluding to the concluding

---

39 The opening episodes of Matthew 26 are organized in a fairly neat chiasm:

chapters of Deuteronomy, where we learn that Moses' words are "complete" or "perfected." Jesus has said all that must be said; His discourses to Israel are perfect, and, like a new Moses, He is getting ready to complete His work by His death, and then to send His disciples, like a new Joshua, off to disciple the nations.

During the next several chapters, Jesus says almost nothing. He has been talkative throughout the Gospel; He has offered long discourses, and when the Pharisees charge Him, He defends Himself. He does not do that any more. He says only one word during His trial before the high priest – a warning that the Son of Man will be enthroned, and that the high priest will see it. He says even less before Pilate. He has finished *all* His words.

This is an announcement of final judgment against Israel. From the beginning of His ministry, Jesus has been talking – He has laid out a way of righteousness and peace for Israel, commissioned His disciples, disclosed the secrets of the king of heaven, told His disciples how to govern their communities and about the demand for forgiveness, and the demand to avoid offense to children. Israel never listens. Instead, the Pharisees try to catch Him in His words; priests and elders plot against Him; they accuse Him of being in league with the devil. So Jesus announces the judgment that waits for Israel, and then stops talking. He has no more words for Israel, and when He again turns to teaching, at the end of Matthew's gospel, He sends His disciples to the nations, the Gentiles, to teach them all that He has commanded.

A. Passover, delivered up, chief priests, plot, 26:1-5
(*paradidomi*, v. 2; *archiereus*, v. 3)
    B. Woman pours myrrh on Jesus, 26:6-7 (*muron*, v. 7)
        C. Disciples complain: give to poor, 26:8-9
        (*ptochos*, v. 9)
            D. Jesus: She has done a good deed, 26:10
        C'. Poor always with you, 26:11 (*ptochos*, v. 11)
    B'. Woman poured perfume to prepare for burial, 26:12-13
    (*muron*, v. 12)
A'. Judas and the priests: chief priests, deliver, 26:14-16
(*paradidomi*, vv. 15, 16; *archiereus*, v. 14)

He has said all He will say to Israel, and now He turns from them and provokes them to jealousy by directing His attention to the Gentiles. When God stops speaking to His people, when Israel's husband stops speaking to His bride, it is a sign that His patience has come to an end.

That opposition and those plots have intensified as a result of Jesus' preaching in the temple. Since Jesus arrived in Jerusalem on Palm Sunday, He has been embarrassing and enraging the chief priests, scribes, Pharisees, elders. Even the Sadducees and Herodians have taken their licks. He made a ruckus in the temple, turning over tables and stopping the traffic of sacrificial animals, an enacted announcement of the doom of the temple. They tried to trap Him, but He turned the tables and trapped them. They had to slink away in silent shame when He asked them questions they could not answer. Then He launched into a scathing condemnation of the scribes and Pharisees before stalking out of the temple. He delivered the Olivet Discourse in private, only to the disciples, but there was no doubt that Jesus had come to the temple as a Jeremiah, ready to announce its destruction.

Instead of fearing the judgment of God, or repenting, the priests and elders of the people gathered together to plot against the Lord and His anointed. Herod (2:4) and the Pharisees (12:14) plotted against Jesus before, but now the priests and elders of Israel conspire in earnest, gathering in the court of the High priest like the Gentiles who gather against the Lord's anointed (Psalm 2; cf. Psalm 31:13 and many others). Jesus' assault on the temple has stung them, and they have to put Him down.

Jesus finishes speaking, and instead of being an active teacher, He is reduced almost to an object. Instead of speaking to adoring and attentive crowds, Jesus is passed from hand to hand to hand. The verb "deliver up" is used some fifteenth times in these chapters, often translated as "betray." Jesus says He will be delivered up (Matt. 26:2), then Judas offers to deliver Jesus into the hands of the Jews (26:15-16). Once He is arrested, His captors led Him away and delivered Him to Pilate, who sees that they have delivered Him up out of envy (27:2, 18). He passes from the hands of the soldiers arresting Him, to the hands of the priests, into the hands of Pilate, and finally, at the climax, Pilate "delivered Him up to be crucified" (27:26). Jesus, who seemed so much in charge in the temple, turns passive. Jesus the man of bold speech and action enters into passivity, into Passion.

Matthew makes it clear that this is not the whole story, however. Jesus turns passive; He appears to lose control. But Matthew makes it clear that Jesus continues to be in control. Jesus knows that He is going to be delivered up, and He announces it again, as He has repeatedly, to His disciples. "After two days," the Passover begins (26:2). That is, on the "third day," Jesus the Passover Lamb will be slaughtered, just as He will be raised on the "third day." His deliverance comes as no surprise. More than that, Matthew subtly shows that the chief priests and elders are not in charge of their own plot. The *one* element of the plot that we know about has to do with the timing, and they stick with that plan for the space of about ten verses before they begin changing course. Once Judas appears, the priests and elders abandon their careful plans and carry out their plot during Passover. Worse, they do not avoid what they were trying to avoid. The key element of the plan is announced in verse 5: "Not during the festival, lest a riot occur among the people." The word for "riot" occurs only one other time in Matthew, where it describes the "uproar" among the Jews who are rioting in front of Pilate's Praetorium (27:24). Because of the uproar, Pilate washes his hands and delivers Jesus up to the Jews.

The conspirators are not in charge. Their plots are ineffective. They gather, they plot, they attack the Lord and His anointed. But the one who sits in heaven laughs at them. He knows that their plots amount to nothing, that what really determines the future is the word of God, the fulfillment of Scriptures, the plots of Jesus.

Besides, the whole series of events is already scripted. It fulfills Scripture, down to the tiniest detail. Judas goes to the chief priests and offers his services in handing Jesus over, and they give Him thirty pieces of silver (26:15). The amount of the payment takes us back to Exod. 21:32 and Zech. 11:12-13. In Exodus, this money appears in a law dealing with dangerous animals. An ox that is wild and dangerous, and is in the habit of goring people has to be restrained. If such an ox kills someone, then the owner is responsible. If the dead person is free, the punishment can take the form of a ransom payment, whatever the family of the dead person demands. If the person gored is a slave, the owner of the ox pays the slave's owner thirty shekels of silver as compensation. Thirty pieces of silver is thus the price of a slave; that is how much Judas values Jesus. And the thirty pieces of silver evokes the larger concerns of the law. Animals are supposed to be submissive to their owners, and animals that go wild and kill people are like the serpent, a beast of the field who attacked Adam and Eve. Israel is supposed to be like the Lord's work animal, plowing and threshing the world in obedience to Yahweh, but Israel has become a demon-possessed, goring ox. Jesus charges that Israel is an ox that has a *habit* of goring. Every prophet, every servant that Yahweh sends ends up dead, gored by the ox that is Israel. Jesus, too, will be gored, surrounded, as Psalm 22 says, by the bulls of Bashan whose mouths are like the mouths of lions.

Matthew is tracking Zechariah 9-14 throughout the latter part of His Gospel. In Zechariah 11, the Lord has seen that the shepherds – the rulers, kings, and priests – afflict the people, traffic in sheep, buying and selling sheep and boasting about how rich they have gotten by preying on the flock. So the Lord sends His own shepherd, but Israel becomes weary of Him. Finally, the shepherd quits, breaks his staff that is called "favor," and asks for His wages. They weigh out thirty pieces of silver, and the shepherd sarcastically calls it a "lordly price." Jesus is the true Shepherd, but He is the rejected shepherd, the shepherd that the chief priests value at thirty pieces of silver.

There are a lot of ideas floating around today about how the world works, about who is in charge. Some are true, or largely true; some have a grain of truth; some are just nutty. Whether real or not, though, they do not make that much difference. Whatever the plots of men, they are overridden by the Lord's plan, and in the end they are buffoonish posturing. Plots are re-plotted against the plotters, traps trap the trappers, and the wicked fall into the pit they made. Just as Jesus turns the verbal attacks of the Pharisees and scribes against them, so He turns their plots against them.

The Passion Narrative is of course about Jesus' arrest, trial, and death; it is about the Son of Man being "delivered up." But Matthew wants us to realize that there's a lot more going on, that the story is actually woven of several distinct stories. In these opening scenes of his Passion Narrative, Matthew introduces several characters or sets of characters. I have already mentioned the priests. They have their agenda, but their plot is not under their control; they are unwilling and unconscious participants in the Lord's Passover plot. We have already noted Judas; keep your eye on him as well. In the middle of the story, though, two other characters are introduced – on the one hand the woman who anoints Jesus and on the other hand the Twelve. This is not the last time we will see women, nor the last time we see the Twelve. Notice not only that they keep coming up, but notice how they interact with each other.

The disciples and a woman are central to the story in Matt. 26:6-13. During the last week of Jesus' life, He has been traveling back and forth from Bethany to Jerusalem (v. 17). After He ends His discourse, He and the disciples go back to the village to stay with Simon, identified as a leper (v. 6). Apparently, he is a cleansed leper; it is unlikely that a leper would host a dinner party. Healed or not, he is one of the marginal, "poor" Israelites with whom Jesus identifies. While the chief priests and elders gather to plot in the official palace of the high priest, at the center of Israel's religious power-structure, Jesus gathers at a meal with a leper. At dinner, a woman anoints Jesus' head with oil (v. 7), an extravagant act of devotion. Her action in itself is worth considering.

Jesus says it is for His burial (v. 12). The woman is the only one at the table who has believed what Jesus has been telling everyone for a long time – that He has come to Jerusalem to die. The disciples have heard this again and again, but even when Judas shows up with the soldiers in Gethsemane, the disciples try to fight them off. They do not really believe that Jesus is headed to the grave, but the woman does. Her good work is proclaimed with the gospel because she is the only one to believe the gospel. She announces Jesus' death ahead of time, just as women will be the first witnesses of the resurrection and the first of the church's evangelists. The anointing also identifies Jesus as King and Priest. He goes to the grave not as a victim but as a triumphant conqueror, the Christ, the son of David. He looks passive, as He gets traded from hand to hand. But He is the good Shepherd who lays down His life of His own accord. His death is not a tragedy; it is not a sorry episode; it is not sad. It is the last triumph of Jesus, the Son of Man.

The story turns on the question of the price the woman paid for the perfume. The woman has spent a great deal of money, and her prodigality highlights another part of her role in the story, in contrast to the disciples. Matthew simply tells us that it was "very costly," but John says that the disciples estimate the value at three hundred denarii, nearly a year's worth of wages for a day worker. The perfume is worth thousands of dollars, and it all pours out in a few minutes, all poured out on Jesus' head and, John tells us, on His feet. It is an act of extreme extravagance, and the disciples are indignant. They say that the gift is excessive, extravagant, obscene. The same money could have been distributed to the poor, put to use, invested, shared, used in ministry. It is easy to scoff at the disciples, but we would likely share their very practical objections.

The contrast with Judas is even sharper. The woman has spent a year's wage honoring Jesus, preparing Him for death. Judas accepts thirty pieces of silver to hand Jesus over. Not every disciple is a Judas, of course, but eventually they will forsake Jesus and run away. Besides, they, like Judas, apply standards of value that do not fit. The Twelve complain about the extravagance of the woman's offering. They value the perfume monetarily; how much does it cost – too much? If so, we can choose something more prudent and reasonable to offer Jesus. They place too little value on Jesus, just as Judas does. Judas is the extreme example of a mindset that all the disciples share, a tendency to judge value in monetary terms.

Jesus defends the woman. She has done a "good deed" (26:10). Jesus' words sound cold, as if He is telling the poor to wait their turn while He bathes in luxury. Of course, the church's first love is Jesus, her Lord, but in the previous chapter, Jesus identified ministry to the poor and ministry to Him (25:31-46). The issue is one of timing. Timing is a key issue in the entire passage. Passover has come, so it is time for Jesus to be delivered up. The priests plot to set the time for capturing Jesus. Judas looks for an opportune time. And when Jesus responds to His disciples, He also talks about timing. They do not know what time it is; they do not know that this is the time for Jesus' burial; they do not know that the time of Jesus' presence with them is running out. "The poor you will always have; but you will not always have Me."

Another key to understanding Jesus' words is to notice his reference to His body in Matt. 26:12. The woman anoints His head, but He speaks of His body. That helps us get a handle on what Jesus is saying. The key is to recognize the double body of Christ. While Jesus sits at table, the woman pours perfume on His body for burial. Soon that body will not be there, but Jesus says at the close of the gospel that He will continue to be with them (28:18-20). How? Not in the buried body, but in the risen body, which is present through the power of the Spirit, and which is also present in the Spirit-filled body of disciples. I will not always be with you, Jesus says, but I will be with you in the body, in the poor, the "least of these My brothers." In the end, extravagant generosity to Jesus' poor brothers and extravagant devotion to Jesus amount to the same thing.

We are at the beginning of the Passion narrative, the climax of the story of Jesus, the climax of all human history. We are about to hear the story of man putting God on trial, man rejecting God, man putting God to death on a cross, but also of a God whom death cannot hold, a God who will not accept man's rejection but goes through death to deliver us. Here is great mystery, and we start out the narrative with stories about a woman who wastes a year's wages on a consumable gift for Jesus, about disciples complaining about the extravagance, about Judas haggling over

Jesus' blood money and getting a bad deal of it. We are entering on great mysteries, but Matthew wants to talk about money. We are tempted to be cynical: of course, Matthew wants to talk about money — he is a tax-collector.

Matthew is not obsessed with money. The issue is that following Jesus, being a disciple, taking up the cross and following Him to His death and grave requires a transvaluation of our values. Judas is the negative example, of course, but the disciples are only lesser versions of Judas' system of values. The model is the woman. She is heedless of money. She is only interested in honoring Jesus, in what amounts to an act of worship. The woman approaches Jesus, draws near like a priest to the temple. According to John's account, the fragrance of the perfume fills the whole house, like the shining glory of the Lord descending on the temple. She draws near as the bride Israel to anoint and minister to her Lord. She gives extravagantly, imprudently, because she is giving to Jesus. She values heavenly treasures; her scale of values places Jesus at the top, far more precious that gold, silver, precious stones, or perfume, even the poor. He is so valuable that He is worth everything, worth the extravagant prodigality of the costly perfume. This sets the tone for the following chapters: the whole Passion narrative challenges us to revise our values, calling us to invert normal expectations and normal standards.

Jesus is anointed as King. We expect Him to do something kingly. Instead, He is delivered over to the Jews, does not fight back, does not even let His disciples fight back. Jesus has power: OK, let us see Him use it. But He refuses. Jesus can defend Himself in debate: Let us see Him silence the Jewish accusers, just like He has done again and again. But He falls silent. We are back to where we started, with Jesus' silence: He finished *all* these words. He will no longer speak to Israel. He has nothing left to say. All that can be said has been said, and Israel will not have it or Him. He no longer speaks, but instead He acts, but the *way* He acts is crucial.

After the scathing rhetoric of the Olivet Discourse, we expect an act of judgment, and His silence is judgment. But we expect more. We expect Him to cast Israel out. He has come to His own; His own have rejected Him; He has denounced them; He has written them off, washed His hands of them. Let the Son of Man gather those armies to the walls of Jerusalem *now*. We are all Jonahs, and we want to see some fireworks. Instead, His activity is passivity. When He stops speaking, He begins to be passed from hand to hand to hand until He is finally delivered up to the cross. We expect Jesus to cast Israel out; instead *He* is cast out. We expect another exile for Israel; instead, Jesus is exiled. We expect Israel's destruction; we see instead Jesus'.

The woman is commended because she understands. She understands that Jesus is beyond price, and that He deserves everything we have, and more than we can give. She understands that if we want to follow Him our scale of values has to be remade from top to bottom. If we want to be Jesus' disciples, and follow the woman's example of "good deeds," we must be prepared to follow *this* king, the king who is delivered up, and up, and up, finally delivered up to the cross. We need to learn to imitate her extravagance, which is the extravagance of Jesus Himself, the Good Shepherd who gives Himself for His flock.

Body and Blood
Matthew 26:17-30

[17] Now on the first day of Unleavened Bread the disciples came to Jesus and asked, "Where do You want us to prepare for You to eat the Passover?" [18] And He said, "Go into the city to a certain man, and say to him, 'The Teacher says, My time is near; I am to keep the Passover at your house with My disciples.' [19] The disciples did as Jesus had directed them; and they prepared the Passover. [20] Now when evening came, Jesus was reclining at the table with the twelve disciples. [21] As they were eating, He said, "Truly I say to you that one of you will betray Me." [22] Being deeply grieved, they each one began to say to Him, "Surely not I, Lord?" [23] And He answered, "He who dipped his hand with Me in the bowl is the one who will betray Me. [24] The Son of Man is to go, just as it is written of Him; but woe to that man by whom the Son of Man is betrayed!

It would have been good for that man if he had not been born." ²⁵ And Judas, who was betraying Him, said, "Surely it is not I, Rabbi?" Jesus said to him, "You have said it yourself." ²⁶ While they were eating, Jesus took some bread, and after a blessing, He broke it and gave it to the disciples, and said, "Take, eat; this is My body." ²⁷ And when He had taken a cup and given thanks, He gave it to them, saying, "Drink from it, all of you; ²⁸ for this is My blood of the covenant, which is poured out for many for forgiveness of sins. ²⁹ But I say to you, I will not drink of this fruit of the vine from now on until that day when I drink it new with you in My Father's kingdom." ³⁰ After singing a hymn, they went out to the Mount of Olives.

The very first time Jesus mentions the cross, He says nothing about His own death. In Matthew 10, Jesus gives instructions to the Twelve about their mission to the lost sheep of the house of Israel. They will be persecuted and opposed, and Jesus describes that suffering and opposition as the cross. Only those disciples who are willing to take up the cross and follow Me are worthy of Jesus (10:38). Nowhere in this passage does Jesus mention that *He* will also bear a cross. In Matthew 10, it is only the disciples. Even when He begins talking about His own cross, the literal crucifixion that awaits Him in Jerusalem, He emphasizes that the disciples will share in it. At Caesarea Philippi, in the shadow of one of Caesar's great monument cities, Jesus says that He goes to Jerusalem to suffer, to be killed, to rise on the third day. And when Peter protests, Jesus repeats what He said to the Twelve as they left on their mission: "If anyone wishes to come after Me, let him deny himself, and take up his cross, and follow Me" (Matt. 16:24).

Jesus predicts His own crucifixion for the first time on His way to Jerusalem: "we are going up to Jerusalem, and the Son of Man will be delivered to the chief priests and scribes, and they will condemn Him to death, and will deliver Him to the Gentiles to mock and scourge and crucify Him, and on the third day He will be raised up" (20:18-19). The disciples have not gotten the point. Right after Jesus' first announcement that He will be crucified, the mother of James and John comes asking for special privileges for her sons. "Take up your cross" is first a statement about discipleship, and in the first instance, it refers to the literal risk that the disciples are taking. They are headed to Jerusalem with Jesus, who is deeply hated by the Jewish leaders. Jesus has been popular with crowds, and the Romans are no doubt keeping an eye on Him to see if He will create a disturbance that will have to be suppressed. In the end, the Jews accuse Him of being opposed to Caesar, a rebel, something that is far more accurate a description of them than of Jesus.

If the disciples follow Jesus, and stay with Him, and do not flee when He is arrested, they face the literal prospect of crucifixion. The Romans frequently suppressed Jewish rebellions not only by killing the leader but by destroying the followers. "Take up your cross" does refer to all sorts of suffering we might endure as followers of Jesus. But it is in the first instance a political exhortation: it is about staying close to a controversial and politically disruptive Jesus even when the Romans threaten to nail you to a cross.

Jesus is in Jerusalem with His disciples, and the Passover is approaching. As Jesus says to His disciples, his "time is at hand." That means the time of the cross, the time of crisis, a time of crisis not only for Jesus Himself but also for His disciples. If the Teacher is going to the cross, the disciples run the same risk. All this means that the Passion narrative is not just the story of Jesus going to the cross, but the story of the disciples. The story of the Passion is the story of Jesus, but it is also the story of the sifting and maturation and transformation of the apostles. They are not simply recipients of the work of Jesus; they are participants in the event of the atonement.

Matthew announces this when he tells us that it is the "first of unleaven." In Jerusalem, it is a festival season, the feast of the first month, which begins with the celebration of Passover on the 14th of the first month and continues with the Feast of Unleavened Bread for the following week. As I've noted, ancient leaven was not yeast. Israelites would reserve a bit of an earlier batch of bread dough to insert into the next batch to leaven it. Leavening would continue from loaf to loaf to loaf, from dough to dough to dough. But during the week of Unleavened Bread, they ate only unleavened bread and purge the house of all leaven. "Seven days you shall eat unleavened bread, but on the first day you shall remove leaven from your houses" and "Seven days there shall be no leaven in your houses" (Exod. 12:15, 19). Anyone who had leaven would be cut off from the people; they had to purge leaven from their houses on pain of excommunication. When the week was over, they had to start over. They still could not go down to the local supermarket, so they had to leave a lump of dough exposed, so that airborne yeast spores could get into it. Then they would start over, and keep the leaven going from dough to dough to dough until the next year.

The Feast of Unleavened Bread marked a new beginning for Israel. When they left Egypt, they were supposed to leave Egypt behind. They cut off the leaven of Egypt and made a new start. They were supposed to abandon the permeating influences of Egyptian culture and religion. But even that new lump became corrupt over the year, and so a new beginning had to be made every year. Paul applies this to the church in his first letter to the Corinthians. Christ the Passover has been sacrificed, Paul says, and that means that Christ has initiated a new Feast of Unleavened Bread. Therefore, Paul says, purge the old leaven, the leaven of malice and wickedness; keep the feast instead with unleavened bread, the "unleavened bread of sincerity and truth" (1 Cor. 5:6-8).

Matthew tells us that the disciples prepare the Passover on the "first of unleavened," the Passover evening. But Matthew uses a rather unusual phrase to describe this first day. The word "day" is not found in the text, nor the word "feast." Mark calls it the "day" of unleavened, and Luke uses the word "feast." Matthew's phrase is more stark and unusual: It is the "first of unleavened." What is Matthew getting at? "First" (*protos*) is used here not as an adjective modifying "day" but as a noun, and as such it may carry the connotation of "beginning" or "initiation." And the word "unleavened" is also used without modification. "In the beginning of the purgation of leaven" or "at the start of the unleavening" captures the sense. Matthew announces that the beginning of this week is the beginning a process of purgation; old leaven is going to be cast out, and a new leaven begun.

Earlier in Matthew, Jesus has used "leaven" as an image of both the kingdom (13:33) and of the teaching of the Pharisees and Sadducees (16:6-12). The latter leaven is the leaven that needs to be purged. Why would Matthew want to remind us of the leaven of the Pharisees and Sadducees at this point in the story? . The answer comes in the previous section of Matthew 26, where Judas approaches the chief priests and elders and offers to betray Jesus. Judas has been infected and permeated by the leaven of the scribes and Pharisees. He has been filled with the revolutionary zeal of the Pharisees. Like the Pharisees (Luke 16:14), Judas loves money, and so is willing to give Jesus up for a few pieces of silver.

During the Passover feast, Jesus will be slaughtered for the sins of His people. During the Feast of Unleavened Bread, the loaf of the disciples is going to be purged. Old leaven is going to be cast out, and there will be chance for new leaven to begin. In 1 Corinthians, Paul is speaking about a sinful *person* as leaven; the wicked man that is tolerated in the Corinthian church is the leaven that might leaven the whole lump. Here too, during the unleavening, the disciples are going to be purged of their Pharisaism and half-hearted devotion. Judas is going to be cast out, the little leaven that might leaven the whole lump. But the rest of the disciples will be tested too.

How are the disciples going to do? How are they going to fare during this process of purging and unleavening? Jesus predicts that they will not do well. While Jesus is eating, He informs the disciples that one of the Twelve will deliver Him up (Matt. 26:20, 23-24). This little episode is carefully put together. Jesus announces that someone will betray Him; the disciples become deeply saddened by the news, and each in turn asks "Is it I?" Jesus reiterates his initial statement, but deepens it – the one to betray Him is someone who has "dipped his hand" in the bowl, someone who has shared the common plate of food. So far, Jesus has not told them who it is, and we are left in suspense. Which one is it? Then Jesus reiterates His initial prediction, but with a woe attached to it, and this time Judas asks, Is it I? Jesus answers by identifying Judas as the traitor.

The episode has some suspense and uncertainty if read by itself, but Matthew does not put it by itself. We already know from the previous episode, and in fact from virtually every mention of Judas in the gospel, that Judas is the betrayer. Judas is explicitly identified as the "one who was betraying Him" in verse 25. Why the suspense if we already know this? Does Matthew want to make us smug because we know something the disciples do not know? Are we supposed to say, "Do not worry Peter; do not worry James and John and Andrew and all the rest. It is all OK. We already know who the traitor is, and it ain't you. You can relax"? Quite the contrary. Matthew has written this little passage to make it clear that Judas is *not* alone. Both Judas and the rest of the twelve are going to betray Jesus, at one level or another. There is no suspense for Judas. We know he is the traitor too. But there is suspense for the other disciples. They have to take up the cross: Will they? They have to purge the old leaven of the scribes and Pharisees: How will that go? Will they make a clean break with the Pharisees? Or will they join with the Pharisees and turn on Jesus?

It also leaves us in suspense about ourselves. The episode is told to raise questions about the reader. We are not allowed to rest content in not-being-Judas. It is *good* not to be Judas. But it is not enough, because the others will betray and deny and abandon Jesus in lesser ways. They may not be filled with the leaven of the scribes and Pharisees, as Judas is, but they are certainly not making a clean break with the old leaven.

So far, we are simply in suspense. We know Judas is a traitor, but cannot tell about the rest of the disciples. Their track record is not encouraging, but perhaps they will rise to the occasion. But after the Passover meal, Jesus makes the point explicit. Jesus and His disciples leave the upper room, singing, and climb to the Mount of Olives. The last time they were on the Mount, Jesus predicted the destruction of a temple. He said that not one stone will be left on another that will not be thrown down. His return to the mountain marks the initial fulfillment of that prophecy. He reiterates the Olivet discourse in a different way. On the Mount of Olives, Jesus announces that He the shepherd will be struck. He is the temple, and the temple of His body will be torn down, but it will be raised up again on the third day.

But it is not only Jesus that will be torn down. He is the temple, but His disciples also form a temple around Him. This temple too will be scattered. In fulfillment of the Scriptures, in fulfillment specifically of the prophecy of Zechariah about the scattering of the flock, all the disciples will fall. All are going to be "scandalized" this night; all will stumble over the stumbling block that is Jesus. Judas alone sells Jesus; Judas alone identifies Jesus. But Judas is *not* alone in setting Jesus aside. *All* the disciples forsake Him. Not one stone will be left on another that will not be torn down. Not even Peter, the rock on whom Jesus builds His church, will remain.

This is the setting for Matthew's account of the Last Supper, and the institution of the Lord's Supper. Verses 26-29 have been studied and debated and examined for two millennia. They are some of the most often-repeated and best known and most studied verses in the Scriptures. Of course, this meal is the new Passover. Of course, it is a new Sinai, since Jesus alludes to the Sinai covenant of Exodus 24 in the phrase "blood of the covenant." The reference to forgiveness reminds us not only of the blood of the sacrifices but also of the prophetic promise of a new covenant that will deal with sin once for all, a promise of blood that will cleanse the conscience from dead works. Of course, the Supper displays the death of Jesus, and of course it also points ahead to the great feast in the Father's kingdom. All that is true, but in Matthew, these rich and deep words of institution are surrounded by warnings and predictions about betrayal and about the treachery of Judas, the close table companion who turns against the Christ, words about the weakness and frailty of the other disciples, who will flee as soon as the shepherd is struck.

That context lends an important nuance to our understanding of Jesus' words and to our understanding of the Supper. Jesus breaks the bread, and says: "This is my body." That is His body given in death on a cross, but it is also the fragmentation of the body of the disciples, which is also broken, scattered, shattered, torn down. The behavior of the disciples, their weakness and denial and betrayal – that is all part of the suffering that Jesus will endure. It is part of the breaking of His body. When Jesus first mentions the cross, He has a specific form of suffering in mind: the division of family members from one another because of the gospel (Matt. 10:34-39). Jesus knows that cross too. He knows the pain of the sword that divides members of a single house, the house that is made of the brothers, mother, and sisters who do His will. Yet, as Jesus takes this bread, the body that will be torn on the cross, the body of disciples that will flee, as He takes that bread that will be broken, He *gives thanks*. And He offers that body to the disciples as food. As He finishes the meal – the meal that He knows will be followed by arrest, trial, torture, and the cross – He goes out singing. He goes out to the garden where He will be arrested; He goes to unjust trial and beatings; He goes to the cross and the grave, and *He goes out singing*. He goes out for the joy that is set before Him.

In all likelihood, the disciples sing the Hallel, Psalms 113-118, which climaxes with the marvelous news that the rejected stone has become the chief cornerstone of the temple (Psalm 118:22-24). Jesus gives thanks for the body that will be broken, His own body and the body of disciples. He goes out singing because He knows that this is the "first of unleavening," the purging of the old leaven and the beginning of new, a new beginning for Israel, an Israel fermented by the leaven of the kingdom instead of the leaven of scribes and Pharisees. He goes out singing because He trusts His Father that the scattered disciples will be scattered, the fragmented body restored`, the dead raised again. He goes out singing because He knows that the temple of His body, though torn so that not one stone will be left on another, will be rebuilt, a glorious house, and that the rejected stone will become the chief cornerstone.

In Gethsemane
Matthew 26:31-56

⁳¹ Then Jesus said to them, "You will all fall away because of Me this night, for it is written, I will strike down the Shepherd, and the sheep of the flock will be scattered. ³² But after I have been raised, I will go ahead of you to Galilee." ³³ But Peter said to Him, "Even though all may fall away because of You, I will never fall away." ³⁴ Jesus said to him, "Truly I say to you that this very night, before a rooster crows, you will deny Me three times." ³⁵ Peter said to Him, "Even if I have to die with You, I will not deny You." All the disciples said the same thing too. ³⁶ Then Jesus came with them to a place called Gethsemane, and said to His disciples, "Sit here while I go over there and pray." ³⁷ And He took with Him Peter and the two sons of Zebedee, and began to be grieved and distressed. ³⁸ Then He said to them, "My soul is deeply grieved, to the point of death; remain here and keep watch with Me." ³⁹ And He went a little beyond them, and fell on His face and prayed, saying, "My Father, if it is possible, let this cup pass from Me; yet not as I will, but as You will." ⁴⁰ And He came to the disciples and found them sleeping, and said to Peter, "So, you men could not keep watch with Me for one hour? ⁴¹ Keep watching and praying that you may not enter into temptation; the spirit is willing, but the flesh is weak." ⁴² He went away again a second time and prayed, saying, "My Father, if this cannot pass away unless I drink it, Your will be done." ⁴³ Again He came and found them sleeping, for their eyes were heavy. ⁴⁴ And He left them again, and went away and prayed a third time, saying the same thing once more. ⁴⁵ Then He came to the disciples and said to them, "Are you still sleeping and resting? Behold, the hour is at hand and the Son of Man is being betrayed into the hands of sinners. ⁴⁶ Get up, let us be going; behold, the one who betrays Me is at hand!" ⁴⁷ While He was still speaking, behold, Judas, one of the twelve, came up accompanied by a large crowd with swords and clubs, who came from the chief priests and elders of the people. ⁴⁸ Now he who was betraying Him gave them a sign, saying, Whomever I kiss, He is the one; seize Him." ⁴⁹ Immediately Judas went to Jesus and said, "Hail, Rabbi!" and kissed Him. ⁵⁰ And Jesus said to him, "Friend, do what you have come for." Then they came and laid hands on Jesus and seized Him. ⁵¹ And behold, one of those who were with Jesus reached and drew out his sword, and struck the slave of the high priest and cut off his ear. ⁵² Then Jesus said to him, "Put your sword back into its place; for all those who take up the sword shall perish by the sword. ⁵³ Or do you think that I cannot appeal to My Father, and He will at once put at My disposal more than twelve legions of angels? ⁵⁴ How then will the Scriptures be fulfilled, which say that it must happen this way?" ⁵⁵ At that time Jesus said to the crowds, "Have you come out with swords and clubs to arrest Me as you would against a robber? Every day I used to sit in the temple teaching and you did not seize Me. ⁵⁶ But all this has taken place to fulfill the Scriptures of the prophets." Then all the disciples left Him and fled.

When John the Baptist was in prison, he sent disciples to ask Jesus, "Are you the expected one, or shall we look for another?" Jesus answered by summarizing His ministry: He gives sight to the blind, makes the lame walk, cleanses lepers, opens the ears of the deaf, raises the dead, preaches the gospel to the poor. He quotes from Isaiah, a prophecy about the anointed Servant of Yahweh who will do all that Jesus has done. Then He adds, "Blessed is he who is not offended over Me" (11:2-6). Blessed is He who does not stumble over Me; blessed is the one who is not scandalized by Me. Why would anyone be scandalized by Jesus? He is doing miracles, signs and wonders, preaching the good news that the kingdom is at hand. Why would anyone find that hard to swallow? In Matthew 11, the problem is that John is in prison. How can Jesus be fulfilling all the hopes of Israel, if John is languishing in prison? Is not the Messiah coming to *release* prisoners? How can the Forerunner of the Messiah end up dead?

Jesus returns to the same topic as He and His disciples leave Jerusalem, their Passover meal, and cross the valley to the Mount of Olives. He predicts the fall of His disciples. All His disciples will stumble and fall because of Him this night. As in Matthew 11, the terminology that Jesus uses is the source of our English word "scandal." The disciples will be "scandalized" by Jesus. The word literally refers to a stone that someone stumbles over. Lev. 19:14 commands Israel not to lay a "scandal" in the way of the blind man to make Him stumble. All the disciples will be "scandalized" by Jesus; instead of a rock of refuge, they will find Him a stone of stumbling (26:31, 33).

They stumble for the same reason that John and his disciples were in danger of being scandalized. A Messiah who leaves suffering and imprisonment in His wake does not seem to be much of a Messiah. A Messiah who gets seized and tried and crucified, and does not do anything in his own defense – that is not the kind of Messiah any Jew wants. Paul said that he preached Christ crucified, foolishness to Greeks and a stumbling block to the Jews. The disciples are typical Jews in this regard, offended by a suffering Messiah.

The word "deny" is crucial, used in Matthew only in contexts where Jesus commands His disciples to deny themselves and take up the cross. There are only two choices, as far as Jesus is concerned: Either deny one's self, give up all hope of security and safety, and follow Jesus to the cross; or, deny Jesus, and find safety among the multitude in the court of the high priest. The disciples will fail; they will not deny themselves, but deny Jesus.

As always, Jesus sees these events in the light of prophecy. The prospect that the people of God will be scandalized, will stumble over a stumbling stone, is nothing new. Yahweh threatened to set up stumbling stones in the way of His unfaithful people. When they turn from Him, and refuse to repent, He threatens to make them stumble and fall once and for all, by setting up a stone to make them fall. Jesus is that stumbling stone. The specific prophecy that Jesus has in mind is from Zechariah. The rejected Shepherd-King that Yahweh placed over Israel (Zech. 11:4-17) will be struck, and the people scattered into the fire of exile (Zech. 13:7-9). In Zechariah, the scandal, the stumble, is not permanent. The scattered people will return, refined. Jesus sees this as a prediction of the disciples' failure, their faithlessness to Jesus. But it is also a prophecy that the disciples will go through a process of scattering, a process of purification, but that this dispersion will end in regathering, the fire of exile will purge and purify the disciples so that they will lead a *new*, purified Israel.

Zechariah predicts fall and restoration, but beyond that it is a prediction that, despite their denials and stumbling, the disciples *will* share in the sufferings of Jesus. For now, they scatter, but they are the one-third that is left to be refined like silver and tested like gold. This night, Jesus will be alone; this night in the garden, Jesus will be alone before his captors. But the remnant will not escape purging and purification. Peter says he will die with Jesus, and that is true: he will die as the feeble disciple he has been, and rise with Jesus to become the leader of the Twelve. On this night, he will stumble; on this night, the disciples all will scatter. But eventually they will all be regathered, and sent to make disciples of the nations.

Based on this prophecy, Jesus predicts a mini-exile, but also an eventual "return from Babylon," as the disciples gather with Him in Galilee (Matt. 26:32). This is the way God always works. He never glorifies His people, or extends His kingdom, in a straight line. For our God, the way to glory, to life, to health, to safety, to salvation is always a crooked path. There is always a deviation through exile, through scattering, through the waters and the wilderness, through death. Glory is always on the far side of the cross; to have a bride, you always have to be taken near death and torn in two; to have day, you have to pass through night. This is the lesson that Jesus learns in the garden, in His prayer to His Father. This is part of the process of Jesus' perfecting. Through His experience in the garden, through the prayers He offers, He learns obedience, He learns that His Father never brings glory in a straight line. He has to learn the crooked way to glory.

This may sound like an odd way to put it. Is not Jesus God? How can He learn anything? Is not Jesus always faithful, sinless, completely obedient? How can He learn obedience? Was not He perfect from the get-go? How can he be "perfected" or "made perfect"? We do not have space to go into all the theological niceties here, and even if we had world enough and time, we would be far from understanding the mystery of Gethsemane. What we can say, with assurance, is that Jesus learned obedience by His sufferings, and particularly in the prayers that He offers here. This is part of His qualification to be our priest.

The writer of Hebrews refers directly to this event (Heb. 5:7-10). Jesus asks for the cup to be removed; the Father does not answer. He prays three times, and the Father does not deliver Him from death. He will have to drink the cup; the only way for the cup to "pass away" is for Jesus to drink it. He submits to His Father, praying the prayer that He taught the disciples, "Thy will be done." He denies Himself, and takes up His cross, in submission to the Father's will. The author of Hebrews seems to be reading an alternative account.

The author of Hebrews says that "He was heard because of His piety." Matthew seems to record the opposite: the Father did not hear or answer. There is no voice from heaven, no splitting of the sky, no sudden rescue, no invasion of twelve legions of angels. But Hebrews is right, of course: Jesus is delivered from death. The Father does hear Him. Jesus is delivered from death, however, only after going *through* death. He does not sidestep the grave, but is taken to it. He learns that the way to life is not a straight line; the way to life deviates through death. The way of life is always a crooked way. Paul also prayed three times for deliverance. The Lord gave him a thorn in the flesh to prevent him from becoming proud; it was a "messenger from Satan." Three times Paul prayed for deliverance, and finally the Lord answered: "My grace is sufficient; power is perfected in weakness." He was delivered from the thorn, but not by having it removed. He was delivered by enduring it in faith. This is the lesson Jesus learns in the garden: "power is perfected in weakness."

The last time Jesus was with these three disciples, Peter, James, and John, there was transfigured glory, a voice from heaven, a bright light, an answer from the Father. The last time Jesus was with these three, they saw a glimpse of Jesus' glory. This seems completely opposite. Nothing could be more different. Instead of glory, Jesus grieves to the point of death. Instead of the voice of the Father, there is silence. Instead of light brighter than the sun, the night remains dark, and the powers of darkness seem to be in charge.

Not that the disciples see it anyway. When He arrives at the garden, Jesus takes Peter, James, and John with Him to pray (Matt. 26:36-37). He warns them to watch with Him as He prays. But they cannot. Three times he finds them sleeping. They are not alert, watchful, waiting. In the Olivet Discourse, Jesus warned the disciples to be alert and prepared for the coming of the bridegroom (25:1-13), but the disciples do not watch and pray with Him but instead fall asleep. Those warnings were in the context of the destruction of the temple, and the coming of the Son of Man in AD 70. But the Son of Man is coming here in Gethsemane as well. This is the hour of the Son of Man, just as much as His hour of the destruction of Jerusalem. Here is a temple falling, and the disciples are not watchful. The disciples can stay awake for a light show on the mount of transfiguration. That is dazzling, and even though they are drowsy they are instantly awake. But a Jesus groaning and crying and sweating blood and speaking cryptically of a cup that He has to drink – that cannot hold their attention.

If they had been able to watch, though, they would have observed something even more awesome than the transfiguration. On the mount of transfiguration, Jesus was glorified and illuminated by obvious, self-evident glory. The glory is not apparent at all on the Mount of Olives, in Gethsemane. But this is true glory, the glory of the Son's submission to the Father, the glory of the Son willing to drink the cup. This is not straight-line glory, but it is glory, the Triune glory of the God who gives Himself for His people, the Shepherd struck for His sheep, the glory of power made perfect in weakness.

Power perfected in weakness: that is the theme of the last episode as well. Judas has been enticed by money, like the seed among thorns that is choked out by love of riches (13:22). The other disciples are like seed on stony ground, which withers when persecution arises (13:21). Here they stumble and fall. Here they deny Jesus. There is the obvious stumbling. They leave Jesus behind and flee. Jesus says, "Take up your cross and follow Me," which is to say, "Be willing to die with me." Instead the disciples flee. The disciples who have left everything to follow Jesus *leave* Jesus.

For one disciple at least (John tells us it is Peter), the fall takes a paradoxical form. The fall takes the form of an effort to *defend* Jesus. An unnamed disciple cuts off the ear of the high priest's slave, but this is also an abandonment of Jesus and of the Father's purposes (26:51-52). The word "sword" is used six times in Matt. 26:47-56, three times in verse 52 alone. (Otherwise, Matthew uses the word only once, in Matt. 10:34). The mob comes to arrest Jesus with "swords and clubs" (26:47, 55), and right at the center of the account one of the disciples draws a sword. Even though he intends to defend Jesus, this is in fact another form of denial. A disciple with a sword has in effect joined the mob that opposes Jesus. Jesus warns that those who take up the sword will perish with the sword. In the immediate scene, it is the crowd "from the chief priests and elders of the people" who are holding swords (26:47). Now they form a mob to kill Jesus, who has presented to Israel a way of righteousness and peace. Within a generation, though, they will be in danger from Roman swords.

Jesus' words hint at the alternative. "Take up" is what disciples are supposed to do with the cross (10:32), not with the sword. Those who take up cross rather than sword are the ones who are disciples of Jesus, and true opponents of Roman paganism. The mob comes against Jesus as if he was a "thief" (*lestes*), and Jesus will die like a brigand between two brigands. But they are the true brigands, the revolutionaries who will be slaughtered by Roman swords. At the center of the whole passage comes the chief denial of Jesus, the reliance on the sword as a means of victory rather than the cross, the confidence in the strength of the arm, the chariot, the horse, rather than confidence in the strength of God, the strength that is perfected in weakness.

But there is likely another dimension to this. Jesus warns His disciples that those who rely on physical or military power will die by the same. He warns the Jewish mob that their swords and clubs will only lead to them being killed by swords and clubs in the future. (They are armed with swords and "crosses.") Jesus has also come with a sword, a sword that divides between father and son, mother and daughter, sister and brother. Jesus comes with the sword of the Spirit. Those who live by that sword can also expect a sword. Those who live by the sword of the Spirit can expect to be attacked and hated and crucified, as Jesus is. That sword, the sword of Jesus, the sword of the Spirit, is the victorious sword. When disciples of Jesus rely on that sword, they can expect persecution, but also expect that the cross they suffer will lead to glory. Because the way of the Spirit, the way of Jesus' sword, is the Father's crooked path to glory.

God on Trial
Matthew 26:57-27:2

⁵⁷ Those who had seized Jesus led Him away to Caiaphas, the high priest, where the scribes and the elders were gathered together. ⁵⁸ But Peter was following Him at a distance as far as the courtyard of the high priest, and entered in, and sat down with the officers to see the outcome. ⁵⁹ Now the chief priests and the whole Council kept trying to obtain false testimony against Jesus, so that they might put Him to death. ⁶⁰ They did not find any, even though many false witnesses came forward. But later on two came forward, ⁶¹ and said, "This man stated, 'I am able to destroy the temple of God and to rebuild it in three days.'" ⁶² The high priest stood up and said to Him, "Do You not answer? What is it that these men are testifying against You?" ⁶³ But Jesus kept silent And the high priest said to Him, "I adjure You by the living God, that You tell us whether You are the Christ, the Son of God." ⁶⁴ Jesus said to him, "You have said it yourself; nevertheless I tell you, hereafter you will see the Son of Man sitting at the right hand of power, and coming on the clouds of heaven." ⁶⁵ Then the high priest tore his robes and said, "He has blasphemed! What further need do we have

of witnesses? Behold, you have now heard the blasphemy; [66] what do you think?" They answered, "He deserves death!" [67] Then they spat in His face and beat Him with their fists; and others slapped Him, [68] and said, "Prophesy to us, You Christ; who is the one who hit You?" [69] Now Peter was sitting outside in the courtyard, and a servant-girl came to him and said, "You too were with Jesus the Galilean." [70] But he denied it before them all, saying, "I do not know what you are talking about." [71] When he had gone out to the gateway, another servant-girl saw him and said to those who were there, "This man was with Jesus of Nazareth."[72] And again he denied it with an oath, "I do not know the man." [73] A little later the bystanders came up and said to Peter, "Surely you too are one of them; for even the way you talk gives you away." [74] Then he began to curse and swear, "I do not know the man!" And immediately a rooster crowed. [75] And Peter remembered the word which Jesus had said, "Before a rooster crows, you will deny Me three times." And he went out and wept bitterly. [27:1] Now when morning came, all the chief priests and the elders of the people conferred together against Jesus to put Him to death [2] and they bound Him, and led Him away and delivered Him to Pilate the governor.

"Evening and morning were the first day."

In Genesis 1, time begins in darkness, at night, and moves toward daylight. The days of creation moved from evening to morning. Creation began in utter darkness, and then the Lord spoke and there was light. As the creation week continued, the light increased, as each day displayed more and more glory. History moves in the same direction. The Old Covenant was a time of relative darkness, its calendar pegged to the moon, but with the coming of the Word of God in the flesh, day dawns. Israel's history also began at night, on the night of the Passover. During that night, the angel of death stalked through Egypt, killing the firstborn in any house that did not have the blood of a lamb spread on the door posts and lintel. During that same night, Israel packed up, plundered the Egyptians, and began their journey toward the Promised Land. Israel crossed the sea during the night as well, and when the day dawned, Pharaoh and his hosts were drowned. In the morning light, Israel sees only the corpses of their enemies floating on the waters. For Israel as for the whole creation, "evening and morning," evening *to* morning makes the first day, the day of Israel's formation as a people, the day of their creation.

Jesus' trial also moves from darkness to light. Jesus shares the Passover meal with His disciples, and then heads out to the Mount of Olives. On that same night Jesus prays in Gethsemane. On that same night, Judas brings the Jewish mob with swords and clubs to arrest Jesus. Still on that same night, the Sanhedrin meets to put Jesus on trial, and Peter denies Jesus three times. It is not until all that has happened that the cock crows to announce the beginning of a new day, and only in the morning do the chief priests and elders of the people hand Jesus over to the Roman authorities for a trial before Pilate.

The trial before the Sanhedrin takes place in darkness. The priests, scribes, and elders assemble together as a duly constituted law court. There were assemblies of judges in each town of Israel, but the Great Sanhedrin was the supreme court of ancient Israel. That is the court in Jerusalem before which Jesus is tried. It was a collection of some seventy Jewish leaders who provided a degree of self-governance for the Jews under Roman rule. The Sanhedrin is no longer a mob, no longer a group "of the people," like the mob that arrested Jesus in the garden. This is a court, a duly constituted assembly, gathered together.

As such, they need to follow rules and procedures. They need to follow the law. They cannot simply condemn Jesus to death without any trial or evidence or witnesses. They know that the law requires two or three witnesses. They know that they have to find Jesus guilty of something worthy of death. This is a court, and a court is supposed to bring things to light. It is supposed to expose works of darkness and dispel the darkness. But this court is in the dark.

Though constituted as a proper law court, a meeting of the supreme court of Israel, the priests, elders, and scribes do not follow accepted procedures. They know the outcome they want before they begin. They offer false witnesses in the hope that they can find sufficient evidence to put Jesus to death. The fixed goal is to kill Jesus. The verdict and the sentence are pre-determined, and all they have to do is to find the means to get to that verdict and that sentence. Once they determine that Jesus is worthy of death, the Jewish court begins to torture and mock Jesus. They spit on His face and slap Him and beat Him with fists, and mock His claims to be a prophet. The darkness of injustice also hangs over them, also the darkness of ignorance. When Jesus testifies that He is the Christ, the Son of God, and that He will be exalted as the Son of Man, the high priest considers it blasphemy. That cannot be true, the high priest assumes. But it is true. Jesus really is all He claims to be, and He will soon sit at the right hand of the Power.

They are ignorant of their own Scriptures. They fulfill prophecy even as they spit and slap and beat Jesus. Isaiah wrote of the Servant of Yahweh, "I gave My back to those who strike Me, And My cheeks to those who pluck out the beard; I did not cover My face from humiliation and spitting" (Isa. 50:6). By shaming Jesus, they are proving that He is the Suffering Servant who bears the sins of Israel. They are fulfilling Jesus' own prophesies. He has been telling His disciples for a long time that He would be handed over to the chief priests and elders, put on trial, eventually put to death on a Roman cross. He has predicted that He would be mocked and scourged by the Gentiles. The Jews are surrounded by fulfillments of Jesus' prophecies. Their own actions are just what Jesus predicted. Yet they stumble about in darkness.

The darkness of this night is even deeper than that. It is not just that the court is a kangaroo court, determined to reach a predetermined verdict and sentence before they begin to hear evidence. It is not just that they are ignorant of the truth, even though they are fulfilling it. Israel was created in the darkness of the first Passover, and on this night, that whole process is being reversed. All that made Israel "Israel" is being stripped away. Israel is systematically divesting herself of all her privileges, all her reason for being. Israel is undoing herself on this night, in a great anti-Passover.

For instance: The high priest hears what he thinks is the blasphemy of Jesus, and he tears his priestly robes. This is strictly forbidden in the law (Leviticus 21), and amounts to a symbolic renunciation of the priesthood. A priest without his robes of glory and beauty is no more useful than a temple with a rent veil.

Then the Jewish leaders hand over Jesus to the Romans, the climax of this inverted Passover. On the first Passover, Israel was delivered from the angel of death and separated from Egypt. In Exodus 12-14, the night of Passover continues, narratively, until the day after the crossing of the sea. Chronologically, it is not the same night; but in the narrative there is no explicit reference to dawn until Pharaoh and his hosts drown in the sea (Exod. 14:27). Evening of Passover, morning of Exodus: one day. Matthew's account of Jesus' trials also moves from night to day. Jesus celebrates Passover with His disciples, prays in Gethsemane, is arrested and tried by the Sanhedrin, all on the same night. Day does not dawn until the Jews hand Jesus over to the Romans (Matt. 27:1-2). Passover is turned inside out: on the first Passover/Exodus, dawn found Israel delivered from a defeated Gentile power; on this Passover/Exodus, Israel lets herself be reabsorbed into the nations: "We have no king but Caesar." Israel spends this night renouncing the Lord who delivered them on the night of Passover. Yahweh shows up, and Israel puts Yahweh on trial.

Strangely, the leaders' effort to organize a kangaroo court does not work! Two sets of witnesses are mentioned in Matthew 26. The first set is explicitly called "false witnesses" (vv. 59-60). But Matthew says "the whole Sanhedrin was seeking false testimony against Jesus . . . and they did not find any" who could present united testimony (vv. 59-60). At this point, they are still keeping up the appearance of following Torah's requirement of two or three witnesses. But they are not actually seeking truth or justice. Their procedural justice is cover for convicting an innocent man. Woe to the sticklers.

When they cannot find suitable testimony, they are stymied, albeit briefly. They call a second set of witnesses, two witnesses, who come "later" (26:60). These witnesses bring a united testimony, one that passes the procedural test, the rules of evidence, the requirement of two or three witnesses. And, even better, their testimony happens to be *true*. They claim that Jesus said He was able to destroy the temple and rebuild it in three days. Matthew does not record this statement, but it is the kind of thing Jesus might say, and John records that He actually did say it, though He was talking about the temple of His own body, not the physical temple of Jerusalem.

Here is something the Sanhedrin can work with, and the high priest presses the point with Jesus. Did you say this? Do not you have anything to say in your defense? What did you mean by this? When Jesus does not answer, the high priest places Jesus under oath, and demands to know whether or not Jesus is the Christ, the anointed One, the Son of God who according to Scripture will come to build the temple. Jesus acknowledges that the high priest has spoken correctly: He is the Son of God, the temple-building Son of David. And then Jesus, as He so often does, raises the stakes. Instead of backing off and qualifying and softening His claims, He intensifies them by adding that He is not only the Messiah but that someday the high priest himself will perceive that Jesus is the Son of Man, the one exalted to the ancient of days in the prophecy of Daniel. He claims He is the Lord who sits on the right hand of Yahweh, as Psalm 110 prophesies.

These titles did not mean for the Jews what they mean for us. In the Old Testament, "Son of God" is not a statement about divine nature; it is a Messianic title, a title that identifies the descendant of David who, Yahweh predicted, would build the temple. "Son of Man" does not mean "human nature," though it does identify a human being. "Son of Man" means "last Adam," and it specifically refers to the vision of Daniel where he sees "one like the Son of Man" exalted to receive authority over the nations. This is the climax of Jesus' teaching about Himself as the "Son of Man," which has been a thread of His teaching from the beginning. The Son of Man has nowhere to lay His head, the Son of Man has authority to forgive sins, the Son of Man is Lord of the Sabbath, the Son of Man will be three days and three nights in the heart of the land, the Son of Man will suffer many things, but will rise from the dead, the Son of Man will come in His kingdom with His angels. That whole storyline of the Son of Man, Jesus says, will come to its climax when He is exalted at the right hand of the "Power" and share the authority of the God of Israel, the Creator.

This testimony finally convicts Jesus: the testimony of two witnesses who quote something Jesus actually said, something true; and Jesus' own testimony to His status as Son of Man and Davidic Son of God. Jesus is not convicted by all the false testimony, but by true testimony.

Everything has been done correctly here. Procedurally, the trial ends up impeccable; they get two witnesses who agree on their testimony. Their witness is true, and then the witness is confirmed by the testimony of the accused Himself. Best of all, it is a capital crime, blasphemy. Everything is right here, everything impeccably done – except that in convicting Jesus, they are convicting Yahweh incarnate. They follow the law to a tee, and end up convicting the lawgiver of blasphemy.

Modern atheism boasts about putting God on trial. God does not measure up to their standards. A triune God does not measure up to their standards of rationality: How can three be one? A God who expresses jealous wrath against His enemies and His people, or a God who orders the slaughter of the Canaanites, does not measure up to their standards of morality. Atheists think they are being daring, cutting edge, innovative, creative, when they subject God to their own standards, and find that He does not measure up. Hardly. Modern atheists are simply repeating the gestures that we find in the gospel story itself.

The God of Israel comes to Israel, and Israel puts Him on trial. They condemn God incarnate on the basis of true testimony – His claim to be able to destroy and rebuild the temple. Jesus really claims such power, and He really has it, as He has demonstrated again and again. But the Sanhedrin does not want such a God, a God who commits the blasphemy of destroying and rebuilding temples.

This is what the Sanhedrin really objects to. How dare Jesus, how dare *God*, knock down *their* temple? They want a god of guarantees, whose entire reason for being is to ensure that their temple will stand and keep standing, no matter what. Like all pagans, they want a god who ensures the persistence of the past, not a God who breaks down the present to make a new future. For them, a God who destroys and raises up is a blasphemous God. That is what Sanhedrins of every age long for: a god who sanctions their traditions. They will always send a God who kicks over their little monuments to the cross.

But the God who destroys His own temple is the only God there is. This is the God of Israel, not a God who exists to prop up our world, to keep things steady as she goes. The God of Israel is a disruptive God, who stirs things up, who forms worlds and tears them apart, who builds temples and destroys them when they get corrupt. The only God is the God who wrenched Israel away from Egypt on the first Passover and at the sea, the God who is wrenching a new Israel out of the old on this night, another night of Passover, a night that is for the rising and falling of many in Israel.

Innocent Blood
Matthew 27:1-10

> ¹ Now when morning came, all the chief priests and the elders of the people conferred together against Jesus to put Him to death; ² and they bound Him, and led Him away and delivered Him to Pilate the governor. ³ Then when Judas, who had betrayed Him, saw that He had been condemned, he felt remorse and returned the thirty pieces of silver to the chief priests and elders, ⁴ saying, "I have sinned by betraying innocent blood." But they said, "What is that to us? See to that yourself!" ⁵ And he threw the pieces of silver into the temple sanctuary and departed; and he went away and hanged himself. ⁶ The chief priests took the pieces of silver and said, "It is not lawful to put them into the temple treasury, since it is the price of blood." ⁷ And they conferred together and with the

money bought the Potter's Field as a burial place for strangers. [8] For this reason that field has been called the Field of Blood to this day. [9] Then that which was spoken through Jeremiah the prophet was fulfilled: "And they took the thirty pieces of silver, the price of the one whose price had been set by the sons of Israel; [10] and they gave them for the potter's field, as the Lord directed me."

As we have seen throughout this commentary, Matthew is organized around five discourses, which trace out the history of Jesus as a recapitulation of the history of God and Israel in the Old Testament. Jesus first speaks as a new Moses, instructing His disciples on a mountain about a righteousness that surpasses the righteousness of the scribes and Pharisees. Then Jesus is a Moses or Joshua, sending out His apostles to announce the kingdom and carry out a gracious conquest of the lost sheep of the house of Israel. He speaks about His kingdom in parables and dark sayings, like Solomon the sage-king. He instructs His disciples about forgiveness and discipline within the new Israel, like a new Elisha leading a band of sons of the prophets. Finally, he is a new Jeremiah announcing the doom on the temple and the city of Jerusalem, warning that the temple is going to be torn down and there will not be one stone left upon another. If Matthew is following the history of the Old Testament, the next thing that should happen is a destruction of a temple and an exile. It has already begun, in Matthew 26. When Judas leads the temple guard to Gethsemane to arrest Jesus, the disciples flee, leaving Jesus the shepherd to be struck instead of the scattered sheep. That is the beginning of the diaspora of the Twelve, the beginning of the destruction of the temple of Jesus personal and corporate body.

This storyline continues into Matthew 27. At Jesus' trial before the Sanhedrin, the charge is that He said he would destroy the temple and rebuilt it in three days (26:61). While Jesus hangs on the cross, this is the focus of the Jews' mockery of Jesus: "You who are going to destroy the temple and rebuild it in three days, save Yourself!" (27:40). That is the meaning of the narrative that surrounds these two statements. What we are witnessing in Matthew 27 is the collapse of a temple, the fall of a house, and great is its fall.

This is true in two senses. On the one hand, this chapter is about the fall of the temple of Jesus' body, the rending of that temple until there is nothing left. Matthew makes this point by carefully tracing the passage of time. As I noted above, the passion of Jesus moves from darkness to light. Jesus celebrated Passover with His disciples in the evening (26:20), and during the night He was arrested and tried before the Sanhedrin, while Peter denied Him outside in the high priest's courtyard. Now day dawns (27:1), a harbinger of hope. Dawn means a new day, light shining in darkness and overcoming the darkness. But this day will not remain day. This day turns to a darkness darker than night, darkness visible (27:45). The Jews might think this is the beginning of their new day: they will get rid of Jesus and everything will brighten up. But this is the Lord's day, and that is a day of darkness and gloom, a day of clouds and thick darkness (Zeph. 3:14-15). Israel has become Egypt, and before the Passover Lamb is slaughtered and His blood displayed, Israel undergoes a plague of darkness.

Matthew describes a three-day sequence. From the evening of Jesus' Last Supper to the day of His crucifixion is Day One; Matt. 27:62 mentions a "next day" when a guard is set at the tomb; then in Matt. 28:1 there is another dawn on the day after the Sabbath. That is a *real* dawn, a dawn on the third day. In the creation week, the earth began to bring forth its fruit and produce on the third day. So too on Matthew's third day, the earth yields up the first fruits of the dead, and on the next recorded day, symbolically the fourth, Jesus declares that He is like the Sun, given all authority in heaven and on earth. Matthew shows us the destruction and rebuilding of the temple, and makes clear that it takes three days to accomplish. What Jesus predicted comes true, just as He predicted, for He was speaking about the temple of His own body.

Just as importantly, these chapters are about the destruction of another temple, the looming destruction of the Jerusalem temple. When Jesus dies, that temple is ruined by the earthquake that tears the veil in two. Temple veils are barriers, keeping people out of God's presence, and without veils the temple in Jerusalem is pointless. That is the climax, but Matthew 27 prepares for that temple destruction.

Blood is a key theme of this section (27:4, 6, 8). Everyone in the story tries to escape responsibility for shedding Jesus' blood, but Jesus' blood clings to everyone who touches him. It will be charged to Jerusalem, the city of blood (23:34-35). When Judas recognizes that his betrayal has led to Jesus' condemnation, he acknowledges that he is under a curse. Deuteronomy curses those who accept bribes to strike down the innocent (cf. Deut. 27:25). Judas knows that the temple authorities conspired with him, and he throws the blood money where it belongs – into the temple (27:5) – where is came from in the first place. He throws the money into the temple, which puts the blood money – the innocent blood of Jesus – right before the face of God, where it will arouse God's wrath against His temple.

For their part, the chief priests deny any involvement in the matter, but they implicitly admit their guilt when they hastily remove the blood/money before it can defile (27:6). They even concede that they cannot remove the curse from Judas (Matt. 27:4). The blood of their sacrifices cannot remove high-handed sin. "See to that yourself," they tell Judas, and Judas does, taking his own life in a desperate attempt to pay for Jesus' blood with his own (cf. Num. 35:33; Lev. 24:21). The Jews try to escape bloodguilt, but they cannot escape it any better than Judas can, and they eventually spread the guilt out on the whole nation, and their children (Matt. 27:24-25). Ultimately they give up and accept the blood, and not merely Jesus' blood. The first time Matthew mentions blood is in Matthew 23, where Jesus warns that all the righteous blood from Abel to Zechariah the son of Berechiah will be charged to "this generation," the generation that completes the story of righteous blood, the generation that brings the sin of the Israelites to fullness. The Jews finally accept that blood on themselves and their children.

Everyone feels the contamination of the blood of Jesus. Judas wants to get rid of the money because it bought Jesus' blood. The Jews do not want the money because it is blood money. Pilate knows that Jesus is innocent, and so he tries to wash off the blood of Jesus. Everyone wants to scrape off the blood. But it comes back, again and again, and it will be charged to "this generation."

Matthew, as always, sees the events as fulfillments of prophecy. Many of his prophetic citations are puzzling and difficult, but the reference here is more difficult and puzzling than most. There are many questions here. Matthew attributes the quotation to Jeremiah, but then quotes from Zechariah. Why? When we look back at the source in Zechariah, the links between Zechariah and Matthew's story seem pretty arbitrary. There are some words in common - thirty pieces, throw, potter – and that is striking, but does the story of Zechariah 11 hang together with the story of Jesus, Judas, and the chief priests?

We can gain clarity if we recognize that this Old Testament citation points back again to the threat to the temple. Matthew claims to quote from Jeremiah, but actually quotes from Zech. 11:12-13 – though even that is not an exact quotation. Matthew knows what he is doing, and he is doing something that he and other New Testament writers do elsewhere. Mark begins his Gospel with a quotation he attributes to Isaiah, but which includes some wording from Malachi and an allusion to Exodus 23. In Matt. 21:5, Matthew conflates Isa. 62:11 ("say to daughter Zion") with Zech. 9:9 ("your King is coming to you," etc.). Matt. 2:5-6 quotes from Micah, but the line "who will shepherd my people Israel" is from 2 Sam.5:2. Yet, Matthew says that this quotation was written by "the prophet." Here in Matthew 27, Matthew is doing it again. He quotes from Zechariah but evokes passages in Jeremiah at the same time. Several passages in Jeremiah refer to potters and pottery, fields and purchases, and innocent blood (Jer.

18-19; 32:6-15). Whenever Matthew or another New Testament writer gives us these mixed quotations, they want us to consider the passages together.

What are the prophecies from Jeremiah and Zechariah about? Both warn about the breaking of a covenant, the shattering of Israel, because of their hostility to Yahweh and because of their shedding of innocent blood. To get the connections between Zechariah and Matthew, we need to start further back, at the beginning of Matthew 26, when Judas first has contact with the chief priests and elders. The story of Zechariah 11 begins with the Lord instructing the prophet to feed and pasture the sheep that are destined for slaughter. The Lord is angry with the shepherds who are selling and slaughtering the sheep, showing no pity to the flock that they are to care for. The prophet takes up his work of shepherding the flock doomed to destruction, using two staffs – which he named Favor and Union. Zech. 11:10-11 says, "And I took my staff, Beauty, and cut it in two, that I might break the covenant which I had made with all the peoples. So it was broken on that day. Thus the poor of the flock, who were watching me, knew that it *was* the word of the LORD." Whatever else we learn from Zechariah 11, we learn that the Lord is withdrawing His favor from the people of Israel. Matthew wants us to see that in the story of Judas and the chief priests: Because they shed the innocent blood of Jesus, a sin that defiles the land, they are doomed.

Zechariah goes on (Zech. 11:12): "Then I said to them, 'If it is agreeable to you, give *me* my wages; and if not, refrain.' So they weighed out for my wages thirty *pieces* of silver." This is virtually identical to Matthew 26, where Judas asks what the chief priests will give him for betraying Jesus, for slaughtering *the* Lamb. Judas is the instrument of the false shepherds who slaughter the flock and buy and sell them to enrich themselves. Zechariah goes on (Zech. 11:13-14): "And the LORD said to me, 'Throw it to the potter'—that princely price they set on me. So I took the *thirty* pieces of silver and threw them into the house of the LORD for the potter. Then I cut in two my other staff, Bonds, that I might break the brotherhood between Judah and Israel." This is the portion that Matthew quotes, and again it closely resembles what happens with Judas. But the Zechariah prophecy shows that the money thrown into the temple treasury, to the potter, is a sign that the bonds between Israel and Judah are going to be shattered. Israel will fight with Israel, as the Lord raises up a shepherd who will not care for the flock but will eat their fat and tear their hooves. That is what lies in store for the Jews, and Judas' blood-money in the temple is a sign of that doom.

The relevant Jeremiah passages are not about shepherds and pieces of silver, but about potters and innocent blood. Jeremiah warns that Israel will be shattered like a clay pot because they worship idols and shed innocent blood (Jer. 19:4, 10-11). In the later passage, Jeremiah purchases a field and stores the deed in a pot, a sign that Yahweh will one day restore His people to their land. The Lord says:

> Because they have forsaken Me and made this an alien place, because they have burned incense in it to other gods whom neither they, their fathers, nor the kings of Judah have known, and have filled this place with the blood of the innocents (they have also built the high places of Baal, to burn their sons with fire for burnt offerings to Baal, which I did not command or speak, nor did it come into My mind), therefore behold, the days are coming, says the Lord, that this place shall no more be called Tophet or the Valley of the Son of Hinnom, but the Valley of Slaughter. Then you shall break the flask in the sight of the men who go with you, and say to them, "Thus says the Lord of hosts: 'Even so I will break this people and this city, as one breaks a potter's vessel, which cannot be made whole again; and they shall bury them in Tophet till there is no place to bury.'"

Tophet was a place of idolatrous worship, where Israel offered human sacrifices. Because they had set up places of human sacrifice in the valley of Tophet, and shed innocent blood there, they will be shattered. Jeremiah dramatizes this doom by shattering a clay pot – representing Israel, formed by Yahweh as a new Adam – in the valley of Tophet. In Jesus' day, the Jews have become like the nations, plotting against the Messiah, offering a human sacrifice. And so they will be shattered (Psalm 2). Because they destroy the temple of Jesus' body, they will themselves be destroyed. Because they offer the firstborn, they will be slaughtered.

These Old Testament passages, particularly Zechariah, throw one last bit of light on Matthew's Passion story. All the early church debates about Christ revolved around this one question: Who suffered and died on the cross? *Jesus* is the answer, of course, but who is Jesus? All the heretics of the early church tried to create some space, put a buffer, between Jesus and God. Arians said that Jesus was only a creature, and Nestorius re-located the buffer so that it was between Jesus' divinity and humanity. They wanted to avoid one very offensive conclusion: that the suffering man on the cross is God, that God the Son died on the cross. The heretics make sense. After all, how can God die? That cannot be God, the sovereign Creator and King of the universe, with that mangled, bloody, torn body. That cannot be God crying out, "My God, My God." That cannot be God breathing His last.

We confess the opposite. Trace back the antecedents of the pronouns in the Nicene Creed. "And in one Lord Jesus Christ, the only-begotten Son of God . . . very God of very God . . . being of one substance with the Father . . . who for us men and for our salvation came down from heaven and was incarnate . . . and was crucified for us under Pontius Pilate." Who is the one on the cross? It is none other than the only-begotten Son of God, very God of very God, the Son who is "one substance" with the Father, the One who created all things. That Son of God is on the cross.

That creedal confession fits the prophecies of Zechariah and Jeremiah The ultimate solution to the "shepherd problem" of Zechariah, the ultimate solution to the false shepherds who destroy the people and prey on them, is for Yahweh Himself to become the Shepherd of Israel. *He* is the shepherd valued at thirty shekels, the shepherd who is struck, the one pierced. Yahweh Himself took that role. God's blood is shed, the most innocent of innocent blood. And that leads to two results. Matthew has written this portion of his Gospel to highlight the similarities and differences between two disciples, Judas and Peter. Peter is a lot like Judas. Peter betrayed Jesus; his betrayal was also predicted by Jesus; Peter too brought down curses with his self-maledictory oaths (Matt. 26:69-75). But Peter turned not to the priests but to Jesus, whose blood is poured out for forgiveness (Matt. 26:28). And so Peter was restored to favor.

Jesus' blood is inescapable. Everyone in the story is going to come under the blood of Jesus, one way or another. It is going to be charged against those who conspire to kill Jesus, or it is going to be the blood of the covenant, shed for the forgiveness of sins, for those who turn to Jesus. Either way, the blood will be on you and your children. Those who try to remove it, throw it away, wash it off – those are the ones who are doomed. Those who receive Jesus' blood will have robes of white washed in the blood of the Lamb. Jesus closes out the history of blood that began with Abel: His righteous blood is also charged to Jerusalem, and cries out for vengeance against Jerusalem. But to those who receive Jesus and trust Him, it speaks a better word than the blood of Abel, a word of forgiveness and pardon.

King of the Jews
Matthew 27:11-26

[11] Now Jesus stood before the governor, and the governor questioned Him, saying, "Are You the King of the Jews?" And Jesus said to him, "It is as you say." [12] And while He was being accused by the chief priests and elders, He did not answer. [13] Then Pilate said to Him, "Do You not hear how many things they testify against You?" [14] And He did not answer him with regard to even a single charge, so the governor was quite amazed. [15] Now at the feast the governor was accustomed to release for the people any one prisoner whom they wanted. [16] At that time they were holding a notorious prisoner, called Barabbas. [17] So when the people gathered together, Pilate said to them, "Whom do you want me to release for you? Barabbas, or Jesus who is called Christ?" [18] For he knew that because of

envy they had handed Him over. [19] While he was sitting on the judgment seat, his wife sent him a message, saying, "Have nothing to do with that righteous Man; for last night I suffered greatly in a dream because of Him." [20] But the chief priests and the elders persuaded the crowds to ask for Barabbas and to put Jesus to death. [21] But the governor said to them, "Which of the two do you want me to release for you?" And they said, "Barabbas." [22] Pilate said to them, "Then what shall I do with Jesus who is called Christ?" They all said, "Crucify Him!" [23] And he said, "Why, what evil has He done?" But they kept shouting all the more, saying, "Crucify Him!" [24] When Pilate saw that he was accomplishing nothing, but rather that a riot was starting, he took water and washed his hands in front of the crowd, saying, "I am innocent of this Man's blood; see to that yourselves." [25] And all the people said, "His blood shall be on us and on our children!" [26] Then he released Barabbas for them; but after having Jesus scourged, he handed Him over to be crucified.

Israel was supposed to be different. Yahweh called Abram at the beginning of Israel's history, calling him out from among the nations, out from among the idols, to worship the living God. When Israel gathered at Sinai, Yahweh declared that they were to be a separate people, a holy people, devoted to Him, serving Him instead of idols. Her whole life as a nation was to be shaped by the covenant with Yahweh. From her worship to her treatment of strangers and widows to the punishments inflicted on criminals to the laws of property – everything in Israel's national life was to be distinct from the surrounding nations, a model for the surrounding nations. Israel was to be the covenanted bride of the living God, devoted to her husband.

The Old Testament is a long story of Israel's accommodation to the nations, her growing resemblance to the Gentiles. That story comes to a climax here, before Pilate, at the trial of Jesus. Jesus is moved from the Sanhedrin to the court of Pilate (27:2), so that He stands before the Roman governor (27:11). Jesus is tried by the Jews, and He is tried by the Gentiles. But there is really no change, no progression or regression. The same cast of characters is present in both trials – the chief priests and elders. In both, people testify against Jesus and call Him Messiah. In both, Jesus speaks little, and in both He says "You have said." In both, Jesus is condemned to death, and both courts permit Jesus to be mocked and tortured. The Jewish trial is just as brutal and unjust as the Roman trial. In fact, it is worse. The Jews had already decided what to do with Jesus before the trial, and all they had to do was arrange testimony to get to the prearranged verdict. Pilate at least tries to investigate. Israel was supposed to be different. Israel was supposed to be devoted to justice and fairness, to hear testimony before deciding, to avoid condemning the righteous. But Israel's court has become a mirror image of the Roman court, or worse.

But the reversals for Israel are even more basic than this. It is not merely that Israel fails to live up to the covenant. They actively renounce the covenant, actively reverse all that they were called to be and do. When Israel came to Sinai, they were covenanted to Yahweh by the covenant-cutting rituals. They gathered at the mountain, as the "congregation" (*synagoge*) of Yahweh. They sacrificed animals, Moses ascended the mountain to receive the law that He delivered to the people, Moses sprinkled blood on the people, and they all cried out that they would keep all the words of the covenant. In the presence of Yahweh their King, they covenanted to be His bride.

All that is overturned in the trial before Pilate. Israel gathers before Pilate; Matthew uses the verb form for the word "synagogue" (27:17). The Jews are forming a "worshiping" assembly in the presence of Pilate. Their king is there, but instead of swearing loyalty to him, they want to get rid of Him. He has no beauty that they should desire Him. Instead of crying out their agreement to keep the words of the covenant, they cry out, "Crucify Him, Crucify Him." They are sprinkled with blood in the end, but it is the innocent blood of Jesus, which will condemn them. Pilate offers to "release" a prisoner to them, using a verb that Matthew elsewhere uses for "divorce." At Sinai, Israel cuts covenant with Yahweh; but this is an anti-covenant ceremony, an un-covenanting. At Sinai, Israel entered into a marriage relationship with the living God; but in the court of Pilate, they are released, sent away. This is not a renewal of the marriage covenant. Pilate's court amounts to a divorce court.

The conflict between Jesus and the Jewish leaders is a conflict over the control and leadership of the "crowd." Throughout the Gospel, the multitude has been following Jesus, marveling at His miracles and words. That has provoked the Jews to envy. They want the crowd to follow them; they want the bride of Israel for themselves. And here in Pilate's court they get what they want. They persuade the crowd, the bride, to renounce her royal husband. They persuade the crowd to demand Jesus' death. Like Joseph, Jesus is sold by His brothers, because He is the favored one of His Father.

The Jewish leaders also declare their relationship to Rome. In John's gospel, this is explicit. When Pilate asks, "What shall I do with your king?" they answer, "We have no king but Caesar." The decision is more subtle in Matthew's account. Every Jewish teacher in first-century Israel had to teach his disciples how to respond to the problem of Rome, and Jesus is no exception. When Jesus taught about loving enemies and going a second mile (5:38-48) or told His disciples to return Caesar's coin to Caesar (22:15-22), He was teaching them how to respond to brutal overlords. Jesus helped a Roman soldier, and commended his faith (8:1-13; cf. 2 Kings 5). Now, He stands on trial before Pilate and is mocked by Roman soldiers.

What do the Jews do? Do they want to follow Jesus' instructions about relating to the empire? Their decision is evident in their reaction to Pilate's offer to "release" a prisoner to them. The first Passover involved an exchange of sons: Yahweh took Egypt's firstborn sons, and delivered Israel's. Pilate offers a similar exchange to the Jews, at Passover (27:16-17, 21). This is apparent in the names. Jesus is the son of the Father. Early in his gospel, Matthew identified Him as Israel, the Son that Yahweh brought out of Egypt (2:15). Now Jesus the son stands before Pilate, and another "son" is there too – Barabbas, whose name means "son of the father." Who is the son of Egypt? Who is the son Israel? Which son will Israel acknowledge to be her own? Which son is the favorite son? In choosing Barabbas, the Jews give their answer to that question. They prefer the firstborn of "Egypt" to the firstborn of Israel.

It is also a Day of Atonement. On the Day of Atonement, two animals were brought to the tabernacle or temple; a lot was thrown, and one of the animals was selected as a scapegoat. The scapegoat was sent away to the wilderness bearing the sins of Israel on its head; the other goat was brought to the tabernacle and slaughtered as a sin offering. Barabbas and Jesus are the two goats: one is released, the other killed. Jesus is designated as the sin offering, whose blood will be brought into the Most Holy Place to cleanse all the sins and uncleanness of Israel. Barabbas is the scapegoat, but he is not sent off to the wilderness. He is sent back to Israel, bearing all the sins and guilt of Israel right back to where he came from.

This is not "mere symbolism." What Barabbas represents is unleashed among the people. Barabbas was a Jewish freedom fighter or insurrectionist (Mark 15:7), and so the decision before the Jews is not only a decision between two men but a decision about their future relation to the Roman empire: Will they choose the way of armed revolution or the more revolutionary way of Jesus? They make the fateful choice for Barabbas. They choose the way of armed resistance and violence, rather than the peaceable way of Jesus. And they will pay. In choosing Barabbas, they choose to take up the sword, and Jesus has already warned that those who take up the sword will perish by the sword. Though they choose the way of resistance to Rome, they, more profoundly chose the way of Rome. They choose to resist Rome with Rome's weapons, choose to resist violence with violence. That is fateful, because Rome is always going to win a struggle on Roman terms. They always have more of their kinds of weapons than anyone else has. It is also suicidal: the Jews choose to trust in horses, chariots, insurrectionists, rather than in the way of Yahweh.

While the trial exposes the failures and apostasy of Israel, it also exposes the impotence of the Roman Empire. Pilate has a reputation as a brutal and bumbling Roman governor. We know from Jewish sources – Philo and Josephus – that he had little sympathy for Jewish custom, and did not care to learn. He often offended Jews. When Jews resisted, he put down their resistance with brutal force. In this trial, the bumbling side comes out, which shows itself in cowardice. Pilate quickly assesses the situation, and has the shrewd insight to discern that the Jews are motivated by envy. He knows Jesus is innocent. He tries to release Jesus, and he finally washes his hands of Jesus' blood. His eagerness to get rid of Jesus is intensified when he gets the message about his wife's dream. Like Joseph and the wise men (Matt. 1:20; 2:12-13, 19, 22), she has received revelation in a dream (27:19). All the dreams in Matthew come from God. Dreams are interventions of heaven into the events of earth. All the dreams in the early part of Matthew conspire to keep Jesus alive. God tells Joseph to take Mary as his wife, tells the wise men not to go back to Herod, tells Joseph to flee from Israel, tells Joseph to go back to the land, tells Joseph to go to Nazareth rather than back to Bethlehem. Here again God intervenes to reveal that Jesus is a righteous man. The revelation that this man is innocent comes from outside, from heaven.

Nothing works. Pilate realizes finally that he has no power, and that if he continues to try to release Jesus he will only provoke the Jewish leaders further, who have secured control of the mob (v. 24). He is called "governor" eight times in this story, but with each use of the word, the irony becomes sharper. He is the Roman governor, with a battalion of the best soldiers in the world under his command, but he has no control of this situation. The word "governor" is first used in Matthew 2, in a quotation from the prophet Micah, who tells Bethlehem "Out of you will come a governor." Jesus is that governor, the Son of David, the King of the Jews. He is the one who is truly in charge of this trial, not Pilate. He is the true governor and judge.

When Pilate realizes he can do nothing, he tries at least to slip away from responsibility. So he washes his hands before the people and professes his innocence. This reminds us of Judas' actions in the previous section of the chapter. Judas realized he had betrayed innocent blood, and so he threw the money that had paid for the betrayal back to the temple. The gesture was an attempt to strip the blood from himself, and an attempt to throw the blood where it belonged, into the temple, to the Jewish leaders. Pilate is doing something similar, washing his hands as a sign that the blood of Jesus is not his responsibility.

This is not the only connection between Pilate and the story of Judas and the blood money. When he washes his hands, Pilate echoes the words of the Jewish leaders: "You shall see."[40] That is what the Jewish leaders said to Judas when he tried to bring the blood money back to the temple. But if Pilate is speaking the words of the Jewish leaders, then the Jewish leaders have been cast in the role of Judas. They are traitors, who have shed innocent blood, traitors who have renounced their Master and King. Judas went out and hanged himself, and that is what lies in store for the Jewish leaders. They are committing suicide.

Pilate's hand-washing rite also alludes back to a ritual of the Old Testament. "Blood pollutes the land," Numbers 35:33 says, "and no expiation can be made for the land for the blood that is shed on it, except by the blood of him who shed it." That comes in a passage that deals with cities of refuge. The city of refuge provided a way for the expiation of blood that was shed accidentally. It was the death of the high priest that removed that blood. What happens if blood is shed on the land, and nobody knows who did it? Deut. 21:1-9 gives a ritual for removing the blood guilt: the elder of the nearest city slaughter a heifer and wash their hands and confess before God that they do not know who is responsible. Pilate is unknowingly performing that rite. He wants to save the city from the stain of innocent blood by washing his hands. Of course, the ritual does not fit here. Washing hands

---

40 The passage is structured to bring out the parallel between the Jews and Pilate:

removes bloodguilt only if no one knows who is responsible for the bloodshed. But Pilate knows who is responsible. He is, and so are the Jewish leaders. There is no mystery here. Pilate washes his hands over a "heifer." In this case, the *heifer is Israel* herself, who will receive the blood and bear guilt. Israel is the scapegoat on behalf of Rome. Israel will suffer destruction for the innocent blood shed on the earth. And the Jews accept it. When Pilate cleans off his hands in their presence, they accept the blood, and make a kind of demonic anti-covenant: "His blood be on us and on our children."

So does it all come down to this? Israel was called to be different from all the other nations, called to cling to her Husband, the Creator God, in faith. Now Israel has turned from her King, her husband, at precisely the moment He has come to rescue her. She has chosen Barabbas over Jesus. She has accepted the innocent blood of Jesus on her own head, and on her children. Has it all come down to this? Is this the end of Israel's story? No. Israel *is* different, and they are different precisely here, in Pilate's court. What happens to Israel here reveals the precise difference between Israel and the nations. Israel was called to be a priestly nation. That means that Israel was called to offer sacrifice on behalf of the nations, and to intercede for the nations. But it also means that they are called to bear the sins of the nations. Israel is called to be the global scapegoat. That is the vocation that makes Israel special.

Jesus delivered (*paradidomi*) to Pilate, 27:2
    Judas: betrayed innocent blood (*haima athoon*), 27:4
        Jews: you will see (*su opse*), 27:4
            Pilate: I am innocent of blood
            (*athoos . . . apo tou hamatos toutou*), 27:24
        Pilate: you will see (*humeis opsesthe*), 27:24
    Jews: blood on our heads, 27:25
Jesus delivered (*paradidomi*) to cross, 27:26

Jesus has said this already. *"All the blood"* from Abel to Zechariah will be charged to this generation. *All* the blood?! Did Israel shed the blood of Abel? Was that blood shed in the land of Israel? No, yet Israel is going to be charged with that blood, because that is what Israel is called to do and be. Israel is called to bear the sins of the nations on herself. That is how the Lord deals with sin. But Israel herself sins. How does the Lord deal with *that*? In the Old Covenant, when Israel sins, Israel suffers her sins. She is destroyed, but then raised up. The innocent blood cries out, Yahweh destroys His people and city, scatters them to the winds, but then regathers to rebuild and replant. Will that cycle just go on and on and on forever? Israel destroyed and rebuilt, Israel destroyed and rebuilt? Is that salvation? Is that redemption for the world? Is there no way to remove Israel's sins?

Israel is not the only scapegoat here. Israel is not the only one who accepts blood guilt. Jesus' last words before going to the cross are His answer to Pilate's question. "Are you King of the Jews?" Pilate asks. Jesus answers, *"You say."* This is an affirmative. Jesus does not deny He is a King. Jesus says He is, but says it in a way that emphasizes that *Pilate* is the one who has decided that Jesus is King of the Jews. He designates Jesus as King when he sends Jesus to an innocent death. Pilate will say it again with the inscription that he puts over Jesus on the cross: "This is Jesus the King of the Jews." Being king means being the representative of your people, it means sharing in all that the people suffer. It means suffering first. If Israel is the scapegoat, the heifer who receives the bloodguilt from Pilate, then Jesus is the Chief Scapegoat, the King of Scapegoats. He goes first, and suffers *all* that Israel will suffer. He is the temple that is torn down so that not one stone is left on another. And if Israel gets behind Him, they will be saved.

If Israel herself is going to be saved, there needs to be a perfect Israel. Jesus is Israel. He is the Son called from Egypt. He is Yahweh become Israel to bear the sins of Israel. He is the final sacrifice. Are you the king of the Jews? Pilate asks. Jesus says, "You have said." This is what it means to be king of the Jews. This is what kings do. They take the burdens of their people. To be king of the Jews is to be the sin-bearer for the sin-bearing people. To be king of Israel is to die on behalf of Israel. All the sins of the world are heaped on Israel, and all the sins of Israel are heaped on King Jesus, so that He can bear it all away.

God Is Mocked
Matthew 27:27-44

²⁷ Then the soldiers of the governor took Jesus into the Praetorium and gathered the whole Roman cohort around Him. ²⁸ They stripped Him and put a scarlet robe on Him. ²⁹ And after twisting together a crown of thorns, they put it on His head, and a reed in His right hand; and they knelt down before Him and mocked Him, saying, "Hail, King of the Jews!" ³⁰ They spat on Him, and took the reed and began to beat Him on the head. ³¹ After they had mocked Him, they took the scarlet robe off Him and put His own garments back on Him, and led Him away to crucify Him. ³² As they were coming out, they found a man of Cyrene named Simon, whom they pressed into service to bear His cross. ³³ And when they came to a place called Golgotha, which means Place of a Skull, ³⁴ they gave Him wine to drink mixed with gall; and after tasting it, He was unwilling to drink. ³⁵ And when they had crucified Him, they divided up His garments among themselves by casting lots. ³⁶ And sitting down, they began to keep watch over Him there. ³⁷ And above His head they put up the charge against Him which read, THIS IS JESUS THE KING OF THE JEWS. ³⁸ At that time two robbers were crucified with Him, one on the right and one on the left. ³⁹ And those passing by were hurling abuse at Him, wagging their heads ⁴⁰ and saying, "You who are going to destroy the temple and rebuild it in three days, save Yourself! If You are the Son of God, come down from the cross." ⁴¹ In the same way the chief priests also, along with the scribes and elders, were mocking Him and saying, ⁴² "He saved others; He cannot save Himself. He is the King of Israel; let Him now come down from the cross, and we will believe in Him.⁴³ He trusts in God; let God rescue Him now, if

He delights in Him; for He said, I am the Son of God." ⁴⁴ The robbers who had been crucified with Him were also insulting Him with the same words.[41]

God is not mocked, Paul tells us. The Passion narratives tell a different story. Matthew gives very little information about the physical sufferings of Jesus. Nothing about blood, or exposed ribs, or human flesh flayed to tatters. We can imagine those sufferings from what he records, but his focus is elsewhere. For Matthew, the cross is mainly about man's mockery of God. Pilate knows Jesus is innocent, and he apparently wants to dispose of Jesus quickly. He turns Him over for scourging and crucifixion, and turns a blind eye to what happens within his own Praetorium. "Have nothing to do with that just man," his wife had warned him. Pilate follows her advice. He gives Jesus up to the lions and dogs and wolves, to the strong bulls of Bashan that attack from every side, and washes his hands of the matter.

In the Praetorium, a whole cohort of Roman soldiers – one-tenth of a legion, some six hundred men – relieves its boredom, or unloads its spite, by spending an afternoon in cruel fun. They conduct a coronation layered with mockery. They have heard that Jesus calls Himself a King. So they dress Jesus in a scarlet robe, crown Him with thorns, place a reedy scepter in His hand, and bow proclaiming Him King of the Jews. The robe is the scarlet chlamys of a Roman soldier, so the soldiers mockingly make Jesus one of their own, the chief of the Roman cohort. They are also mocking the Jews: this is just the kind of king the Jews deserve, they imply. They are also playing Jews. Matthew says that they "gather" around Jesus, using the same verb he used for the gathering of the Jews around Pilate, the verb that is the root for the noun "synagogue." Roman soldiers form a macabre synagogue around Jesus, and hail Him as King. They form a parody of a synagogue of Gentile God-fearers.

---

41 A few structural features of the crucifixion narrative in Matthew 27. First, there are several fairly clear chiasms. The scene of mockery in the Praetorium, for instance:

Then they take it all away. They reverse the whole coronation with an anti-coronation. They spit in contempt instead of kneeling in reverence, they pull the scepter from His hand and beat His

---

A. Soldiers gather and strip Jesus, vv 27-28a
   B. Robe on Jesus, v 28b
      C. Crown of thorns on Jesus' head, v 29a
         D. Reed in hand, v 29b
            E. Soldiers kneel, v 29c
               F. "Hail, King of the Jews," v. 29d
            E'. Soldiers spit, v. 30a
         D'. Reed, v 30b
      C'. Beat Jesus' head, v 30c
   B'. Strip robe, v 31a
A'. Replace Jesus' garments, v 31b

The A-B sequences could be seen not as chiastic but as parallel: The scene begins with a stripping and an investiture, and it ends with a stripping and an investiture.

Verses 38-44 also form a fairly neat chiasm:

A. Robbers on Jesus' right and left, v. 38
   B. Passers-by mock Jesus, vv 39-40
      1. Passers by
         2. Destroy temple
            3. If you are Son, come down
   B'. Chief priests and elders mock, vv 41-43
      1. Chief priests and elders
         2. He saved others, cannot save Himself
            3. He said He is Son of God
A'. Robbers insult Jesus, v 44

Overlapping and overarching these chiasms is a roughly parallel pattern:

A. Jesus offered drink, v 34
   B. "You who destroy the temple," v 40
      C. "If you are son of God," vv 40, 43
         D. Robbers insult him, v. 44
A'. Jesus drinks, v 48
   B'. Temple veil torn, v 51
      C. "Truly this was the Son of God," v 54
         D'. Women minister to Him, vv 55-56

crowned head with it, they strip off the scarlet robe and replace it with Jesus' own robe. They remove the veil of irony and reveal what they really think about this King of the Jews, what they think about these arrogant Jews who think themselves the chosen of the earth, what they think about the odd, pathetic God who would choose the Jews.

Once the soldiers are done with Jesus, they lead Him to Golgotha, the place of the skull, and fix Him to the cross, and now it is the turn of the Jews to continue the mockery begun in the Praetorium. As people pass, they "blaspheme" Jesus, shaking their heads and throwing Jesus' words back at Him: "You who destroy the temple and rebuild it in three days, save yourself." Prove yourself the Son of God by coming down from the cross. The chief priests and elders and scribes join in: Come on down from the cross and we'll believe in You. Save yourself, and we'll believe that you can save us. Finally, even the robbers join in. Jesus is numbered with transgressors, flanked on the cross by two "royal attendants," brigands like Barabbas. The cross triptych forms a bizarre parody of the ark of the covenant, Jesus enthroned as King at the center with two rough beasts taking up the position of the cherubim at Yahweh's right and left. The first time Jesus mentioned brigands, He was in the temple, condemning the Jewish leaders for allowing the house of prayer for all nations to be transformed into a "den of robbers" (Matt. 21:31). Now some of the robbers from the den are at His side, as Jesus, the living temple, is torn apart on the cross. The Jews are robbers, Jesus has already charged, and now the robbers join with the Jews, blaspheming Jesus in the same way as the Jews: if you are the Son of God, come down from the cross.

Roman soldiers mock Jesus, random passers-by mock Jesus as He hangs on the cross between heaven and earth, the Jewish leaders mock Jesus, even brigands, true criminals, the scum of the earth, mock Jesus. Jews and Gentiles, governors and criminals, scribes and commoners join in a single chorus of blasphemy. This is what unifies the divided human race: Divided though they are, all races and classes can join together in at least one thing, in blasphemy. It is like a restored Babel, with the cross of Jesus the tower that reaches to heaven.

God is *not* mocked, Paul says. God *is* mocked, says Matthew. Who's right? The two are in perfect harmony, but to see that, we need to run through the passage again. At every point, the mockery is being turned against the mockers. At every point, mockery is turned inside out; injustice becomes the pathway to restoration and redemption, mockery the road to truth.

Start with the soldiers. They mock Jesus, and in mocking Jesus mock the Jews. But their mockery actually reveals the truth, in all sorts of ways. Had they any discernment, the Roman soldiers could have seen the irony of the situation for themselves. During the trial, Pilate ceded authority to the Jewish people. The decision to crucify was theirs, not his, and the solders are essentially acting on orders from the Jews. Pilate has the title "governor," but he does not do much governing here. The Jews are really in charge. So when the soldiers say that Jesus is king of the Jews, they are saying that He is *their* king too: they carry out His orders.

But there are layers here that the soldiers do not grasp. The scarlet robe is the robe of a Roman soldier, but scarlet is also a color of the tabernacle curtains and of the similar robes of the High Priest. In robing Jesus in scarlet, they are dressing Jesus for priestly service, and the priest also wears a crown. On the Day of Atonement, the High Priest stripped off his garments, put on linen garments for the rituals of atonement, then put his normal clothes back on. In stripping, and re-clothing, and stripping and re-clothing again, the Roman soldiers are sending Jesus off to sprinkle His own blood for the covering of sin, once and for all. At the death of the high priest, his robes were stripped and placed on his son, the new high priest. So too, a priesthood is dying here, the priesthood of Aaron and Zadok, and is being replaced by a new priest, the priest after the order of Melchizedek. Scarlet is also the color of the harlot's clothing in Revelation. By dressing Jesus in scarlet, the soldiers are unknowingly confessing that Jesus is the one who takes the harlot's sins, the one who declares "though your sins be as scarlet, they shall be as wool; though they are red like crimson, they shall be white as snow."

Joseph's story was a story of clothing, of robing and disrobing. His father gave him a coat of many colors as a sign of his preeminence among his brothers, but his brothers stripped that coat and sent him naked to Egypt. Potiphar gave him another robe, but Potiphar's wife stripped that from him. Finally, Pharaoh robed Joseph with all the authority of Egypt, and from that position he saved the brothers that had betrayed him and gave food to the world. All unknowing, the Roman soldiers prepare Jesus to be a new Joseph, who will go before His people to prepare a place for them, who will rise to receive all authority and to distribute bread.

At the cross, too, the Roman soldiers and Jews cannot help but fulfill God's purposes. The scene is like casting for a play: they are assigning roles to everyone in this great drama. And, in spite of themselves, everything everyone does casts Jesus as King of the Jews or as the temple of God. The Roman soldiers unwittingly fulfill prophecy. Matthew makes this explicit in verse 35, but it is pervasive. When they give Jesus gall, they fulfill Psalm 69:21. Roman executioners were always allowed to take a criminal's clothing, but their lots fulfill Psalm 22:16. And if the Roman soldiers stand in the place of the ones who persecute the Psalmist, then Jesus stands in the place of the Psalmist, which is to say, in the place of David, the King of Israel, King of the Jews. As Isaiah predicted, Jesus is crucified among transgressors (Matt. 27:38; cf. Isa. 53:12; cf. Matt. 20:21-23). It is not just that they are fulfilling prophecy; Matthew is not making an apologetic point. The irony is deeper. When they fulfill prophecy, they undermine their mockery. Everything the soldiers do proves that Jesus is who He said He is.

The passers-by also fulfill prophecy, and by their mockery not only assume roles but place Jesus in a role as well. Verse 43 is a quotation from Psalm 22:8. In the original Psalm, these words come from people sneering at David. The chief priests and scribes position themselves as enemies of the Lord's Anointed. Their actions and words show that Jesus is indeed "King of Israel," David's Son (Matt. 27:42). "If you are the Son of God" – where have we heard that before? It takes us back to the temptation scene (Matt. 4:3, 6). These are Satanic mockers and accusers, and the chief priests, scribes, and elders join in Satanic scorn (Matt. 27:41). In describing the people as "wagging their heads," Matthew shows that this scene is the fulfillment of Psalm 22. "I am like a worm and not a man," the Psalm says, "A reproach of men and despised by the people. All who see me sneer at me; they separate the lip, they wag the head" (Psalm 22:7). The actions of the mockers place them in the role of the enemies of the Lord's Anointed.

But the other Scriptural references to "wagging" or "shaking" the head are also in the background. When Jerusalem lies in ruins, Jeremiah says, "all who pass along the way will clap their hands in derision at you; they hiss and shake their heads at the daughter Jerusalem: 'Is this the city of which they said, "The perfection of beauty, a joy of all the earth?"'" (Lam. 2:15). Earlier Jeremiah had warned that resistance to Nebuchadnezzar would be disastrous, since Yahweh was determined to make Jerusalem and the temple and the land "a desolation, an object of perpetual hissing. Everyone who passes by it will be astonished and shake his head" (Jer. 18:16). Passers-by mock Jesus for saying He could destroy the temple and rebuild it, but they act the part of those passers-by who saw Solomon's temple in ruins and shook their heads in sadness, or mockery, at the desolation of the once-great city. They mock Jesus' prophecies, even as they fulfill them. They mock Jesus' claims about the temple, but unwittingly treat Him as the temple.

They mock Jesus as if He were an impotent, ruined temple. They should have known better. When Solomon built the temple, he prayed that Yahweh would hear prayers directed toward that place. Even when Israel went into exile, Solomon hoped, Yahweh would still hear the prayers of the people directed toward the temple (1 Kings 8). Israel did go into exile, and left behind the dusty ruins of Solomon's temple, and for seventy years they prayed toward the temple, toward the *ruins* of the temple, hoping that Yahweh would hear and restore them. The temple did not save itself, but that ruined temple did save them: they turned to the temple ruins, prayed for restoration, and were restored. Jesus on the cross is a ruined temple, the ruins toward which we direct our prayers.

The mockery and torture and a kangaroo court and an unjust trial and a vicious execution of an innocent man prove that Jesus is king. All that is what makes Jesus a king. Are you a king? Pilate asks. "*You* say," Jesus answers. Which is to say: It is up to you. You can make me a king, Jesus says, and Pilate does, by delivering him over to the mockery of the soldiers, over to the mockery of the passers by, over to the mockery of the Jewish leaders, over to the mockery of brigands. Pilate's actions, and the rejection and mockery of the Jewish leaders, place Jesus in precisely the position of David and precisely in the position of the Suffering Servant of Isaiah. Mockery is not proof *against* Jesus kingship but the opposite, the fulfillment of the Scriptures that show us the Davidic king in precisely this position, despised by the people, rejected and scorned, trusting in God alone for His vindication!

The crowds, Jewish leaders, and robbers all join in a Satanic temptation. Jesus is Adam at the tree, a tree that has become a means of execution rather than a source of fruit. And the temptation of the Christ is the same as the temptation of the first Adam: Yea, has God said? Did God say that He would rescue you? Where is He? And if Your Father promised a rescue and *does not* come, then can God be trusted? He has sent you to an excruciating death; He has sent you into a place where you are surrounded by a mob of mockers. What kind of Father is that? Can you trust a Father who would lead you *here*? Can you trust a Father who would lead you here and then leave you on your own?

That is the temptation, but Jesus stays on the cross because He trusts that this cross is proof of His sonship, proof of His kingship. And we should too. When we suffer, we are tempted to doubt our Father's word, tempted to doubt our Father's goodness. When the Father puts us on a cross, we want to climb down as quickly as we can. But the cross, with all its pain, shame, humiliation, and mockery, is where we belong, because that is where Jesus is, where our King hangs, displaying His kingship to the world.

Atheists – especially the new atheists – blaspheme, and giggle like schoolboys. They think themselves daring, subversive, so deliciously cunning. But they learned their skills from the gospel story. Matthew beat them to it. Mocking God is not an invention of atheists. It is what Jews do when God comes close, too close for their comfort. It what the religious Romans do in the presence of God. Redemption runs through the trail of blasphemy. Atheists are utterly conventional, very traditional Mocking God, killing righteous men – that is the human project.

More Pelagian than Pelagius, the modern world tells us that we are not so bad, and that where we understandably fail, we have the resources within ourselves to fix things. Whether it is war, or poverty, or racial hatred, or disease and disfigurement, we can fix it with a few quick twists of the dial. Scripture has no patience with such mild optimism. The cross of Jesus is the crux of human history, the deepest revelation of the human condition. At this crossroads, the Bible uncovers the bloody corpse of a righteous man, the twisted and crucified corpse of the eternal Son of the living God. Putting Jesus to death *is* the human project. That is what we do. And this means we are far, far worse than we let ourselves imagine.

When someone comes with the demand that we do justice and love our neighbors, we betray Him, we mock Him, we beat Him on the head and crown Him with thorns, before we pack Him off to death on a cross. We are specialists in destruction. History is a charnel house of ruins, toppled temples, smoldering cities, stinking corpses heaped for burning. This is what we do. That is the human project. Worse, when God the Creator, source of all good and all life, to whom we owe eternal gratitude for our very being, appears in human flesh, we beat Him back with clubs and crosses, until the body of God is a mangled mess. This is the human project. This is what we do.

And let us not fool ourselves into thinking we would have done any differently. Let us not comfort ourselves with the thought that if we have been part of this drama, we would have been Simon of Cyrene, who bears the cross alongside Jesus. No. At best, we would have been cowardly disciples, fleeing from Jesus in the garden, and at worst we would have been the traitor Judas, among the Jewish leaders who stop at nothing to put Jesus on the cross, among the Jewish crowd chanting "Crucify! Crucify!" or among the Roman soldiers genuflecting in cruel deference and acclaiming Jesus King of the Jews.

Left to ourselves, this would be our last word. But God has a different project, and He will not let us get away with ours. The cross of Jesus is the crux of history, but that means the cross of Jesus not only reveals the radical disorder of fallen humanity, but also that it discloses the meaning of the world, the point of creation, the damage done by sin, the hope of glory. God does not simply bypass the human project of destruction. The gospel is not the good news of a new divine fiat, "Let there be peace. Let there be justice." The gospel is the good news that God has entered our story of rage and ruin, offers His cheek to us, and then humbly turned the other cheek, all to invert our project and turn it into His. The path of God's redemption does not bypass blasphemy and destruction, but faces it squarely, endures it, and remakes it from the inside. God does not avoid mockery or smack it down. He over-accepts our mockery to turn it to truth. God *is not* mocked precisely because God *has been* mocked.

Left to ourselves, our contemptuous, vicious, violent "No!" to Jesus would be our last word. But for God, Jesus is "Yes," and in, with, and under our "No," the Father of Jesus transforms our "No" into His resounding, triumphant, eternal "Yes."

The Death of God
Matthew 27:45-54

⁴⁵ Now from the sixth hour darkness fell upon all the land until the ninth hour. ⁴⁶ About the ninth hour Jesus cried out with a loud voice, saying, "Eli, Eli, lama Sabacthani?" that is, "My God, My God, why have You forsaken Me?" ⁴⁷ And some of those who were standing there, when they heard it, began saying, "This man is calling for Elijah." ⁴⁸ Immediately one of them ran, and taking a sponge, he filled it with sour wine and put it on a reed, and gave Him a drink. ⁴⁹ But the rest of them said, "Let us see whether Elijah will come to save Him." ⁵⁰ And Jesus cried out again with a loud voice, and yielded up His spirit.⁵¹ And behold, the veil of the temple was torn in two from top to bottom; and the earth shook and the rocks were split.⁵² The tombs were opened, and many bodies of the saints who had fallen asleep were raised; ⁵³ and coming out of the tombs after His resurrection they entered the holy city and appeared to many. ⁵⁴ Now the centurion, and those who were with him keeping guard over Jesus, when they saw the earthquake and the things that were happening, became very frightened and said, "Truly this was the Son of God!"

"In the beginning God created the heavens and the earth. And the earth was formless and void and darkness was on the face of the deep. And the Spirit of God hovered over the face of the waters." Creation did not come perfectly formed from the hand of God. First Yahweh made a world that required forming, shaping, filling, and, above all, illumination. Creation begins in darkness, then moves to light. On the fourth day, Yahweh delegated the light-keeping role to created lights, to the sun, moon, and stars. These were set up in the firmament to do what God did on the first day, to separate the day from the night, light from darkness. They were set in the firmament as clocks, to keep time, and as rulers, to govern the day and the night.

Creation begins with darkness giving way to light, and when lights go out and the world goes back into darkness, it is a signal that creation is being undone. When the sun, moon, and stars go out or fall from the sky, it is a sign that the work of creation is moving in reverse. Isaiah warns that Yahweh will lift a standard to call a distant nation to invade Judah, a bestial nation that will growl over Judah like the roaring of the sea, and will bring distress to the land: "darkness and distress; even the light is darkened by its clouds" (Isa. 5:30). Because of this invasion, there will be "distress and darkness, the gloom of anguish; and they will be driven away to darkness" (Isa. 8:22). The lights are going out for Judah, and she is entering a dark age. Eventually, Isaiah says, those who suffer through the conquest will see a new day dawn: "the people who walk in darkness will see a great light; those who live in a dark land, the light will shine on them" (Isa. 9:2).

When the day of Yahweh comes, Zephaniah later warns, it will not be a day of deliverance, but "a day of wrath, a day of trouble and distress, a day of destruction and desolation, a day of clouds and thick darkness" (Zeph. 1:15). Judah's day in the sun is ending; night is coming on, and Judah is reverting to the state before creation, to darkness, formlessness, and emptiness. When Yahweh moves against Pharaoh, Ezekiel writes, He "will cover the heavens, and darken their stars." He will "cover the sun with a cloud and the moon will not give its light. All the shining lights of the heavens He will darken over you and will set darkness on your land" (Ezek. 32:7). The sun and moon, which rule and set the times for Pharaoh and for Egypt, are stopping. Her time is over. Instead of light, there is darkness.

The darkness that most thoroughly extinguishes the light is the darkness that awaits every one of us. When Judah's lights go out, Yahweh preserves a remnant. Yahweh brings an end to Pharaoh and puts out the sun and moon, but Egypt is still here even today. Death is utter darkness. Death is the shroud that lays over all people. Those in the shadow of death live in the dark. In the allegory of death at the end of Ecclesiastes, Solomon speaks of the sunlight and moon and stars being darkened. When Jesus speaks of people being handed over to eternal death, he describes it as a place of "outer darkness" where there is weeping and gnashing of teeth. Darkness is the darkness of un-creation. All darkness is the darkness of death.

As Jesus hangs from the cross, darkness descends. For three hours, in the middle of day, from noon when the sun is at its height to three o'clock when the afternoon begins to fade, Jesus hangs on the cross in utter darkness. As Jesus dies, creation is moving in reverse. A world is coming to an end. The sun is blotted out, and the moon does not give her light, the stars fall from the sky. The clock stops for the Jews and Romans who have put Jesus on the cross.

Out of that darkness comes a voice, a loud voice, a voice like thunder, like the sound of many waters. This, too, is following the creation story. When the world was formless, empty, and dark, God spoke. The first work of God, the first word of God in the Bible, the first word spoken into creation, is, "Let there be light." In many of the ancient myths, the order of creation is the result of warfare. Some god has to fight against the powers of chaos, a dragon, or the deep, so that the world can be bright and well-formed. In Genesis, there is no struggle or battle. There are no rivals, there is no violence. With the calm assurance of absolute omnipotence, Yahweh says, "Let there be light" and there is light.

That is *not* the word spoken in the darkness of Golgotha. Jesus' words do not appear to be an Almighty divine fiat. His cry is the cry of a man in distress, the anguished prayer of a faithful, righteous man who has been abandoned by his friends, surrounded by bestial enemies, whose hands and feet have been pierced, whose clothes have been removed and distributed among his enemies. Out the darkness of Golgotha comes a voice that does not break through the darkness and turn it to light. The voice at Golgotha articulates, gives audible shape, to the darkness that surrounds it.

The voice from the darkness does not resemble the calm Almighty voice of the Creator, but more directly recalls another biblical incident when creation turned back, when darkness descended, when all the lights went out. The ninth plague in Egypt was a plague of darkness that came over all the land of Egypt, a "thick darkness" so thorough that Yahweh describes it as a "darkness which may be felt" (Exod. 10:21-22). In Jesus' day, Israel has become an Egypt, and the God of Israel sends a plague of darkness on His own people like the plague of darkness that afflicted Egypt.

The plague that followed the plague of darkness, the Passover slaughter of the firstborn of Egypt, also took place in the darkness, at night. During the night of Passover, as the Israelites celebrated the Passover within their houses of refuge, marked with blood, the angel of death slaughtered all the firstborn of Egypt. Out of the gloom of Passover night a "great cry" arose from the Egyptians (Exod. 12:30), a cry of lamentation from the gloom.

Israel has become an Egypt, and if Israel is an Egypt, then *her* firstborn must die. That can only be Jesus. The cry that pierces the darkness at Golgotha is not the loud voice of a creative fiat. It is the voice of lamentation, lamentation and bitter weeping, the shriek of Egypt lamenting her firstborn. Jesus is the Passover Lamb. He is the true Son, the true Israel. But here on the cross, He stands in for all the Egyptian-Jews who crucify Him, and He takes the cry of Israel on His own lips: "My God, My God, why have you forsaken me?"

Matthew records this cry, taken from Psalm 22, in Aramaic, and because of that we can understand something of the sequel. Some of the people standing by think Jesus has cried out for Elijah. Eli, Eli, "My God, My God," is part of Elijah's name, which means "My God is Yah" or "Yah is my God." How can they miss this? The Jews at the foot of the cross do not recognize Jesus' cry as a prayer from the Psalms. Perhaps they are continuing to mock Jesus. He calls Himself the King of Israel, but He cannot overcome the Romans. He calls Himself Son of God, but God does not deliver Him from the cross. When Jesus cries out the first prayer of Psalm 22, they recognize it, but turn it into scorn. They mock Him for calling out to Elijah: See if Elijah comes.

Perhaps, though, it is also an indication of how dull the Jews have become. Jesus began to teach in parables, He says in Matthew 13, because the people have closed their eyes and ears; they refuse to hear and see, and so Jesus reinforces that blindness and deafness by teaching them in dark sayings that they cannot grasp. They refuse to hear; God judges by making it difficult to hear. He gives them over to their resistance. And now that comes to a climax at the cross. The Jews are surrounded by signals that Jesus is who He says He is, clues that He is the promised Messiah. The Romans give Him wine, and later vinegar, just as David says in Psalm 69. Roman soldiers divide up His clothing and cast lots for it, just as Psalm 22 predicts. The Jewish leaders actually quote the mockery of Psalm 22 against Jesus, deliberately taking up the role of those who mock the Lord's Anointed. When Jesus actually speaks out the words of Psalm 22, they still do not get it. They do not even recognize that Jesus is right in the place where Israel's king is supposed to be, right where David was. Their own Scriptures have become obscure parables.

But the supposition that Jesus cries for Elijah has a significance of its own. Our Old Testament ends with a promise that Elijah is coming "before the great and terrible day of Yahweh" (Mal 4:5). Earlier in Matthew, when the disciples ask about Elijah's coming, Jesus assures them that they have read the Scriptures correctly. Elijah does come "and restores all things," and He identifies John the Baptist as that Elijah (Matt. 17:11). Elijah comes to restore the world, to bring Israel back from exile, to trigger the coming of the kingdom.

The Jews misunderstand or mock Jesus, and yet their misunderstanding ironically captures the truth: Jesus *is* crying for Elijah, not just for personal deliverance, but for the great and terrible day of Yahweh. In the darkness at Golgotha, in the darkness reminiscent of the darkness of the first creation, Jesus cries out for a new creation. The Jews mock. "Let us see if Elijah comes to Him." But that means: "Let us see if His sufferings are the birth pangs of the Kingdom. Let us see if His death is the beginning of the woes that will bring in the great and terrible day of Yahweh."

As it turns out, that is exactly what happens. In this darkness, the world is actually coming to an end, and a new world is emerging. This *is* the great and awesome day of Yahweh, and on this day the whole set of eschatological events that Israel had been hoping for begins to happen. The Jews are waiting for the gift of the Spirit. Ezekiel promised it: "I will put my Spirit within you and cause you to walk in My statutes, and you will be careful to guard my ordinances" (Ezek. 36:27). Joel had promised it: "In the last days, says the Lord, I will pour out My Spirit upon all flesh. Your sons and daughters will prophesy; your old men will dream dreams, and your young men will see visions. Even on the male and female servants I will pour out My Spirit in those days" (Joel 12:28-29). Israel is waiting for the Spirit, and at His death Jesus cries out and "yields up His Spirit." This might be just a way of describing death, but I think Matthew intends something more. This is not just Jesus' death, but the death of Jesus *as* the gift of His Spirit, the Pentecostal cross. Jesus received the Spirit at His baptism, went to the wilderness in the power of the Spirit, preached and taught and healed in the power of the Spirit, and now at His death, yields up that Spirit, giving it to those who receive Him. He is Elijah on the cross, and as He departs He bestows a double measure of the Spirit on us.

Israel is hoping that Yahweh will burst out of His temple, and fill the earth with the knowledge of the glory of the Lord. Ezekiel promised this when He saw the vision of a restored temple, with water flowing from the temple, first a trickle, then a stream, then a river that could not be crossed. The living water finally pours into the Dead Sea, bringing all the fish to life. The life and power of the temple are bursting out of the temple and filling the land, renewing the land as it goes (Ezekiel 47). Israel waits for the world to be filled with the life that flows from the temple, and at the death of Jesus the veil of the temple is torn. This is a sign of judgment on the temple. Jesus goes to the cross as the temple that will be torn down and restored in three days. His cry of dereliction is the cry of the temple being forsaken by its Lord (cf. Ezekiel 8-11). As Jesus gives Himself in the final sacrifice, the architectural temple in Jerusalem is ruined. Yet, this is not just a judgment. Because the architectural temple is removed, and because Yahweh's Spirit is being poured out on *people*, the river of life is going to flow to the ends of the earth. Yahweh has resided in the temple at Jerusalem, but now He is breaking out from the temple, marching out to the ends of the earth. The temple has been a barrier, but it is no longer a barrier. Through the flesh of Jesus, we can draw near in the Most Holy Place.

Israel has been hoping that the world would be shaken. Israel hopes for high places to be brought down and low places raised. Things are not as they should be. Pagan Romans rule the earth. The people of God are slaves. Herod is the King of the Jews. That is not as it should be. But the prophets assured Israel that it would not last forever. "The earth will be broken asunder, the earth is split through, the earth is shaken violently," Isaiah promised," and when this is done, "Yahweh of hosts will reign on Mount Zion in Jerusalem" (Isa. 24:19-20, 23). "Yet once more," Haggai says, "yet once more in a little while I am going to shake the heavens and the earth" (Hag. 2:6). That shaking will topple those who are high and mighty, and make the low places rise up. As the prophets predicted, after Jesus "yields up the spirit," the land is shaken by an earthquake. Earth is supposed to be stable and fixed, but at the death of Jesus, the earth begins to waver. The world begins to fall apart.

Israel has been hoping for resurrection. Ezekiel stood in a valley full of dry bones and was told to prophesy. Ezekiel calls on the wind or breath or spirit, and that spirit blows over the dead and dry bones; there is an earthquake; the wind gives them breath, and the dead rise (Ezekiel 37). This is a vision of the restoration of Israel and Judah from the grave of exile, and that vision is being fulfilled and repeated in the death of Jesus. At the death of Jesus, because the earth is shaken, the living fall, and the dead rise. The tombs of the saints are opened (Matt. 27:51-53), divine signs that vindicate Jesus and explain His death. Already at His death, Jesus triumphs over the grave. Already at His death, He breaks open Sheol and shines the light of life into the darkness of the tomb.

Israel is hoping for the conversion of the nations. In the last days, Isaiah said, Zion would be raised up as chief of the mountains (Isa. 2:1-4). That is what will happen when Yahweh has shaken the earth and changed its political topography. Zion will become the chief of the mountains, and all the nations will stream into Jerusalem to learn of the Lord and His ways, so that they will beat their swords to plows and their spears to pruning hooks. At the death of Jesus, the centurion and his soldiers confess Jesus as Son of God (Matt. 27:54), the first fruits of the Psalm's promise that "all the families of the nations shall worship before Him" (Psalm 22:27).

At the death of Jesus, when Jesus cries out a second time with a loud voice from the darkness, everything is shaken. From the veil of the temple above, to the earth beneath, to the tombs under the earth, the whole world is shaken and begins to fall, so that a new world can take its place. Everything the Jews have been hoping for begins to happen, or happens in symbol, at the death of Jesus. "Let us see if Elijah will save Him," the Jews say. "Let us see if His death will bring in the end times." And it does. It does.

In the midst of the darkness, apparently overwhelmed by darkness, Jesus overcomes the darkness. His cry matches the original divine fiat that broke the darkness of the first creation. But He does not overcome that darkness by a calm omnipotent word. Jesus overcomes the darkness by entering the darkness. He overcomes the darkness by sharing the darkness. He overcomes the darkness by speaking the darkness in his prayer of lamentation and forsakenness. He overcomes the darkness of uncreation, and makes a new creation, by entering fully into the God-forsakenness of *our* condition.

There is no rupture in the Trinity here; God does not cease to be Triune for the few hours that Jesus dies on the cross, reduced to the Father and Spirit. To speak of the "death of the Son of God" is not to say that the Son of God ceased to exist. Even normal human beings do not cease to exist at death. But we should not let that necessary qualification minimize the mystery of what is happening here. God the Son died on the cross. He entered fully into the God-forsaken condition of humanity, so that He can restore communion between God and man. God the Son entered so fully that He endured a human death, to triumph over death. He entered into our death, so that He could shake death and burst it from the inside. He entered the darkness, articulated the darkness, to turn darkness to light.

When Yahweh first created, He spoke in the calm power of a fiat, "Let there be light." That is the way the world was made. It is *not* the way the world is remade. The world is remade from a cross. The world is remade when God the Son enters the darkness, suffers the darkness, passes through the dissolution of uncreation, in order to triumph over it.

This is the cross that Jesus calls us to share. Bearing the cross as a follower of Jesus means sharing the darkness, sharing in His cry.

We do not want things this way. When things get gloomy for us, we want to be able to say "Let there be light." And if we cannot say it, we want *God* to say it. When God puts us on the cross, we want to get down. We want to remake the world by coming down from the cross. It is not possible. The world was made light with a calm divine fiat. Worlds are remade otherwise, only as those who have the Spirit, who bear crosses after Jesus, enter into the darkness, and cry out from that darkness the prayer of Jesus, only as we enter the gloom and the God-forsakenness and cry out to the God who makes light shine in the darkness.

Dead and Buried
Matthew 27:55-66

⁵⁵ Many women were there looking on from a distance, who had followed Jesus from Galilee while ministering to Him. ⁵⁶ Among them was Mary Magdalene, and Mary the mother of James and Joseph, and the mother of the sons of

Zebedee. ⁵⁷ When it was evening, there came a rich man from Arimathea, named Joseph, who himself had also become a disciple of Jesus. ⁵⁸ This man went to Pilate and asked for the body of Jesus. Then Pilate ordered it to be given to him. ⁵⁹ And Joseph took the body and wrapped it in a clean linen cloth, ⁶⁰ and laid it in his own new tomb, which he had hewn out in the rock; and he rolled a large stone against the entrance of the tomb and went away. ⁶¹ And Mary Magdalene was there, and the other Mary, sitting opposite the grave. ⁶² Now on the next day, the day after the preparation, the chief priests and the Pharisees gathered together with Pilate, ⁶³ and said, "Sir, we remember that when He was still alive that deceiver said, 'After three days I am to rise again.' ⁶⁴ Therefore, give orders for the grave to be made secure until the third day, otherwise His disciples may come and steal Him away and say to the people, 'He has risen from the dead,' and the last deception will be worse than the first." ⁶⁵ Pilate said to them, "You have a guard; go, make it as secure as you know how." ⁶⁶ And they went and made the grave secure, and along with the guard they set a seal on the stone.

Psalm 22 provides the narrative substructure for Matthew's account of the crucifixion of Jesus. The Psalm begins with "My God, My God, why have you forsaken Me," the words of Jesus from the cross. "Why are you so far from saving me, from the words of my groaning? O my God, I cry by day, but you do not answer, and by night, but I find no rest" (vv. 1b-2). But David does not stay in that state of isolation, fear, distance, and despair. The Psalm begins "My God, My God, why have you forsaken me?" but it ends in praise: "I will tell of your name to my brothers; in the midst of the congregation I will praise you" (v. 22) It ends with the hope that "all the ends of the earth shall remember and turn to the Lord," and that even those "who go down to the dust" shall bow before Yahweh (v. 27, 29). Psalm 22 begins in despair and anguish but moves to triumph and hope. Psalm 22 not only provides a few lines and specific predictions of the crucifixion, but provides the whole story-line, because Jesus' crucifixion also moves from isolation, anguish, and despair to hope and confidence. "My God, My God, why have you forsaken Me?" Jesus cries from the cross, but when He cries again His God answers by shaking the earth, opening tombs, bringing the bodies of saints out and sending them to the holy city. Jesus' death too moves from humiliation to exaltation. Before He is brought down from the cross, His triumph is already evident.

Psalm 22 provides background for the crucifixion in another way as well. The Psalm is not only about David's deliverance from suffering. It has a corporate dimension. David begins alone, attacked by enemies, but ends with brothers and friends gathered around Him. In the Psalm, Yahweh extracts David from a hostile mob and places Him among his brothers. In his suffering, David is surrounded by beasts. "Many bulls encompass Me; strong bulls of Bashan surround Me; they open wide their mouths at Me, like a ravening and roaring lion" (vv. 13-14). "For dogs encompass me; a company of evildoers encircles me; they have pierced my hands and feet" (v. 16). David's prayer is that he would be delivered from these beasts: "But you, O LORD, do not be far off! O you my help, come quickly to my aid! Deliver my soul from the sword, my precious life from the power of the dog! Save me from the mouth of the lion! You have rescued [answered] me from the horns of the wild oxen!" (Psalm 22:19-21). He hopes to be restored to *human* community. He wants to be another Adam, a beast-tamer.

Yahweh hears the king's prayer, and as soon as He answers, David is surrounded by a different crowd. "You have answered Me," he says, and immediately "I will tell of your name to my brothers; in the midst of the congregation I will praise you" (vv. 21-22). He is surrounded by those who fear Yahweh, by the seed of Jacob; He praises Yahweh in the "great congregation" among "those who fear" the Lord. Yahweh takes David from the beasts that want to devour Him and places him in the company of the faithful. He is delivered from the zoo and brought into a liturgical gathering.

This is precisely what happens to Jesus. During His trial and sufferings, Jesus is surrounded by raging Jewish leaders, a mob clamoring for a cross, scornful Roman soldiers, by jabbering and gibbering and jeering. At His death, all that changes. Jesus has been surrounded by priestly bulls and Gentile dogs, but when He dies He is immediately surrounded by faithful human beings. He is immediately put into an assembly of the seed of Jacob, the assembly of brothers.

But these are not the brothers that one would expect. This is not the assembly that we have seen around Jesus throughout the gospel. Early in the gospel, Jesus chose the Twelve to be with Him. The Twelve were the inner circle when He gave the Sermon on the Mount. The Twelve were the ones sent to the lost sheep of the house of Israel. The Twelve were the ones who heard Him talk about the destruction of the temple. The Twelve have been witnesses of His miracles; they have been His closest students; they have participated in His ministry of preaching, healing, exorcism. But they have been absent since the Garden of Gethsemane. They fled instead of taking up the cross to suffer alongside Jesus in His trials and death. Even when Jesus dies, they do not immediately materialize. Eventually, they will be restored to Jesus' inner circle, will receive the great commission, and will go off to fulfill that commission. For now, they are still absent.

Instead, the congregation of "brothers" and "those who fear God" that surrounds Jesus includes a Roman centurion and his cohort of Gentile solders, women who have followed Jesus from Galilee, and Joseph of Arimathea, identified as a "disciple" but, as John tells us, a "secret disciple for fear of the Jews," a disciple who has listened to and followed Jesus at a distance. None of these characters were important before Jesus' death. They have been in the background, or hidden, or actively opposed to Jesus. By His death, Jesus brings things out into the open – dead bodies, Gentile believers, Sanhedrin members who are secret followers, women disciples. Those who are far off suddenly come to center stage.

The women become especially prominent at the cross and the tomb. Women have been in the background of Matthew's gospel (14:21; 15:38; but cf. 9:20-22; 15:21-28; 26:6-13), but now they come to the forefront. We know that there have been crowds following Jesus in Galilee and from Galilee, and we know from a couple of references that there were women in the crowds. When Matthew has mentioned women, they have been almost an afterthought. He calculates the number of *men* fed in the wilderness at five thousand, and then adds, "besides women and children." The women are with the children, off to the side, on the margins. In the inner circle are the Twelve, then the five thousand men, and later the four thousand men, whom Jesus feeds, and then out on the outer edges of the multitude are women and children.

Though virtually invisible in the Gospel, the women are doing what disciples are supposed to do. As Matthew says, they have "followed" Jesus from Galilee, all the way to the cross. They have followed Jesus further than the Twelve. After Jesus is buried, they still follow Him, sitting opposite the tomb (27:61). They follow Jesus all the way to the grave, and are there again on the day after the Sabbath to hear the announcement of Jesus' resurrection from the angel. They pass through His entire Passion with Him.

While they have been following Jesus, they have been serving Him. Importantly, the mother of the sons of Zebedee is among them. The first time we met her in the Gospel story, she was asking Jesus to give her sons prominent positions in His kingdom. At that time, Jesus said that they would instead have to suffer with Him and Jesus emphasized that the "great" in the kingdom would not be lords but servants: "whoever wishes to become great among you shall be your servant, and whoever wishes to be first among you shall be your slave" (20:26-27). The sons of Zebedee are not there at the cross, but their mother is, among the women who have done what Jesus said, who have "served" Jesus while following Him.

Even the earlier references to women, the ones that seem to be demeaning, are in fact complimentary. Women are almost invisible in the earlier part of the story. They are in the background, *with the children*. But Jesus tells His disciples to become like children. At one point, he pulls a child from the back and sets him in front of the disciples, saying: "Unless you are converted and become like children, you will not enter the kingdom of heaven. Whoever humbles himself as this child, he is the greatest in the kingdom of heaven" (18:3-4). And later, "Let the children alone . . . for the kingdom of heaven belongs to such as these" (Matt. 19:14). The women who are with the children are where all disciples should be, not proudly putting themselves forward but humbly serving. Matthew has set us up. All along, we thought that the main characters of the story were men like Peter, James, John, Judas. Now at the climax, he shrewdly levels us with a punch line: the truest disciples are the ones we have barely noticed. We must re-read the entire Gospel from these margins, with the insight that the invisible women are the most inspiring models of discipleship.

But there are also symbolic reasons for the prominence of women here at the tomb. Two of the women are named "Mary." One is Mary Magdalene, who suddenly appears here for the first time in the gospel. There is another Mary, identified as the "mother of James and Joseph." Earlier in the gospel, people marvel at Jesus' teaching and ask, "Is not his mother called Mary, and his brothers, James and Joseph and Simon and Judas?" (13:55). I think the "other Mary" in Matthew 27-28 is Mary the mother of Jesus. Even if that is not the case, the name Mary occurs twice, and the name Joseph also occurs twice – Joseph the son of Mary and Joseph of Arimathea. That immediately draws us back to the early part of the gospel, where the names Mary and Joseph are used repeatedly. The names take us back to the birth narrative, and if the "other Mary" is indeed Jesus' mother, the association between death and birth is even stronger. Mary, who bore Jesus in her womb, is there with Jesus at the tomb. She is there because this tomb is going to become a womb, as Jesus emerges as the "firstborn of the dead" on the third day. It is a new tomb, a *virgin* tomb. But this virgin, like Mary, becomes fruitful. Once Jesus the Seed of Abraham is planted in it, He will burst out and produce much fruit.

The women watch the cross from a distance. When Jesus is buried, they sit opposite the grave, and they return to the tomb on the first day of the week. They watch, as the soldiers did at the cross, but they are waiting, perhaps knowing that Jesus promised to come back on the third day. They form the nucleus of the new community established by the death of Jesus.

Matthew gives us two other responses to the death of Jesus. Joseph of Arimathea approaches Pilate and asks for the body of Jesus. He wants to honor Jesus. Matthew tells us that Joseph was rich, and elsewhere we learn that he was a member of the council, the Sanhedrin, that condemned Jesus. This fulfills prophecy. As Isaiah predicted, the Servant who suffers alongside transgressors is with a rich man in His death (Isa. 53:9). He died as a brigand, on a Roman cross. He died the death that the insurrectionist Barabbas deserved. But after His death, He is honored with a noble burial in a tomb cut from the rock. Joseph is from Arimathea, the hometown of Samuel the prophet ("Ramathaim," 1 Sam. 1:1), the prophet who raised David from the sheepfold and made him king. Joseph too is a king-maker.

Matthew goes into detail describing how Joseph prepares the body. Receiving permission from Pilate, Joseph personally prepares Jesus' body and lays it in the tomb, and rolls a large stone in front (Matt. 27:58-60). Jesus has already broken rocks and opened tombs by His death (Matt. 27:51-52), so it is unlikely that this tomb will hold Him. Joseph simply wants to do homage to the dead. Whether Joseph knows it or not, he is preparing Jesus for priestly ministry. Clean linen cloth reminds us of the priestly attire at the temple, the linen clothing that the high priest wore on the Day of Atonement when he entered the Most Holy Place to sprinkle blood toward the ark. The stones of the temple were "hewn" and the stones of the foundation were "large stones," eight to ten cubits high (1 Kings 7:10). John makes this point in his account of the resurrection, when he shows the tomb to be like the Most Holy Place, and the slab on which Jesus lay to be the ark, flanked by two angels.

What is happening here seems to be the opposite. This is not a living priest but a dead man, crucified as a criminal. This is not a temple or most holy place, but the opposite of a holy place, a tomb. It is a new tomb, undefiled by other dead bodies, but as soon as the dead body of Jesus enters, it becomes defiled. But Jesus' death reverses everything. Women rather than disciples stay at the grave. A rich man rather than a poor disciple gives Jesus a tomb. Most importantly, the place of death is being transformed into a place of life, the place of intense impurity into a Most Holy Place. That is what God is up to. In the death and burial of Jesus, God is at work to transform crosses into instruments of life and tombs into wombs.

The Jews want to arrest that process. They want the dead to remain dead, graves to remain defiled. They are already Judaizers, who want the old system to remain intact, no disruptions, no transformations, no resurrections. The priests and Pharisees take Jesus' prophecy of resurrection seriously, more seriously than the disciples (27:63-64). They gather before Pilate (27:62), as they had gathered before him in his court (27:17), forming an infernal "synagogue." It is fitting that the Pharisees reappear here. The Pharisees were last mentioned in Jesus' denunciation of the scribes and hypocrites, where He condemned the Pharisees and scribes for erecting monuments to the prophets, the very prophets they kill (Matthew 23). Now they have approved the killing of another prophet, the greatest prophet, the final prophet, and they want to seal His tomb.

The Pharisees are supposed to believe in the resurrection of the dead. That is the great doctrinal difference between Pharisees and Sadducees, the Sadducee party that makes up the majority party among priests. Now Pharisees and Sadducees are banding together. They might disagree about the resurrection in general, but they agree on one thing: Jesus cannot come out of the grave unless the disciples steal His body. Their professed desire to avoid deception and fraud (27:64) is ironically overturned later when they themselves perpetuate a false report about the resurrection (28:11-15).

And then there is the tragicomedy of the Jews' interaction with Pilate. They address him as "Lord," using the word *kyrios*. That is the term one would use to show respect to an official. It can mean something as colorless as "Sir." But throughout Matthew's Gospel, people have generally addressed Jesus as *kyrios*, as Lord. The Jews have made their commitment. They have a Lord, and it is not Jesus. They have chosen Caesar as their king.

They want Pilate to seal the tomb to thwart grave-robbers. But we know what Jesus really intended to do, namely, to come out of the tomb, to burst it from the inside. Against that kind of power, Pilate is wholly powerless. He can seal the tomb all He wants. He can place all the guards He has at the entrance. But the entrance is still going to be a door, an exit. Jews rely on Roman power to keep Jesus in check, as they will attempt to do for a century after Jesus rises. But it will not work. Pilate is not the lord of the dead.

For his part, Pilate is in typical form. He will not take responsibility for anything. The Jews want him to be Lord of the dead, but he washes his hands of this plan as thoroughly as he tried to wash his hands of the blood of Jesus. "You see to it," he said during the trial, foisting responsibility onto the Jewish leaders (27:24). He does the same here: "You have a guard," adding, as if he knows it will not work, "make it as secure as you know how" (M27:65). Give it the old college try. You can use my soldiers. See if you can keep a dead man dead.

Human beings can kill. Human beings can bury. And we can respond to death in various ways. Matthew shows us three responses to the death of Jesus – the waiting women, Joseph who honors Jesus, the Jews who want to make sure that Jesus stays in the tomb. We can, like Joseph, do honor to the body, wrap it in clean linen and place it in a new tomb hewn from the rock. We can, like the Pharisees and chief priests, do everything we can to close the books on the dead. We can, like the women, sit in silent mourning, waiting. But what are we waiting for? The only way for human beings to empty tombs is to become resurrection men, grave-robbers like Dickens' Jerry Cruncher.

What we cannot do is turn the tomb into a womb. What we cannot do is open up the earth that receives the dead so that the dead come out. What we cannot do is roll away the stone. What we cannot do is shake the earth so that the rocks break and the dead saints emerge. That is something only God can do. And He has. Jesus the God-man was put on trial. Jesus the God-man suffered and died on the cross. Jesus the God-man went into the tomb, into Sheol. But death could not hold Him, and instead of being swallowed by death, He swallowed death in victory. He turned the tomb into a womb, death into a transition to new life. He turned the place of death and defilement into a Holy of Holies. Jesus proved Himself the Lord of death.

And that is why Jesus emerges with all authority in heaven and on earth. His authority extends from heaven, where He reigns with His Father, to earth, where He reigns by His Spirit, to the world of the dead, the world under the earth, which He conquered in His burial.

8

He Is Risen!

He Is Risen
Matthew 28:1-10

¹ Now after the Sabbath, as it began to dawn toward the first day of the week, Mary Magdalene and the other Mary came to look at the grave. ² And behold, a severe earthquake had occurred, for an angel of the Lord descended from heaven and came and rolled away the stone and sat upon it. ³ And his appearance was like lightning, and his clothing as white as snow. ⁴ The guards shook for fear of him and became like dead men. ⁵ The angel said to the women, "Do not be afraid; for I know that you are looking for Jesus who has been crucified. ⁶ He is not here, for He has risen, just as He said. Come, see the place where He was lying. ⁷ Go quickly and tell His disciples that He has risen from the dead; and behold, He is going ahead of you into Galilee, there you will see Him; behold, I have told you." ⁸ And they left the tomb quickly with fear and great joy and ran to report it to His disciples. ⁹ And behold, Jesus met them and greeted them. And they came up and took hold of

His feet and worshiped Him. ¹⁰ Then Jesus said to them, "Do not be afraid; go and take word to My brethren to leave for Galilee, and there they will see Me."

Jesus' resurrection is a return to the beginning. In virtually every detail, Matthew takes us back to the beginning of His Gospel. In the end is the beginning, because in the beginning is the end. Two Marys come to the tomb on the first day of the week. One of them is Mary Magdalene, the "other Mary" is Mary the mother of James and Joseph, who is (I believe) Mary the mother of Jesus. Mary was there at the beginning of the gospel story, at the beginning of the life of Jesus, when He first emerged from her womb into the world. Mary is here again as He emerges from the tomb into a new world. It is a new beginning.

An angel appears, descending from heaven to roll away the stone and to announce that Jesus is risen. We have seen something descend from heaven before, something with wings! When Jesus was baptized, when He began His ministry, He went to John to be baptized in the Jordan, and as He was coming out of the water the heavens were split and the Spirit of God descended from heaven in the form of a dove. Now that Jesus has endured the baptism of blood on the cross, now that He has drunk that cup, an angel descends from heaven to roll away the stone. Angels appear repeatedly in the early chapters of Matthew. When Joseph learns that Mary is pregnant, and is ready to put her away quietly, an angel of the Lord appears in a dream to assure Joseph that the child is conceived by the Spirit (Matt. 1:20). Obeying the angel's instruction, Joseph takes Mary as his wife. When the magi deceive Herod and return home without telling Herod where the king of the Jews was born, an angel of the Lord appears again to Joseph in a dream and tells him to flee to Egypt to escape the sword of Herod (Matt. 2:13). Once Herod is dead, an angel of the Lord appears again to Joseph telling him to return to the land (Matt. 2:19). No angels appear between the birth story of Jesus and the narrative of His resurrection. The coming of an angel from heaven takes us back to the beginning of the story. It is a new beginning.

And it is not just the presence of the angel that takes us back. It is what the angel says. An angel came to Joseph in dreams to direct his movements and actions: Take Mary as your wife; go to Egypt; go home. The angel was a traffic director, showing Joseph where to go and when. And here too an angel of the Lord appears at the tomb of Jesus and gives directions. Go here, do this, go there, he tells the women.

When Joseph returned from Egypt, he settled his family in Nazareth in Galilee, and when Jesus began His ministry, He began it in his own territory, in Galilee. Through the early part of the gospel, Jesus carried out His ministry of healing, exorcism, preaching in Galilee, but after His transfiguration He began making His way toward Jerusalem. Galilee fades into the background. Now that He is raised, it is all about getting back to Galilee, all about getting back to the beginning. "Tell the disciples that Jesus is risen.," the angel tells the women, and that He is going into Galilee. When Jesus appears to the women, He has the same message: "Take word to my brethren to leave for Galilee, and there they shall see me." At the very end of the gospel, when the disciples have gathered to see Jesus, they are commissioned from a mountaintop in Galilee.

Jesus' journey to Jerusalem began with the transfiguration, when Jesus' face shone like the sun and His garments became white as light. As soon as Jesus had appeared in glory, He began a journey from Galilee toward Jerusalem. Now an angel appears, whose appearance and form are bright as dawn in a dark sky, and whose garments are white as snow. And this transfigured angel tells the women to tell the disciples to retrace their steps, to go back to the beginning, to reverse Jesus' progress by going from Jerusalem back into Galilee.

The sequence of events in that first Galilean ministry is being replayed. Jesus battles Satan in the wilderness, resisting His temptations and proving Himself the true Son, the true Israel of God. Then He withdraws into Galilee, and begins preaching the gospel of the kingdom. "Repent," he says, "for the kingdom of heaven is at hand." The end is the beginning. The end is a new beginning. In Jerusalem, Jesus battles Satan. In Jerusalem, the Jews challenge Jesus' claim to be Son of God, just as Satan did. In Jerusalem, the Jews ask for a sign, just as Satan did. In Jerusalem, the Jews demand that Jesus come down from the cross, just as Satan tempted Him to avoid the cross altogether. Jesus' trials in Jerusalem are a second entry into the wilderness to battle Satan, and now that He has emerged victorious, He goes to Galilee, begins proclaiming the gospel, and sends His disciples to all the Gentiles throughout the earth. Jesus' ministry has not ended with His death. Because of His resurrection, His ministry starts over again. We are back to the beginning; it is a new beginning.

The beginning that is announced here is not, however, simply a return to the beginning of the Gospel. The end of Matthew's Gospel reaches not just back to the beginning of the gospel story, but to the beginning of all beginnings, back to the beginning when God created the heavens and the earth. Matt. 28:1 literally says "on the Sabbath, after it began to dawn toward the first of the Sabbaths." Jesus rises on the day after the Sabbath, but that is also the beginning of new Sabbath. The day after the Sabbath, the first of the Sabbaths, is the first day of a new creation, and this new creation is not just a return to the old creation but an improvement on it.

We can see that it is an improvement on the old creation by looking at what Genesis says about heaven and earth, and what Matthew says about it.[42] At the beginning of the Bible, God created the heavens and earth, two zones, two regions. Heaven was Yahweh's place, and earth was given to the sons of men. In Genesis 1, one day comes to an end without the declaration that Yahweh saw that it was good. That is Day 2, when Yahweh inserts a firmament, a boundary, between the waters above and the waters below, between heaven and earth. This is not declared to be good, because it is not permanent. Heaven and earth are created separate; the firmament keeps them separate. But that is not yet good, not yet the fulfillment of God's purpose for creation.

---

42 Heaven and earth are used in combination eight times in the gospel, and those uses fall out into a nearly chiastic pattern:

God's purpose from the beginning is to bring heaven to earth, and to raise earth to heaven. His purpose from the beginning is to rend the veil of the firmament that separates heaven and earth, so that God and creation could enjoy un-mediated fellowship, so that His will would be done on earth as it is in heaven.

More than any other gospel, Matthew is about the fulfillment of this expectation and purpose.[43] Matthew uses the word "heaven" over seventy times, more than any other book of the New Testament, and twice as much as any of the other gospels. In Matthew, Jesus proclaims the kingdom of heaven, tells His disciples about their Father in heaven, speaks of the angels in heaven, assures His disciples that what they bind on earth will be bound in heaven. According to Matthew, the story of Jesus is about heaven coming to earth, heaven invading earth, heaven renewing earth. When heaven invades earth, the powers of earth are shaken down. Easter is about this fundamental shift in the balance of power. Easter is about the God of heaven overthrowing the powers of earth.

    A. Heaven and earth pass away, 5:18

        B. Will done on earth as in heaven, 6:10

            C. Praise Father, Lord of heaven and earth, 11:25

                D. Keys of kingdom of heaven (heaven/earth/heaven/earth/heaven), 16:19

                D'. Binding and loosing (earth/heaven/earth/heaven/earth/heaven), 19:18-19

            C'. Call no one father but Father in heaven, 23:9

    A'. Heaven and earth pass away, 24:35

        B'. All authority in heaven and earth to Jesus, 28:18

If this structure works, then the authority given to Jesus is authority given to fulfill the prayer of Matt. 6:10. Jesus receives authority so that the will of the Father will be done.

43 Jonathan Pennington, *Heaven and Earth in Matthew's Gospel* (Grand Rapids: Baker 2009).

Jesus' resurrection is an earthquake that shakes the powers until they shatter. One by one, the powers that conspired to kill Jesus are toppled. We think big stones represent power and solidity. Large stones are used to built temples and towers and city walls and skyscrapers and fortresses. Jesus' grave is locked tight like a fortress, but when an angel descends from heaven, he pushes away the stone like a feather and uses it for a throne. We think that the guy with the biggest army, the guy with the biggest arsenal, the guy with the most nukes and drones and troops, is the most powerful. We think we are secure from terrorists if we have men with machine guns patrolling our airports. We have learned to trust in horses and chariots. But when an angel descends from heaven, brave and battle-hardened guards fall to the ground as dead men.

If there is one thing on earth that seems to hold absolute power, it is death. Tyrants rise and fall; Presidents come and go; celebrities are quickly forgotten – and they all fall before the most resolute and relentless power on earth, the power of death. But when an angel descends from heaven, he empties tombs. For the first time in history, Death yields up a victim; for the first time, a man is raised. Jesus is not raised like others have been raised, not raised like the child raised to life by Elijah or like Lazarus. He is raised to a life beyond the reach of Death; He died once, and will die no more, and has the power of indestructible life. He is permanently beyond the reach of death. The powers that have oppressed earth are overthrown by an invasion of heaven's King. What looked like strength is exposed in its impotence, while, on the other hand, what looked like defeat and weakness is transformed to power.

Women are weak, and the women in Matthew's gospel story have been helplessly watching since they came into the story. They sit watching Jesus on the cross, watch Jesus put into the tomb, watch the grave. They can do nothing. But when an angel descends from heaven, passive, weak women are mobilized and dash off to tell the disciples, knowing that the whole mission of the church depends on them getting a message to the disciples.

Women are weak, dead men are weaker. Dead men have *no* power. Crucified men do not stroll through the streets of the capital. But when an angel descends from heaven, the powerless are empowered, and the dead rise. A crucified man, still bearing the scars of His execution, appears in a garden to Mary, walks through doors, eats fish with His disciples, claims to have inherited all authority in heaven and on earth. When the angel descends from heaven, women become braver than soldiers; the dead more lively than the living; the cross more potent than all the weapons man can produce.

Men have always dreamed of a new beginning. They have always wished that time could be run in reverse and we could have a new start on the sorry spectacle of history. Those who pursue that dream usually end up with more of the same, only worse. They end up entrenching Death's power even more securely. The old week of human history ended in a cross, and the dream of going back to Day One has ended with guillotines and Gulags. But that sobering reality should not lead to despair. We cannot reverse time, return to Eden, and make sure that this time round Adam stays clear of that tree until it is time. Earth cannot start earth's history over again. We cannot turn the clock back and make a new, and better, beginning. *We* cannot, but the God of heaven *can*, and Easter announces that He *has*.

Go!
Matthew 28:11-20

[11] Now while they were on their way, some of the guard came into the city and reported to the chief priests all that had happened. [12] And when they had assembled with the elders and consulted together, they gave a large sum of money to the soldiers, [13] and said, "You are to say, 'His disciples came by night and stole Him away while we were asleep.' [14] And if this should come to the governor's ears, we will win him over and keep you out of trouble." [15] And they took the money and did as they had been instructed; and this story was widely

spread among the Jews, and is to this day. ¹⁶ But the eleven disciples proceeded to Galilee, to the mountain which Jesus had designated. ¹⁷ When they saw Him, they worshiped Him; but some were doubtful. ¹⁸ And Jesus came up and spoke to them, saying, "All authority has been given to Me in heaven and on earth. ¹⁹ Go therefore and make disciples of all the nations, baptizing them in the name of the Father and the Son and the Holy Spirit, ²⁰ teaching them to observe all that I commanded you; and lo, I am with you always, even to the end of the age."

Two groups rush away from the empty tomb. Both of them have news. The women came to the tomb looking for Jesus, but now they have heard the angel's announcement that Jesus is risen, and obey the angel's command to go to the disciples and announce the resurrection to them. Along the way, Jesus Himself appears to them and repeats the instructions. Matthew uses a verb that contains the word "angel," which in Greek simply means "messenger." They go off to "report" (v. 8), and then Jesus tells them to "report" (v. 10). Both verses use the verb *apaggelo*. Having listened to the angels, the women become angels, messengers taking the Easter gospel to the disciples.

But there is another group heading off from the empty tomb too, and they too have a "report." They too have become "messengers" or "angels." Matthew uses the same verb — *apaggelo* — to describe the guards who go into the city to "report" to the chief priests. The soldiers and the women have been contrasted before. The soldiers sat watching Jesus at the foot of the cross, while the women sat watching Jesus' death from a distance. Once Jesus' body has been placed in the tomb, the women watch the tomb, while Pilate sends a detachment of guards to the tomb to prevent the disciples from stealing Jesus' body.

Both of them have seen the angel's appearance. Both saw that the angel's face was like lightning, and that his garments were glistening white like snow. Both were afraid. The soldiers fell as dead men, but the women feared and rejoiced and listened to the angel. Now, both the women and the soldiers have become "angels," messengers announcing the news. Both of them go off to report the incident that they have witnessed.

The soldiers start out as faithful witnesses to the resurrection. Matthew tells us that the guards report everything that happened. At the end of Matthew's story of the crucifixion, the centurion who is head of the soldiers at the cross sees "all that had happened," he concludes that Jesus must have been the Son of God. Now other soldiers join him in that confession. The guards tell them all that had happened, everything. They tell the chief priests that they saw an angel come from heaven. They felt the earthquake. They saw the angel roll the stone away and sit on it. They saw the angel's face and his garment.

That can mean only one thing: The God of heaven, the God whom the Jews claim to worship, has intervened on Jesus' behalf, and reversed everything that had happened to Jesus. God has turned around His death, bringing Him back to life; God has turned around His burial, opening the tomb. That can only mean that the judgment against Him was reversed too. God has intervened to overturn the judgments of Pilate and the Jewish leaders, vindicating the condemned Jesus. If an angel from heaven came like lightning, with an earthquake, to open the tomb, that can only mean that the chief priests were completely and utterly mistaken about Jesus.

The chief priests hear all that, but do not believe. They know the whole story of the death and resurrection of Jesus. They are aware of all the signs that Jesus was the prophet of God, the Son of Man. But they will not believe. The guards have the good sense to be afraid when they see the angel, but the chief priests are so hardened that they do not express any fear. They can fix this. A bit of money, and spin control, and it will all go away. It is not surprising then that when Jesus appears to the eleven, He does not send them out to the lost sheep of the house of Israel, as He did earlier in His ministry. He instead sends the disciples out to disciple the nations, the Gentiles. The Jews have rejected their Lord; even when He rises from the dead, they reject Him. And so He turns from them to the nations.

Of course, the Jewish leaders do more than disbelieve. They persuade the soldiers to offer an alternative account of what happened. The guards come to the chief priests reporting all that has happened, but when they leave they are telling a different story (Matt. 28:15). They come in as angels, declaring everything that God has done in Jesus. They leave with a false report, as false angels. It is not a very convincing story, and it does not reflect well on them. They admit that they slept on the job, not a very professional behavior for a guard. Yet, somehow, even though they were asleep, they know exactly what happens at the tomb. They know that someone came to take the body of Jesus, and they know who those someones were – the disciples of Jesus. It is an ironic conclusion to the work of the guards. They were hired to prevent the disciples from stealing the body, but they admit that they failed. They were hired to prevent the disciples from spreading a deception, but they end up spreading a false report themselves.

What transforms their story from a story of angels and earthquakes and rolling stones into a story of deception is *money*. The chief priests have already used money to get their way with Jesus. They paid Judas thirty pieces of silver to betray Jesus. They use their money to buy treachery. They used their control of the mob to pressure Pilate to condemn Jesus. They are able to control the Roman courts, pulling strings from a distance. Now they use money to control the media. The chief priests have their hands on the levers of power. They can purchase alliances, they can pressure the courts, they control the news cycle, so that their "message," their "announcement," their "gospel" gets the most airtime. The effect of this deception is chilling. Jesus gave only one sign to "this generation," the sign of Jonah (Matt 12:38-41). But the men of Nineveh were more responsive than the Jews, for they repented when Jonah rose from the death waters to preach to them. The Jews do not. They conspire to make sure that no other Jews know about the sign.

Two groups of angels, two messages. Even before the disciples see the Risen Jesus, even before they are commissioned to disciple the nations, the gospel has a competitor. There is an alternative explanation of the events of Easter morning, a naturalistic account. The gospel has always been an embattled message. Today there are rivals – heretical groups that claim to be Christian, secular gospels that promise health and salvation without Jesus. But that is nothing new, and it will not go away. From the beginning to the end of the world, there will be different explanations, different reports, different messages, different gospels.

In that context, Jesus' commission and promise are profoundly important. The main target of the women's message is the disciples. The women are the mediators to carry the message of the resurrection back to the original band of Jesus' followers. The women get word to them, and the eleven gather to Galilee, to the mountain where Jesus told them to meet Him. There they see Jesus and worship Him.

This is a richly typological passage. Jesus' appearance to the eleven culminates not only the story of Matthew's gospel, but also shows Jesus as the fulfillment of a host of Old Testament hopes. The Magi were the first to worship the king of the Jews (Matt. 2:2, 11). Now that Jesus has been raised, the eleven remaining disciples join in (Matt. 28:16). This is no ordinary bow; they prostrate themselves in total submission to Jesus, acknowledging that he is God. He was identified as "Immanuel" at the beginning of the gospel (Matt. 1:23), and now He promises that His divine presence will remain with the disciples forever (Matt. 28:20; cf. Deut. 31:23). Jesus is Yahweh on the mountain, a new Mount Sinai, instructing His disciples to keep and teach His commandments; a new Zion, where the disciples worship.

Jesus is the new Joseph. The only other place in the Bible where "eleven" people "worship" is in Genesis 37, when Joseph has a dream that the sun, moon, and eleven stars will fall to worship him. In the story of Joseph, the dream finally comes to fulfillment in Joseph's "resurrection." Joseph's brothers reject him, plan to kill him, sell him into slavery to the Gentiles, but Joseph is raised up and given authority over all Egypt. It is a preview of Jesus' story-line: The disciples have betrayed Jesus, fleeing from Him in the garden; Jesus' Jewish brothers have killed Him, but now God has raised Jesus up and given Him all authority in heaven and on earth. The Joseph story, I think, helps us capture the psychological tone of this moment. When Joseph's brothers finally realized who Joseph was, realized that lost Joseph had been found and "dead" Joseph had risen again, they were afraid. They were the ones who turned Joseph over to the Egyptians. Maybe he is going to get his revenge, they think. But Joseph assures them that the things they intended for evil, God meant for good, to bring salvation to many people. Jesus' disciples also have reason to fear. The last time they saw Jesus was in the garden, and they could only see Him by looking over their shoulders as they fled from the guards arresting Jesus. Now Jesus is back, and He wants to see them in Galilee. What is He going to say? Are they going to hear Him say, "Depart from Me, I never knew you"?

Jesus is the Son of Man. In Daniel 7, the prophet sees a vision of one like the Son of Man inheriting all authority of all the nations. The Risen Jesus is that Son of Man. His death and resurrection have changed everything. Matthew hammers on the point with the repetition of the word "all." Jesus has all authority, sends His disciples to make disciples of all nations, tells them to teach all His commandments, and promises His presence through all ages (Matt. 28: 18-20). These "alls" are linked: Because Jesus has all authority, He sends His disciples to all nations, and all His commandments are weighty.

Jesus is the new world emperor. As we have seen throughout our studies in Matthew, Matthew's gospel recapitulates the history of Israel. Jesus has played the role of Moses, of Joshua, of Solomon, of Elisha, of Jeremiah. He has been through exodus and conquest and kingship and a divided kingdom and He has predicted the fall of the temple. In His death, He has been forsaken by His Father, sharing the exile of His people, but in His resurrection He has returned from the grave of exile. In these last verses, Jesus is the great World Emperor, the new Cyrus, who commissions His disciples to "go" (cf. 2 Chron. 36:22-23): "All the kingdoms of the earth the LORD God of heaven has given me. And He has commanded me to build Him a house at Jerusalem which is in Judah. Who *is* among you of all His people? May the LORD his God *be* with him, and let him go up!"

Cyrus claims to have authority from the God of heaven. He calls on Yahweh to be with his people. He gives a command to go. Jesus is the new Cyrus, but Jesus is greater than Cyrus. He has authority in heaven, and not merely authority from the God of heaven, or authority on earth. Jesus is the God who will be with His disciples. He gives a command to Go, but instead of sending the eleven back to their homeland, he sends them out to places they have never been.

Israel never existed for herself, but for the sake of the nations. Now that Jesus has risen and issues this command as a new Cyrus, that reality is even more pronounced. Even more than Israel, the church exists for the sake of the world. Jesus did not come to be served but to serve. He came to make disciples, and by His resurrection He gives us the privilege of sharing in making disciples of the nations.

No church exists for the sake of church. We are called together to be sent out, called together so that we can be commissioned to fill our town with disciples, and to participate in the making of disciples throughout the world. We can have the best worship imaginable, the best teaching, the deepest fellowship. All those are good things, but if we do not "go" and "make disciples," then we are failing to be the church God wants us to be. As folks in the Emerging/Emergent church say, the church does not *have* a mission; it *is* a mission.

The eleven came to Jesus and worshiped Him. But Jesus did not want them to stay on the mountain to worship Him. He wanted them to go from the mountain, into the valley below, making disciples by baptizing and teaching. We want to stay on the mountain. It is comfortable and safe. Jesus will not let us. Jesus tells us to get out of here.

Cyrus' commission is at the very end of the Hebrew Bible. "Go up," Cyrus says. Then the Hebrew Bible is over. Matthew's gospel ends in the same inconclusive way. "Go," Jesus says, "make disciples." This is not a happily-ever-after ending. It is an open-ended ending, an ending that is really a new beginning. Jesus' death was not the end of His ministry, and neither is His resurrection. Both are beginnings rather than endings. Jesus rose to commission His disciples to carry on His work to the Gentiles. "Go" said the angel; "Go," Jesus repeated to the women; now, again, "Go" and "make disciples" (Matt. 28:7, 10, 19).

Matthew's Gospel leaves us with this challenge: "Will we do it?"

www.ingramcontent.com/pod-product-compliance
Lightning Source LLC
Chambersburg PA
CBHW052011070526
44584CB00016B/1704